Soviet and Post-Soviet Politics and Society (SPPS)
ISSN 1614-3515

General Editor: Andreas Umland,
Stockholm Centre for Eastern European Studies, andreas.umland@ui.se

Commi[ssioning Editor: ...]
London, [...]

EDITORIAL COMMITTEE*

DOMESTIC & COMPARATIVE POLITICS
Prof. **Ellen Bos**, *Andrássy University of Budapest*
Dr. **Gergana Dimova**, *Florida State University*
Prof. **Heiko Pleines**, *University of Bremen*
Dr. **Sarah Whitmore**, *Oxford Brookes University*
Dr. **Harald Wydra**, *University of Cambridge*

SOCIETY, CLASS & ETHNICITY
Col. **David Glantz**, *"Journal of Slavic Military Studies"*
Dr. **Marlène Laruelle**, *George Washington University*
Dr. **Stephen Shulman**, *Southern Illinois University*
Prof. **Stefan Troebst**, *University of Leipzig*

POLITICAL ECONOMY & PUBLIC POLICY
Prof. **Andreas Goldthau**, *University of Erfurt*
Dr. **Robert Kravchuk**, *University of North Carolina*
Dr. **David Lane**, *University of Cambridge*
Dr. **Carol Leonard**, *University of Oxford*
Dr. **Maria Popova**, *McGill University, Montreal*

FOREI[GN POLICY & INTERNATIONAL AFFAIR]S
Dr. **Peter Duncan**, *University College London*
Prof. **Andreas Heinemann-Grüder**, *University of Bonn*
Prof. **Gerhard Mangott**, *University of Innsbruck*
Dr. **Diana Schmidt-Pfister**, *University of Konstanz*
Dr. **Lisbeth Tarlow**, *Harvard University, Cambridge*
Dr. **Christian Wipperfürth**, *N-Ost Network, Berlin*
Dr. **William Zimmerman**, *University of Michigan*

HISTORY, CULTURE & THOUGHT
Dr. **Catherine Andreyev**, *University of Oxford*
Prof. **Mark Bassin**, *Södertörn University*
Prof. **Karsten Brüggemann**, *Tallinn University*
Prof. **Alexander Etkind**, *Central European University*
Prof. **Gasan Gusejnov**, *Free University of Berlin*
Prof. **Leonid Luks**, *Catholic University of Eichstaett*
Dr. **Olga Malinova**, *Russian Academy of Sciences*
Dr. **Richard Mole**, *University College London*
Prof. **Andrei Rogatchevski**, *University of Tromsø*
Dr. **Mark Tauger**, *West Virginia University*

ADVISORY BOARD*

Prof. **Dominique Arel**, *University of Ottawa*
Prof. **Jörg Baberowski**, *Humboldt University of Berlin*
Prof. **Margarita Balmaceda**, *Seton Hall University*
Dr. **John Barber**, *University of Cambridge*
Prof. **Timm Beichelt**, *European University Viadrina*
Dr. **Katrin Boeckh**, *University of Munich*
Prof. em. **Archie Brown**, *University of Oxford*
Dr. **Vyacheslav Bryukhovetsky**, *Kyiv-Mohyla Academy*
Prof. **Timothy Colton**, *Harvard University, Cambridge*
Prof. **Paul D'Anieri**, *University of California*
Dr. **Heike Dörrenbächer**, *Friedrich Naumann Foundation*
Dr. **John Dunlop**, *Hoover Institution, Stanford, California*
Dr. **Sabine Fischer**, *SWP, Berlin*
Dr. **Geir Flikke**, *NUPI, Oslo*
Prof. **David Galbreath**, *University of Aberdeen*
Prof. **Frank Golczewski**, *University of Hamburg*
Dr. **Nikolas Gvosdev**, *Naval War College, Newport, RI*
Prof. **Mark von Hagen**, *Arizona State University*
Prof. **Guido Hausmann**, *University of Regensburg*
Prof. **Dale Herspring**, *Kansas State University*
Dr. **Stefani Hoffman**, *Hebrew University of Jerusalem*
Prof. em. **Andrzej Korbonski**, *University of California*
Dr. **Iris Kempe**, *"Caucasus Analytical Digest"*
Prof. **Herbert Küpper**, *Institut für Ostrecht Regensburg*
Prof. **Rainer Lindner**, *University of Konstanz*

Dr. **Luke March**, *University of Edinburgh*
Prof. **Michael McFaul**, *Stanford University, Palo Alto*
Prof. **Birgit Menzel**, *University of Mainz-Germersheim*
Dr. **Alex Pravda**, *University of Oxford*
Dr. **Erik van Ree**, *University of Amsterdam*
Dr. **Joachim Rogall**, *Robert Bosch Foundation Stuttgart*
Prof. **Peter Rutland**, *Wesleyan University, Middletown*
Prof. **Gwendolyn Sasse**, *University of Oxford*
Prof. **Jutta Scherrer**, *EHESS, Paris*
Prof. **Robert Service**, *University of Oxford*
Mr. **James Sherr**, *RIIA Chatham House London*
Dr. **Oxana Shevel**, *Tufts University, Medford*
Prof. **Eberhard Schneider**, *University of Siegen*
Prof. **Olexander Shnyrkov**, *Shevchenko University, Kyiv*
Prof. **Hans-Henning Schröder**, *SWP, Berlin*
Prof. **Yuri Shapoval**, *Ukrainian Academy of Sciences*
Dr. **Lisa Sundstrom**, *University of British Columbia*
Dr. **Philip Walters**, *"Religion, State and Society"*, *Oxford*
Prof. **Zenon Wasyliw**, *Ithaca College, New York State*
Dr. **Lucan Way**, *University of Toronto*
Dr. **Markus Wehner**, *"Frankfurter Allgemeine Zeitung"*
Dr. **Andrew Wilson**, *University College London*
Prof. **Jan Zielonka**, *University of Oxford*
Prof. **Andrei Zorin**, *University of Oxford*

---

* While the Editorial Committee and Advisory Board support the General Editor in the choice and improvement of manuscripts for publication, responsibility for remaining errors and misinterpretations in the series' volumes lies with the books' authors.

Soviet and Post-Soviet Politics and Society (SPPS)
ISSN 1614-3515

Founded in 2004 and refereed since 2007, SPPS makes available affordable English-, German-, and Russian-language studies on the history of the countries of the former Soviet bloc from the late Tsarist period to today. It publishes between 5 and 20 volumes per year and focuses on issues in transitions to and from democracy such as economic crisis, identity formation, civil society development, and constitutional reform in CEE and the NIS. SPPS also aims to highlight so far understudied themes in East European studies such as right-wing radicalism, religious life, higher education, or human rights protection. The authors and titles of all previously published volumes are listed at the end of this book. For a full description of the series and reviews of its books, see www.ibidem-verlag.de/red/spps.

Editorial correspondence & manuscripts should be sent to: Dr. Andreas Umland, Department of Political Science, Kyiv-Mohyla Academy, vul. Voloska 8/5, UA-04070 Kyiv, UKRAINE; andreas.umland@cantab.net

Business correspondence & review copy requests should be sent to: *ibidem* Press, Leuschnerstr. 40, 30457 Hannover, Germany; tel.: +49 511 2622200; fax: +49 511 2622201; spps@ibidem.eu.

Authors, reviewers, referees, and editors for (as well as all other persons sympathetic to) SPPS are invited to join its networks at www.facebook.com/group.php?gid=52638198614
www.linkedin.com/groups?about=&gid=103012
www.xing.com/net/spps-ibidem-verlag/

Recent Volumes

267 Bohdan Harasymiw
Post-Euromaidan Ukraine
Domestic Power Struggles and War of National Survival in 2014–2022
ISBN 978-3-8382-1798-7

268 Nadiia Koval, Denys Tereshchenko (Eds.)
Russian Cultural Diplomacy under Putin
Rossotrudnichestvo, the "Russkiy Mir" Foundation, and the Gorchakov Fund in 2007–2022
ISBN 978-3-8382-1801-4

269 Izabela Kazejak
Jews in Post-War Wrocław and L'viv
Official Policies and Local Responses in Comparative Perspective, 1945-1970s
ISBN 978-3-8382-1802-1

270 Jakob Hauter
Russia's Overlooked Invasion
The Causes of the 2014 Outbreak of War in Ukraine's Donbas
With a foreword by Hiroaki Kuromiya
ISBN 978-3-8382-1803-8

271 Anton Shekhovtsov
Russian Political Warfare
Essays on Kremlin Propaganda in Europe and the Neighbourhood, 2020-2023
With a foreword by Nathalie Loiseau
ISBN 978-3-8382-1821-2

272 Андреа Пето
Насилие и Молчание
Красная армия в Венгрии во Второй Мировой войне
ISBN 978-3-8382-1636-2

273 Winfried Schneider-Deters
Russia's War in Ukraine
Debates on Peace, Fascism, and War Crimes, 2022–2023
With a foreword by Klaus Gestwa
ISBN 978-3-8382-1876-2

274 Rasmus Nilsson
Uncanny Allies
Russia and Belarus on the Edge, 2012-2024
ISBN 978-3-8382-1288-3

275 Anton Grushetskyi, Volodymyr Paniotto
War and the Transformation of Ukrainian Society (2022–23)
Empirical Evidence
ISBN 978-3-8382-1944-8

Christian Kaunert, Alex MacKenzie, and
Adrien Nonjon (eds.)

IN THE EYE OF THE STORM

Origins, Ideology, and Controversies of the
Azov Brigade, 2014–2023

Bibliographic information published by the Deutsche Nationalbibliothek
Die Deutsche Nationalbibliothek lists this publication in the Deutsche Nationalbibliografie; detailed bibliographic data are available on the Internet at http://dnb.d-nb.de.

Bibliografische Information der Deutschen Nationalbibliothek
Die Deutsche Nationalbibliothek verzeichnet diese Publikation in der Deutschen Nationalbibliografie; detaillierte bibliografische Daten sind im Internet über http://dnb.d-nb.de abrufbar.

Cover picture: ID 255830294 © Tanyalev1978 | Dreamstime.com

ISBN (Print): 978-3-8382-1750-5
ISBN (E-Book [PDF]): 978-3-8382-7750-9
© *ibidem*-Verlag, Hannover • Stuttgart 2024
All rights reserved.

No part of this publication may be reproduced, stored in or introduced into a retrieval system, or transmitted, in any form, or by any means (electronic, mechanical, photocopying, recording or otherwise) without the prior written permission of the publisher. Any person who commits any unauthorized act in relation to this publication may be liable to criminal prosecution and civil claims for damages.

Alle Rechte vorbehalten. Das Werk einschließlich aller seiner Teile ist urheberrechtlich geschützt. Jede Verwertung außerhalb der engen Grenzen des Urheberrechtsgesetzes ist ohne Zustimmung des Verlages unzulässig und strafbar. Dies gilt insbesondere für Vervielfältigungen, Übersetzungen, Mikroverfilmungen und elektronische Speicherformen sowie die Einspeicherung und Verarbeitung in elektronischen Systemen.

Printed in the United States of America

Acknowledgments

We all felt somewhat apprehensive when Andreas Umland approached us in early 2022 — soon after the full-scale Russian invasion of Ukraine and during the COVID-19 pandemic — to compile an edited collection focused on what is now the Azov Brigade. Here we had a military unit that had its origins in fringe, repulsive politics (i.e. the Ukrainian far right) and persisting connections with the wider Azov Movement, even though they continue to be conflated, and the military unit is quite different a decade on from its founding in 2014 for several reasons. Furthermore, the Azov Brigade was a significant subject of Russian propaganda and fought to the bitter end to defend the city of Mariupol, only surrendering in May 2022 after being ordered to by the Ukrainian high command. We were also concerned that, in the heat of the initial Russian onslaught, our book might be rejected by Ukrainians and scholars alike due to it not being the appropriate time for such a pursuit. In what we have produced, we have also had to guard against the current challenge of those on the far right referring to themselves as 'conservatives' or 'nationalists', as well as all soldiers fighting for Ukraine being viewed as heroes regardless of their belief systems due to the total nature of the ongoing war. The Ukrainian government has felt the need to make overtures to problematic sections of its society and embraced some questionable international recruits. We are aware of these potential pitfalls and have attempted to engage with them head-on here, criticising where necessary and correcting where we believe that misinformation has succeeded in clouding an issue. Now, in 2024, after two years and more of fighting in Ukraine, we feel able to release this book in a less frenetic environment and have had time to properly consult, digest, and evaluate information from various outlets that give us confidence in our findings. We assembled an excellent, internationally diverse team of contributors to write the different chapters. They cover many different dimensions of the Azov Brigade and beyond. The chapters offer fascinating journeys through these different aspects of today's Azov Brigade. We are hugely grateful to our contributors for their hard work, patience, and persistence. Not all this book is comfortable reading about Ukraine and its armed forces, and Kyiv has a lot to do if it is to become a fully-fledged Western democracy. Yet, we also believe that many have become too hysterical about the prevalence of far-right politics in Ukraine, with some Western outlets and populaces falling into traps set by, above all, Russian sources and those who do not want to continue providing aid of various kinds to Ukraine. Above all, we hope that we have succeeded in producing a book that is accessible to scholarly and non-scholarly audiences, that will contribute to academic debates, and that will offer an accurate and nuanced account of the Azov Brigade and its development.

Christian Kaunert,
Alex MacKenzie,
and Adrien Nonjon,
August 2024

Funding Acknowledgement:
This work received financial support from the Czech Science Foundation under standard grant no. 24-10160S.

Contents

Acknowledgments 5

Introduction
Christian Kaunert, Alex MacKenzie and Adrien Nonjon 9

1   The Azov Brigade: Origins, Influences and Ideological Development
Przemysław Witkowski 33

2   Defence Bottom-up Volunteer Battalions at the Onset of the Russian War in Ukraine
Rosaria Puglisi 55

3   From Political Outsiders to Military Stalwarts: The Evolving Face of Ukrainian Nationalism
Taras Tarasiuk and Petro Burkovskiy 83

4   Has the Azov Regiment Depoliticized? An Analysis from the Structure to Individual Trajectories
Bertrand de Franqueville 137

5   Ze Double: A Psychodramatic Interpretation of the Azov's Role in the Russo-Ukrainian War
Ivan Gomza 173

6   The War in Ukraine and the Transnational Far-right Extremist Movement
Mollie Saltskog 209

7   No "Far Right Al-Qaeda": Azov's Foreign Fighters
Kacper Rekawek 231

Conclusion
Christian Kaunert, Alex MacKenzie and Adrien Nonjon 259

Introduction

Christian Kaunert, Alex MacKenzie and Adrien Nonjon

"There are always four sides to a story:
your side, their side, the truth and what really happened"
Jean-Jacques Rousseau

Russia and Ukraine

For over ten years, the Russian Federation has been weaving a devious veil of lies about Ukraine to forcefully discredit the awakening of a nation once under its yoke. Distilled in the aftermath of the Maydan Revolution of February 2014, these distortions are based for the most part on a truncated reading of history and today fuel a violent and brutal war, the death toll of which is currently estimated at over 500,000 victims, both Russian and Ukrainian.[1] Beyond any process seeking to justify to different publics that Russia's invasion of Ukraine was legitimate because of the threat it might pose as a member of the North Atlantic Treaty Organisation (NATO) on the western flank of the Federation, Russian rhetoric, which hardly hides its messianic essence, has sought to portray Ukraine as much more than a geopolitical rival. The reader will be spared the civilisational and eschatological discourses which would make this country the ultimate battlefield against a decadent

---

1 Regarding the ongoing nature of the conflict itself and the fact that casualties are part of the information war between the two countries, estimations should be taken with a fair distance. However British and US officials has estimated the number of casualties in the Ukrainian army to 120, 000 (see: Roth, A. (2023)," Battlefield deaths in Ukraine have risen sharply this year, say US officials", The Guardian, 18th August 2023,accessed on 6th May 2024) and 355, 000 Russians killed or wounded in action (see:https://twitter.com/DefenceHQ/status/1764 244391630184736, 3rd March 20-24 (accessed on 6th May 2024). For civilians the HRMMU has estimated the number to more than 30,000 (See:https://www.oh chr.org/sites/default/files/2024-02/two-year-update-protection-civilians-im pact-hostilities-civilians-24.pdf) to which are added the 15,000 victims of the of the first phase of the russo-ukrainian conflict in Donbass from 2014 to 2022.

"collective West", yet[2], putting aside these fabrications, it is essential to concentrate on the resolutely political and contemporary reading of the conflict.

Since 1991 and the collapse of the USSR, Russia has maintained a resolutely imperial stance towards Ukraine. This attitude has much to do with history. Indeed, Russia sees itself as a great power, capable both in terms of the resources made available by its immense territory and the centuries-old cultural heritage shared by over 140 million people. The idea that Russian elites have of the relationship that they should have with the rest of the world is primarily conditioned by the maintenance of Russia's power, or at least its partial restoration in the twenty-first century. Russia's obsessive ambition has a 'natural' outlet in the so-called "post-Soviet space", which is seen as the essential crucible of its power. This 'near abroad', as it is most-commonly described in the Russian concept of the *russkiy mir*, should be understood here, following Serhii Plokhy, as the only space where Russia still seeks to legitimise the imperial nature of its power[3]. Even though the fall of the USSR enshrined the principle of self-determination of peoples and put an end to the multi-state nature that enabled Soviet power to consolidate its imperial dimension, Russia has never really been able to break away entirely from the idea of being a centre around which all the border states should gravitate. In the Russian conception, this is a more than vital interest that its elites have tried to maintain by forming various supra-national initiatives like the Commonwealth of Independent States (CIS) in 1991 or the Eurasian Union project put forward by Vladimir Putin in 2011[4].

Ukraine holds a crucial position in the geographical region bordering Russia. Despite being independent since 1991, Ukraine has always been a direct target of Russian influence. While Mikhail

---

2 Putin, V. (2022), "Obrashchenie Presidenta Possiyskoy Federatsii" [Speech of the Russian Federation President], 24th February 2022, http://kremlin.ru/events/president/news/67843 (accessed on 6th May 2024)
3 Plokhiy, S. (2022) *Aux portes de l'Europe. Histoire de l'Ukraine* (The Gates of Europe. A History of Ukraine], french translation, Gallimard, p.497
4 Putin V. (2011) "Novyï integratsionnyï proiekt dlia Evrasii—boudouchtchee, kotoroie rojdaetsia sevodnia" (A new project of integration in Eurasia—the future is being written before our eyes), *Izvestiia*, October 3 201.

Gorbachev attempted to maintain Russian dominance to the very last moment through the possibility of forming a new union between the two countries, the Russian Federation's first president, Boris Yeltsin, highlighted Ukraine's significance as the cradle of Russian national identity and history. Putin further emphasised the inseparability of Ukraine and Russia, stating that they cannot exist independently. This attachment to Ukraine, which boasts the second-largest population in the region after Russia, arises from both its geopolitical importance to Russia and the deep-seated significance of its identity. Despite formally recognising Ukrainian independence after the Cold War, Russia's acknowledgement contrasts with the viewpoint held by its politicians and intellectuals, many of whom view Ukraine as an artificial and fragile entity destined to fragment along ethnic and regional lines.[5] This perspective stems from the widespread belief in Russia that Ukrainians are an integral part of the Russian nation, rooted in the historical narrative that Kyiv is the cradle of the Russian nation.

While this interpretation has faced challenges, particularly from within Ukraine since the late 19th and early 20th centuries, it remains prevalent in Russia. It fuels significant political tensions, as highlighted by Alexander Solzhenitsyn in 1990, who argued against the separation of Russians and Ukrainians, viewing them all as part of the people of the Rus of Kiev[6]. This historical perspective leads many Russians to believe that Ukraine is not a foreign country and will inevitably return to Russian influence at some point. Although there is no consensus on this analysis, it remains widespread. Such a view has led to an explicit denial of Ukrainian nationhood and sovereignty at the highest levels of government. In April 2008, Putin reportedly told President George W. Bush that "Ukraine is not even a state. What is Ukraine? Part of its territory is Eastern Europe.

---

5   Lester, J. (1994). "Russian political attitudes to Ukrainian independence", *The Journal of Communist Studies and Transition Politics*, vol. 10 n°2, 1994, p.193-232; Miller, A. (1996) «Obraz Oukrainy i Oukraintsev v rossiïskoï presse posle raspada SSSR» [The image of Ukraine and Ukrainians in the Russian press after the collapse of the USSR], *POLIS* 1996 n°2 p.130-135

6   Solzhenitsyn, A. *Comment réaménager notre Russie?* [How can we redesign our Russia?] Fayard, oct. 1990, p.11-13, 19 and 22

And the other part, the biggest part, we gave to them"[7]. Subsequently, in several of his speeches, Putin used the term "Novorossiia" to refer to the south-eastern regions of Ukraine, referred to the "Rus' of Kiev" as the cradle of Russia, and insisted on the idea of a "single people", claiming that Ukraine was part of Russia's "historic territory" and the "Russian world". In the two following decades, Ukraine swayed between Russia and the West. Still, it took a decisive turn towards the latter following the 2013/14 Euromaydan Revolution (also known as the Revolution of Dignity), which led to the exit of the pro-Russian president, Viktor Yanukovych, and the installation of Petro Poroshenko. Yanukovych's refusal to sign an association agreement with the EU, preferring closer ties with Russia, played a vital role in the protests that quickly escalated into violence and brutal police responses, leading to his downfall. Soon after, Russia annexed the Crimean Peninsula in February-March 2014, backed pro-Russian separatists to help establish the semi-states of Donetsk and Luhansk in eastern Ukraine, and continued to support such actors in the years that followed while claiming that Ukraine is part of Russia. In an article entitled "On the Historical Unity of Russians and Ukrainians", published on the Kremlin website on 12 July 2021, Putin reiterated this perspective, arguing that modern Ukraine "is entirely the product of the Soviet era" and that "Russia has been stolen", concluding that "Ukraine's sovereignty is possible only in partnership with Russia". A year earlier, Putin made amendments to the Russian constitution that supported this interpretation of history (article 67 declares that Russia is "united by a thousand years of history"). In 2014, by ordering the annexation of Crimea and intervention in the Donbas, he radically altered the situation by putting this vision into practice and attempting to subjugate Ukraine by force.

These neo-imperial perspectives on Russian policy and their reception in Ukraine have influenced relations between the two states. Russia adopts an "imperial master" stance, seeking to "re-establish political, economic and military control over the former space of the Empire conquered by Moscow from the seventeenth

---

7   Stent, A. (2014) *The limits of partnership*, Princeton University Press, p.168

century onwards"⁸. Described as colonial, imperial, or neo-imperial, this policy is characterised by an asymmetrical relationship. This is manifested in Russia's persistent refusal to recognise Ukraine as a sovereign state and to respect its ability to make internal and external decisions that could distance it from Russia and weaken Russian positions in the post-Soviet space. Since the collapse of the Soviet Union, Russia has pursued a policy towards Ukraine based on these assumptions, notably by refusing to recognise its full sovereignty and interfering in its internal affairs in the name of the historical and cultural proximity between the two peoples. This policy, facilitated by Ukraine's economic dependence on Russia, is marked by blatant condescension and contempt, as demonstrated by the many statements made by Russian political figures, such as former President Dmitri Medvedev and Putin, who, on 7 February 2022, in the presence of Emmanuel Macron, addressed Ukraine with the words of a despicable Russian song: "Whether you like it or not, my beautiful one, you will have to endure"⁹.

The Kremlin's persistent refusal to recognise Ukraine's sovereignty can also be seen in its rejection of the possibility that Kyiv might make choices that could distance it from Russia and weaken Russian positions in the post-Soviet space. Since the 1990s, developments in Ukraine have aroused growing irritation in Moscow, aggravated by the Orange Revolution of 2004 and the Euromaydan protests between 2013-2014. The main concern of Russia's leaders has been to seek to maintain a regime in Ukraine similar to the one in place in Russia and to block Western influences. They have also sought to counter Ukraine's rapprochement with the European Union (EU) and NATO, perceiving these moves as severe threats to Russian interests in the region, however exaggerated.

Indeed, if the 2022 invasion of Ukraine has much to do with the so-called "besieged fortress" syndrome, let us note the preponderant place occupied by memorial antagonisms in the various processes of Russian subversion. Putin gave a striking overview in his

---

8 Plokhiy S. *Aux portes de l'Europe*, op.cit. p.491 et 495, 498-9
9 Gran, I. (2022) *Z comme zombie* [Z like Zombie], POL, p.143

speech on 22nd February 2022, announcing the official recognition of the separatist republics of the Donbas region, the so-called 'people's republics' of Donetsk and Luhansk. Complementing to some extent an article addressed earlier in July 2021 to Russian officers, Putin denies, in the purest imperial and Soviet historiographical tradition, the legitimate existence of Ukraine as a sovereign and real nation because it was "entirely created by Russia, or more precisely, by Bolshevik and Communist Russia" under Vladimir Lenin's aegis.[10] De facto erasing the cultural and linguistic differences between the two nations now merged into a single "Great Russian" whole, the current master of the Kremlin cannot limit himself solely to rewriting Ukrainian national history.

The brutal invasion of Ukraine is undeniably a sign that we are now in an age of "post-truth". In this war, objective facts are replaced by emotions and personal opinions, which are often influenced by the latter. While the Ukrainian far right has always been the subject of rigorous coverage by specialist researchers and a few journalists, it has remained a niche, not to say confidential, subject restricted to the margins of the news since the Maydan Revolution and the first clashes in the Donbas in 2014. By using the pretext of the "denazification" of the country to justify its systemic terror against a nation seeking independence and sovereignty, Russia has primarily truncated the truth about Ukraine's extremists[11]. By playing on the multiple traumas of the Second World War, which saw the horrors of Nazism unleashed on Central and Eastern Europe, Putin has disproportionately exploited the support of specific Ukrainian nationalist organisations for the German occupier. Even if they did not represent the Ukrainian population then, these organisations serve as ideal ideological foils for the Kremlin to justify its claims in what it considers to be its "near abroad". More than any

---

10 Putin, V. (2022), "Stat'ya Vladimira Putina. Ob istoricheskom edintsve russkikh i ukraintsev" [Vladimir Putin's paper. On the historical unity of Russians and Ukrainians] 12th July 2021, http://kremlin.ru/events/president/news/66181 (accessed on 6th May 2024)
11 Zygar, M. (2023), 'Putin's New Story About the War in Ukraine', available at: https://www.foreignaffairs.com/ukraine/putins-new-story-about-war-ukraine (accessed on 17th November 2023).

other region of Europe, Ukraine is directly targeted by this discourse because of the initial proximity of the Organisation of Ukrainian Nationalists (OUN) to the various organs of the National Socialist Reich with its colonial and genocidal ambitions. In the tragic and short-lived episode of the Second World War, collaboration between the OUN and Nazi Germany, the contours of which continue to be debated by eminent historians such as Oleksandr Zaitsev[12], Myroslav Shkandrij[13], John Paul Himka[14], Gregorz Rossolinski-Liebe[15] and Yaroslav Hrystak, nevertheless retained a prominent place in Russian propaganda. During the existence of Soviet Ukraine, the press frequently demonised the nation based on this collaboration — which only accounted for between 50,000 and 200,000 Ukrainians over the entire duration of the war — to establish and maintain an inevitable guilt-inducing domination of Russia. While one might have thought that the collapse of the USSR in 1991 would have put an end to speeches such as Putin's before the invasion of Ukraine, they have retained a certain predominance in Russia. While this strategy may have struck a chord with the Russian public in 2014, where the term resonates sincerely given the "blood price" paid by the USSR in the Second World War — also considered to be its "darkest hour" in the face of the fascist threat[16] — it has also crystallised in Western public opinion, which is unfamiliar with the "war of memories" in Eastern Europe and the literature dedicated to it. A highly controversial figure in the Ukrainian nationalist

---

12 Zaitsev, O. (2015). Fascism or ustashism? Ukrainian integral nationalism of the 1920s–1930s in comparative perspective. *Communist and post-communist studies*, 48(2-3), 183-193.
Zaitsev, O. (2015). De-mythologizing Bandera: Towards a scholarly history of the Ukrainian nationalist movement. *Journal of Soviet and Post-Soviet Politics and Society*, 1(2), 411-420.
13 Shkandrij, M. (2015). *Ukrainian nationalism: politics, ideology, and literature, 1929-1956*. Yale University Press.
14 Himka, J. P. (2021). *Ukrainian Nationalists and the Holocaust*. ibidem.
15 Rossolinski-Liebe, G. (2014). *Stepan Bandera: The life and afterlife of a Ukrainian nationalist*. ibidem.
16 Bakke, K., Rickard, K., and O'Loughlin, J. (2023), 'Perceptions of the Past in the Post-Soviet Space', *Post-Soviet Affairs*, 39(4), 223-256; Tolz, V and Hutchings, S. (2023), 'Truth With a Z: Disinformation, War in Ukraine, and Russia's Contradictory Discourse of Imperial Identify', *Post-Soviet Affairs*, 39(5), 347-365.

movement of the 1930s and 1940s, Stepan Bandera, is now part of an electric debate in the West that goes far beyond his actions during the Second World War and the Nazi occupation. National hero or war criminal?[17] While some are right to highlight the complexity of the figure and his place in Ukrainian national memory, others rightly or wrongly see him as an irremovable stumbling block to Ukraine's entry into Europe and Western support[18].

But above and beyond any dispute over memory[19], which may have widened the European divide, the immediacy of history and the people involved raises the most questions. In the frenzy of combat, many people have wondered about the backgrounds of specific fighting units and their ideological affiliations. Is this a natural reflex fuelled by the sensationalism of a subject or a morbid fascination? Not since the Maydan Revolution has the Ukrainian far-right received so much media coverage. Far from the single Right Sektor, around which several groups had initially coalesced and which Russian propaganda had until then regarded as the architect of a pseudo "fascist coup" in 2014, the Russian invasion of February 2022 saw the designation of the enemy change, this time targeting the Azov regiment.

The Azov Brigade Issue

The Azov regiment — now known as the 3rd Assault Brigade (3-tia okrema chturmova bryhada "Azov") — is probably the most famous unit of the conflict among those responsible for defending Ukrainian territory from the invading Russians. Many people discovered

---

17 Franqueville, B. & Nonjon, A. (2022) "Mémoire et Sentiment National en Ukraine" [Memory and National Sentiment in Ukraine], *La vie des idées*, May 17 2022. Available at: https://laviedesidees.fr/Memoire-et-sentiment-national-en-Ukraine

18 Considered by some as a collaborator, Stepan Bandera is a figure who should not be celebrated in Europe.

19 Cooper, N. and Jones, K (2009), 'Introduction: Memories of Conflict in Eastern Europe', *Journal of Contemporary European Studies*, 17:1, 3-7; Koposov, N. (2017), *Memory Laws, Memory Wars* (Cambridge: Cambridge University Press); Mälksoo, M. (2021). Militant Memocracy in International Relations: Mnemonical Status Anxiety and Memory Laws in Eastern Europe. *Review of International Studies*, 47(4), 489-507. doi:10.1017/S0260210521000140;

Azov during the terrible Battle of Mariupol, which lasted from 22 February to 20 May 2022. Surrounded, outgunned and cut off from supplies at the vast Azovstal steelworks after several weeks of intense fighting, their resistance, seen live on many networks and news channels, became the symbol of Ukrainian resilience in a war against an enemy that was far more powerful[20] and cruel given the resources involved and the many atrocities committed not only in Mariupol but also in Butcha, Borodianka, and beyond. Essentially killed in action or deported to Russia and the separatist entities of the Donbas, the regiment's fighters have acquired the status of martyred heroes in Ukraine and around the world. The powerful mobilisation of Ukrainian society has dramatically enhanced this status to see them released, and also by the disappearance in disturbing circumstances of 53 members of the unit in an explosion in the separatist prison at Olevnika on July 29 2022. Reconstituted in the aftermath of the battle around SSO (*Syly spetsialnykh operatsii Zbroinykh syl Ukrainy*—Special Operations Forces), and territorial defence units, Azov now appears to be an essential unit in the Ukrainian armed forces. Far from relying solely on the local population's support, the brigade enjoys an international aura. When its staff are not simply rewarded by the Ukrainian Presidency, some of its fighters are received abroad in the most prestigious institutions—witness the reception of a delegation on 23 May 2024 by the former British Prime Minister Boris Johnson—to plead the Ukrainian cause. Similarly, many news channels use images broadcasted by the brigade on their own Youtube channel to document the war.[21]

However, the praise and current reputation of Azov are far from unanimous. Since its formation in the spring of 2014, the unit has been the subject of numerous polemics, highlighting its sulphurous past as a paramilitary unit on the far right of the political spectrum. While a simple Google search often shows the Azov Brigade being described as "Nazi" or "neo-Nazi", other research tends

---

20   Reuters (2022), 'Mariupol Defenders Surrender to Russia but Their Fate is Uncertain', available at: https://www.reuters.com/world/europe/ukrainian-troops-evacuate-mariupol-ceding-control-russia-2022-05-17/ (accessed on 17th November 2023).
21   https://www.youtube.com/@ab3army

to show that (para)fascist symbols such as the Idea of the Nation — presented as a Ukrainian variation of the Wolfsangel rune — and the Black Sun, could often be seen on the uniforms, banners and tattoos of some fighters as well. Although these symbols have since been abandoned and even emptied of their radical substance, they pale into insignificance compared to the other evidence put forward to accuse the regiment of extremism. The problem is primarily due to the backgrounds of some of its members, starting with Andriy Biletsky, the colonel initially in charge of commanding the Brigade and a former activist in clearly xenophobic and anti-Semitic organisations such as Patriot of Ukraine and the Ukrainian Social-National Assembly. Despite having founded and then led Azov at the very start of the conflict in 2014, in 2016, Biletsky founded, based on a core group of veterans, the political party National Corps, a party movement with nationalist and revolutionary leanings that placed it among the most radical and even fascist right-wingers. Although this party claims to be autonomous, many have questioned the links that might exist between the Azov regiment, a "normal" and professionalised component of the Ukrainian army, and the National Corps, suggesting that an entryist strategy might threaten the very foundations of the rule of law and Ukrainian democracy. These fears have been reinforced by the international expansion of the movement, which, up until 2022, had several contacts with extremist groups in the West. In 2019, an attempt was even made in the United States to put Azov on the State Department's list of foreign terrorist organisations[22].

---

22 Atlantic Council (2020), 'Why Azov Should Not be Designated a Foreign Terrorist Organisation', available at: https://www.atlanticcouncil.org/blogs/ukrainealert/why-azov-should-not-be-designated-a-foreign-terrorist-organization/ (accessed on 17th November 2023); New York Times (2020), 'We Once Fought Jihadists. Now we Battle White Supremacists', available at: https://www.nytimes.com/2020/02/11/opinion/politics/white-supremacist-terrorism.html (accessed on 17th November 2023); Likhachev, V. (2022), 'What is Azov Regiment? Honest Answers to the Most Common Questions', available at: https://euromaidanpress.com/2022/04/07/what-is-azov-regiment-honest-answers-to-the-most-common-questions/ (accessed on 17th November 2023); McCallum, A. (2022), 'Much Azov About Nothing: How the Ukrainian 'neo-Nazis' Canard Fooled the World', available at: https://lens.monash.edu/@poli

Seemingly legitimate, this debate on the fundamental nature of Azov and its trajectory became more complex considering Russian aggression, creating a cognitive dissonance within the public debate. The Russian horrors legitimised by the fallacious idea of the "denazification" of Ukraine gave rise to reactions that were as justified as they were contradictory. As in the West, Ukrainian society constantly struggles to maintain democratic consensus. As a result, what might broadly be termed the "far right" symbolises the antithesis of the ideas that have dominated since 1945 since it is considered an absolute evil whose influence must be prevented, if not limited, by a range of political, legal and social measures. By passing the Symonenko laws in 2015, condemning the use of both communist and fascist symbols, and rejecting the far-right three times by giving it less than 2% of the vote in the national elections of 2014 and 2019[23], Ukraine has demonstrated strong support for consensus. However, these mechanisms of relegation or containment have been accompanied by a form of prejudice: until 24 February 2022, the Ukrainian far right was regarded by political scientists as an existing political phenomenon, admittedly with neither significant parliamentary representation nor a plausible path to power"[24], but which nevertheless regained a particular importance in the wake of the Maydan and the Russian annexation of Crimea. This proactivity has been widely documented and has given rise to several debates about the far right's potential to cause harm in Ukrainian politics. The Russian invasion of the country has changed this perception, sometimes excessively. Through a perfectly logical rejection of Russian rhetoric—which, incidentally, is finding it hard to hide its radicalism—and support for the dozens of Ukrainian fighters who die every day defending their land, positions denouncing any focus on

---

tics-society/2022/08/19/1384992/much-azov-about-nothing-how-the-ukraini an-neo-nazis-canard-fooled-the-world (accessed on 17th November 2023).
23 Freedom House (2020), 'A New Eurasian Far Right Rising: Reflections on Ukraine, Georgia, Armenia', available at: https://freedomhouse.org/sites/def ault/files/2020-02/FarRightEurasia_FINAL_.pdf (accessed on 17th November 2023).
24 Freedom House (2018), 'Far-Right Extremism as a Threat to European Democracy', available at: https://freedomhouse.org/sites/default/files/2020-02/ukr aine%20brief%20final_1.pdf (accessed on 17th November 2023).

radical nationalists have multiplied, so that after having been everywhere, the Ukrainian far right now seems to be nowhere. It has even become something of a political and academic taboo.

Writing on the Ukrainian Far-Right: Necessity and Challenges

The far right, whether French, British, American or Russian, is a legitimate subject for study. Many Western states are sensitive to the issue because of their histories. Several have recently either elected far-right politicians in some form or they have become a normalised component of political landscapes. Giorgia Meloni, Prime Minister of Italy and leader of the Brothers of Italy is one such example, with Geert Wilders, leader of the Party for Freedom in the Netherlands, attempting to negotiate with potential coalition partners as the largest party after 2023's national election. The continuing popularity of Donald Trump could spell serious trouble for NATO and the US foreign commitments should he be elected in November 2024, not least due to his penchant for cosying up to autocrats. Should he return to office, he is also very likely to focus his efforts on getting revenge on domestic political opponents and behaving in an authoritarian manner more generally. Significant events have undoubtedly contributed to support for extremists in the West, such as the Global Financial Crisis, Eurozone Crisis, and Refugee Crisis. Far-right political violence has also been rising in some states, although this is a contentious issue.[25] Indeed, some argue that we are approaching, if not in, a so-called 'fifth wave' of terrorism, the underlying energy of which is right-wing extremism.[26] Some European states have also pointed to rising plots by far-right individuals or cells, although remaining secondary to jihadi ones.[27]

---

[25] Ravndal, J., Tandberg, C., Sessolo, S., Jupskås, A., Bjorgo, T. (2023), *RTV Trend Report 2023: Right-Wing Terrorism and Violence in Western Europe, 1990-2022*, available at: https://www.sv.uio.no/c-rex/english/groups/rtv-dataset/2023-rtv-trend-report.pdf (accessed on 15th January 2024).

[26] Auger, V. (2020), 'Right-Wing Terror: A Fifth Global Wave?', *Perpsectives on Terrorism*, 14(3), pp.87-97.

[27] Europol (2023), *Terrorism Situation and Trend Report 2023*, available at: https://www.europol.europa.eu/cms/sites/default/files/documents/European%20

Unlike in the West, the Ukrainian far right is no longer a subject. Studying it is now seen as "moral procrastination"[28]. Faced with such an emotionally charged subject, given the atrocities committed by the Russians in the name of 'denazification', researchers often find it difficult to assert their expertise and avoid suspicion when they do so, despite the minority nature of the phenomenon under study. Post-2014 radical Ukrainian nationalism is a complex and protean political category. Without ignoring its ideological basis and often violent militant practices, we could observe that it had gradually assimilated into the patriotic consensus born in reaction to the war. Today, all Ukrainians fight at the front, regardless of their ideals. Azov is the most representative unit of this trend, becoming a "Special Purpose Regiment" of the National Guard in November 2014 and, in 2023, a brigade—still under the auspices of the Ukrainian government. Its recruitment has expanded based on an elitist and disciplined image in stark contrast to the rest of the Ukrainian army in the 2010s, attracting non-politicised fighters. Therefore, a study of the Ukrainian far-right would be less relevant in light of this reality.

Similarly, it isn't easy to justify an interest in the far right in Ukraine when this same movement has infiltrated the ideological representations and axioms of the Russian government. How, then, can we equate the existence of quasi-groupuscular movements in Ukraine with the explicitly genocidal allegations of Sergeytsev[29],

---

Union%20Terrorism%20Situation%20and%20Trend%20report%202023.pdf (accessed on 15th January 2024).

28 Shekhovtsov, A. (2022), "How the West enabled genocide in Mariupol with its misguided Azov obsession", Euromaidan Press, April 2 2022. Available at: https://euromaidanpress.com/2022/04/02/how-the-west-enabled-genocide-in-mariupol-with-its-misguided-azov-obsession/

29 Sergeytsev, T. (2022), "Chto Rossiia doljna sdelat s Ukrainoï" [What Russia should do with Ukraine', *Ria Novosti*, April 4th 2022. Available at: https://ria.ru/20220403/ukraina-1781469605.html?_x_tr_sl=ru&_x_tr_tl=fr&_x_tr_hl=fr&_x_tr_pto=sc

Medvedev[30], Solovyov[31] or Krassovsky[32], whose stated aim is to wipe Ukraine off the map and, if necessary, kill anyone who resists their re-education? This dichotomy of facts immediately distorts the scientific debate. Even admitting that there is a radical fringe in Ukraine sharing a common minimum of nationalism, xenophobia or populism, it is unthinkable today to elaborate on it as a serious subject at the risk of being accused of reductio ad hitlerum or *rucism*[33].

The reductio ad hitlerum is one of the main arguments in the Russian-Ukrainian conflict. This truncated reasoning stems, as we have said, from the status of Absolute Evil acquired by the crimes perpetrated by the fascist and Nazi regimes in Eastern Europe. Expressing legitimate fears in the light of the intense disinformation campaign Russia is waging around the world, this reductio ad hitlerum leads us to evaluate this Absolute Evil by the yardstick of false propaganda, which has become the decisive criterion for judging the acceptability of opinions, particularly concerning nationalism in its various forms. Intellectual and moral disqualification is, therefore, not uncommon. Any attempt to analyse and understand

---

30 Domańska, M. (2022), Medvedev escalates anti-Ukrainian rhetoric, *OSW*, May 4th 2022, Available at: https://www.osw.waw.pl/en/publikacje/analyses/2022-04-05/medvedev-escalates-anti-ukrainian-rhetoric
31 Petrovskaya, H. (2024). Media Framing of the Russian Invasion of Ukraine: An Analysis of the TV Program 'Evening with Vladimir Solovyov'. Available at: https://research.library.fordham.edu/international_senior/157/
32 Kalikh, A. & Djibladze I. "L'incitation au génocide contre les Ukrainiens dans la propagande russe", *Desk Russie*, April 14 2024, Available at: https://desk-russie.eu/2024/04/14/lincitation-au-genocide-contre-les-ukrainiens.html
33 Popularized in Ukraine in the wake of the Russian invasion, it's a neologism formed from the words "Russian" and "racist", or rashizm in Ukrainian. It was defined on March 13, 2023, in a bill tabled by the Verkhovna Rada, as "the totality of principles and practices as totalitarian and misanthropic", mobilized by Russia in the context of the conflict. These include: the systemic violation of human rights and fundamental freedoms; the cult of power and militarism; the cult of the leader's personality and the sacralization of state institutions; the self-aggrandizement of Russia and Russians through violent oppression and/or the denial of the existence of other peoples; an expansionist state policy implemented through the spread of the Russian language, culture, the Orthodox Church, the media, political and public institutions, and through the promotion of the ideas of the Russkiy mir (Russian world) among other peoples; the systematic violation of the norms and principles of international law, of the sovereign rights, territorial integrity and internationally recognized borders of other states, and of the principle of non-use of force or the threat of force.

the Ukrainian nationalist phenomenon, however objective and nuanced, would be equated with a pro-Russian position. The significant result of this suspicion of crypto-fascism or crypto-*rashizm* is the creation of an ineffective form of anti-fascist consensus, as well as the inability to understand the past and future of the Ukrainian far right. For example, by practising reductio ad hitlerum, it becomes difficult, if not impossible, to grasp the power stakes of the last ten years between the far right and the government on military issues, or to understand the complex relationship between Andriy Biletsky and Arsen Avakov[34], the former mayor of Kharkiv and a previous Minister of the Interior.

Similarly, it is impossible to recognise certain troubling occurrences that seem to indicate persistent connections, such as the National Corps—despite being an independent political movement—regularly claiming to have links with the military unit, Biletsky visiting and taking photos with active soldiers, ongoing conferences with well-known extremists such as the Russian neo-Nazi Alexey Levkin, and more[35]. These formulations suggest that evil cannot and must not be located in Russia. To take an interest in the Ukrainian far right would be to deny specific trajectories in Russia, such as the neo-Nazi Dimitri Rogozine, appointed by Putin to head Roskosmos, Pavel Goubarev, the first governor of Donetsk and a former member of the racist neo-Nazi party Russian National Unity, or quite simply the Wagner Group—now part of the Russian army—or Rusich, a regular neo-Nazi unit specialising in the torture of Ukrainian prisoners commanded by the notorious St Petersburg neo-Nazi Alexeï Milchakov, who declares himself as such in interviews[36] in which he talks about his cut ear collections and his taste

---

34 Gomza, I., and Zajaczkowski, J. (2019). Black Sun Rising: Political Opportunity Structure Perceptions and Institutionalization of the Azov Movement in Post-Euromaidan Ukraine. *Nationalities Papers,* 47(5), 774.
35 Atlantic Council (2020), 'The Azov Regiment has not Depoliticised', available at: https://www.atlanticcouncil.org/blogs/ukrainealert/the-azov-regiment-has-not-depoliticized/ (accessed on 30th November 2023).
36 Kozhurin, Dmitry (2022). "Who Are The Neo-Nazis Fighting For Russia In Ukraine?". Radio Free Europe/Radio Liberty, 27 May 2022. Available at https://www.rferl.org/a/russian-neo-nazis-fighting-ukraine/31871760.html

for the smell of burning flesh[37]. The resulting intellectual pattern is evident at this challenging time when Ukraine has to fight in the information theatre: guilt by association and transitivity. This line of reasoning, based on the idea that the Ukrainian far right constitutes a relatively narrow and marginal milieu—which is true—leads to unfounded associations. Thus, slanderous reasoning with no head or tail, added to the idea of implicitly supporting Russian imperialism, deprives several studies on the Ukrainian far right of much of their validity.

Finally, how can we fail to mention the opposite reactions, which complicate the study of such a phenomenon and reinforce suspicion? Some perceive refusing to work on the Ukrainian far right as a break from the scientific ideal, not to say it is an inevitable collaboration with the subject of study on the pretext of being loyal to the Ukrainian cause. Whether it is the first or the second form of suspicion, the result remains the same: blocking research and debate rather than facilitating them. So what should we do? Is it coherent to continue contributing to the study of a phenomenon and educating people about it when various media campaigns have been implemented to ensure that it is no longer covered or misinterpreted? Should we wait until the end of the conflict and lose precision? Or risk opprobrium all the same? The current situation in Ukraine and beyond is highly dynamic and subject to many changes. This underlines the importance of staying alert and informed, seeking out reliable sources of information and analysing events with a critical mind. Narratives can often be shaped to serve particular interests, and a nuanced understanding of the historical, political and social contexts is essential to grasp the complex issues facing the world today fully. As a result, if specialists fail to speak out, these attitudes reinforce the risk of disinformation through the proliferation of fake news and conspiracy theories, rendering any form of argumentative deconstruction of Russian propaganda ineffective. This is a huge mistake, both because it gives Russia an advantage on the ground and because it prevents the democratic consensus in Ukraine from being maintained.

---

37   https://x.com/nexta_tv/status/1563793653025456129

This volume aims to plunge into the "eye of the storm", exploring the origins, evolution and controversies surrounding the Azov Brigade to bring a degree of order and clarity to an issue that confuses and obscures, especially given the different narratives defended by the leading players in the ongoing war between Russia and Ukraine. We thought it would be helpful to attempt to describe, based on the research experience of several renowned researchers. These various polemical processes contribute to establishing a permanent logic of suspicion, through which the study of the Ukrainian far right often loses the serenity and perspective needed to understand the phenomenon. We cannot stress enough that Russia's invasion of Ukraine in 2022 — and indeed its broader activities in the post-Soviet space — has much to do with historical and resurgent imperialism and the drift towards authoritarianism[38]. We cannot attribute the primary responsibility for the conflict to any country other than Russia.

Furthermore, we express our concern about the situation turning in Russia's favour, as is happening at the time of writing. We believe that Western states should continue to support Ukraine with military and economic aid. Nevertheless, we cannot overlook the fact that Ukraine does have an extreme right wing and that this should be a concern for Ukrainians and non-Ukrainians alike for several reasons. It could even grow in the years to come if Russia succeeds in winning the present war and Ukrainians feel abandoned or betrayed by the West. That being the case, several questions remain legitimate and need to be asked.

---

[38] Dylan, H., Gioe, D., and Grossfeld, E. (2023), 'The Autocrat's Intelligence Paradox: Vladimir Putin's (Mis)management of Russian Strategic Assessment in the Ukraine War', *The British Journal of Politics and International Relations*, 25(3), 385-404; Erdinger, H. (2023), 'Offensive Ideas: Structural Realism, Classical Realism, and Putin's War on Ukraine', *International Affairs*, 98(6), 1873-1893; Götz, E. and Staun, J. (2022), 'Why Russia Attacked Ukraine: Strategic Culture and Radicalized Narratives', *Contemporary Security Policy*, 43(3), 482-497; Kuzio, T. (2023), 'Imperial Nationalism as the Driver Behind Russia's Invasion of Ukraine', *Nations and Nationalism*, 29(1), 30-38; Oksamytna, K. (2023), 'Imperialism, Supremacy, and the Russian Invasion of Ukraine', *Contemporary Security Policy*, 44(4), 497-512.

To begin with, to what extent does the Ukrainian far right pose a problem? The state is becoming more democratic but has faced challenges from its far right for some time. Indeed, Ukraine has a history of such movements, notably the OUN, as mentioned above, led by Bandera during the Second World War, which collaborated with the Nazis. However, some of today's organisations have local support and mayors in some parts of Ukraine. In addition, there are discernible transnational far-right networks involving Ukraine, whether concerning mixed martial arts, music festivals, or other shared interests[39]. It is also true that some volunteer battalions established in 2014 as a result of internal unrest, Russian interference, and the sorry state of the Ukrainian army can trace their origins to far-right movements, such as what was the Patriot of Ukraine, founded in 1999 and defunct in 2014. The Azov Battalion, as it was called at the time, was one of these volunteer battalions. Still, there were also many others and different ones at the time, from those organised by extremists to those created by foreigners opposed to Russia[40], such as the Georgian National Legion. The leaders that formed these units could also be very different politically from individuals that joined them, with reputation, location and other factors influencing volunteers' decisions. Given the clear propaganda value of the volunteer battalions for Russia, the dangers to the Ukrainian state, and the commitments made under the Minsk I and II agreements (2014 and 2015, respectively), the Ukrainian government quickly placed the Azov Battalion and other units under state control in the months and years that followed[41]. It may even be the case that another volunteer unit, the Ukrainian Volunteer Corps of the Right Sector, continues to operate independently, albeit in

---

[39] Bellingcat (2020), 'Dispatches from Asgardsrei: Ukraine's Annual Neo-Nazi Music Festival', available at: https://www.bellingcat.com/news/2020/01/02/dispatches-from-asgardsrei-ukraines-annual-neo-nazi-music-festival/ (accessed on 30th November 2023).

[40] Umland, A. (2019), 'Irregular Militias and Radical Nationalism in Post-Euromaydan Ukraine: The Prehistory and Emergence of the 'Azov' Battalion in 2014', *Terrorism and Political Violence*, 31(1), 105-131.

[41] Russia Matters (2020), 'Is Ukraine a Hub for International White Supremacist Fighters', available at: https://www.russiamatters.org/analysis/ukraine-hub-international-white-supremacist-fighters (accessed on 17th November 2023).

cooperation with the Ukrainian armed forces[42]. In view of the above, we recognise that Ukraine faces challenges from the far right—as do many Western states today—and must confront them if it is to strengthen its democratic credentials. Still, there is little evidence to support the Kremlin's claims about the country, given the electoral unpopularity of far-right political parties and that the Azov Brigade is now just one of hundreds of units in the Ukrainian armed forces.

Thus, the focus on the unit likely exceeds its military and political significance. In addition, some foreign fighters from the West served in the unit or had links with it or other far-right organisations in Ukraine[43]. However, their numbers probably never exceeded a few hundred in total. In contrast, the Azov Movement, while undoubtedly an offshoot of the Azov Battalion, given its success and fame, is a collection of organisations and was perhaps made up of around 20,000 people in 2018. Specifically, there is a political party, the National Corps, and a national paramilitary group, the National Militia, which has now been replaced by the Centuria[44]. The main question here is the extent to which connections continue to exist between the entities mentioned, given that the military unit is now under state control. Starting at the top, the leadership has undoubtedly changed. The actual leadership of the Azov Brigade has changed chiefly, including founder Biletsky, who subsequently left to form the National Corps party. It has also been pointed out that the Ukrainian government eliminated the extreme elements and foreign fighters following the absorption of the Azov Battalion into the state forces, finding alternative employment for the former group.[45] While some of this exploits the Azov Brigade's

---

42 Mutallimzada, K., and Steiner, K. (2023), 'Fighters' Motivations for Joining Extremist Groups: Investigating the Attractiveness of the Right Sector's Volunteer Ukrainian Corps', *European Journal of International Security*, 8(1), 47-69.
43 Rekawek, K. (2023), *Foreign Fighters in Ukraine: The Brown-Red Cocktail* (Abingdon: Routledge).
44 Stanford University (2022), 'Azov Movement', available at: https://cisac.fsi.stanford.edu/mappingmilitants/profiles/azov-battalion (accessed on 30th November 2023).
45 Mironova, V. and Sergatskova (2017), 'How Ukraine Reined in its Militias: The Lessons for Other States', *Foreign Affairs*, available at: https://www.foreignaff

fame, it's essential to ask how the organisational changes and personnel losses suffered by the unit—certainly since the Russian invasion of 2022—have changed it, if at all. Consequently, it may be essential to take seriously the view that "[e]ach year the connections (between regiment and movement) are looser"[46]. Nevertheless, it is valuable to explore in detail the history of key individuals and organisations, their actions since the formation of the unit, and ideological development, and to establish what connections, national and transnational, do or do not persist today given the need to cut through the fog and contradictions of Russian disinformation efforts. At the same time, we are cautious not to neglect the Ukrainian far right, as seems to be happening in some Western media and supportive governments during the war to maintain support for the country. Ultimately, it is essential to cut through the narratives promoted by the different players to understand events in Ukraine better for the benefit of several audiences, from Ukrainian citizens to Western decision-makers.

Outline of the Book

The primary purpose of this book is to investigate the changing Azov military unit, from battalion to brigade. We consider several dimensions in depth, from those who established it and their ideologies through why volunteer battalions came to be in Ukraine, Russian perceptions of the unit, and political views held within it in recent years. This book brings together many experts of Ukrainian politics who approach Azov from different angles and enrich our knowledge of the unit through diverse methodologies, from interviews within the unit to content analysis of Russian media channels. Specifically, our book is structured in seven very different chapters. As editors of this volume, we allowed our authors

---

airs.com/articles/ukraine/2017-08-01/how-ukraine-reined-its-militias (accessed on 30th November 2023).

46 CNN (2023), 'A Far-Right Battalion Has a Key Role in Ukraine's Resistance. Its Neo-Nazi History Has Been Exploited by Putin', available at: https://edition.cnn.com/2022/03/29/europe/ukraine-azov-movement-far-right-intl-cmd/index.html (accessed on 30th November 2023).

significant leeway out of interest as to what they would find. We only gave them rough chapter titles and questions to answer. How exactly they undertook their chapters was left up to them to decide.

The first chapter, by Przemyslaw Witkowski, investigates the far-right thinkers who animate the beliefs of those who created the then Azov Battalion. It considers how much people were catapulted into the spotlight during the Euromaydan Revolution. Finally, it considers the changing connections between the Azov military unit and Ukrainian far-right movements and those abroad, such as in Poland. He sees the Azov Brigade as continuing to connect with the wider Azov Movement, but these have lessened over time.

Rosaria Puglisi provides our second chapter, which focuses on how and why volunteer battalions appeared in Ukraine in 2014. The chapter goes beyond the Azov Battalion. Puglisi views this as a 'bottom-up' phenomenon, with Ukrainians mobilising themselves because the state could not. Such societal action is not just a feature of recent years but a pattern in Ukrainian history. It is very much a story that distinguishes it from Russia's 'top-down' history. Puglisi also argues that, while it would be easy to dismiss these units as a ragtag bunch of right-wing extremists, this is far from accurate. Indeed, despite the significant focus on units like Azov and Right Sector, these were a minority of the total number formed. These volunteers may well have helped lay the foundations for the resistance the Ukrainian armed forces offered since the Russian invasion in 2022.

Thirdly, Taras Tarasiuk and Petro Burkovskiy contribute a chapter concerned with the evolution of Ukrainian nationalism. Of course, scholars point to how those on the far right are increasingly referring to themselves as 'nationalist' or 'conservative'. Tarasiuk and Burkovskiy begin with an outline of far-right organisations in Ukraine today and explore how participants in such circles have become of military significance, even the 'tip of the spear' against Russia. Their activities in the armed forces and potential appeal to wider audiences are thus worthy of close observation. Furthermore, if Ukraine is intent on becoming a liberal democracy aligned with the West by joining the European Union, its leaders will need to think carefully about how to deal with these formations, which may be seen as heroes in the long term.

The fourth chapter is by Ivan Gomza, who offers a stellar psychodramatic interpretation of Azov's role in the Russia-Ukraine War. The symbolic dimension of the conflict is of great significance in a period where misinformation is rife and even a significant part of the conflict. In this way, Gomza expertly engages with Russian digital media and assesses responses to Azov. Peculiarly, the unit is given attention far beyond its military significance in these spaces, likely due to the circumstances of its creation and the need for Putin to render believable his claim that Ukraine is Nazified. Russian representations and beliefs about the unit also have many peculiarities and contradictions.

Bertrand de Franqueville, in the fifth chapter, moves on to consider the crucial question of whether the Azov Brigade is now a depoliticised entity. After having conducted extensive fieldwork and interviewed several members of the unit, he reached the problematic conclusion that far-right elements and linkages between the unit and the Azov Movement still exist, but other people originally joined and continue to enter the formation with entirely different political views, from anarchists to liberals. Furthermore, some became involved due to geographical proximity or attention garnered by the unit regarding its military successes. Rather than the whole unit being 'Nazified'—ubiquitous in Russian propaganda—de Franqueville recognises the 'messy' nature of the unit's evolution and membership.

The sixth chapter concerns whether Ukraine has become a hub for the transnational far right and is by Mollie Saltskog. In 2019, the Soufan Group published a report on the rise of white supremacy extremism. Saltskog builds on that work, finding that Ukraine certainly has some troubling far-right connections, yet Russia has stronger ties still. Not only this, but the rise of the Ukrainian far right must also be seen in the context of the growing popularity of right-wing extremism and dissatisfaction with economic, political, and social events in Western democratic states.

The seventh and final chapter is by Kacper Rekawek, who has written extensively on foreign fighters that have participated in the conflict in Ukraine. His chapter specifically focuses on those who travelled to join the Azov military unit between 2014 and 2022. Ultimately, Rekawek finds little evidence of the formation being some 'far-right Al Qaeda' that would somehow orchestrate attacks in the West when foreign fighters returned to their home countries. Indeed, the Azov Battalion attracted only a handful of such fighters over the years, and, to date, very little has materialised in the way of violence by returnees.

We then draw the book to a close with our conclusion.

1 The Azov Brigade
Origins, Influences and Ideological Development

Przemysław Witkowski

Introduction

The Azov **Brigade** is a unique military unit in contemporary Europe. It was established in May 2014 as a paramilitary, independent volunteer battalion, whose members were initially mainly nationalists, Neo-fascists and football hooligans, in reaction to growing pro-Russian separatism in eastern Ukraine. In September 2014, it was transformed into a regiment and became part of the armed forces of Ukraine. Its numbers increased significantly, and most of the new soldiers no longer had anything to do with the original ideology of the unit's creators. In January 2023, the unit received the status of an assault brigade, was enlarged, and volunteers were again accepted into its ranks. In this context, it is worth asking the question: what is the ideological character of this armed unit today?

The **Brigade**, now part of the armed forces of a democratic state, started as an extremist group and is still controversial for this reason. In this context, accurate information is mixed with rumours, misinformation, and slander. In the Russian media, the Azov **Brigade** is portrayed as being composed of Nazis, Neo-Nazis, and extremists.[1] In turn, some Ukrainian and Western media tend to omit controversial elements of their symbolism or ideological references in their descriptions of this unit.[2] Other media, which try to balance the image of this milieu, face accusations of favouring Russia or, at

---

1 И. Петров (2022), „Верховный суд РФ признал украинский нацполк "Азов" террористической организацией", *ВЕРХОВНЫЙ СУД РОССИЙСКОЙ ФЕДЕРАЦИИ*, 3 August, Available at: https://vsrf.ru/press_center/mass_media/31424, (Accessed: 19 January 2023).

2 O. Kuzmenko (2020), 'The Azov Regiment has not depoliticized', *Atlantic Council*, 19 March, Available at: https://www.atlanticcouncil.org/blogs/ukraineale rt/the-azov-regiment-has-not-depoliticized (Accessed: 1 December 2023).

best, suggestions that "this is not the time" because a defensive war is underway[3], in which Azov is actively involved. At the same time, the leaders of the Azov Movement themselves, in the official communiqués of the unit and its civilian sister party of the National Corps, have been trying to present themselves primarily as veterans and patriots for several years.[4]

In the last few years, the Azov **Brigade** has increasingly become the object of research, both scientific and journalistic investigations. Michael Colborne devoted a book to the Azov Movement, and large fragments about **the Brigade** can also be found in Kacper Rekawek or texts by Adrien Nonjon, Anton Shekhovtsov, Andreas Umland, Vyacheslav Likhachev, and numerous publications by the investigative journalism group Bellingcat and the Ukrainian independent media websites Zaborona, Hromadske and analyses of centres dealing with political extremism, such as the Center for Analysis of Radical Right or Counter Extremism Project.[5]

---

3   O. Katerji (2022) 'By focusing on the Azov Battalion we are falling into Putin's trap', *The New Statesman*, 12 April. Available at: https://www.newstatesman.com/world/europe/ukraine/2022/04/why-focusing-on-the-azov-battalion-means-we-are-falling-into-putins-trap (Accessed: 1 February 2023).
4   Azov Regiment (2021) 'ATTENTION! THE AZOV REGIMENT'S RESPONSE TO THE ALLEGATIONS PUBLISHED IN "TIME" MAGAZINE. Available at: https://azov.org.ua/the-azov-regiments-response-to-the-allegations-published-in-time-magazine (Accessed: 1 February 2023).
5   M. Colborne (2022) *From the Fires of War. Ukraine's Azov Movement and the Global Far Right*. Stuttgart and Hannover: ibidem Press.; K. Rękawek (2022) *Foreign Fighters in Ukraine. The Brown–Red Cocktail*. London: Routledge; A. Nonjon (2020) 'Olena Semenyaka, The "First Lady" of Ukrainian Nationalism', *Illiberalism Studies Program Working Papers*, September. Available at: https://www.illiberalism.org/wp-content/uploads/2020/10/Nonjon-Olena-Semenyaka-The-First-Lady-of-Ukrainian-Nationalism.pdf (Accessed: 1 February 2023); A. Shekovtsov (2020) 'Why Azov Should Not be Designated a Foreign Terrorist Organisation'. Available at: https://www.atlanticcouncil.org/blogs/ukrainealert/why-azov-should-not-be-designated-a-foreign-terrorist-organization/ (Accessed: 18 January 2024); A. Umland, (2019) 'Irregular Militias and Radical Nationalism in Post-Euromaydan Ukraine: The Prehistory and Emergence of the 'Azov' Battalion in 2014', *Terrorism and Political Violence*, Vol. 31, no 1, pp. 105-131.; V. Likhachev (2015) 'The "Right Sector" and others: The behavior and role of radical nationalists in the Ukrainian political crisis of late 2013–Early 2014', *Communist and Post-Communist Studies* vol. 48, no. 2-3, pp. 257–271.; K. Kovalenko (2020) 'Fight for the white race. How the Russian neo-Nazi Denis Nikitin promotes his ideas in Ukraine, and why the Azov Regiment', *Zaborona*, 12 June. Available at:https://zaborona.com/en/fight-for-the-white-race-how-

Also crucial for understanding the ideological positioning of the Azov **Brigade** on the map of political thought is a more detailed description of the structure of the Azov movement. The military unit is not a completely independent political entity, separated from other movement branches, but a larger whole, a network of entities connected by leaders, symbolism, or jointly implemented activities. Therefore, an essential clue to understanding the ideological turn of the Azov **Brigade** is the choice of patrons of the movement from previous generations of Ukrainian nationalists, books published by Azov-related publishing houses, cultural, political, and sports events organised in its social centres, as well as the activities of famous former and current militants (also in groups seemingly independent of the Brigade). The very structure of the **movement** is not a random choice but is also the result of the ideology professed by its activists and **context**, and as such, must also be discussed in this text. This structure can also be found in other far-right political groupings related to the Azov Movement, drawing on the example of the autonomous nationalist, such as CasaPound Italia or the Polish Stormtroopers movement.[6] This structure allows for avoiding easy destruction of the movement by changing its construction from hierarchical to networked and dividing it into thematic segments that are formally independent. Also, it makes it possible to bring to the fore the parts of the movement that are more acceptable to public opinion while hiding those that are more extremist in nature or even officially denying any connections with

---

[6] the-russian-neo-nazi-denis-nikitin-promotes-his-ideas-in-ukraine-and-why-the-azov-regiment (Accessed: 1 February 2023).; V. Engel (2019) 'Zelensky Struggles To Contain Ukraine's Neo-Nazi Problem', *Center for Analysis of Radical Right*, 30 November. Available at: https://www.radicalrightanalysis.com/2019/11/30/zelensky-struggles-to-contain-ukraines-neo-nazi-problem (Accessed: 1 February 2023); K. Rękawek (2022) *Western Extremists and the Russian Invasion of Ukraine in 2022 – All Talk, But Not a Lot of Walk*, Counter Extremism Project. C. Froio, G. Castelli, G. Bulli, M. Albanese (2020) *CasaPound Italia : contemporary extreme-right politics*, Abingdon: Routledge.; R. Schlembach, (2013) 'The 'Autonomous Nationalists': new developments and contradictions in the German neo-Nazi movement', *A Journal For And About Social Movements*, Vol. 5 (2): 295–318.; P. Witkowski (2019) '„Europa będzie biała albo bezludna", czyli szturmowcy', *Krytyka Polityczna*, 30 April, Available at: https://krytykapolityczna.pl/kraj/szturmowcy-przemyslaw-witkowski (Accessed: 1 February 2023).

them. At the same time, it is also divided into layers in which, depending on public visibility, the professed ideology is presented differently. Such an approach to discussing the Azov Brigade can allow us to answer questions about its ideological nature, provide a basis for sound conclusions, and reduce speculation.

The ideological evolution of the Azov Movement will be presented here, from its Neo-Nazi roots, through the formation of the movement based on the cadre of skinheads and stadium hooligans, and the influence of new Western currents of Neo-fascism, to the period of transition to the mainstream, initiated by the participation of activists of the movement in the EuroMaydan Revolution. Following these events and the unrest in eastern Ukraine exacerbated by Russia in 2014, the Azov Brigade was born as a 'volunteer battalion'. Since then, it has proceeded through expansions (from a battalion to a regiment to a brigade as of 2024) and has been brought under state control. In this analysis, it is essential to remember that the current patriotic attitude of the Azov Brigade (but still based on nationalism) is a stage that has lasted only a few years. It was preceded by a long ideological evolution, starting with the most extreme currents of the right, and, along with the inclusion of this military unit, a large part of the extremist references were eliminated in the unit itself, shifting them to the activities of the National Corps party, the paramilitary group Centuria and other elements of the Azov movement. At the same time, if we want to maintain scientific integrity, it is impossible to separate the Brigade from the milieu associated with it in the Azov Movement, as by the very choice of the model of building the movement, they are inherently linked.

This text is an attempt at sketching an overview of Azov's Brigade ideological background and analysis of the evolution of this milieu from the mid-90s (the Patriot of Ukraine/SNA era) to today, where Azov has allegedly evolved to a kind of "mainstream patriotism". At the same time, I try to answer the following questions in this chapter: Which individuals and movements have mainly influenced Azov's ideology, way of conducting political work, and movement structure?; What role did the Ukrainian far-right (especially those related to/preceding Azov) play in the EuroMaydan Revolution?; and how did the EuroMaydan Revolution and war with Russia impact the Ukrainian far-right and the Azov Brigade's ideology and whether today's Azov Movement has kept some of its earlier revolutionary and extremist aspects?. The author puts forward the thesis that although the brigade itself has moved away from extremist content in its communications, adopting at most a perspective of nationalistically tinged patriotism, several prominent figures from the Azov leadership remain part of the network of the Azov Movement, which remains neo-fascist in essence and training centres and shares social centres, with some soldiers participating in sports competitions, concerts and other public activities organised by the wider Azov Movement. This text investigates the organisational and ideological development of the Azov Movement, then the influence of The EuroMaydan Revolution on the creation of the Azov Battalion, and then moves on to discuss the impact of earlier generations of Ukrainian nationalists and non-Ukrainian currents of political thought on the formation of Azov's ideology. Finally, I ask whether the Azov Brigade 2021 made an ideological move towards mainstream political discourse.

The EuroMaydan Revolution and the Creation of the Azov Battalion

To understand the Azov movement's ideological roots and geopolitical positions, it is essential to note what kind of Ukrainian nationalism they represent. Azov ideology is not a typical position for this current in Ukraine, especially regarding relations with neighbouring nations. The earlier incarnations of Ukrainian nationalism, in particular Stepan Bandera's Organization of Ukrainian Nationalists (OUN) and its military arm, the Ukrainian Insurgent Army (UPA) from the 1930s and 1940s, took an ethnocentric (Ukrainian-centric) position, directing their aversion equally towards Russia (or its geopolitical successor, the USSR) and Poland.[7] Most contemporary Ukrainian nationalist organisations refer to this tradition

---

7   See further: G. Rossolinski-Liebe (2014) *Stepan Bandera: The Life and Afterlife of a Ukrainian Nationalist. Fascism, Genocide, and Cult*, Stuttgart and Hannover: ibidem Press.

today, such as the Ukrainian National Assembly – Ukrainian People's Self-Defense (UNA-UNSO), All-Ukrainian Union Svoboda or Right Sector, and whose traces can also be found in groups such as Batkivshchyna.[8] Hence, the position of the Azov Movement is specific and unusual in this context, as I demonstrate.

Initially, in the 1990s, the future leaders of the Azov Regiment tried to participate in the creation of a traditional, hierarchical and centralised party typical for this aforementioned ideological current. They were active in the Social-National Party of Ukraine (SNPU), established in 1991. Its militia was founded in Lviv in 1996 under the Society for Supporting the Ukrainian Army and Fleet Patriot of Ukraine, later called Patriot of Ukraine for short. At the beginning of the 21st century, the party began moving away from Neo-Nazism and towards nationalist positions. This process led to its transformation in 2004 into the All-Ukrainian Svoboda Union, led by Oleh Tiahnybok. This move resulted from Tiahnybok's ambition to become a mainstream politician. The SNPU militia—Patriot of Ukraine—was too extreme and violent for the mainstreaming plans of Tiahnybok and was disbanded. Some of the younger activists from Kharkiv, including Andriy Biletsky, Mykola Kravchenko, and Oleh Odnorozhenko, did not accept this. They recreated the Patriot of Ukraine organisation, re-establishing it in 2008 as the Neo-fascist party Social-National Assembly (SNA) based on its branches from eastern Ukraine.[9] The attempted move to the centre initially brought success to the new Tiahnybok party. In the first fifteen years of the twenty-first century, it recorded results in the parliamentary elections in western Ukraine in the range of 5-7%, with a record 34.69% in local elections in the Ternopil district (2009). In presidential polls, Tiahnybok reached 28% of support (December 2013). At the same time, SNA remained on the fringes of the Ukrainian political scene.

When on November 21, 2013, protests began in Ukraine due to the failure to sign the Association Agreement with the European

---

[8] W. Dobrowolski (2022) *Ruch Azowski. Ideologia, działalność i walka ukraińskich nacjonalistów*. Warszawa: Capital, pp.17-20.
[9] Ibidem, pp.21-25.

Union by the then President of Ukraine, Viktor Yanukovych, the group led by Biletsky was still a mixture of former skinheads and football hooligans, ideologically led primarily in the spirit of National Socialism. It was a group whose values revolved around the idea of a hierarchical society, authoritarianism, and calls for national rebirth, with a penchant for direct action combined with a paramilitary flair. Since 2011, the group has faced repression from the authorities, including the imprisonment of its leaders, noticeably Biletsky (from 27th December 2011 to 24th February 2014) . So long as Ukraine was ruled by the team of corrupt President Viktor Yanukovych, balancing between the West and Russia, the group remained on the margins of the political scene, one of many organisations of the Ukrainian extreme right.

The social protests in 2013 and 2014 shifted the Biletsky group towards a 'military' attitude. From this point, its paramilitary structure and ultra-patriotic phraseology began to gain visibility and importance. The nationalist and Neo-fascist milieu played a visible role in the protests related to the EuroMaydan and the overthrow of the pro-Russian president Viktor Yanukovych in 2013 and 2014.[10] Most Ukrainians protesting then were prepared only for peaceful, liberal protests. They were surprised by the brutality of the authorities' reaction, which was sent against them by special police units, including snipers and groups of paid aggressive hooligans, commonly known as 'titushky' in Ukraine. As a result, it was the nationalists and Neo-fascists who became the core of the EuroMaydan self-defence forces, grouping themselves into paramilitary units, which were called 'hundreds'. Unlike most other protesters, they were equipped with firearms. Many had received regular training under the guidance of veterans of the war in Afghanistan, had experienced direct clashes with the police, and many of them regularly trained in combat sports. It was mainly thanks to them that the protesters managed to survive the massive attack of the pro-government police on the Euromaidan protesters on 18th/19th February

---

10 A. Umland (2019) 'Irregular Militias and Radical Nationalism in Post-Euromaydan Ukraine: The Prehistory and Emergence of the 'Azov' Battalion in 2014', *Terrorism and Political Violence*, Vol. 31, no 1, pp. 105-131.

2014, which resulted in the deaths of almost 100 protesters and 13 police. It is worth noting, however, that the escalation of protests from peaceful to attacks on pro-government police in the initial period of the EuroMaydan was also primarily the result of the actions of nationalists and Neo-fascists, who were the first to start this type of activity, attacking with batons or Molotov cocktails.[11]

During the protests, an initially informal coalition of nationalist and Neo-fascist groups, Right Sector, was formed in March 2014 and transformed into a political party. It was joined by the leading groups representing these circles in Ukraine, i.e. UNA-UNSO, SNA and several smaller ones (Trident, Carpathian Sich, White Hammer).[12] However, high visibility in the protests did not translate into electoral successes. In the 25 May 2014 presidential race, Right Sector leader Dmytro Yarosh received 127,000 votes, 0.7% of the total cast. In the October elections, Svoboda and Right Sector, which went into the election separately, won 6 and 1 seats in the 450-seat parliament, which can be considered a devastating defeat, especially since Svoboda lost 31 seats compared to the previous election result. Ideological differences between the Bandera heritage current (UNA-UNSO and Svoboda) and the Azov current (Patriot of Ukraine — later the National Corps) of Ukrainian nationalism, internal conflicts between the leaders and the prominent leader's (Yarosh) departure from the party at the end of 2015 ended the existence of the Right Sector. Although the party still exists on the Ukrainian political scene with former UNA-UNSO activists as its members, the Right Sector is of little significance today.

At the same time, in February 2014, on the initiative of the Kharkiv Neo-fascists and football hooligans of the FC Metalist Kharkiv club from the "Sect 82" group, armed city defence units were formed against the forces of Russian-backed separatists. Initially under the name 'Black Corps' in April, they were recognised

---

11   BBC (2014) 'Groups at the sharp end of Ukraine unrest', *BBC*, 1 February. Available at: https://www.bbc.com/news/world-europe-26001710 (Accessed: 1 February 2023).
12   V. Likhachev (2015) 'The "Right Sector" and others: The behavior and role of radical nationalists in the Ukrainian political crisis of late 2013–Early 2014', *Communist and Post-Communist Studies* vol. 48, no. 2-3, pp. 257–271.

by the Ukrainian Minister of Internal Affairs, Arsen Avakov, as a unit of the 'Special Tasks Patrol Police'. On the 5th of May 2014, they began using the name Azov Battalion. It was financially supported by the Ukrainian financial magnate Ihor Kolomoyskyi.[13] The group was taken under the protection of the leader of the right-wing populist Radical Party, Oleh Lyashko, former UNA-UNSO leader Dmytro Korchynsky, party deputy Yulia Tymoshenko Batkivshchyna and the then governor of the Donetsk district, businessman Serhiy Taruta, and the Minister of Internal Affairs. Instructors who trained Azov often had experience in the Georgian Armed Forces.[14] The Azov Battalion proved itself in the battles with the separatists in Kharkiv, Novoazovsk, Donetsk and Mariupol. In November 2014, it was incorporated into the National Guard of Ukraine as the Azov Regiment. As a result of its involvement in fighting and the courage of its soldiers on the battlefield, Azov became widely known in Ukraine, becoming, for many, a symbol of resistance to separatists' actions. Azov's deputy commander, Vadim Troyan, became the police chief of the Kyiv district in 2014 (however, not including the city of Kyiv itself). Its commander, Biletsky, was 2014 elected from a single-mandate constituency to the Ukrainian parliament from the lists of the Popular Front of the future Prime Minister of Ukraine, Arseniy Yatsenyuk.

The Influence of Ukrainian and non-Ukrainian Currents of Political Thought on the Formation of Azov's Ideology

The intellectual roots of the people who created the Azov Brigade can be traced by taking a closer look at books published by the Azov Movement's publishing houses (i.e. "Plomin", "Orientyr", and "Nouvi Arditi"). First, there are books by Ukrainian nationalists

---

13   J. Cohen (2015) 'In the battle between Ukraine and Russian separatists, shady private armies take the field', *Reuters*, 5 May. Available at: https://www.reuters.com/article/idUS60927080220150505 (Accessed: 1 February 2023).
14   A. Nemtsova (2017) 'War and Murder in Eastern Ukraine', The Daily Beast, 27 May 2014, updated 12 July 2017. Available at: https://www.thedailybeast.com/war-and-murder-in-eastern-ukraine (Accessed: 1 February 2023).

from the 1930s. Works by authors such as Yuri Lypa, Dmytro Dontsov, Yaroslav Stetsko, Mykhailo Kolodzinsky, and Mykola Stsiborskyi have been published. The choice of these texts is not accidental and differs from the ideological patterns for varieties of Ukrainian nationalism that predated the Azov Movement. Of course, they were known, but a particular specificity of their selection by the Azov Movement is noticeable here, manifesting itself primarily in the location of geopolitical accents in the texts of these ideologists and the resulting ideological ones. Lypa, military MD and nationalist activist created The Black Sea Doctrine, which made it possible to lay new geopolitical axes towards which Ukraine was to orient itself. It would be pan-Slavism, no longer understood as pro-Russian, or capitulation to Polish imperial ideas, or a broader choice for this region for centuries — westernisation or a Eurasian centre with Moscow at its core, but an independent existence of Ukraine in connection with other countries of Central and Eastern Europe (also recognised as the Baltic-Black Sea region), to put a stop to Russian aggression.[15] Geopolitically, it was a very original position within Ukrainian nationalism and created a different geopolitical perspective than that represented by most of this environment at that time. As a result, this approach of Lypa allows Azov to strengthen the foundations of an independent, nationalist path for Ukraine, placing this country at the centre of geopolitical processes and not its periphery.

Similar geopolitical threads the Azov emphasises in Dontsov's political thought. The latter, in turn, emphasised Ukraine's links not with the Eurasian continental planes but with the cultural and civilisational continuity between the basins of the Ukrainian rivers — the Dnieper and the Dniester with the river system of Poland and Lithuania, resulting in a civilizational connection with Central and Eastern Europe (and thus with the West), and not with the East. At the same time, in his opinion, Ukraine is to fulfil the historic mission of being a shield for Europe against Russia and its aggressive expansion. This role is crucial because Dontsov wrote: "The keys to

---

15 See further: Y. Lypa (2007). *All Ukrainian Trilogy. Vol. 2: Mission of Ukraine; The Black Sea Doctrine*; Division of Russia. Kyiv: MAUP.

the mastery of the Slavs, and through this to the whole Europe, can only be obtained by the one who owns Ukraine".[16] Dontsov also points to a potential partner in constructing the shield against Russia — Poland. Here, despite numerous conflicts, the perception of a common enemy will prevail. Similarly to Lypa, Dontsov proposed the construction of a Central European bloc stretching from the Baltic Sea to the Black Sea. This element plays an essential role in the geopolitical thought of the Azov Movement. Contrary to other Ukrainian nationalist groups, they seek to extinguish disputes with the Polish side and see its nationalists as the main ally in building a Central European federation. Donstov, the Ukrainian nationalist and ideologist, like Lypa, broke away from the standard East-West axis in this current political thought and, as a result, relying on his concepts, offers the original contribution of the Azov Movement to contemporary Ukrainian nationalism.

Yaroslav Stetsko also appears as an essential figure for the Azov Movement, not only because of his combat and independence activities during the Second World War, his national-socialism approach to the state ideology but also for geostrategic reasons and his vision of building alliances reaching directly beyond the region of Central and Eastern Europe. In 1946, Stetsko headed the Anti-Bolshevik Bloc of Peoples (ABN), whose president he was until the end of his life in 1986. ABN united representatives of nations under SSSR rule. ABN's goal was the destruction of Bolshevism and the disintegration of the Soviet Union. According to Dorril, this organisation initially cooperated with the British and American Secret Service[17], and according to George F. Kennan, it had significant influence in Congress.[18] Here, the geopolitical aspect is also crucial for the Azov movement. The ABN envisioned a federation of independent states in Eastern Europe after it broke up the Soviet Union

---

16 See further: D. Dontsov (1957). *The Basis of Our Politics*. New York: ODFFU.
17 S. Dorril (2002). *MI6: Inside the Covert World of Her Majesty's Secret Intelligence Service*. New York: Simon and Schuster, pp. 234-235.
18 Ch. Simpson (1988). *Blowback: America's Recruitment of Nazis and Its Effects on the Cold War*. New York: Grove Atlantic, p. 271.

to be called the "New Order".[19] The ABN publications excluded Russia from this future federation and gave essentially racist justifications pointing to the "Asian roots" of the Russians[20]. At the same time, Stetsko's political ideas are essential for the Azov Movement today: the indication of alliances with the Anglo-Saxon world, the vision of building a Central European federation, and the justifications for excluding Russia from it.

Therefore, based simultaneously on these concepts and the current geostrategic calculation geopolitically, the movement now promotes the ideas of the Intermarium (geopolitical plan to unite former Polish–Lithuanian Commonwealth lands within a single polity). While this is drawn from the ideas of the Polish dictator in the 1920s and 1930s, Józef Piłsudski[21], Azov modifies them by moving the Intermarium's centre from Poland to Ukraine and sketching a north–south axis, referring to the vision of Gothic wanderings from antiquity—from the Baltic to the Greek colonies in the Crimea.[22] At the same time, in the Ukrainian centre, they see a place for the rebirth of Europe, according to the ideologues of the movement—Semenyaka, Kravchenko, or Zaikovskyi—decadent, corrupted by liberalism, homosexuality, or gender movements. Hence, the aim of the movement is a pan-European reconquista and the impulse for it, which is to flow after a successful nationalist revolution from "young" Eastern Europe to "old" Western Europe, from the creation of a local Polish-Belarusian-Lithuanian-Ukrainian federation (led by the latter) to visions of unifying Europe[23] in the spirit

---

19 A. Holian (2011) *Between National Socialism and Soviet Communism: Displaced Persons in Postwar Germany*. Ann Arbor: University of Michigan Press, p.129.
20 Ibidem, p.128.
21 See further: P. Okulewicz (2001) *Koncepcja „Międzymorza" w myśli i praktyce politycznej obozu Józefa Piłsudskiego w latach 1918–1926*, Poznań: Wydawnictwo Poznańskie.
22 A. Nonjon (2020) 'Olena Semenyaka, The "First Lady" of Ukrainian Nationalism', *Illiberalism Studies Program Working Papers*, September. Available at: https://www.illiberalism.org/wp-content/uploads/2020/10/Nonjon-Olena-Semenyaka-The-First-Lady-of-Ukrainian-Nationalism.pdf (Accessed: 1 February 2023).
23 Ibidem.

of pan-European fascism sketched by Francis Parker Yockey and Oswald Mosley.[24]

The Azov Movement publishing house also published the nationalist leader of the pre-Second World War organisation The National Defense Organization "Carpathian Sich" Mykhailo Kolodzinsky's book *Ukrainian Military Doctrine* (1939), directly postulating ethnic cleansing of the Jewish and Polish population, including murder.[25] But here, the crucial part is not underlining the genocidal element, but rather the Messianism and geopolitical approach similar to Lypa and Dontsov, in Kolodzinsky's view also seeing the central point of the geopolitical approach based on the Black Sea and the Crimea. As the Azov Movement is a movement critical of capitalism, it must rely on ideas combining nationalism with a social approach. Hence, the emphasis on their ideological roots in the notion of "Natiocracy" by Mykola Stsiborskyi is essential for the Azov Movement. According to Stsiborskyi, democracy and capitalism were inseparable and fundamentally flawed. He felt that democracy and capitalism required equal rights and freedoms while, at the same time, nature was inherently not equal. He was similarly critical of communism and socialism, seeing Italian fascism as an alternative to the abovementioned systems.[26] In a book by Orientyr, Stsiborskyi writes that fascism is "first and foremost an idealistic and spiritual reaction to the contemporary condition created by democracy, socialism, and communism". Towards the end of the 2010s, there was a practical parting of the paths of nationalists in the tradition closer to Bandera with that represented by the Azov Movement. The Azov Movement is now more a Ukrainian version of a pan-European "conservative revolution" rather than just the voice of Ukrainians and their narrowly perceived national interests.

---

24   1st Paneuropa Conference Report,' Reconquista Europe", 15 June 2017, archived 13 June 2018, https://web.archive.org/web/20180613133924/http://reconquistaeurope.tumblr.com/post/161847863121/1st-paneuropa-conference-report-the-1st-paneuropa
25   M. Wojnar (2020) 'Myśl polityczna Organizacji Ukraińskich Nacjonalistów w drugiej połowie lat trzydziestych w świetle nowych dokumentów', *Studia z Dziejów Rosji i Europy Ś rodkowo-Wschodniej*, vol LV, no 2, pp. 95-115.
26   M. Stsiborskyi (1935). НАЦІОКРАТІЯ, Ukrlife.org, no date, http://ukrlife.org/main/evshan/natiocracy.htm, (Accessed: 1 July 2023).

This trend is also visible in other countries (e.g., Poland, Italy, Spain, or France). The new generation of the extreme right is seen instead as a broader, paradoxically international movement of a pan-European, or often also pan-white character, rather than an independent political force of one specific nation, hence its involvement in international alliances or participation in global initiatives, which is much rarer in the older generation of activists.

Hence, from then on, Azov began to draw more heavily from Western political thought, which was mainly related to neofascism, conservative revolutionaries, and integral traditionalism. Publishing houses associated with the Azov Movement have published *Revolt Against the Modern World* by the Italian baron, lecturer at the SS school, and spiritual father of Neo-fascism, Julius Evola (1898-1974). The founders of the "Plomin" publishing house opened a bar in Kyiv with a large portrait of Evola as its centrepiece wall.[27] Evola's picture was also hung in the Militant Zone shop in Azov's social centre, "Cossack House".[28] At the same time, another clear ideological component visible in the inspirations of the Azov movement is the French *nouvelle droite* (the French New Right, which emerged in the 1960s). Publishers associated with the movement have released three books by former OAS and Europe Action member Dominique Venner (*A Western Samurai; For a Positive Critique;* and *The Rebel Heart*). As a result of the movement's activities, Venner is also on the list of literature recommended for sergeants of the Ukrainian Armed Forces. The movement's publishing houses also published texts by GRECE (Groupement de Recherche et d'Études pour la Civilisation Européenne, Eng.: "Research and Study Group for European Civilization") members George Dumézil and Mircea Eliade. They planned to publish translations of texts by Alain de Benoist, which Zaikovskyi did not finish due to his death. It was also intended to publish a magazine modelled on the French

---

27 M. Colborne (2022) *From the Fires of War. Ukraine's Azov Movement and the Global Far Right*. Stuttgart and Hannover: ibidem Press, p. 43.
28 M. Colborne (2020) 'Dispatches From Asgardsrei: Ukraine's Annual Neo-Nazi Music Festival', *Bellingcat*, 2 January. Available at: https://www.bellingcat.com/news/2020/01/02/dispatches-from-asgardsrei-ukraines-annual-neo-nazi-music-festival (Accessed: 1 February 2023).

journals nouvelle droite *Éléments* or *Nouvelle école*.[29] They have also published two books by Ernst Jünger (for example, *Fire and Blood*, for which Olena Semenyaka wrote a preface) and calendars with images of Oswald Spengler and Martin Heidegger. These authors were highly critical of liberal democracy and called for the revival of conservative values or the rebirth of the state based on the nation or the army. In Ukraine, seen by the Azov activists as plagued by corruption and weakened by emigration and armed conflict, this set of authors has proven very persuasive for activists of the Azov Movement. The authors mentioned above supported militarism, highly valued the "warrior spirit", and praised the hierarchical and authoritarian ruling style. All this provided strong support for the war-defense ideology created by Azov.

Azov's Ideology After 2021

The Azov Brigade itself has been in the last five years focused more on military issues since the formation of its sister party, the National Corps; the military unit emphasised less ideological and more patriotic matters. Nonetheless, it is only possible to accurately characterise the ideological position of the Azov movement by focusing on the Brigade itself, by discussing its peripheral groups, or by taking account of its structure resulting from the ideological pillars of the movement. Therefore, the very structure of the movement deserves a broader discussion in this context. Its branched, networked character allows the movement to present some parts as its official, extremist-free representation. At the same time, other parts, which are still its immanent element, remain in the shadows. Nonetheless, the Azov Movement continues its extremist activities, both in the field of practical action and drawing inspiration and influence from extremist ideologies. Thus, the following are characteristic of the Azov Movement: high fragmentation, an attempt to serve various segments of Ukrainian society, blurred dividing lines

---

29 J. Ostrogniew (2022) 'Polegli w obronie Ukrainy', *Szturm,* No data. Available at: https://www.szturm.com.pl/index.php/miesiecznik/item/1514-polegli-w-obronie-ukrainy (Accessed: 1 February 2023).

between multiple entities (Brigade, political party, social centres, veteran organisations, sports associations, militia, informal groups), programs, and initiatives of the movement (devoted to sport, seniors, children, public health issues), as well as a division into more publicly acceptable entities constituting the "front" of the movement and more extremist ones forming its direct "backstage" (like Nord Storm, Freikorps or Wotan Jugend).

The official Azov Brigade website currently contains only entries about the war, with nothing about politics. However, the Brigade is not the only movement activity related to the military. The Veterans Brotherhood group plays an essential role in the movement, and it is also active in the Veterans' Movement of Ukraine (VMU), a leading Ukrainian veteran umbrella group. Also, the March of Defenders — a public march and demonstration held on the Independence Day of Ukraine, which honours all the veterans and serving personnel of the Armed Forces of Ukraine, is organised by Dmytro Shatrovskyi, an Azov Brigade veteran.[30] The Azov Movement also runs a rehabilitation center for soldiers in Kharkiv, Brothers' Citadel[31], as well as two military courses — the School of Sergeants, named after Yevhen Konovalets, and the School of Warrant Officers, named after Mykola Stsiborskyi.[32] Both patrons of the schools are historical leaders of Ukrainian nationalism (OUN), and military training in these universities is intertwined with the ideological formation in the spirit of nationalism. Officially, the Brigade presents itself as a purely patriotic formation while striving to dominate the movement of military veterans. Still, it continues military training of an ideological nature in the back room[33].

Several factors contribute to the declarative refusal of the extremism of the Azov Movement. The National Corps and many from far-right circles became significantly less popular after Volodymyr Zelenskyy's presidential victory in 2019. This is due to the

---

[30] M. Colborne (2022) *From the Fires of War. Ukraine's Azov Movement and the Global Far Right*. Stuttgart and Hannover: ibidem Press, p. 59.
[31] W. Dobrowolski (2022) *Ruch Azowski. Ideologia, działalność i walka ukraińskich nacjonalistów*. Warszawa: Capital, p103.
[32] Ibidem, pp.187-188.
[33] Ibidem.

general right-wing, patriotic turn to political discourse in Ukraine since 2014. Theses and positions on the Russian threat, the need to militarise society, the fight against traitors, and ultra-patriotic rhetoric have become much more visible on the Ukrainian political scene, and more prominent players have taken over these slogans. They know how to play them better politically, thanks to more outstanding funds and political experience. This is evidenced by the election defeat in the 2019 local elections of the following parties: National Corps (2.5% support), Right Sector (2.15% support), and Svoboda (2.15% support). Their mutual squabbles and program differences do not allow them to form a single electoral coalition, dooming them to the fate of being extra-parliamentary groups.

The resignation of Avakov from the post of Interior Minister in July 2021 was also a significant blow to the Azov movement. This multi-millionaire and businessman had supported the Azov movement for several years and, according to press reports, while still running his business in Kharkiv, home to the leaders of the Azov Movement, he used the help of the movement's militants in combating competition. As minister from 2014 to 2021, he allegedly extended a protective umbrella over it and supported it financially from the very beginning.[34] Thanks to his support, many of Azov's veterans found work in public institutions related to security. Vadym Troyan, the former chief of staff of the Azov Battalion, made a spectacular career as deputy chief of police and later as acting chief of police and deputy minister of internal affairs.[35] Avakov also assigned Azov veteran Serhiy Bondarenko as the deputy head of the Kyiv region police. Other veterans found employment as senior police officers in Kyiv, Kharkiv, and Poltava.[36] Also, one of the founders of Azov, ex-neo-nazi Sergey Korotkikh enjoyed the patronage of Avakov. Korotkikh used to work as a top police official

---

34 M. Colborne (2022) *From the Fires of War. Ukraine's Azov Movement and the Global Far Right*. Stuttgart and Hannover: ibidem Press, p. 59.
35 Interfax-Ukraine (2017) 'Cabinet appoints Troyan as deputy interior minister of Ukraine', Kyiv Post, 8 February. Available at: https://www.kyivpost.com/post/9415 (Accessed: 1 February 2023).
36 Bellingcat (2019) [Twitter] 15 February. Available at: https://twitter.com/bellingcat/status/1096449188051775488 (Accessed: 1 February 2023).

under Avakov and calls himself a friend of his son Oleksandr.[37] Avakov's resignation started the Azov movement's subsequent complaints of "repression" from Zelenskyy's government.[38] The arrest of several National Corps members by the Ukrainian SBU in August 2021, alleged to be part of a racketeering and extortion ring, was one of the signs of this process.[39]

The reactions of Ukraine's Western allies, especially the USA and Canada (where a large Ukrainian diaspora lives), were also significant. Ukraine's military resistance to the Russian invasion depends heavily on the supply of Western military equipment and intelligence support. Azov and its associated organisations were some of the central public relations problems for Ukrainian governments between 2014 and 2022. On the one hand, its political positions were reported by the democratic Western press, primarily the Bellingcat portal. On the other hand, the extremist connections of the Azov Movement, its symbolism, and ideological roots, as well as the participation of Russian Neo-Nazis in it, allowed the Russian authorities to attack Ukraine.[40] As a result of the publication of the results of the investigations of the Hromadskie, Zaboronna, and Bellingcat portals, and the ensuing pressure from the West, the Azov Movement began to publicly distance itself from its most controversial participants, such as Levkin or Nikitin/ Kapustin[41] and in 2022 dropped from its insignia the neo-nazi symbols,

---

[37] Kyiv Post (2021) 'Suspicious deaths around Azov fighter remain uninvestigated', The Kyiv Post, 1 October. Available at: https://www.kyivpost.com/post/6745 (Accessed: 1 February 2023).

[38] M. Colborne (2022) *From the Fires of War. Ukraine's Azov Movement and the Global Far Right*. Stuttgart and Hannover: ibidem Press, p147.

[39] M. Laryš (2022) 'Far-Right vigilantes and crime: law and order providers or common criminals? The lessons from Greece, Russia, and Ukraine', *Southeast European and Black Sea Studies*, vol. 22, no. 4, pp. 479-502.

[40] Euractiv (2022) 'Russia designates Ukraine's Azov Regiment a 'terrorist' group', *Euractiv*, 3 August. Available at: https://www.euractiv.com/section/global-europe/news/russia-designates-ukraines-azov-regiment-a-terrorist-group (Accessed: 1 February 2023).

[41] A. Nonjon (2020) 'Olena Semenyaka, The "First Lady" of Ukrainian Nationalism', *Illiberalism Studies Program Working Papers*, September. Available at: https://www.illiberalism.org/wp-content/uploads/2020/10/Nonjon-Olena-Semenyaka-The-First-Lady-of-Ukrainian-Nationalism.pdf (Accessed: 1 February 2023).

substituting it with a golden trident (Ukraine coat of arms), three swords and other non-extremist symbols.[42] This has had some effect. With the increasing involvement of the West in the war in Ukraine, more and more entities removed the Azov Brigade from their lists of extremist organisations (Japan and the Anti-Defamation League).[43] Leading members of both main US political parties met in October 2022 with high-ranking soldiers of the Azov at the Capitol in Washington D.C.[44] Veterans of Azov participated in a similar tour of Israel in December 2022.[45]

It should also be noted that the ideological attitude of the Brigade was influenced by the deaths of several of the essential ideologues of the Azov movement. Since the Russian invasion, the prominent ideologue of the movement, organiser of the "Orientyr" publishing house and vice-chairman of the National Corps, Mykola Kravchenko, as well as the leading propagator of the idea of the third position in Ukraine and the nouvelle droite leader of the "Plomin" club, the "Nuovi Arditi" publishing house and the Avant-garde Cultural Association, Serhiy Zaikovskyi, and the leader of the Kharkiv group Freikorps, Georgiy Tarasenko, died on

---

42   T. Ball (2022), 'Azov Battalion drops neo-Nazi symbol exploited by Russian propagandists', *The Times*, 30 May, Available at: https://www.thetimes.co.uk/article/azov-battalion-drops-neo-nazi-symbol-exploited-by-russian-propagandists-lpjnsp7qg (Accessed: 1 February 2023).
43   Al Mayadeen English (2022) 'ADL refuses to call Ukraine-Pentagon Azov Battalion a "neo-Nazi" unit', *Al Mayadeen English*, 9 December. Available at: https://english.almayadeen.net/news/politics/adl-refuses-to-call-ukraine-pentagon-azov-battalion-a-neo-na (Accessed: 1 February 2023); K. Azari (2022) 'Ukrainian Azov Battalion removed from Japan's International Terrorists' list', *Arab News*, 10 April. Available at: https://www.arabnews.jp/en/japan/article_69828 (Accessed: 1 February 2023).
44   J. Crosse (2022) 'Congressional leaders of both parties welcome members of neo-Nazi Azov Battalion to Washington', *World Socialist Web Site*, 7 October. Available at: https://www.wsws.org/en/articles/2022/10/07/pndc-o07.html (Accessed: 1 February 2023).
45   A. Winstanley and A. Abunimah (2022) 'Israel helps Ukraine whitewash its Nazis' *The Electronic Intifada*, 23 December. Available at: https://electronicintifada.net/content/israel-helps-ukraine-whitewash-its-nazis/36911 (Accessed: 1 February 2023).

the battlefield.[46] Indeed, of the most important intellectual leaders of the Azov Movement, only Semenyaka remains alive.

There is also a growing conflict within the movement between supporters of Biletsky and Korotkikh.[47] From late 2020 and into 2021, Korotkikh appears to have become close with other neo-nazi Russian exiles in Ukraine as well, including Levkin, Denis Nikitin/Kapustin, and Mikhail Shalankevich. Korotkikh, thus, is building a separate base within the movement under his patronage. People faithful to Korotkikh led the group towards Neo-Nazism and criminal activity, following the example of similar organisations operating in Polish Białystok or Gdańsk.

The party led by Biletsky is trying to shift its message towards the mainstream. Electoral defeats and US pressure have additionally forced a softening of the tone, eschewing open violence and downplaying revolutionary change, at least in the short term. They appear to be counting on the National Corps being one of the major political movements in Ukraine when the war ends. At the same time, far-right activists joining Ukrainian units currently choose Battalion Revenge, associated with the Tradition and Order group[48], or the Da Vinci Wolves Battalion[49], which, although in practice are subordinated to the Ukrainian armed forces, are not formally part of it like the Azov Brigade.

---

46 J. Ostrogniew (2022) 'Polegli w obronie Ukrainy', *Szturm,* No data. Available at: https://www.szturm.com.pl/index.php/miesiecznik/item/1514-polegli-w-o bronie-ukrainy (Accessed: 1 February 2023).

47 The Marker (2021) '"AZOV NEEDS A WAR." AN INTERVIEW WITH MICHAEL COLBORNE', The Marker, 29 December. Available at: https://violence-marker.org.ua/en/2021/12/29/azov-needs-a-war-an-interview-with-michael-colborne, (Accessed: 1 February 2023).

48 P. Witkowski (2023) 'Skazany z Mariką Matuszak neofaszysta przeszedł w Ukrainie szkolenie bojowe', *Polityka,* 23 lipca 2023, Available at: https://www.polityka.pl/tygodnikpolityka/kraj/2220822,1,skazany-z-marika-matuszak-neofaszysta-przeszedl-w-ukrainie-szkolenie-bojowe.read (Accessed: 1 August 2023).

49 T. Gibbons-Neff (2023), 'Nazi Symbols on Ukraine's Front Lines Highlight Thorny Issues of History', *The New York Times,* 5, January https://www.nytimes.com/2023/06/05/world/europe/nazi-symbols-ukraine.html (Accessed: 1 August 2023).

Summary and Conclusions

However, the distinction between the military unit and the broader political movement is an important issue that eludes most writing about the Azov Brigade. Most writers focus on the Brigade to the exclusion of the network of organisations that were built around it. And while in the case of the Brigade itself, which is part of the Ukrainian armed forces, it is difficult to talk about its extremist character, in the case of the entire movement, of which the Azov Brigade is the central part (where it plays the role of a "clean" front for the movement), it is still legitimate. On the one hand, we have the "front stage" of the movement, which presents it to a broader audience, voters, key elites, opinion formers, or Western allies. In this sphere, mainly Azov's soldiers and veterans, who present themselves as heroic patriots, and few elements can be disturbing with their extremist character.

Meanwhile, "backstage," we have many such elements. These are alliances with other extremist organisations from Europe and America. These are conferences devoted to characters or topics characteristic of Neo-fascist circles. These are concepts proclaimed by the ideologues of the movement straight from the writings of the Nazis, revolutionary nationalists, fascists and Neo-fascists, conservative revolutionaries, or integral traditionalists. This publishing and concert activity is typical of extremist circles. It is impossible to shift such an extensive and multithreaded movement from one ideology to another as it would be possible in a centrally controlled party. This is almost impossible in the two years since the last new-right, Neo-fascist events organised by the Azov Movement. Therefore, the numerous comments after the start of the Russian invasion claiming that the Azov Movement had already lost its extremist character can be referred only to the Brigade itself. The movement as a whole still presents itself as one of the factions of contemporary Neo-fascism. In the last two years, no significant declarations have indicated a change in the ideology of its foundations.

2 Defence Bottom-up
Volunteer Battalions at the Onset of the Russian War in Ukraine

Rosaria Puglisi*

In her "*Naydovsha Podorozh*" ("The Longest Journey"), written from her Polish exile in the early months following the Russian large-scale invasion of Ukraine in February 2022, the Ukrainian writer Oksana Zabushko chronicles the story of her country's struggle for independence against enduring Russian imperial ambitions as a people's history. This history is of a community that acts harmoniously as a single-willed creature.[1] It is a deep-seated "altruistic collectivism", as opposed to the *vertikal vlasti*, the rigidly hierarchical structure of power that characterises Russia, she argues, that, through the Orange Revolution and the Euro-Maidan, prompted Ukrainians to organise spontaneously in forms of "direct democracy".

> "Always strong at a horizontal level [...] and fully capable to get organised autonomously and act at the level of local communities, communicate, and establish flexible and effective, provisional, or regular networks fit to pursue complex objectives, the Ukrainians have never trusted the '*vertikal*'".[2]

According to some Ukrainian thinkers, the contrast between a horizontal and a vertical power system sets apart their country's political culture from Russia's: the former is intrinsically competitive and, therefore, democratic in its social and political expressions,

---

* This chapter is an updated version of a working paper published in 2015 with the Rome-based Istituto Affari Internazionali, to which I am grateful. The research is based on interviews with Ukrainian officials, civil society representatives and Western diplomats conducted by the author in Kyiv in January and February 2015 and online in the summer of 2022. I feel indebted to all those who have shared their time and thoughts during these interviews. For confidentiality's sake, sources have been anonymised.
1 Oksana Zabuzhko (2022) "Naydosha Podorozh", here referred to in its Italian edition "Il viaggio piu' lungo", Einaudi, p. 39.
2 *Ibd. p.70*

whereas the latter is hierarchic and ultimately authoritarian. "You do not expect orders in Ukraine; you do not act based on orders, many times you act against orders", — points out philosopher and historian Volodymyr Yermolenko, ascribing Ukrainians' independence of action to their country's historical roots.

The protracted absence of a unified state entity, in Yermolenko's view, and Kyiv Rus' multiple centres of interest, a *de facto* pluralist construct, prompted individuals to organise themselves autonomously instead of, or even despite, the state. Precursors to the rich network of civil society organisations that since the 2013-14 Euro-Maidan have proven indispensable participants in the country's security and defence, structures alternative to the state and the church, the *brastvo*, developed already in the Middle Ages to address communities' needs. Deprived of identity and self-rule, the Ukrainians came to see statehood and nation as separate entities.[3]

Zabuzhko recognises a deeply rooted sense of distrust towards the state in the process that brought about the "resuscitation of the army" following the institutional meltdown precipitated by President Yanukovich's flight in the winter of 2014, the Russian takeover of Crimea, and the beginning of the hostilities in the Donbas. At that point, she remarks, it had become clear that nobody would defend people and country, and the Ukrainian spirit of self-preservation kicked in again.

> "[…] when there is a really dangerous situation, Ukrainians' traditional mistrust towards the State becomes paradoxically advantageous, an element of strength rather than weakness: without waiting for the leadership to take the situation in their hands, the Ukrainian people acted in the country's defence on its own initiative".[4]

The reconstruction of the army, "shaken and demoralised by the government's betrayal", became a widely shared exercise in the

---

[3] Volodymyr Yermolenko and Tetiana Ogarkova, "Who are the Ukrainians and What do They Want", podcast series Exploring Ukraine, episode 132, 11 August 2022, https://ukraineworld.org/podcasts/ep-132. On the role of civil society as a security actor see Rosaria Puglisi "A People's Army: Civil Society as a Security Actor in Post-Maidan Ukraine", IAI Working Papers 15, 23 July 2015, https://www.iai.it/en/pubblicazioni/peoples-army

[4] *Ibd. p. 85*

hands of volunteers, somehow the "continuation of Maidan". Equally, the decision to defend the country and push back the Russian attacks in the Donbas was made "bottom-up", the result of a "popular plebiscite".[5] In Zabuzhko's recount of "altruistic collectivism", there prevails a narrative that has become dominant in Ukraine and, to a certain extent, foundational of the modern Ukrainian state: that the volunteer battalions, as part of the broader volunteer movement, saved the nation and restored its dignity.

In their brief lives, which spanned roughly from April 2014 until, formally, June 2015, the volunteer battalions encapsulated a much larger spectrum of the contradictions that characterise post-independence Ukraine: the nation vs. the state, the centre vs. the periphery, the aspiration to modernise vs. the resistance to reform, the pressure of vested interests vs. the prevalence of collective interest.

Surrounded by a halo of confusing information and deliberate propaganda, the emergence of volunteer military units in post-Maidan Ukraine and their engagement in military operations in the Donbas proved contentious, both internationally and domestically. At a time when international partners were considering whether to provide Kyiv with defensive lethal weapons to withstand the offensive in the east, the question as to whether the Ukrainian forces were cohesive, disciplined, law-abiding and loyal to the country's institutions appeared unquestionably crucial. As a commentator in *The Guardian* put it, as long as "militias" hung out uncontrolled, Ukraine remained an unreliable interlocutor.[6] At the same time, Moscow repeatedly referred to "illegal military formations" to undermine the credibility of the Ukrainian military efforts and question Kyiv's capacity to reign in fanatic right-wing anarchic tendencies.[7]

---

5   *Ibd. p. 87*
6   "*The Guardian* view on the Ukraine conflict: Swift action needed," *The Guardian*, 5 February 2015, http://www.theguardian.com/commentisfree/2015/feb/05/guardian-view-ukraine-conflict-swift-action-needed.
7   TASS Russian News Agency, "Lavrov expects EU mission in Ukraine will decide on status of volunteer battalions," 12 January 2015, http://tass.ru/en/world/770766.

At home, the volunteer battalions, or "dobrobaty", also attracted their fair share of criticism. Accused of being highly politicised, self-congratulatory, undisciplined and hostile to the military command, they saw not only the legitimacy of their requests for heavy military equipment but their very utility questioned.[8] Demonstrations, episodes of street violence and the vocal political activism of some of the commanders fuelled speculation that a military coup was in the making and that irregular militias would become involved in criminal wars.

Against the background of a deteriorating economic situation, growing misgivings on the conduct of the military operations in the east, primarily the emotional defeats in Ilovaisk, Debal'tseve and the siege of the Donetsk airport, popularly ascribed to the military command's corruption, incompetence or lack of patriotic commitment; and intense dissatisfaction with the slow pace of reforms throughout 2015, the Ukrainian authorities became increasingly alarmed of the potential risks posed by unchecked paramilitary units[9]. The stabilisation of the combat operations and the Minsk II protocol provision envisaging the "disarmament of all illegal groups" offered opportunities to gradually subsume the majority of the battalions under the authority of the Ministry of Defence (MoD) or the Ministry of Interior (MoI). This move brought all the legally registered formations under the chain of Command of the Anti-Terroristic Operation (ATO) first and the Joint Force Operation (JFO) later.

Nine years after the start of the war, it would be mistaken to dismiss the *dobrobaty* as a ragtag army of uncontrolled right-wing extremists. Indeed, the fragmentation of the different units in terms of training, discipline and military equipment, as well as their reluctance to accept coordination and a proper chain of command,

---

8 Yurii Butusov, "Dobrovol'chi batal'yoni: struktura, strakhi, problemi boyvoho zastosuvannya" [Voluntary battalions: structure, fears problems of employment in combat], ZN.ua, 29 August 2014
9 On the criticism against the military leadership see Rosaria Puglisi "General Zhukov and the Cyborgs: A Clash of Civilisation within the Ukrainian Armed Forces", IAI Working Papers 15, 17 May 2015, https://www.iai.it/sites/default/files/iaiwp1517.pdf

made them rapidly redundant on the battlefield. The engagement of some individual groups in support of powerful vested interests or criminal gangs turned them all into potential sources of instability, too.

At the same time, however, the volunteer battalions contributed to the military operations' early convulsed days. By questioning the authority and modus operandi of the armed forces, they added to the process of modernisation and de-bureaucratisation that has made the Ukrainian military highly effective and ultimately capable of pushing back Russia's full-scale invasion in 2022. Furthermore, by mobilising society around the country's defence, the volunteers helped bridge the gap between the people and the institutions, increase social cohesion, and eventually create resilience. With all their contradictions and shortcomings, the *dobrobaty* planted the seeds of Ukraine's resilience today, with lessons also being learnt at an institutional level.

This chapter looks back at the establishment and the role of the volunteer battalions between 2014 and 2015 and their dismantling from mid-2015. It also briefly considers their legacy in light of the 2022 Russian invasion.

From Maidan to the ATO

The war in Ukraine started unexpectedly. The 2012 Military Doctrine of Ukraine defined as "unlikely" in the medium term the possibility of an "armed aggression that resulted in a local or regional war."[10] The 2012 National Security Concept listed "the continuing deterioration of the Armed Forces of Ukraine and the defence industry" among the country's security threats.[11] When the security situation in the Donbas started worsening in the spring of 2014, and hostilities degenerated into an armed conflict, the Ukrainian military, plagued by years of underfunding, corruption, patronage and Russian infiltration, was not combat-ready.

---

10 P. Fluri, M. Koziel and A. Yermolaiev (eds), *The Security Sector Legislation of Ukraine*, Center for Army, Conversions and Disarmament Studies, Kyiv, 2013, p. 141.
11 *Ibid.*, p. 128.

The total number of combat-ready troops and equipment in the ground forces amounted nominally to 80,000 personnel, 775 tanks, 51 helicopters, fewer than 1,000 artillery pieces and 2,280 armoured personnel carriers. In fact, due to a combination of lack of training and inadequate and poorly maintained equipment, the size of the combat-ready force was only 6,000 troops.[12] The Ministry of Interior (MoI) special forces, like the anti-riot Berkut units, were dissolved after the shootings in Maidan. Between 25 and 30% of police and security forces in the Donbas region had defected to the separatist side, according to a MoI estimate.[13]

On 7 April, acting President Turchynov established the anti-crisis headquarters; on 12 April, Russian-backed separatist forces led by Igor Strelkov took control of Slovyansk; on 15 April, President Turchynov announced the beginning of the Anti-Terrorist Operation. Volunteer battalions started emerging between April and May 2014, building on the experience of the Maidan self-defence groups and gathering primarily Maidan activists. A parliamentary decree on 1 April imposed the demobilisation of all armed formations that had emerged as a result of the confrontation and the unrest in Maidan.[14]

Territorial defence battalions (under the Ministry of Defence or MoD), special police battalions, and reserve battalions of the National Guard (under the MoI) were established at a regional level based on the 1991 law on the Defence of Ukraine, a 2014 Presidential Decree on Mobilisation, and MoI and MoD instructions.[15]

---

[12] Dmitry Gorenburg, "Ukrainian Military Capabilities," Web blog post, *Russian Military Reform*, 22 December 2014, https://russiamil.wordpress.com/2014/12/22/ukrainian-military-capabilities/.

[13] Aleksandr Khodakovsky, head of the Ukrainian Security Services in Donetsk, for example, became the commander of the notorious pro-Russian Vostok battalion. Catherine A. Fitzpatrick, "Russian-Backed Separatist Leader Khodakovsky Changes His Story to Reuters—or Does He?," *The Interpreter*, Institute of Modern Russia, 24 July 2014, http://www.interpretermag.com/russian-backed-separatist-khodakovsky-changes-his-story-to-reuters-or-does-he/.

[14] Decree of the Verkhovna Rada of Ukraine, "On the Immediate Disarmament of Illegal Armed Formations in Ukraine," Відомості Верховної Ради (диовн No. 18-19, 2014, ст14, http://zakon4.rada.gov.ua/laws/show/1174-18.

[15] "V 19 oblastyakh Ukrainy sformirovany dobrovolcheskie otryady- Rechinskiy" ["In 19 regions of Ukraine volunteer units are being established—Rechinskiy"],

Battalions reporting to the MoI were placed under the authority of the regional head of police, while those reporting to the MoD were placed under the regional military enlistment offices. Funded nominally through the regional budget, they were armed by the MoI or the MoD and equipped almost exclusively through civil society organisations' donations or the financial support of local businesses (including local oligarchs). The Dnipro 1 and Dnipro 2 special police battalions, for example, were funded by Dnipropetrovsk governor and oligarch Ihor Kolomoisky. According to governmental sources, all battalions were trained in MoI or MoD training facilities before deployment. However, the effectiveness of this training was disputed by media reports highlighting the disparity across different formations, as battalions were ultimately responsible for instructing their recruits.[16]

By the summer of 2014, the MoD had established 32 territorial battalions, including servicemen recalled as part of the first wave of mobilisation. Of these 32, 10 were volunteer battalions, including, for example, the 20 Dnipropetrovsk, the 11 Kyiv and the 24 Luhansk (Aidar) battalions.[17] In October, the numbers went up to 44 territorial defence battalions under the MOD, 32 special police battalions, three volunteer national guard battalions and at least three unregulated battalions that had no direct chain of command (*DUK Pravy Sektor*).[18] In early November, Minister of Defence Stepan Poltorak ordered territorial defence battalions to be absorbed into the formal structures of his ministry and threatened action

---

Censor.net 15 April 2014, http://censor.net.ua/news/281231/v_19_oblastyah_ukrainy_sformirovany_dobrovolcheskie_otryady_rechinskiyi.

16 Michael Cohen and Matthew Green, "Ukraine's Volunteer Battalions", Infantry, April-July 2016, pp. 66-69
17 "Po vsey Ukraine sozdayut'sya bata'lyony territoryalnoi oborony" [Everywhere in Ukraine territorial defence battalions are being established"], *Censor.net*, 30 April 2014, http://censor.net.ua/news/283361/po_vseyi_ukraine_sozdayutsya_batalony_territorialnoyi_oborony.
18 Michael Cohen and Matthew Green, "Ukraine's Volunteer Battalions", Infantry, April-July 2016, pp. 66-69 The total number of individual combatants involved is, instead more difficult to estimate, as no official recording was set at the time.

against those that failed to comply or refused to disband.[19] This was the first step in the disarmament and reintegration process that proved less straightforward and more uneven than the authorities liked to portray it.

A militarised police corps akin to European gendarmeries, the National Guard was set up in March 2014 based on the recently dissolved internal troops. It was placed under the MoI. Three volunteer and reservists' battalions were established under the National Guard but later transformed into special-purpose regiments: the Donbas, the General Kul'tchisky and the Azov. Thirty-three battalions were set up as special police battalions, tasked to maintain law and order in the regions and equipped exclusively with light infantry weapons.[20] Dnipro 1 was, for example, originally part of the Dnipropetrovsk police and was later sent to patrol in the ATO zone.[21]

In 2015, the overall number of MoI and MoD volunteer battalions was assessed at between 40 and 50. They varied in size, from the hundreds in the Donbas battalion to the dozens in the Kyiv-based Holy Mary battalion, established as late as February 2015.[22] According to military analyst Yurii Butusov, the size of territorial defence battalions was later standardised to be 426 servicemen, and

---

19 "Poltorak: Dobrovol'cheskie batal'yony budut potchinyat'sya Ukrainskoi armii" ["Poltorak: Volunteer battalions will report to the Ukrainian army"], *Ria-Novosti*, 11 November 2014 http://ria.ru/world/20141111/1032695742.html.
20 "Avakov: Seichas' deystvuyut 34 dobrovolcheskikh battal'yona. Odin rasformirovan v svyazy s neobratimymi protsessami" ["Avakov: 34 volunteer battalions are currently working. One was dissolved in connection with irreversible processes"], *Censor.net*, 26 September 2014 and Yurii Butusov, "Dobrovol'chi batal'yoni: struktura, strakhi, problem boyvoho zastosuvannya" ["Volunteer Battalions: structure, fears, problems of their employment in combat], Zerkalo Nedeli 29 August 2014http://censor.net.ua/news/304387/avakov_seyichas_d eyistvuyut_34_dobrovolcheskih_batalona_odin_rasformirovan_v_svyazi_s_ne obratimymi_protsessami.
21 *Vice News*, "Flying Drones with the Dnipro Battalion: Russian Roulette (Dispatch 93)," Video, 15 February 2015, https://news.vice.com/video/flying-drones-with-the-dnipro-battalion-russian-roulette-dispatch-93.
22 "Dobrovol'cheskoe formirovanye "Svyataya Mariya" offitsyal'no stalo podrazdeleniem NVD" [The volunteer formation Holy Mary has officially become a unit of the MoI"], *Ukrainska Pravda*, 3 February 2015 http://www.pravda.co m.ua/rus/news/2015/02/3/7057382/.

National Guard battalions were 460. Police volunteer battalions could include between 33 and 400 individuals.[23]

Membership in the volunteer formations was socially, linguistically, nationally and politically varied. Battalions practiced a non-ethnically, non-nationally exclusive recruitment policy.[24] They comprised primarily Maidan activists with a background as diverse as police or army veterans, small entrepreneurs and students, but also, admittedly, individuals with a criminal record and, later on, internally displaced people from the Donbas and Crimea. *Dobrobaty* included Russian speakers from the east, like the Donbas, the Dnipro 1 and the Azov battalion, and Ukrainian speakers from the West, like the L'viv battalion. The Crimea battalion included Muslim Tatars from the peninsula who had sworn to retake their homeland once the war in the Donbas was over.[25] Calls were heard, at one point, for the establishment of an all-Jewish battalion.[26]

Although most combatants were Ukrainian citizens, unspecified numbers of Georgians, Russians and other European passport

---

23 "Dobrovol'cheskie Batal'yony: struktura, strakhi, problemy boevogo primeneniya" ["Volunteer battalions: structure, concerns, problems of their employment in battle"] *Censor.net,* 29 August 2014 http://censor.net.ua/resonance/300275/dobrovolcheskie_batalony_struktura_strahi_problemy_boevogo_prim eneniya

24 Emmanuel Karagiannis, "Ukrainian Volunteer fighters in the Eastern Front: Ideas, Political-Social Norms and Emotions as Mobilisation Mechanisms", Southeast European and Black Sea Studies, 2016, Vol. 16, n. 1, 139-153

25 "Komandir sotni "Krym": "Kadyrovtsy — ne muzhchiny, oni psy" ["Commander of the Hundred "Crimea": Kadyrov fighters are not men, they are dogs"], *Inforesist,* 22 January 2015 http://inforesist.org/komandir-sotni-krym-kadyrovcy-ne-muzhchiny-oni-psy-kotorym-skazali-fas/. ""Krymchanie ne separatisty i ne predately. Reshim vopros na Donbasse i budem osvobozhdat' polustrov" — Komandir battal'yon Krym ["Crimeans are neither separatists or traitors. We will solve the problem in the Donbas and will free the peninsula" — the Commander of the Crimea battalion"], *Censor.net,* 15 January 2015, http://censor.net.ua/video_new s/320068/krymchane_ne_separatisty_i_ne_predateli_reshim_vopros_na_donba sse_i_budem_osvobojdat_poluostrov_komandir.

26 ""Eto nasha strana i eto nash dom": v Ukraine formiruyet'sya noviy dobrovol'cheskiy evreyskiy batal'yon "Matilan"" ["This is our country and this is hour home": in Ukraine the new Jewish battalion Matilan gets established"], *Censor.net,* 17 July 2014 http://censor.net.ua/news/293781/eto_nasha_strana_i_ nash_dom_v_ukraine_formiruetsya_novyyi_dobrovolcheskiyi_evreyiskiyi_ba talon_matilan.

holders were reported to have joined the battalions.[27] The Azov battalion was reputed to be the most international, while the Dudaev battalion was mainly composed of veterans of the Chechen wars who fought against Moscow. This was the case, for example, for commander Isa Munayev—Brigadier General of the Republic of Ichkeria, Minister of Interior under Dudaev, and Grozny military commander—who was killed around Debal'tseve in early February 2015.[28]

Volunteers covered a wide spectrum from an ideological point of view as well. Azov battalion commander Andrii Biletsky was a well-known extreme right activist and founder of the organisation Patriot of Ukraine.[29] *DUK Pravy Sektor* was established on the basis of the nationalist party organisation that is its namesake. Its commander Dmytro Yarosh, defined by analysts as a "mainstream Ukrainian nationalist," received 127,000 votes, equivalent to 0.7% of the total, in the 25 May 2014 presidential elections.[30] In an

---

[27] Media reports talk of at least 100 Georgians fighting on the side of the Ukrainian forces in the Donbas. See "Gruziya ne nakazhet svoikh grazhdan za uchastie v boevykh desviyakh za granitsey" ["Georgia will not punish its citizens for the participation in military operations abroad"], *Ukainska Pravda*, 31 January 2015 http://www.pravda.com.ua/rus/news/2015/01/31/7057012/.

[28] "Battal'yon im. Dudaeva vozglavil chechenets, obvinyaemyy v pokushenii na Putina" ["The Dudaev battalion was run by a Chechen accused of an attack against Putin"], *Ukrainska Pravda*, 3 February 2015 http://www.pravda.com.ua/rus/news/2015/02/3/7057284/. Munayev was replaced by another Chechen leader, Adam Osmaev, who was accused by the Russians to be responsible for a failed terrorist attack against President Putin. "Komandyrom batal'yona im. Dzhiokara Dudaeva stalo Adam Osmaev, korotogo rossiyanie podozrevali v podgotovke pokusheniya na Putina" ["Adam Osmaev, whom the Russian suspected of plotting an attack against Putin, has become the commander of the Dudaev battalion"], *Censor.net* 3 February 2015 http://censor.net.ua/video_news/322894/komandirom_batalona_imeni_djohara_dudaeva_stal_adam_os maev_kotorogo_rossiyane_podozrevali_v_podgotovke.

[29] While Biletsky and the top leadership of the Azov are defined by experts as "biological racists," it is generally excluded that the whole battalion is aligned along the same ideological lines. Hromadske International, *Azov Battalion Is Not Neo-Nazi, But Some People In Battalion Are- Umland*, Video, 15 December 2014, https://www.youtube.com/watch?v=dvDlIuAXjSI. For an overview of the far right in Ukraine and its overall relations with volunteer battalions.

[30] Devin Akles, "A Guide to Ukraine's Far Right," Hromadske International, *Medium*, 13 December 2014, https://medium.com/@Hromadske/ukraines-far-right-explained-438857ec9aae.

interview with the Ukrainian TV Hromadske International, Maxim, a left-wing historian from Simferopol volunteering in the Aidar battalion, referred to different political groups within his battalion that were united by the sole objective of fighting against the Russian invasion.[31]

At least six battalion commanders were elected to parliament in the October 2014 elections spread across then Prime Minister Yatsenyuk's *Narodniy Front* (Yurii Beryoza from the Dnipro 1 battalion and Andrii Teteryuk from the *Mirotvorcheskii*), the conservative party *Samopomich* (Semen Semenchenko from the Donbas), and *DUK Pravy Sektor* (Dmytro Yarosh). Andrii Biletsky from Azov and Serhiy Mel'nychuk from Aidar were registered as independents on Parliament's list.[32]

More than their political orientation, Ukrainian observers contested voluntary formations' connections with oligarchic interests and their potential role as their sponsors' private army. Media reported regularly and critically on their occasional engagement in settling oligarchs' business and political disputes.[33]

---

31 Margo Gontar, *How Ukrainian Left Activist 'Goes to Fight Russian Imperialism*, Hromadske International, 26 January 2015, http://int.hromadske.tv/articles/show/ukraine_left_activist_fights_russia_imperialism.

32 "Novye Litsa: radi chego kombaty idut v bol'shuyu politiku" ["New faces: why are volunteer battalions commanders going into big politics"], *Ukrainska Pravda*, 20 October 2014, http://life.pravda.com.ua/person/2014/10/24/182635/.

33 The Ukrainian press has reported allegations that Rinat Akhmetov offered $25 million to the Aidar battalion to gain access to his power plant in Shchastiya ("U Akhmetova prokommentirovali zayavleie o tom chto yakoby predlagal dengi Aidaru" [Akhmetov's assistants commented on the statement that in a way he gave money to Aidar"], *Inforesist*, 23 January 2015 http://inforesist.org/u-axmetova-prokommentirovali-zayavlenie-o-tom-chto-on-yakoby-predlaga l-dengi-ajdaru/). The Azov and Dnipro 1 battalions have been accused of providing active support to different presidential candidates during the May 2014 elections ("V Donbasse aktivno "pomogali" provesti vybory dobrovol'cheskie batal'yony" ["In the Donbass volunteer battalions helped "actively" to conduct elections"], *Zerkalo Nedeli*, 2 November 2014 http://zn.ua/VYBOR Y2014/v-donbasse-dobrovolcheskie-batalony-aktivno-pomogali-provesti-vyb ory-157753_.html). The Donbas battalion's obstruction to humanitarian assistance from the Rinat Akhmetov foundation to the Donbas has also been presented as part of an intra-oligarchic dispute. Accused of taking the side of Akhmetov's opponent, the battalion claimed it was instead trying to prevent the smuggling of alcohol and other expensive goods across the internal administrative border (Evgeniy Shibalov, "Gumanitarnaya blokada" ["Humanitarian

Battalions in combat operations

Despite their differences, what brought the volunteers together in the spring of 2014 was generally a high motivation and patriotic commitment to fighting what they saw as their country's first war of independence. In the spring and early summer, volunteer battalions initially took the brunt of a war that the Ukrainian security sector was unprepared to sustain. Under-equipped and lightly armed, they held the front against Russian and Russian-supported separatist troops, thus giving the Ukrainian authorities time to regroup and organise a defence. Many in Kyiv, including Member of Parliament and former Adviser to the MoI Anton Gerashenko, believe that had it not been for the volunteers, the line of demarcation with the separatist forces would be frozen further west and run along the Dnipro River.[34]

To counter the deterioration of the security situation in the Donbas and the pro-Russian forces' occupation of Slovyansk, two National Guard battalions composed of Maidan activists were quickly set up and sent to the east together with the Omega police special operation unit.[35] As military analyst Yurii Butusov put it, these were the only formations that could be deployed rapidly and were combat-ready. Nothing else was available. Moved to the east, these units were engaged in activities that would generally be

---

blockade"] *Zerkalo Nedeli*, 19 December 2014 http://gazeta.zn.ua/internal/gu manitarnaya-blokada-_.html).

34 "Esli by ne dobrovol'cheskie batal'yoni, razmezhevanie s rossiskimi terroristami prokhodilo by gde-to po Denpru — Anton Gerashenko" ["If it had not been for the volunteer battalions, the line of demarcation with Russian terrorists would be somewhere on the Dnipro River"] *Censor.net*, 9 November 2014 http://censor.net.ua/news/311039/esli_by_ne_dobrovolcheskie_batalony_ra zmejevanie_s_rossiyiskimi_terroristami_prohodilo_by_gdeto_po_dnepru.

35 "S nachalo ATO Natsgvardiya ne byla gotova k boyam, k pervye dni rabotal tolko Spertsnaz — Poltorak" ["The National Guard was not combat-ready at the beginning of the ATO. In the first days only the special forces worked — Poltorak"], *Censor.net*, 21 October 2014 http://censor.net.ua/news/308023/s_nacha la_ato_natsgvardiya_ne_byla_gotova_k_boyam_v_pervye_dni_rabotal_tolko_ spetsnaz_poltorak; "Paruby: Srochno komplektuem novy batalyony Natsgvardii i vydvigaemsiya na peredovuyu" ["Poruby: We will quickly set up the National Guard battalions and we'll then move forward"], *Censor.net*, 18 April 2014 http://censor.net.ua/photo_news/281820/parubiyi_srochno_komplekt uem_novye_batalony_natsgvardii_i_vydvigaemsya_na_peredovuyu_foto.

assigned to the army had a state of war been declared. The Donbas battalion was explicitly established to replace the Donetsk police special units that had deserted.[36]

Most personnel in volunteer battalions were employed in law-and-order functions, manning the checkpoints and patrolling liberated areas, or were tasked with supporting the armed forces.[37] Some battalions, however, played a crucial role in several direct combat operations, like Donbas, Dnipro 1 and Azov in the Ilovaisk battle and *DUK Pravy Sektor* in the Donetsk airport battle (where commander Dmytro Yarosh was injured). The Azov battalion launched a major counteroffensive east and northeast of Mariupol on 10 February 2015.[38]

Initially armed exclusively with light weapons, territorial defence battalions were later provided with armoured vehicles.[39] Yet, the issue as to whether volunteer battalions, in general, should receive more substantial equipment remained a bone of contention. The shift from a police to a fully-fledged military operation, starting in July 2014, justified some of the battalions' requests for heavy artillery provisions.[40]

---

36 "Dobrovol'cheskie Batal'yony: struktura, strakhi, problemy boevogo primeneniya" ["Volunteer battalions: structure, concerns, problems of their employment in battle"] *Censor.net,* 29 August 2014 http://censor.net.ua/resonance/300275/dobrovolcheskie_batalony_struktura_strahi_problemy_boevogo_pri meneniya.

37 See, for example, James Sprankle's photo essay on L'viv battalion patrolling in Debaltseve: "Defending Debaltseve," *Foreign Policy,* 5 February 2015, http://foreignpolicy.com/2015/02/05/defending-debaltseve-ukraine-russia/?utm_content=bufferf53e4&utm_medium=social&utm_source=facebook.com&utm_campaign=buffer.

38 "A glimmer of hope—the Azov counteroffensive," Web blog post, *Conflict Report,* 10 February 2015, http://conflictreport.info/2015/02/10/the-azov-counteroffensive-ukraine-fights-back/.

39 "Dobrovol'cheskiy batal'yon s tankami na voruzhenie sozdayut v Zaporozhskoi oblasti" ["A volunteer battalion equipped with tanks is being established in the Zaporozhzhya region"], *Censor.net,* 8 September 2014 http://censor.net.ua/news/301738/dobrovolcheskiyi_batalon_s_tankami_na_voorujenii_sozda yut_v_zaporojskoyi_oblasti.

40 "Dobrovol'cheskie Batal'yony: struktura, strakhi, problemy boevogo primeneniya" ["Volunteer battalions: structure, concerns, problems of their employment in battle"] *Censor.net,* 29 August 2014 http://censor.net.ua/resonance/300275/dobrovolcheskie_batalony_struktura_strahi_problemy_boevogo_pri meneniya.

Dobrobaty were officially part of the same chain of command as other MoI or MoD forces and claimed to coordinate their operations through the anti-terrorist centre in Kyiv and the local anti-terrorist command in the field. This applied also to *DUK Pravy Sektor* that, although still formally independent, coordinated its activities with the ATO combat command, the Ukrainian armed forces brigades and the voluntary battalions of the MoD and the MoI, according to Commander Yarosh.[41] However, the lack of coordination among the volunteer battalions and between the latter and the army turned the successful operation for the recapture of Ilovaisk into a tragic debacle in August 2014.[42] Ilovaisk was an eye-opener for many and marked the beginning of the volunteer battalions' dismantling and legalisation.[43]

Contracted by the MoI and the MoD, volunteers were theoretically subject to the same legislative provisions and disciplinary regulations as other forces engaged in the ATO.[44] In case of alleged

---

[41] Dmytro Yarosh, "Bahato khto zaraz prosit' prokomentuvati…" ["Many are now asking to comment on…"], Facebook status update, 2:31 pm, 13 February 2015, retrieved from https://www.facebook.com/dyastrub/posts/782660468477506.

[42] Michael Cohen and Matthew Green, "Ukraine's Volunteer Battalions", Infantry, April-July 2016, pp. 66-69 The total number of individual combatants involved is, instead more difficult to estimate, as no official recording was set at the time.

[43] Fought from early August to early September 2014, the battle for Ilovaisk proved to be a watershed in the war in the Donbas. Not only did Ukrainian forces report for the first time the massive presence of Russian soldiers fighting on the side of the separatists, but there was also large scale shelling on their positions from behind the border with Russia. Furthermore, from an operational point of view, the battle dramatically highlighted the weaknesses of the Ukrainian forces. It marked clearly, for the first time in the military campaign, the contrast between what the public came to characterise as the courage and the sense of duty of the soldiers, the officers and the generals who had kept their positions in the battlefield until the end, and the lack of competence and responsibility of top officials engaged at the decision-making and military management level in the capital. Rosaria Puglisi "General Zhukov and the Cyborgs: A Clash of Civilisation within the Ukrainian Armed Forces", IAI Working Papers 15, 17 May 2015, https://www.iai.it/sites/default/files/iaiwp1517.pdf

[44] "Dobrovolcheskie batal'yony prinimayushchie uchastie v ATO perekhodyat na kontraktnuyu sluzhbu v Natsgvardiyu i VSU" ["Volunteer battalions participating in the ATO take up contract service in the National Guard and the Ukrainian Army"], *Censor.net*, 19 January 2015 http://censor.net.ua/news/

violations, they were thus liable to be investigated by the competent prosecutor office: the military prosecutor in the case of MoD battalions and the civilian prosecutor in the case of MoI battalions. Human rights abuses allegedly perpetrated by volunteers were brought to light by human rights organisations and regularly reported by the Ukrainian press.[45] A September 2014 Amnesty International report called on the Ukrainian authorities "to bring Aidar and other volunteer battalions under effective lines of command and control, promptly investigate all allegations of abuses, and hold those responsible to account. "The Ukrainian authorities," the report continued, "cannot afford to replicate in the areas they retake the lawlessness and abuses that have prevailed in separatist-held areas. The failure to eliminate abuses and possible war crimes by volunteer battalions risks significantly aggravating tensions in the east of the country and undermining the proclaimed intentions of the new Ukrainian authorities to strengthen and uphold the rule of law more broadly."[46]

Kyiv subsequently made efforts to enforce discipline on volunteer formations. The December 2014 Report of the UN Human Rights Monitoring Mission in Ukraine registered the government's commitment to investigate allegations of human rights abuses.[47] Restored in August 2014, the military prosecutor's office also dealt with cases relating to several *dobrobaty*.[48] With fifty members

---

320551/dobrovolcheskie_batalony_prinimayuschie_uchastie_v_ato_perehod yat_na_kontraktnuyu_slujbu_v_natsgvardiyu.

45   Lyudmila Klochko, "Report on the human rights mission to the Donetsk and Luhansk oblasts," Kharkiv Human Rights Protection Group, 1 January 2015, http://khpg.org/en/index.php?id=1420140250; http://gazeta.zn.ua/internal/zachistka-stanicy-_.html; Artem Chapai, "Sluzhili dve Aidarovtsy. O chom prinyato molchat' na voine" ["Two Aidar servicemen. What is generally kept quite during a war"], *The Insider*, 5 January 2015 http://www.theinsider.ua/politics/54a9af9fa9f76/.

46   Amnesty International, "Ukraine: Abuses and war crimes by the Aidar volunteer battalion in the north Luhansk region," 8 September 2014, https://www.amnesty.org/en/documents/EUR50/040/2014/en/.

47   Office of the United Nations Commissioner for Human Rights, "Report on the human rights situations in Ukraine," 15 December 2014, http://www.ohchr.org/Documents/Countries/UA/OHCHR_eighth_report_on_Ukraine.pdf.

48   Mariya Zhartovskaya and Pavel Sheremetev, "Glavniy voenniy prokuror: vsegda vynovat to kto komanduet" [The Military chief prosecutor: who

accused of looting and vandalism, the Shakhtarsk battalion was disbanded in October 2014,[49] when an investigation was also opened against the Prykarpattya battalion, accused of desertion in the battle of Ilovaisk.[50] Several criminal investigations were conducted against Aidar members for illegal deprivation of liberty and a case of murder.[51]

To improve discipline, provisions to reintroduce military administrative detention were discussed and approved by Parliament. Yet, as opposed to a formally declared state of war, the status of the Anti-Terroristic Operation created a degree of legal ambiguity and, according to critics, allowed the authorities the freedom of manoeuvre to close an eye on some unorthodox behaviours while remaining verbally committed to punishing war crimes.[52]

---

commands is always guilty"], *Ukrainska Pravda*, 5 March 2015 http://www.pravda.com.ua/rus/articles/2015/02/10/7058074/.

49 "Avakov raspustil batal'yon Shakhtersk iz-za morodestva" ["Avakov dissolved the Shakhtersk battalion because of looting"], *Censor.net*, 17 October 2014, http://censor.net.ua/news/307488/avakov_raspustil_batalon_shahtersk_iz za_maroderstva

50 "Voennaya prokuratura shchitaet dezertirstvo batal'yona Prikarpat'e pervoprichinoi tragedii pod Ilovaiskom" ["The military prosecutor believes the Prekarpat'e battalion desertion is the main reason for the Ilovaisk tragedy"], *Censor.net*, 7 October 2014, http://censor.net.ua/news/306001/voennaya_pro kuratura_schitaet_dezertirstvo_batalona_prikarpate_pervoprichinoyi_tragedi i_pod_ilovayiskom.

51 "Otkrili 57 ugolovnykh del v otnoshenii lits predstavlyavshkhsya boyzami "Aidara"" [57 criminal cases opened against individuals who present themselves as Aidar battalion combatants"] *Lb.ua* 20 October 2014, http://society.lb.ua/life /2014/10/20/283146_otkriti_57_ugolovnih_del_otnoshenii.html; Olga Zhaldak, "Voennaya prokuratura i SBU opredelyat sudbu dvukh boytsov Aidara, kotorykh zaderzhala militsiya- A. Gerashenko" ["The Military prosecutor and the SBU will decide about the two Aidar combatants who were arrested by the police — A. Gerashenko"] *UNN*, 4 October 2014, http://www.unn.com.ua/ru/ news/1392331-viyskova-prokuratura-i-sbu-viznachat-dolyu-dvokh-biytsiv-ay daru-yakikh-zatrimala-militsiya-a-geraschenko; "Voennaya Prokuratura rassleduet 27 ugolovnykh del protiv 13 boitsov Aidara" [The military prosecutor is investigating 27 criminal cases against 13 Aidar combatants"], *Nezavisimoe byuro novostei*, 22 December 2014 http://nbnews.com.ua/ru/news/139383/

52 Ilmari Kaihko, "A Nation-in-the.making, in arms: control of force, strategy and the Ukrainian Volunteer Battalions", Defence Studies, 2018, Vol. 18, no 2, 147-166 (p 153)

The politicisation of the volunteer battalions

While detractors dismissed their role in combat operations as "overestimated", and their military strength was believed to be limited, volunteer battalions acquired a degree of notoriety and levels of popular trust that put them in the potential position of kingmakers at home. According to an opinion poll published in December 2014, *dobrobaty* ranked second, after civil society organisations, and before the church and the army, among the institutions the Ukrainians trusted the most.[53] Another survey published in February 2015 ranked them first.

Essentially part of the civil society mobilisation that in Maidan and afterwards had called for radical changes in the functioning of the state, volunteer battalions were seen by the public as addressing state institutions' systemic failures. Having stepped in at a moment when the Ukrainian authorities were unprepared to face the military threat in the east, voluntary formations embodied for many Ukrainians the heroic spirit of Maidan. In addition to their military role, society seemed to appreciate their tendency to open traditionally closed political processes to the public and divulge information that ministries would prefer to keep quiet. In the general public's view, their presence inside the system had the advantage of maintaining institutions in check.

Following several military setbacks after the Minsk I agreement in September 2014, accusations against the inadequacy of the army leadership and recriminations against the alleged weakness of President Poroshenko as Chief Commander of the Army raged. Uncertainties deriving from an impending economic default, dissatisfaction with the slow pace of reforms and diverging interpretations as to the costs for Ukraine of the Minsk II agreement seemed to work as powerful catalysts of popular discontent throughout 2015.

Often savvy social network users, volunteer battalion commanders established comprehensive communication platforms and loyal political constituencies, also made necessary by persistent

---

53 "Voina" ["War"], *Zerkalo Nedeli*, http://opros2014.zn.ua/war.

fundraising needs to procure equipment for their units. Shifting nonchalantly between the Parliament and the front, between grey suits and military fatigues, most appeared to provide the vision and the inspiration that many in society missed at such a difficult time. They became compelling, although far from always reliable, political actors. Some of the commanders, particularly those who acquired parliamentary seats, took a vocal role in policy debates, promoting at times unreasonable conflict resolution proposals, like, for example, the sealing off of the whole Donbas region, as was proposed by the Donbas battalion commander Semen Semenchenko.[54]

Volunteer battalions, reservist battalions and veterans' organisations became involved in spectacular demonstrations in the capital, rekindling not-too-distant memories of urban guerrilla warfare that the Kyivites would rather forget. Whether calling for an early de-mobilisation, demanding guarantees for the future of the Aidar battalion or appealing for the introduction of the state of war, the violence of these demonstrations prompted conspiracy theories of external intervention and resulted in criminal investigations.[55]

---

54 See, for example, Semenchenko's participation in the TV show "Shuster," which aired live on the Ukrainian TV channel Inter on 19 December 2014 on How to save the Donbas from the humanitarian catastrophe. Television show, http://24tv.ua/home/showSingleNews.do?vipusk_shuster_live_za_19_grudnya_viz hiti_na_donbasi_lyustratsiya_poukrayinski&objectId=523222. See also his interview with Ukrainiska Pravda on 23 December 2014, http://www.pravda.c om.ua/rus/articles/2014/12/23/7053033/.

55 See for example, the discussion around the National Guard's strike on 13 October 2014, which was organised, according to Minister of Defence Poltorak as well as Minister of Interior Avakov, by an FSB agent. "Gruppa boytsov Natsgvarii pod AP trebuyut provesti demobilizatsiyu" ["A group of National Guard servicemen outside the presidential administration demand demobilisation"], Censor.net, 13 October 2014 http://censor.net.ua/news/306862/grup pa_boyitsov_natsgvardii_pod_ap_trebuyut_provesti_demobilizatsiyu; "Diskreditirovatsk dobrovol'cheskie batal'yony pytayutsya segodnya ili duraki ili vragi Ukrainy. Ob ix rospuske rech ne idiot—Avakov" ["Today it is either the idiots or the enemies of Ukraine who are trying to discredit the volunteer battalions. There is no discussion about their disbandment—Avakov"], Censor.net, 11 November 2014, http://censor.net.ua/news/311356/diskreditirovat_dobr ovolcheskie_batalony_pytayutsya_segodnya_ili_duraki_ili_vragi_ukrainy_ob _ih_rospuske; "Aktsiya gvardeytsev-srochnikov ne spontanna, no im ochen' khotelos' popast' v televizor, kak kombatam-dobrovol'tsam—zamgenprokurora Matios" ["The demonstration of National Guard draftees is not spontaneous, they were dying to appear on TV as volunteer combatants—deputy

In late 2014, physical threats—like the picketing of state institutions and the setting on fire of tyres—or more intangible threats—like statements that volunteers will "bring the fight to Kyiv" — generated widespread concerns that the battalions might be hatching a military coup.[56] A *Washington Post* commentator went as far as claiming that "warlords and armed groups" were undermining the rebuilding of Ukraine.[57] Concerns that the volunteer battalions might represent more a domestic source of instability than a practical element within the framework of the country's security system were also harboured within the presidential administration.[58]

Consistent political attacks on the president, the government and specific ministries were certainly shaking and undermining an already fragile institutional structure. Conflicting political and economic clan interests were clearly at play in mobilising and politicising volunteer battalions. Demagogic leaders tried to take advantage of a unique platform that could further their political ambitions and promote previously unthinkable careers.

At the same time, however, the lack of sweeping reforms and tangible results—especially in the fight against corruption—

---

prosecutor general Matios"], *Censor.net*, 15 October 2014, http://censor.net.ua/video_news/307177/aktsiya_gvardeyitsevsrochnikov_ne_spontanna_no_im_ochen_hotelos_popast_v_televizor_kak_kombatamdobrovoltsam;
"Sotrudnitsa rossiskikh spetsluzhb Yuliya Kharlamova aktivno uchastvovala v "bunte" Natsgvardii i verbovala soldat" ["The Russian special services agent Yuliya Kharlamova was an active participant in the National Guard strike and was recruiting soldiers"], *Censor.net*, 16 October 2014 http://censor.net.ua/photo_news/307397/sotrudnitsa_rossiyiskih_spetsslujb_yuliya_harlamova_aktivno_uchastvovala_v_bunte_natsgvardii_i_verbovala.

56 Jamie Dettmer, "Ukraine Militias Warn of Anti-Kiev Coup," *The Daily Beast*, 28 November 2014, http://www.thedailybeast.com/articles/2014/11/28/ukraine-militias-threaten-anti-kiev-coup.html?source=facebook&via=mobile   and Shaun Walker, "Azov fighters are Ukraine's greatest weapon and may be its greatest threat," *The Guardian*, 10 September 2014, http://www.theguardian.com/world/2014/sep/10/azov-far-right-fighters-ukraine-neo-nazis.

57 Adrian Karatnycky, "Warlords and armed groups threaten Ukraine's rebuilding," *The Washington Post*, 30 December 2014, http://www.washingtonpost.com/opinions/the-rise-of-warlords-threatens-ukraines-recovery/2014/12/30/a23b2d36-8f7b-11e4-a412-4b735edc7175_story.html?postshare=2981419988538209.

58 Sergey Rakhmanin, "Tretiya mirovaya igra" [Third world game"], *Zerkalo Nedeli*, 7 November 2014 http://gazeta.zn.ua/internal/tretya-mirovaya-igra-_.html.

provided "warlords and armed groups" ammunition to challenge the leadership. Ukraine was fighting two wars: the east against the Donbas separatists and the second in Kyiv against a political leadership and an administrative bureaucracy that had only partially changed and appeared unwilling or unable to embrace substantial transformations.

At the end of 2014, 32.6% of Ukrainians described themselves as disappointed at the lack of reforms: the economic situation had deteriorated in the previous six months, while levels of corruption had remained the same. This data stands against 17.9% of respondents who ascribed the country's difficulties to the last government and Putin's aggressive policy. 14.7% of those polled concluded that things would change in Ukraine only with a new political generation in power. 46.8% of respondents identified the destruction of networks of corruption in the country as one of the main objectives of the Maidan movement.[59]

Consolidated vested interests and a pervasive system of corruption made it difficult to achieve the necessary level of consensus that would allow the implementation of the reforms the Maidan "Revolution of Dignity" fought for. Unwittingly, the volunteer battalions and their commanders became part of the complicated balancing game between the MoD and the MoI, between President Poroshenko, who supported the former and Prime Minister Yatsenyuk, who supported the latter. They were also caught in the mechanisms of the Soviet-style, unreformed machinery of decision-making and resource allocation that they thought, perhaps naively, they had brought down in Maidan.

Some street protests throughout 2015 involving volunteers, reservists and war veterans appeared staged by internal or external actors. They were likely an attempt to introduce an influential variable in the ongoing power struggle between political and oligarchic interests in the country. Although their demonstrations could

---

[59] Tomasz Piechal, "Disappointment and fear—the public mood in Ukraine," Centre for European Studies (OSW), 14 January 2015, http://www.osw.waw.pl/en/publikacje/analyses/2015-01-14/disappointment-and-fear-public-mood-ukraine.

be politically instrumentalised, veterans nonetheless expressed some legitimate concerns. Most of them had a direct, brutal experience of the inadequacy of the Ukrainian state.

Both volunteers and army servicemen were clothed, equipped, and fed thanks to the generosity of friends and family and the relentless activism of the vast network of civil society organisations that emerged at the beginning of the hostilities in the Donbas. In the early days of the ATO, life-saving flak jackets and helmets (not to mention night visors or other non-lethal equipment) were in short supply. Summer military uniforms were delivered when it was already snowing. Under the heat of summer, water provisions were brought to the front by support groups rather than by military logistic units. Volunteers mobilised to buy blankets, sleeping bags and essential medicine. US-donated meal-ready-to-eat rations never made it to the front. They were instead commercially sold by the superintendent of the food warehouse of one of the military units.[60]

A military commander engaged in the ATO would receive a salary of €300. National Guard reservists were paid about €150 for two months of service and a total of €20 as travel allowance for the same period.[61] No provisions were in place to define the status of participants in the ATO, and social security protection provisions remained unspecified for a long time. Women, for example, served as snipers while were not even legally authorised to be involved in combat roles and were registered as administrators or seamstresses. Once demobilised, they struggled to see their status as combatants recognised.[62]

---

[60] Myron Spolsky (ed.), "Criminal Scheme of Commercial Sales of American Rations Donated to Ukrainian Army Uncovered," *Euromaidan*, 8 June 2014, http://euromaidanpr.com/2014/06/08/criminal-scheme-of-commercial-sales-of-american-rations-donated-to-ukrainian-army-uncovered/.

[61] Dmytri Sinyak, "Kak maidanovtsy srazhayutsya s separatistami i na ch'ei storne okazalos' Minoborony" ["How Maidan activists are fighting against separatists and on whose side is the Ministry of Defence"], *Focus*, 10 July 2014, http://focus.ua/society/309870/.

[62] See for example, Olesya Khromeychuk, "The Death of a Soldier Told by his Sister" 2022, (Monoray), chapter "Masha".

The lack of a legal status affected all volunteers and was only partially regularised. This was despite President Poroshenko's promises in June 2015 that every serviceman involved in military operations in the Donbas would be granted recognition and the relative benefits and privileges.[63] Coming back from the front, even amputees have had to fight against bureaucracy and red tape to seek healthcare assistance.[64]

A journalist summed up this collective sense of dismay:

> "They were besieged, saw death and suffered, but they stood for themselves, for Ukraine and its people. The ATO combatants are heroes because they were not afraid to take up weapons and stand up in defence of their own country. Yet, when they return home, not all of them will be rewarded with medals. The majority will be facing a new war. This time, it was on the administrative front, with the bureaucratic machine of the state apparatus. For the right to receive the status of a participant in the military operation."[65]

Although most likely motivated by scepticism towards what they saw as unreliable paramilitary formations, the military leadership's protracted reluctance to provide volunteers with heavy weapons intensified a mutual sense of distrust. Wild rumours circulated among volunteers that the army command deliberately sent them to the front lines unequipped to have them killed in action. According to volunteers, this would be part of an unspoken strategy for the old, pre-Maidan security structures to rid themselves of the nuisance represented by the *dobrobaty*.[66]

---

63 "Vse zadeistvovannye v ATO poluchat status uchastnika boevykh deistvii — Prezident" ["All those serving in the ATO will receive the status of participants in military operations — the President"], *Censor.net*, 18 June 2014 http://censor.net.ua/news/290466/vse_zadeyistvovannye_v_ato_poluchat_status_uchastnika_boevyh_deyistviyi_prezident.
64 Anna Nemtsova, "It's Time to Call Ukraine a War," *The Daily Beast*, 4 February 2015, http://www.thedailybeast.com/articles/2015/02/04/it-s-time-to-call-ukraine-a-war.html.
65 Lesiya Vasilenko, "Uchasnik boevykh deistvii. Nereal'naya mechta uchastnika ATO" ["Participant in military operations. The unreal dream of a participant in the ATO"], *Zerkalo Nedeli*, 10 October 2014 http://gazeta.zn.ua/internal/uchastnik-boevyh-deystviy-nerealnaya-mechta-uchastnika-ato-_.html
66 Dmytri Sinyak, "Kak maidanovtsy srazhayutsya s separatistami i na ch'ei storne okazalos' Minoborony" ["How Maidan activists are fighting against separatists and on whose side is the Ministry of Defence"] *Focus*, 10 July 2014, http://focus.ua/society/309870/.

"We can go into battle, defend the motherland, get injured and even die, but we are not authorised to receive weapons through which we can defeat the enemy and escape death," commented a volunteer who had himself been injured in battle.[67]

Disarmament and Integration

Traditionally sceptical towards their authorities, Ukrainians' trust in their country's institutions remained low even after the Maidan and the coming to power of President Poroshenko. In December 2014, 24.5% of respondents in a national poll proclaimed their absolute confidence in the volunteer battalions. Still, only 8.3% declared the same degree of unwavering faith in the president, 7.5% in the prime minister, 4% in the Cabinet of Ministers and 3% in the Parliament.[68]

Authorities in Kyiv were well aware of the risk that widespread resentment and dissatisfaction posed in terms of further destabilisation of the country. In the face of an economic contraction of 20% in early 2015, Prime Minister Yatsenyuk called for the whole country to mobilise in a spirit of "unity and solidarity" to face necessary austerity measures and painful reforms.[69] Attempts were also made to de-escalate the volunteers' discontent with promises that their status would finally be regularised and that a way forward for integration or demobilisation would be defined.

According to Anton Gerashenko, member of parliament and adviser to Minister of Interior Avakov, with the Ukrainian defence forces back on their feet, inviting foreign combatants to leave the battalions and to depose their weapons was the first priority. The

---

67 "Idti v boy i umrat' mozhno, a moshnoe i nadezhnoe oruzhie — ne polozheno — boets dobrovol'tsego batal'yona" [It's possible to go into battle and to die, but to get powerful and useful weapons is not allowed — a combatant of a volunteer battalion"], *Censor.net*, 21 August 2014 http://censor.net.ua/video_news/298 995/idti_v_boyi_i_umirat_mojno_a_moschnoe_i_nadejnoe_orujie_ne_polojen o_boets_dobrovolcheskogo_batalona.
68 "Narod i vlast'" ["The people and the power"], *Zerkalo Nedeli*, http://opros20 14.zn.ua/authority.
69 Victoria Petrenko, "Yatsenyuk calls for nation to mobilize," *KyivPost*, 11 February 2015, http://www.kyivpost.com/content/ukraine/yatsenyuk-calls-for-nation-to-mobilize-380297.html

second step was setting up provisions for volunteers and reservists interested in taking up a permanent position in the army or the police to integrate into the system fully. Regarding social security, Prime Minister Yatsenyuk announced in late January 2015 the creation of a single national register for military personnel in the ATO. Legislation was drafted for regional administrations to provide financial resources towards accommodation expenses for the families of servicemen killed in action, thus delegating to local authorities financial commitments they were not necessarily equipped to honour[70]. Legal steps were also considered in parliament regarding the status of volunteers and social protection for them and their families.[71]

On 1 February, a decree was signed stipulating that servicemen would be paid double when serving in the ATO and would receive a daily compensation of about €40 for each day in the area of operations. The decree also listed a range of financial incentives for successful military operations and the capture or destruction of enemy military equipment.[72] On 17 February, Minister Avakov handed out medals and apartments to the National Guard and police personnel injured in the ATO, including those serving in the Azov, Donbas, *Mirotvorets* and General Kul'chinsky battalions.[73]

With Kyiv's fears of destabilisation, the change of the operational requirements in the ATO created the conditions to set in

---

[70] "V Ukraine sozdadut edinyi reestr boitsov pogibshikh v ATO" ["In Ukraine a single register of servicemen who died in the ATO is being established"], *Ukrainska Pravda*, 1 February 2015 http://www.pravda.com.ua/rus/news/20 15/02/1/7057085/.

[71] Dmytro Yarosh, "Bahato khto zaraz prosit' prokomentuvati…" ["Many are now asking to comment on…"], Facebook status update, 2:31 pm, 13 February 2015, retrieved from https://www.facebook.com/dyastrub/posts/7826604684 77506.

[72] "Yatsenyuk: Boitsam v zone ATO zaplatyat vdvoe bol'she" ["Servicemen in the ATO zone will be paid double"] http://www.pravda.com.ua/rus/news/2015 /02/1/7057087/.

[73] Arsen' Avakov, "Segodnya vruchal ranenim boitsam nagrady I kvartiry" ["Today I handed out to injured servicemen medals and apartments"], Facebook status update, 3:26pm, 17 February 2015 https://www.facebook.com/arsen. avakov.1/posts/787412071348901.

motion the process that would lead to the disarmament and the integration of the *dobrabaty* in the armed forces.

Starting from the summer of 2014, the character of the combat operations in the East changed. When the Anti-Terrorist Operation was set up, and the decision was made to send volunteers, the fighting had the character of a large-scale police operation. Small groups carrying out security checks, guarding checkpoints or undertaking sabotage actions proved expedient.[74] Yet, in the summer, positions consolidated, and skirmishes became fully-fledged military operations for which the volunteers were neither trained nor equipped. The disaster of Ilovaisk, with all its coordination problems, proved the *dobrobaty's* limitations. With the signature of the Minsk II protocol, the frontlines' stabilisation necessitated the service of a thoroughly professional army. International partners' traditional resistance to train and equip irregular military formations marked this definite change of direction.[75]

In November 2014, Minister of Defence Poltorak ordered territorial defence battalions to be absorbed into the formal structures of his ministry or disbanded. Azov was the first to be integrated into the National Guard with its 500 members elements.[76] In the spring of 2015, independent groups were withdrawn from the frontlines. An outpouring of volunteers was registered around this time. Some returned to civilian life; others signed up for the army motivated to professionalise and change the defence structures from within, acquire practical training and equipment, and see their efforts recognised through an official status that would grant them social protection.

Disbanding and integrating all volunteer combatants proved a gradual and uneven process, with most battalions allowed to

---

[74] Yurii Butusov, "Dobrovol'chi batal'yoni: struktura, strakhi, problemi boyvoho zastosuvannya" [Voluntary battalions: structure, fears problems of employment in combat], ZN.ua, 29 August 2014
[75] In 2018 the US Congress formally banned assistance to the Azov battalion. "Congress bans arms to Ukraine Militia linked to neo-Nazis", The Hill, 27 March 2018 https://thehill.com/policy/defense/380483-congress-bans-arms-to-controversial-ukrainian-militia-linked-to-neo-nazis/
[76] Vera Mironova and Ekaterina Sergatskova, "How Ukraine Reined in its Militias", Foreign Affairs, August 1, 2017

maintain their distinctive identity even within the official structures they joined. Despite Commander Yarosh's commitment to the process and the bulk of the battalion's decision to join the Security Services of Ukraine (SBU) as the special Unit Alpha, *DUK Pravy Sektor* proved the most resistant to legalisation. Critical of what they continued to view as a "Soviet" military leadership, a part of those who did not join Alpha splintered in several special-purpose battalions. With some *DUK Pravy Sektor's* members involved in the July 2015 armed clashes in Mukacheve, President Poroshenko announced his intention to bring to parliament legislation defining as terrorists all "illegal armed groups".[77] In 2016 and 2018, *DUK Pravy Sektor* attracted the condemnation of both Military Prosecutor Matios and Commander of the Joint Forces Operations (JFO) for their unwillingness to "make up their mind" and continuing to roam the warzone as "unknown individuals with illegal arms".[78] In autumn 2022, media reports still listed *DUK Pravy Sektor* as one of the groups informally operating in the combat zone.[79]

Legacies

Despite spectacular protests and explicit discontent, fears of a military coup staged by volunteer battalions proved unfounded. Most volunteer commanders were painfully aware of the costs that an open confrontation with the authorities, the army and the police might have for the country. Having become members of Parliament, some acquired a stake in the continuation of this system, despite their repeated calls for reforms.

---

77 "Poroshenko khochet predlozhit' schitat' terroristami vsekh nezakonno vooruzhennykh lits" ["Poroshenko wants to propose to call terrorists all the individuals illegally armed"], Ukrainska Pravda, 15 July 2015
78 "Matios nazvan DUK PS nezakonnym vooruzhennym formirovaniem" ["Matios called DUK PS illegal armed formations"], Ukrainska Pravda 2 February 2016 and "U Naeva nazrel conflict s dobrovoltsami Pravogo Sektora" ["A conflict exploded between Naeva and Pravy Sektor's volunteers"], Ukrainska Pravda, 18 July 2018
79 Igor Burduga, "Nevidimiy legion: Ukrainiski Dobrovol'tsi, yaki ne khocut' legalizuvatysya" ["Invisible legion: the Ukrainian Volunteers who do not want to be legalised"], DW.com, 30 October 2022

When asked whether volunteer battalions would be preparing a putsch against the national authorities, the commander of the Mirotvorets battalion, Andrii Teteryuk, excluded the possibility emphatically. "You need to understand," he told reporters, "that the volunteer battalions are [composed of] the most patriotic Ukrainians, those who love their motherland the most. In no case would they do anything that would damage the country?"[80]

As with every revolutionary or extraordinarily tragic public event, Maidan and the eruption of hostilities in the Donbas brought to the fore a mixed bag of eloquent populists, romantic visionaries, cunning adventurers and committed patriots. Populism and demagoguery have proved an easy temptation for many. Yet in the complex, pluralistic and vehemently confrontational Ukrainian political landscape, post-Maidan media and civil society actors demonstrated themselves to be alert and critical, ready to challenge and undo unconvincing heroes.[81]

As a product of Maidan, most volunteers brought Jacobin attitudes to the frontlines of the "Revolution of Dignity." Generally motivated by patriotism and the urgency for change, most of them proved to be an extraordinary resource for the country at a time of need. Yet, their full integration into formal military units was indispensable. Many volunteers would say they fought in Maidan for a modern, functional, corruption-free country. Their aspirations were heeded and, with the support of Ukraine's international partners, defined the backbone of the reforms that, in the nine years since the beginning of the war, have generally transformed the army and the security sector. Volunteerism has become an inextricable component of Ukraine's modern identity, part of the narrative

---

80 "Rossiskie SMI publikuyut "vbrosy", chto dobrovol'cheskie batal'yony poidut na Kiev. Etogo nikogda ne budet—kombat "Mirotvortsa"" ["The Russian media publish speculations that the volunteer battalions will march against Kyiv. This will never happen—the Commander of the *Mirotvorets* battalion"], *Censor.net*, 17 September 2014, http://censor.net.ua/news/303114/rossiyiskie_smi_publikuyut_vbrosy_chto_dobrovolcheskie_batalony_poyidut_na_kiev_etogo_nikogda_ne_budet.
81 See, for example, the bruising attitude of the journalists who interviewed Donbas battalion Commander Semenchenko for Ukrainska Pravda on 23 December 2014: http://www.pravda.com.ua/rus/articles/2014/12/23/7053033/.

on resistance and resilience. Military volunteerism is memorialised in the official holiday of the Day of Volunteer Fighters on 14 March and recognised in the establishment in January 2022 of a Territorial Defence aimed at channelling the volunteers' commitment in formal structures. Most importantly, the volunteers' engagement in the security sector, both in terms of combatants and of the societal networks that have continued to provide vital material support to the army, has helped modernisation and de-bureaucratisation. Protracted social activism has brought into the military innovative methods and practices from the civilian world, for instance, in procurement, digital transformation and disinformation.[82]

Finally, volunteer experience in combat operations has contributed to the attainment of full recognition of the role of women in the military. Ukraine adopted UN Security Council Resolution 1325 on women's peace and security in 2016 and made it the cornerstone of its commitment to women's engagement in security and defence. 37,000 women currently serve in the army, 1000 in leading positions, all on the frontlines. Rectifying previous provisions, the parliament has issued legislation authorising women to participate in combat operations, attend military schools and pursue a military career.[83]

---

[82] See Rosaria Puglisi "A People's Army: Civil Society as a Security Actor in Post-Maidan Ukraine", IAI Working Papers 15, 23 July 2015, https://www.iai.it/en/pubblicazioni/peoples-army
[83] Author's interview, 13 July 2022

3 From Political Outsiders to Military Stalwarts

The Evolving Face of Ukrainian Nationalism

Taras Tarasiuk and Petro Burkovskiy

Introduction

In the context of the tense Russian invasion in 2022, Ukrainian nationalist movements played a pivotal symbol in military mobilisation and resistance against Russia. They evolved from political outsiders to a crucial component of the Armed Forces of Ukraine (AFU), transforming into expansive mobilisation networks and highly proficient combat units. They formed units, which are the symbol of Ukrainian military professionalism and heroism. They were involved in the most important battles and operations after the start of a full-scale invasion, as the true spear of Ukrainian resilience. Nationalists are nominally the foundation for two assault brigades (Azov 12th Brigade, 3rd Separate Assault Brigade), heavy mechanized brigades (67th Separate Mechanized Brigade "Right Sector"). They quickly created volunteer units under Territorial Defence Forces (TDF), which rapidly became a part of the elite units of the Special Operations Forces of Ukraine (formerly SSO "Azov-Kharkiv," "Azov-Kyiv," along with the "Lubart" unit). They form significant detachments and particular purpose units (14th Regiment). Some of them are part of the armed formation of the Main Intelligence Directorate of Ukraine ("KRAKEN" special unit, tactical group "Revansh," "Brotherhood" battalion).

This chapter highlights some of the main factors for their success, including extensive continuous training, advanced mobilization, a networked command and communication structure, rapid adoption of new technologies, and the ability to adapt to new types of heavy equipment. Additionally, although the chapter emphasizes military training and activities, its purpose is not to establish a direct causal relationship between the actions of these movements and the battlefield successes of nationalist units. While we recognise the indisputable high regard and evaluation of these units' performance in combat, our primary focus is on the movements' preparations for a war in which they fervently believed. The evolution of these units over the past nine years likely significantly impacted their operational effectiveness. In this chapter, we intentionally refrain from scrutinising the ideology behind these movements. Instead of delving into the ideological underpinnings of these movements, our discussion adopts a utilitarian perspective, examining them primarily in terms of their effectiveness as tools for training and mobilising participants. This means we focus on the practical outcomes of their actions and strategies, such as how they prepare participants for combat, rather than engaging in a deeper analysis of the ideological motivations or beliefs of Ukrainian nationalism. It is also worth noting that the chapter primarily focuses on combat units that arose from or were formed based on nationalist and right-wing movements in Ukraine. This does not imply that such practices are exclusive to nationalist units; instead, we suggest that their leading role in innovative training stems from practices cultivated within these nationalist movements. However, this does not mean other units did not employ similar mechanisms and practices. These were also evident among the veteran community in Ukraine after 2014.

Nevertheless, nationalist groups stand out in their meticulous preparation for war, unlike other social movements. This distinct approach to war preparation sets them apart, making them a unique example of this phenomenon. In this sphere, nationalists demonstrate institutionalisation uncommon in social movements, evolving into significant actors in the war. Additionally, their integration into the army is a testament to their effectiveness and the seriousness with which they approach their military objectives. This dual role of political and military engagement distinguishes them from other groups, underlining their unique position in the context of Ukrainian nationalist movements. Not all aspects of the hostilities are currently known, and the constant changes in the situation can significantly alter the nature and role of nationalist movements in the new phase of the Russian-Ukrainian war. However, we can argue that the nationalist movement has become a visible component of the resistance and an example of professionalism.

For this purpose, we will answer several important questions. How did these formations, opposing the government, integrate into the Armed Forces as regular units? Why were most of them incorporated in 2022? How did the nationalist movements avoid dissolving into the general political agenda of existential confrontation with the Russian Federation, a stance currently shared by most Ukrainians? Why could this particular political spectrum survive and become a productive force of opposition against the Russian Federation?

We aim to focus on the apparent reasons for the high motivation and quality preparation of Ukrainian nationalists within the Armed Forces of Ukraine, particularly in the context of their activities. This is primarily a question of facts that attest to the nationalist movements' understanding of the threat posed by the Russian Federation and their persistent, long-term, and systematic preparation of their activists for potential armed confrontation. I underline several key facts that demonstrate the clear advantages of nationalist formations relative to other political movements in the context of the conflict. In our opinion, the main aspects that describe why, in the most dangerous and dark times for Ukrainians in 21 century, the nationalist movement became the tip of the spear in this war.

The case of Ukrainian nationalist units

Since the onset of the conflict with Russia in 2014, Ukrainian nationalists have been actively participating in hostilities. Establishing the first volunteer battalions marked a significant step in forming new professional military units. They have quickly demonstrated their value as a recruitment resource for the Armed Forces of Ukraine, particularly during the initial months of 2022. Their renown and popularity as highly professional units have not only bolstered their standing but also served as a rallying call for broader mobilisation into the ranks of the Ukrainian army, predominantly forming elite and professional units. Following this initial phase, the integration of these nationalist battalions with the Armed Forces of Ukraine gradually intensified. The transition from independent volunteer groups to integral components of the military was marked by a strategic blending of their unique combat experience with the structured environment of the armed forces. This seamless integration underscores the evolving role of these units, cementing their status as essential elements of Ukraine's military infrastructure in response to the ongoing conflict. Therefore, it is necessary to start with a brief review of the significant organisations of the Ukrainian right and nationalists, which represent the overwhelming majority of movements in the arena of socio-political movements of nationalist orientation in Ukraine:

- **The Svoboda party founded in 1991,**[1] is the oldest nationalist political party in Ukraine. In 2014, VO "Svoboda" decided that all party members should join the Armed Forces or serve as community volunteers to support the Ukrainian army.[2] The movement presented as three battalions — "Sich" under the command of the Ministry of Internal Affairs, battalion "Svoboda" as part of the 4th Separate Assault Brigade "Rubizh" and as a separate tactical group (STG) "Karaptska Sich" as a special unit in the 93rd Mechanized Brigade.[3]
- **Ukrainian National Assembly — Ukrainian People's Self-Defence (UNA-UNSO)** is the oldest Ukrainian paramilitary organisation, founded in 1990.[4] Its members

---

1 Istoriia VO SVOBODA [The history of VO SVOBODA], Sovoboda party official page, accessed May 28, 2023, available at: https://svoboda.org.ua/party/history/
2 Pryshtunova Viktoria, "Kombatant's'ke ob'yednannya biytsiv "Lehion Svobody"" [Combatant association of fighters "Legion of Freedom"], UNIAN, April 27, 2015, accessed May 28, 2023, available at: https://photo.unian.ua/photo/627332-the-union-of-soldiers-legion-of-liberty
3 Istoriia batalyoniv [The history of battalions], Svoboda.army, accessed May 28, 2023, available at: https://svoboda.army/history/
4 "Stislyi kurs istorii UNA-UNSO..." [Concise Course of UNA-UNSO History], UNA-UNSO, accessed May 28, 2023, available at: http://una-unso.com/styslyi-kurs-una-unso

participated in conflicts against Russia in Georgia (1993)[5] and Ichkeria (1994-1995).[6] In 2014, UNA-UNSO created a volunteer battalion, which eventually transformed into the 131st separate reconnaissance battalion[7] and presented as the joint battalion "UNSO".[8]

- **"Brotherhood"** is a neoconservative group founded by charismatic leader Dmytro Korchinsky in 2004.[9] In 2014, the "Brotherhood" fought in Azov and participated in creating volunteer paramedic units and military formations.[10] In February 2015, it established a separate unit called the "Christian Volunteer Battalion Saint Maria."[11] After 2022, they formed the battalion "Bratstvo".[12]

---

5 "Stislyi kurs istorii UNA-UNSO..." [Concise Course of UNA-UNSO History], UNA-UNSO, accessed May 28, 2023, available at: http://una-unso.com/stysl yi-kurs-una-unso
6 "Stislyi kurs istorii UNA-UNSO..." [Concise Course of UNA-UNSO History], UNA-UNSO, accessed May 28, 2023, available at: http://una-unso.com/stysl yi-kurs-una-unso
7 "Slavetni chastyny rozvidky 131 okremyy rozviduval'nyy batal'yon" [Glorious pieces of intelligence. 131 separate reconnaissance battalion], Main Intelligence Service of Ukraine, accessed May 28, 2023, available at: https://gur.gov.ua/co ntent/131-okremyi-rozviduvalnyi-batalion.html
8 "Robota BPLA Zvedenoho pidrozdilu UNSO" [Operation of UAVs by the Consolidated Unit of UNSO]), January 29, 2023, accessed May 28, 2023, Link: http://unso.org.ua/uk/new/robota-bpla-zvedenogo-pidrozdilu-unso
9 "Vseukrayins'ka Politychna Partiya Bratstvo" [All-Ukrainian Political Party Brotherhood], YouControl, accessed May 28, 2023, available at: https://youco ntrol.com.ua/catalog/company_details/33105589/
10 Nazarov Oleksandr, "Batal'yon 'Svyata Mariya' provely na pidhotovku do ATO" [The 'Svyata Mariya' battalion conducted training for the ATO], Hromadske, February 3, 2015, accessed May 28, 2023, available at: https://hrom adske.ua/posts/batalion-sviata-mariia-provely-na-pidhotovku-do-ato
11 Sirko Askold, "Rozvidka ta dyversiya—zavdannya batal'yonu 'Svyata Mariya'" [Reconnaissance and sabotage—the tasks of the 'Svyata Mariya' battalion], Radio Svoboda, September 22, 2014, accessed May 28, 2023, available at: https:// www.radiosvoboda.org/a/26598626.html
12 Svyrydiuk Yuriy, "U batal'oni 'Bratstvo' zayavlyayut, shcho Tkachenko zaboronyv vidsypivuvaty ikhnikh viys'kovykh u Lavri. Minkult tse zaperechuye" [In the 'Bratstvo' battalion, they claim that Tkachenko banned singing by their soldiers in Lavra. Ministry of Culture denies it], Suspilne, March 7, 2023, accessed May 28, 2023, available at: https://suspilne.media/406254-u-bataljoni-bratstvo -zaavlaut-so-tkacenko-zaboroniv-vidspivuvati-ihnih-vijskovih-u-lavri-minkul t-ce-zaperecue/

- **DUK-PS / Right Sector (Volunteer Ukrainian Corps-Right Sector)** emerged in 2014 as a leading organisation that incorporated several smaller and lesser-known nationalist movements, such as the "Trident" named after Stepan Bandera, UNA-UNSO, Separate Tactical Group (STG) "Carpathian January," and football fans/ultras from Kyiv, Kharkiv, Dnipro, and Donetsk.[13] The initial goal was to protect Maidan residents from special divisions of "Berkut." After the onset of the Russian intrusion, it transformed into DUK-PS, which consisted of several voluntary military units.[14] Since 2022, nearly all active members of the HONOR movement, along with leader Serhii Filimonov, have joined the Kotsyubailo subdivision.[15] In November 2022, the DUK-PS was legalized and transformed into the 67th Separate Mechanized Brigade.
- **The Ukrainian Volunteer Army (UDA)** under Dmytro Yarosh: Formed as a volunteer military unit in Ukraine, the Ukrainian Volunteer Army (UDA) was officially established in December 2015.[16] Following the onset of Russia's full-scale invasion of Ukraine on February 26, 2022, UDA Commander Dmytro Yarosh announced the deployment of several battalions, including the 1st and 3rd "Volyn," the 5th and 7th separate "Arey" battalions (integrated into the

---

13 Nayem Mustafa, "Za lashtunkamy Pravoho sektoru" [Behind the Scenes of Right Sector], Ukrayinska Pravda, April 1, 2014, accessed May 28, 2023, available at: https://www.pravda.com.ua/articles/2014/04/1/7020952/
14 "Byi roti 'Gonor', batalyonu 'Vovki Da Vinchi', za ostannu dorohu v Bakhmut" [The Battle of the "Honor" Detachment, the "Wolves of Da Vinci" Battalion, for the Last Road in Bakhmut], Argument, April 21, 2023, accessed May 28, 2023, available at: https://argumentua.com/video/b-i-roti-gonor-batalionu-vovki-da-v-nch-za-ostannyu-dorogu-v-bakhmut
15 Novynarnia. "DUK 'Pravyy sektor' stav 67-yu mekhanizovanoyu bryhadoyu ZSU." [DUK Right Sector become a 67th mechanized brigade of Armed Forces of Ukraine], December 12, 2022. Accessed May 28, 2023, available at: https://novynarnia.com/2022/12/12/duk-pravyj-sektor-stav-67-yu-mehanizovanoyu-brygadoyu-zsu/
16 "Pro UDA" [About UDA], uda.army, accessed May 28, 2023, available at: https://uda.army/sample-page/; "Yarosh pishov z PS i oholosyv pro stvorennya novoho rukhu" [Yarosh left PS and announced the creation of a new movement], Ukrainska Pravda, December 28, 2015, Accessed May 28, 2023, available at: https://www.pravda.com.ua/news/2015/12/28/7093943/

129th TDF brigade as of August 30, 2022), the 8th battalions, the combined UDA "South" unit, and separate combat groups, alongside the "Hospitaliers" medical battalion.[17] The UDA structure also encompasses a training centre[18] and ancillary entities such as the internal security service.[19]
- **The "Azov" movement was formally established in May 2014** as a separate volunteer militia unit under the Ministry of Internal Affairs.[20] Between 2014 and 2021, the movement evolved into a broad network of political and public organizations founded by Ukrainian-Russian war veterans. In addition, some participants in the Azov movement continued their professional military service in a separate "Azov" 12th brigade of the National Guards of Ukraine.[21] Azov veterans and movement members also formed or mostly presented in the GUR MO unit "KRAKEN" and in the SSO unit "Lubart". The central part of activists and veterans nowadays is in the 3rd Separate Assault Brigade (SAB).[22]
- **The "Tradition and Order" Movement and the Conservative Party** started from Euromaidan as the Revansh group and was renamed in 2016.[23] In December 2021, the movement evolved into the Conservative Party but conducted only a few activities following the introduction of this new

---

17 ""Smert' moskovs'kiy ordi!"": Yarosh rozpoviv, de yoho syly pidtrymuyut' ZSU" ["Death to the Moscow Horde!"]: Yarosh told where his forces support the Armed Forces], Ukrainska Pravda, February 26, 2022, Accessed May 28, 2023, available at: https://www.pravda.com.ua/news/2022/02/26/7326062/
18 "Navchal'nyy tsentr" [Training center], uda.army, accessed May 28, 2023, available at: https://uda.army/navchalnyy-tsentr/
19 "Structure UDA" [The structure of UDA], uda.army, accessed May 28, 2023, available at: https://uda.army/struktura/
20 Pro Azov [About the Azov], Azov brigade official page, accessed May 28, 2023, available at: https://azov.org.ua/pro-nas/
21 "Bat'alyon 'Azov' stav polkom" [Azov Battalion becomes a regiment], UkrInform, September 18, 2014, accessed May 28, 2023, available at: https://www.ukrinform.ua/rubric-other_news/1708734-batalyon_azov_stav_polkom_1973681.html
22 "Pro Brygadu" [About the brigade], ab3.army (official site of 3rd Assault Brigade), accessed May 28, 2023, available at: https://ab3.army/pro-brigadu/
23 "Tradition and Order—Radical right-wing group active in disrupting civil society events", Reporting Radicalism, accessed May 28, 2023, available at: https://reportingradicalism.org/en/dossiers/groups/tradition-and-order

brand.[24] Following the invasion's commencement, the movement formed the "Revansh" unit,[25] which later evolved into a separate tactical group. This group functions as a special unit within the Intelligence Directorate (GUR) of the Ukrainian Ministry of Defense.[26]

- **Future Society Movement and C14:** originating from the C14 movement, the Future Society is a predominantly Kyiv-based ultra-conservative movement. Its formation involved members from C14 and local council deputies from the Svoboda and European Solidairty parties, with Yevhen Karas as leader.[27] In the early stages of the war, the C14 volunteer unit was established, which subsequently evolved into the 14th separate regiment of the Armed Forces of Ukraine by the end of August 2022, commanded by Yevhen Karas.[28] detailed information regarding the regiment's specific roles or engagements in the conflict remains undisclosed.

Despite their highly active presence across key frontlines, nationalist volunteers represent a minor fraction of the total volunteer force in Ukraine. The Deputy Minister of Defense reported that approximately 100,000 citizens have volunteered for the Territorial Defense Forces, with this being a prevalent and accessible pathway to join

---

24 "Pid Ofisom prezydenta vidbulas' aktsiya «Konservatyvnoyi partiyi». Shcho vymahaly?" [An action of the "Conservative Party" took place under the President's Office. What was demanded?], Hromadske, December 28, 2021, accessed May 28, 2023, available at: https://hromadske.ua/posts/pid-ofisom-prezidenta-vidbulas-akciya-konservativnoyi-partiyi-sho-vimagali
25 "Revansh: Taktychna Hrupa (t.me/revanche_tactical)Uvaha! Total'na militaryzatsiya! «Revansh» povertayet'sya!" [Attention! Total militarization! Revenge is back!], Telegram, February 28, 2022 at 21:55, accessed May 28, 2023, available at: https://t.me/revanche_tactical/5
26 Revansh official site (main page), accessed May 28, 2023, available at: https://www.revanshua.com/
27 ""C14" oformlyayet'sya v politychnu partiyu" ["C14" is registered as a political party], Livyy Bereh, October 03, 2019, accessed May 28, 2023, available at: https://lb.ua/news/2019/10/03/438905_c14_oformlyaetsya_politicheskuyu.html
28 14 polk, "14 polk ZSU. Posvyata." [14th regiment of the Armed Forces. dedication], Youtube, 2:06:00, August 22, 2023, accessed November 28, 2023, available at: https://www.youtube.com/watch?v=opttzTrHa54

the regular army.[29] In October 2023, Serhiy Rakhmanin, a member of the Committee of the Verkhovna Rada of Ukraine on National Security, Defense and Intelligence, indicated that the Ukrainian army includes about 400,000 volunteers.[30] A substantial portion of these individuals likely possess prior military experience, having participated in hostilities or served as former military personnel. Considering that there were around 423,000 individuals holding certificates of participation in hostilities,[31] and with the regular army numbering about 250,000 as of February 24, 2022, the proportion of nationalists within the Ukrainian military is relatively small. Their notable distinction lies in their concentration within specific subdivisions.

To gauge the actual representation of military nationalists, we can approximate the size of their units. This includes two Azov brigades—the 3rd Assault Brigade and the 12th Azov Brigade, the 67th Mechanized Brigade of the DUK-PS, the 14th Regiment under Yevgeny Karasya, and the Brotherhood, Tradition and Order, Kraken battalions, all subordinate to the Main Intelligence Directorate. Additionally, there are 2 Svoboda battalions, the Karpatska Sich battalion and Taras Deyak's SSO Lubart and Karpatska Sich unit. Estimations suggest that a brigade during peacetime exceeds 5,000 personnel, while battalions typically comprise around 250 members, though this number can fluctuate, particularly under

---

29 "Mayzhe 100 tysyach dobrovol'tsiv pryyshly u teroboronu odrazu pislya vtorhnennya rf—Minoborony" [Almost 100,000 volunteers joined the Teroboron right after the Russian invasion—Ministry of Defense], Ukrinform, April 03, 2022, accessed November 28, 2023, , available at: https://www.ukrinform.ua/rubric-ato/3682476-majze-100-tisac-dobrovolciv-prijsli-u-teroboronu-odrazu-pisla-vtorgnenna-rf-minoboroni.html
30 Sereda Sofia, "Serhiy Rakhmanin: Zaraz TTSK ne mozhut' chitko porakhuvaty lyudey, yaki pidlyahayut' mobilizatsiyi" [Serhii Rakhmanin: Currently, the Territorial Centers for Recruitment and Social Support cannot accurately count the people subject to mobilization], Ukrainska Pravda, October 25, 2023, accessed December 17, 2023, available at: https://www.pravda.com.ua/articles/2023/10/25/7425712/
31 "Svizha statystyka shchodo kil'kosti uchasnykiv ATO/OOS stanovy na 2021 rik" [The latest statistics on the number of ATO/OOS participants are for 2021], Legal Hundred NGO, August 05, 2021, accessed November 28, 2023, , available at: https://legal100.org.ua/svizha-statistika-shhodo-kilkosti-uchasnikiv-ato-oos-stanovi-na-2021-rik/

intelligence command. Regiments likely maintain a strength of at least 1,000 personnel. Analysis of photographic evidence suggests that SSO units are approximately company-sized, with up to 250 individuals.[32] Factoring in the potential strength of the UDA, estimated at around six battalions (inclusive of approximately 500 light infantry battalions and 300 in the Hospitaller battalions as of 2022),[33] the number of personnel in nationalist units could be around 20,000. Considering the expansion of brigades during martial law and the inclusion of other units aligned with nationalist ideologies or simply representatives of the movement within the Armed Forces, their numbers could range from 20,000 to 30,000. Consequently, nationalist volunteers constitute less than 1% of the total volunteer force. This observation presents a pivotal question for our research: How did such a relatively small group emerge as a paradigm of a professional army and as a symbol of resistance against the Russian Federation amidst hundreds of thousands of volunteers and within the broader context of nationwide mobilisation against aggression?

---

32 OZSP «Lyubart» (t.me/ozspLubart) "Dlya bahat'okh iz nas viyna pochalas', shche dev"yat' rokiv tomu" [For many of us, the war began nine years ago], Telegram, February 24, 2023, 20:23, accessed November 28, 2023, available at: https://t.me/ozspLubart/277; "Prosto khoroshe foto maybutnikh serzhantiv batal'yonu «Revansh»."KHODAKOVSKY (t.me/BKhodakovsky) "Prosto khoroshe foto maybutnikh serzhantiv batal'yonu «Revansh»." [Just a good photo of the future sergeants of the "Revenge" battalion], Telegram, May 27, 2023, 10:01, accessed November 28, 2023, available at: https://t.me/BKhodakovsky/2547

33 «Tam TikTok znimaiut'. Yak «Arey» pryyshov, pochynayut' plakaty» — rozpovid' biytsiv pro zvil'nennya ta polonenykh u Neskuchnomu" ["TikTok is filmed there. When "Arei" came, they started to cry" — the story of the fighters about the liberation and prisoners in Neskuchny], Suspilne, September 14, 2023, accessed November 28, 2023, available at: https://suspilne.media/571735-tam-tik-znimaut-ak-arej-priihav-pocinaut-plakati-rozpovid-bijciv-pro-zvilnenna-ta-polonenih-u-neskucnomu/; "Yana Zinkevych: «Velyka kil'kist' medykiv zahynuly, velyka kil'kist' — v poloni. I vse tse shchodnya zminyuyet'sya ne na nashu koryst'»" [Yana Zinkevich: "A large number of doctors died, a large number were captured. And all this changes every day not in our favor"], Livyy Bereh, June 13, 2022, accessed November 28, 2023, , available at: https://lb.ua/society/2022/06/13/519824_yana_zinkevich_velika_kilkist.html

The reason for the importance

Their contribution, particularly the nationalist volunteer units, was crucial for success in the battles for the strategic cities of Ukraine (for example, Kyiv and Kharkiv defence operations) and for slowing down the advancement of the Russian army. Many members of nationalist movements (primarily members of the Azov Regiment) were also involved in the defence operation of Mariupol, which became one of the symbols of Ukrainian resistance. In this battle, Ukrainians had less than 5000 soldiers (including more than 1000 Azov regiment personnel under the command of Denys Prokopenko, whereas the Russian group had from 14 to 20 thousands personnel). After two months, three weeks and five days, Russian troops still could not capture the main defence base—Azovstal, which is 11 km² or five times bigger than Monaco, nearly the area of Beverly Hills, or more than half of Salzburg in Austria.

The 3rd Assault Brigade has provided a successful offensive around Bakhmut from May 2023, after more than 9 months of Russian offensive attempts. Other nationalist formations in this city also include the Karpatska Sich unit under the command of Taras Deyak and SOF unit Lubart. STG Karpatska Sich, led by Oleh Kutsyn and composed of Svoboda party and affiliates, was one of the most critical units that defended Barvinkove, 214 which helped to protect Ukrainian Forces from encirclement in Donbas. After all of this, nationalist units present as one of the most popular for volunteers, as adequate and well-trained soldiers. The head of the Main Intelligence Directorate of Ukraine, Kyrylo Budanov, named the Kraken unit as one of the most capable in the Defence Forces of Ukraine (DFU), which actively participated in the Kharkiv defence operation and in the summer counteroffensive in the Kharkiv region.[34] Also, at the Kherson counteroffensive operation, an important role belongs to the Revansh and Bratstvo battalions and

---

34 Svit Navvorit, "RIK—avtors'kyy dokumental'nyy proekt Dmytra Komarova. Chastyna druha" [YEAR—the author's documentary project of Dmytro Komarov. Part two], Youtube, 1:20:02, February 24, 2023, accessed 20 August 2023, available at: https://youtu.be/rlkzADUfb3s?t=2892

SOF units of the Azov movements. They were primarily special operations troops and units coordinating artillery with UAVs.

The importance and symbolism of nationalists are also presented in international negotiations between Ukraine, Russia and Turkey. After the fall of Mariupol, the Azovstal commanders (including the command staff of the Azov Regiment) were evacuated to Turkey under the personal guarantees of Erdogan. Despite the guarantees that commanders in Turkey would remain there until the end of the war, on the 8th of July 2023 President Zelensky personally met the commanders, who were transferred to Ukraine with an official ceremony in Lviv.

According to public opinion polls by the Democratic Initiative Foundation, the Ukrainian Defence of Mariupol was the third (28% of respondents) most memorable moment of the current war.[35] The most popular social network in Ukraine – Telegram (more than 70% of the country)[36] – shows that more people subscribe to the 3rd Assault Brigade Telegram channel (more than 200 000 subscribers)[37] than the channels of the most popular media in the country,[38] such as Ukrainska Pravda, which has less than 150 000,[39] or Censor.net (below 190 000).[40] Two commanders of nationalist units – Denys Prokopenko and Petro Kuzyk – were nominated in the top 25 most influential Ukrainian military for the version of the Novoe Vremya journal. Just these few examples show the level of importance, popularity and respect of them. Active participation in

---

35 "Symvoly, podiyi ta osobystosti, yaki formuyut' natsional'nu pam"yat' pro viynu z Rosiyeyu" [Symbols, events and personalities that form the national memory of the war with Russia], Democratic Initiatives Foundation, May 8 2023, accessed January 18, 2023, available at: https://dif.org.ua/article/simvoli-podii-ta-osobistosti-yaki-formuyut-natsionalnu-pamyat-pro-viynu-z-rosieyu
36 "Media Consumption In Liberated And Frontline Territories" [Media Consumption In Liberated And Frontline Territories], KIIS, October 27, 2023, accessed January 18, 2023, available at: https://www.kiis.com.ua/?lang=ukr&cat=reports&id=1308&page=1
37 https://t.me/ab3army
38 According to the Similar Web rating, accessed 17 January 2024, available at: https://www.similarweb.com/top-websites/ukraine/news-and-media/
39 Ukrainska Pravda (t.me/ukrpravda_news), Telegram, accessed January 18, 2023,
40 Cencor.NET (t.me/censor_net), Telegram, accessed January 18, 2023

primary military operations, particularly the heroic defence of Mariupol, has become a significant symbol of the capabilities of nationalist units. Although they often constituted only a segment of the various military formations, their involvement notably received the most attention and was associated with the success of operations. However, why have they incorporated into the regular army, which is far less motivated and trained than them?

Forced Unity: Nationalists and Army Meets War

To understand the formation of nationalist units, it is essential to comprehend the institutional and political background of Ukraine's security and defence sector. The Ukrainian army has a dynamic history that dates back to the collapse of the USSR in 1991. Initially one of the largest armies in Europe and possessing the world's third-largest nuclear arsenal, the Ukrainian Armed Forces gradually stagnated until 2014. They were not a primary focus of political authorities for most of Ukraine's independence. Before the annexation of Crimea and the war in Donbas, Ukraine did not spend more than 1% of its GDP on the Armed Forces,[41] which notably degraded during the rule of Viktor Yanukovych. It is telling that the head of the Minister of Defense Pavlo Lebediev in Mykola Azarov's cabinet withdrew into Russia after the Revolution of Dignity.[42] Most brigades wore uniforms similar to Soviet ones, and units (especially brigades) carried banners and were named after operations of the Red Army during the Second World War.[43] For instance, the former

---

41 "2012 roku finansuvannya ukrayins'koyi armiyi bude rekordno nyz'kym" [Funding for the Ukrainian army in 2012 will be at a record low], Ekonomichna Pravda, May 19, 2011, accessed May 28, 2023, available at: https://www.epra vda.com.ua/news/2011/05/19/286335/

42 Pokrovsky Andriy, "Pavlo Lebedyev—nevydymyy dlya pravosuddya eks-ministr-utikach" [Pavlo Lebedev is a fugitive ex-minister invisible to justice], Radio Svoboda, May 1, 2017, accessed on 20 August 2023, available at: https://www.radiosvoboda.org/a/28462011.html

43 Slobodyanyuk Mykhailo, "Istoriya Pivnichnoho operatyvnoho komanduvannya Sukhoputnykh viysk Zbroynykh Sil Ukrayiny. 1 chastyna" [History of the Northern Operational Command of the Ground Forces of the Armed Forces of Ukraine. Part 1], Ukrainian Military Pages, May 22, 2022, accessed

14th Mechanized Brigade named after Prince Roman the Great (founder of the Ruthenian Kingdom)[44] was previously called "the 51st Separate Guards Perekop-Kharkiv Prague-Volyn Order of Lenin twice of the Order of the Red Flag, Order of Suvorov and Kutuzov Mechanized Brigade".[45] The downsizing of the armed forces was justified by the expectation of the impossibility of a new large war in Europe and the preparation for a transformation into smaller contract-based formations,[46] ostensibly for their further integration into peacekeeping operations and rapid response forces of NATO.[47]

However, these 'reforms' were neither completed nor financed and during the Yanukovych period, the potential of the Ukrainian army degraded to its maximum at the beginning of 2014, weakening the Armed Forces of Ukraine as much as possible,[48] the first phase of Russian aggression in 2014 showed the results for the Kremlin. According to the published transcripts of the National Security and Defense Council (RNBO) in 2014, only about 5,000 Ukrainian military personnel were ready to resist Russian

---

May 28, 2023, available at: https://www.ukrmilitary.com/2022/05/pivnicne-ok-histo.html

44 "14 Bryhada Za Chyselnistiu budye sche bil`shoyu nizh kolyshnya 51-a " [14th Brigade will be larger in size than the former 51st], Volyns'ki Novyny, January 15, 2015, accessed May 28, 2023, available at: https://www.volynnews.com/news/society/14-a-bryhadu-formuvatymut-iz-novykh-mobilizovanykh/

45 "51-a okrema mekhanizovana bryhada" [51st Separate Mechanized Brigade], Militarnyi, February 15, 2010, accessed May 28, 2023, available at: https://mil.in.ua/uk/articles/51-a-okrema-mehanizovana-brygada/

46 Radomska Olha, "Ostannii pryvoz: Ukraïna perexodyt' na kontraktnu armiü" [The Last Draft: Ukraine Transitions to a Contract Army], BBC News Ukraïna, October 1, 2013, accessed May 28, 2023, available at: https://www.bbc.com/ukrainian/entertainment/2013/10/131001_contract_army_or

47 "Pro zatverdzhennya planu zakhodiv z vykonannya Richnoyi natsional'noyi programy spivrobitnytstva Ukrayina—NATO na 2012 rik" [On Approving the Action Plan for the Implementation of the Annual National Cooperation Program Ukraine—NATO for 2012], Rozporyadzhennya No. 720, August 22, 2012, accessed May 28, 2023, available at: https://zakon.rada.gov.ua/laws/show/720-2012-%D1%80#Text

48 Sanders Deborah, "Ukraine's third wave of military reform 2016–2022—building a military able to defend Ukraine against the Russian invasion," Defense & Security Analysis, Vol. 39, No. 3, 2023, pp. 312-328, DOI: 10.1080/14751798.2023.2201017.

aggression.[49] During this time, Ukrainian nationalists began actively creating volunteer formations. Despite the popular opinion of complete independence, the vast majority had to be formally at least incorporated into the Ministry of Internal Affairs (MIA) or as territorial defence units within the Ground Forces of the Armed Forces of Ukraine.[50] Thus, well-known battalions such as "Azov," "Saint Mary," "OUN,"[51] and the Volunteer Ukrainian Corps (DUK) were formed.[52] However, despite their necessity during the initial active phases of the war in 2014-16, the government primarily focused on reforming existing units rather than building new volunteer-based formations.

Despite this, Ukrainian military service members highlighted problems such as bureaucracy, the underappreciation of combat experience by deeply institutionalised representatives of the rear services, and issues with equipment supply, particularly for personnel.[53] For instance, as of 2019, volunteer organisations such as the Come Back Alive Foundation provided approximately half of all thermal optics in the Joint Forces Operation (OOS) area.[54] All of this

---

49 Shtohrin Irina, "Chomu ne vtrymaly Krym: stenohrama RNBO vid 28 lutoho 2014 roku" [Why Crimea was not held: transcript of the National Security and Defense Council meeting on February 28, 2014], Radio Svoboda, February 27, 2019, accessed May 28, 2023, available at: https://www.radiosvoboda.org/a/29794488.html

50 Shurkhalo Dmytro, "Dobrovolchi batal'yony — mizh viynoyu ta politykoyu" [Volunteer battalions — between war and politics], Radio Svoboda, August 15, 2014, accessed May 28, 2023, available at: https://www.radiosvoboda.org/a/26531775.html

51 Shtekel Mykhailo, "Dobrovoltsi legalizuyut'sya v Zbroynykh sylakh Ukrayiny" [Volunteers are being legalized in the Armed Forces of Ukraine], Radio Svoboda, April 8, 2015, accessed May 28, 2023, available at: https://www.radiosvoboda.org/a/26944303.html

52 "Dobrovol'chyj Ukrayins'kyj Korpus 'Pravyy Sektor'" [Volunteer Ukrainian Corps "Right Sector"], Pravyy Sektor, accessed May 28, 2023, available at: https://pravyysektor.info/dobrovolchyy-ukrayinskyy-korpus-pravyy-sektor

53 "Whe servicemen leaving the armed forces?", NGO "Come Back Alive", March 01, 2020, accessed May 28, 2023, available at: https://savelife.in.ua/en/materials/research-en/why-are-servicemen-leaving-the-armed-for/

54 "Teplovizory ZSU: dvi pravdy vid Genshtabu i volunteriv" [Thermal imagers of the Armed Forces of Ukraine: two truths from the General Staff and volunteers], Novynarnia, April 14, 2016, accessed May 28, 2023, available at: https://novynarnia.com/2016/04/14/teplovizori-zsu-dvi-pravdi-vid-genshtabu-y-volonteriv/

maintained a specific authority for volunteer militants, who, despite not having many privileges, still enjoyed greater freedom of action and could also be present directly in the combat zone instead of serving for several years far from the frontlines.[55]

However, the increased attention to the security and defence sectors also uncovered significant corruption and political scandals. In particular, the most important was the investigation of Gladkovskii, the son of the head of the auto concern "Bohdan Motors" and the first deputy of the head of the RNBO under Petro Poroshenko.[56] Journalists from the "Schemes" program exposed an investigation into the younger Gladkovsky's purchase of defective equipment components at significantly higher prices, including from the Russian Federation.[57] These elements are an essential aspect of the understanding and criticism of Ukraine's political authorities by nationalist movements, the partial distrust of combatants towards Kyiv, and the indisposition of most representatives from volunteer units from integration with the Armed Forces.

For the authors of this chapter, as for Ukrainian researchers, the full inclusion of nationalist movements in a full-scale war with the Russian Federation in 2022 is somewhat self-evident. However, it is essential to note that right-wing factions in Ukraine have almost always remained on the periphery of the political preferences of Ukrainians. The nationalists achieved their best results during the

---

55 Sinchenko, Dmytro. "Na front bez povistky. Chomu na dev'iatomu rotsi viyny vse shche isnuyut dobrobaty." August 10, 2022. Accessed May 28, 2023. https://tyzhden.ua/na-front-bez-povistky-chomu-na-dev-iatomu-rotsi-vijny-vse-shche-isnuiut-dobrobaty/

56 "Rik skandalu dovkola Hladkovskoho ('Svynarchuka'): chy zminylosia shchoś pry Zelenskomu" [A year of scandal around Hladkovsky ('Svynarchuk'): has anything changed under Zelensky], Radio Svoboda, March 4, 2020, accessed May 28, 2023, available at: https://www.radiosvoboda.org/a/svynarchuk-gladkovsky-zelenskiy-poroshenko/30466745.html

57 "Druzi Prezydenta kradut' na oborontsi (sekretni perepysky, ch.1-2)" [Friends of the President steal in defense (secret correspondence, part 1-2)], Bihus Info, February 25, 2019, accessed May 28, 2023, available at: https://www.youtube.com/watch?v=lGTf2nUyxfw; "Koruptsiia v oborontsi—prodovzhennia. Hladkovskyi i UkrOboronProm (taimna perepyska, ch.3)" [Corruption in defense—continuation. Hladkovskyi and UkrOboronProm (secret correspondence, part 3)], Bihus Info, March 4, 2019, accessed May 28, 2023, available at: https://www.youtube.com/watch?v=7w2-JWkoI3Y

presidency of the pro-Russian President Viktor Yanukovych when the Svoboda party received more than 10% of the vote in the 2012 parliamentary elections.[58] However, by 2014, at the height of these movements' development and active participation in the war with the Russian Federation in Donbas, none of the nationalist parties made it to parliament.[59]

Still, the nationalist movement experienced a kind of "renaissance" in the first years following the Revolution of Dignity, peaking in 2017-18 with the widespread expansion of the Azov movement and an attempt to unify all the main political parties on the eve of the 2019 presidential elections.[60] The traditional primary argument of nationalist movements revolved around national security interests, the safety of Ukrainians,[61] and the need for combat readiness.[62] This was reflected in nationalists' perception of Russia as the USSR and the Russian Empire and the modern Russian Federation, which stood against Ukrainian independence movements and elites. The influence of Ukrainian nationalism from the

---

58   "Vybory narodnykh deputativ Ukrainy 28 zhovtnia 2012 roku" [Elections of People's Deputies of Ukraine, October 28, 2012], Central Election Commission, accessed May 28, 2023, available at: https://www.cvk.gov.ua/vibory/vibori-narodnih-deputativ-ukraini-28-zhovtnya-2012-roku.html
59   Central Election Commission, "Pozacherhovi vybory narodnykh deputativ Ukrainy 26 zhovtnia 2014 roku", accessed May 28, 2023, available at: https://cvk.gov.ua/vibory/pozachergovi-vibori-narodnih-deputativ-ukraini-26-zhovtnya-2014-roku.html
60   "Natsionalistychni orhanizatsii idut na vybory yednym spyskom, pershyy nomer – Tiagnybok" [Nationalist organizations run for elections on a single list, first number – Tiagnybok], Radio Svoboda, June 9, 2019, accessed May 28, 2023, available at: https://www.radiosvoboda.org/a/news-natsionalisty-vybory/29989654.html
61   Biletsky Andriy, "Dlia nykh viiny nemaye" [For Them, There Is No War], Ukrainska Pravda. Blogs, August 29, 2021, accessed May 28, 2023, available at: https://blogs.pravda.com.ua/authors/bileckyj/612b4d5a84675/; Tiagnybok Oleh, "Nova Konstytutsiia: zhodnoho osoblyvoho statusu okupovanomu Donbasu!" [New Constitution: No Special Status for Occupied Donbas!], Ukrainska Pravda. Blogs, July 16, 2015, accessed May 28, 2023, available at: https://blogs.pravda.com.ua/authors/tiahnybok/55a7478fb4bde/
62   "Yaku programu predstavyv 'Natsionalnyi korpus' Biletskoho" [What Program Did the 'National Corps' of Biletsky Present], Slovo i Dilo, October 14, 2016, accessed May 28, 2023, available at: https://www.slovoidilo.ua/2016/10/14/novyna/polityka/yaku-prohramu-partiyi-predstavyv-naczionalnyj-korpus-bileczkoho

activities of the Organization of Ukrainian Nationalists and the Ukrainian Insurgent Army during the Second World War also plays a part in defining the enemy. Since the 1990s, UNSO has highlighted the threat of the occupation of Crimea[63] and supported the rebels in Chechnya.[64] Azov drew on its unit's history, which added prestige irrespective of political activity.[65] Nationalist movements criticised the low social mobilization[66] and the state of the military-industrial complex.[67] Since 2014, most nationalist movements have directed their rhetoric toward the security and defence sector.

In recent years, the veteran policy has gained relevance, particularly where the Azov movement attempted to position itself as founded by veterans of the Azov NGU regiment and as a representative of the entire social stratum of veterans. Consequently, the National Corps was one of the primary stakeholders of the veterans' march,[68] an action established in 2019 as a public response to

---

63 "Stislyi kurs istorii UNA-UNSO..." [A Concise Course in the History of UNA-UNSO], UNA-UNSO, accessed May 28, 2023, available at: http://una-unso.com/styslyi-kurs-una-unso
64 "Stislyi kurs istorii UNA-UNSO..." [A Concise Course in the History of UNA-UNSO], UNA-UNSO, accessed May 28, 2023, available at: http://una-unso.com/styslyi-kurs-una-unso
65 "Chleny TSK "Azov" ta veterany odnoymennoho polku stvoryly politychnu partiyu "Natsional'nyy korpus"" [Members of the Central Committee of Azov and veterans of the Azov Regiment formed the political party 'National Corps'], Interfax-Ukraine, October 14, 2016, accessed May 28, 2023, available at: https://interfax.com.ua/news/political/376701.html
66 Biletsky Andriy, "Oholoshuyu mobilizatsiyu!" [I Announce Mobilization!], Ukrayinska Pravda. Blogy, October 8, 2019, accessed May 28, 2023, available at: https://blogs.pravda.com.ua/authors/bileckyj/5d9c59093a33b/
67 Biletsky Andriy, "Stan ukrayinskoho oborono-promyslovoho kompleksu ta viyna z Rosiyeyu: dyversiya chy sabotazh?" [The State of the Ukrainian Defense Industry and the War with Russia: Diversion or Sabotage?], Ukrayinska Pravda. Blogy, January 26, 2022, accessed May 28, 2023, available at: https://blogs.pravda.com.ua/authors/bileckyj/61f10fd717669/
68 Natsional'nyy Korpus (t.me/nationalcorps), "S'ohodni u Kyyevi aktyvisty Natskorpusu y veterany polku 'Azov' razom zi svoyim pershym komandyrom Andriyem Bilets'kym, doluchylys' do Marshu zakhysnykiv Ukrayiny" [Today in Kyiv, Activists of the National Corps and Veterans of the 'Azov' Regiment Joined the March of Defenders of Ukraine with Their First Commander Andriy Biletsky], Telegram, August 24, 2019 at 16:24, accessed May 28, 2023, available at: https://t.me/nationalcorps/4796

the cancellation of the military parade that year[69]. The Kyiv organisation C14, led by Yevhen Karas, systematically sought inclusion in the public council under the Ministry of Veterans and was also actively involved in human rights activities for ATO/OOS[70] veterans.[71] The former head of the Right Sector, Dmytro Yarosh, attempted to introduce a project of law regarding volunteer corps to legalize the status of combatants.[72] However, the general mobilization of society, and veterans in particular, in 2022 left nationalist movements with no choice but to join the armed confrontation with the Russian Federation in the form of armed formations. Firstly, a significant proportion of the movement's active participants were official combatants, which meant a mandatory requirement to report to the military commissariats in the first days following the declaration of martial law in the country.[73]

Secondly, movements like Azov used the history of their combat unit (for example, during the annual marches in honour of the

---

69 Shtohrin Iryna, "Reaktsiya veteraniv na vidmovu vid provedennya paradu i zaplanovani OP zakhody do Dnya Nezalezhnosti" [Veterans' Reaction to the Refusal to Hold a Parade and Planned OP Events for Independence Day], Radio Svoboda, August 13, 2019, accessed May 28, 2023, available at: https://www.radiosvoboda.org/a/30106357.html
70 Anti-Terrorist operation on Donbass (2014-2018) and Joint Forces Operation after 2018
71 Proskuryakov Samuil, "Pravoradykaly potrapyly do Hromads'koyi rady pry Ministerstvi veteranyv Ukrayiny. Zaborona rozpovidae, khto same, ta chomu tse problema" [Right-wing Radicals Got into the Public Council at the Ministry of Veterans of Ukraine. Zaborona Explains Who Exactly and Why It's a Problem], Zaborona, March 23, 2021, accessed May 28, 2023, available at: https://zaborona.com/pravoradikali-potrapili-do-gromadskoyi-radi-pri-ministerstvi-veteraniv-ukrayini/
72 Dym Nestor, "Yarosh pominyav sudovu reformu na zakon pro svoyu armiyu?" [Yarosh Sacrificed Judicial Reform for a Law on His Army?], Novynarnia, June 17, 2016, accessed May 28, 2023, available at: https://novynarnia.com/2016/06/17/yarosh-pominyav-sudovu-reformu-na-zakon-pro-svoyu-armiyu/
73 General Staff of the Armed Forces of Ukraine, Military Staff Order No. 154, Appendix 1 to the Directive of the General Staff of the Armed Forces of Ukraine, "Features of Recruitment and Maintenance of Military Records of Reservists of the First-Line Operational Reserve during a Special Period," July 10, 2013, accessed May 28, 2023, available at: https://www.mil.gov.ua/content/other/dodatok1_7%20.pdf

liberation of Mariupol in 2014)[74] as a critical prestige indicator for the movement, despite the Azov NGU regiment's actual independence and autonomy from political activities.[75] Thirdly, as mentioned before, nationalist movements criticised the low social mobilisation and state policy in the face of confrontation with the Russian Federation. Low military spending, the absence of some aspects of the military-industrial complex, and delays in approving annual defence purchases were criticised. *In essence, the nationalist movement had no other option but to integrate directly into Ukraine's Defense Forces, as narratives opposing Russia were the primary thesis for mobilising supporters.* They expected this movement's development and were a consistent evolution of their survival strategy as political actors. This strategy intensified against the gradual decline of the prominent nationalist organisations of this period and the impossibility of conducting any political activity during a full-scale war.

Forming their units, offering support and assistance to existing units in AFU, and the active involvement of nationalist organisations and their leaders, particularly in direct combat actions, is a consistent result of the movements' rhetoric and strategy since 2014. Mass mobilisation and the implementation of martial law limited the political opportunities for opponents of the authorities, leaving them with no window to take political measures and criticise the confrontation with Russia.

Indeed, a further interpretation of the movement's progression might be framed in terms of its ongoing evolution. Specifically, the Azov movement, which has been militarily engaged, has experienced a plateau since 2019 and has yet to attain electoral success

---

74 "Na chest' s'omoyi richnytsi zvil'nennya Mariupolya v misti vidbuvся viys'kovyy parad. FOTO, VIDEO" [In Honor of the Seventh Anniversary of Mariupol's Liberation, a Military Parade Was Held in the City. PHOTO, VIDEO], Novynarnia, June 13, 2021, accessed May 28, 2023, available at: https://novynarnia.com/2021/06/13/mariupol-free/

75 Likhachov Vyacheslav, "Polk 'Azov' ne ye neonatsystskym: vidpovidi na naiposhirenishi zapytannya" [The 'Azov' Regiment is not Neo-Nazi: Answers to the Most Common Questions], Zmina, April 4, 2022, accessed May 28, 2023, available at: https://zmina.info/columns/polk-azov-ne-ye-neonaczystskym-vidpovidi-na-najposhyrenishi-zapytannya/

since its establishment.[76] Dmytro Yarosh's Ukrainian Volunteer Army (UDA) has also been gradually stagnating, as demonstrated by the degradation of its infrastructure by 2021.[77] Political parties like the Right Sector can be considered politically defunct,[78] and their presence at the front as combat units have decreased. The Svoboda party has only sustained itself through a network of regional deputies and community representatives in a few cities. Lastly, the most rudimentary but equally valid explanation is the existential threat of Russian occupation to nationalist movements and their participants. Russia has demonised Ukrainian nationalists, especially the Right Sector, which was portrayed as a symbol of neo-Nazism during the Maidan protests.[79] Dmytro Yarosh, the leader, was depicted as a menace on Russian television.[80] The Azov battalion, later the Azov Regiment and the 12th brigade, was branded as neo-Nazi and was relentlessly discredited by the Russian media

---

76 Gomza Ivan, "Too Much Ado About Ukrainian Nationalists: the Azov Movement and the War in Ukraine," Krytyka, April 2022, accessed May 28, 2023, available at: https://krytyka.com/en/articles/too-much-ado-about-ukrainian-nationalists-the-azov-movement-and-the-war-in-ukraine
77 "UDA vikhodyt iz frontu—kudy, navishcho y koho 'valityme'. Interv`iu" [UDA Leaves the Front—Where, Why and Whom Will 'Throw'. interview], Novynarnia, October 18, 2018, accessed May 28, 2023, available at: https://novynarnia.com/2018/10/18/uda-vihodit-iz-frontu-kudi-navishho-y-kogo-valitime-interv-yu/
78 "Chomu 'Praviy Sektor' ne peremahaye na viborakh?" [Why Doesn't the 'Right Sector' Win Elections?], Praviy Sektor, December 26, 2021, accessed May 28, 2023, available at: https://pravyysektor.info/chogo-pragnemo-partiya-novyny/chomu-pravyy-sektor-ne-peremagaye-na-vyborah
79 According to the interview
80 "Eks-glava 'Pravogo sektora' stal sovetnikom glavkoma VSU" [The Former Head of 'Right Sector' Became an Advisor to the Commander-in-Chief of the Armed Forces of Ukraine], 60 minut, smotrim.ru, November 2, 2021, accessed May 28, 2023, available at: https://smotrim.ru/video/2353631

both domestically[81] and internationally.[82] Nationalists' rhetoric, especially regarding the Ukrainian language, was used by the Russian Federation to intimidate the population of Donbas.[83] Pro-

---

81 Oleg Borisovich Nemenskiy, "Neonatsizm na sovremennoy Ukrainye," voprosy natsionalizma 2019, no. 1: 1-18; "Yarosh Dmitrii Anatol'ievich", Tribunal, accessed May 28, 2023, available at: https://tribunal.ru/dossier/yarosh-dmitriy-anatolevich; " Yarosh ugrozhayet Kiyevu vyvodom vooruzhennykh neonatsistov na ulitsu" [Yarosh threatens Kyiv with the withdrawal of armed neo-Nazis to the street], Regnum.ru, accessed May 28, 2023, available at: https://regnum.ru/news/2273092; Kustov Maksim "Kak Ukraina stala eksportorom smerti" [How Ukraine became an exporter of death], Zvezdaweekly.ru, October 08, 2022, accessed May 28, 2023, available at: https://zvezdaweekly.ru/news/20 229261539-a123X.html

82 "Sociedad Histórica Militar Rusa: los neonazis ucranianos "no escaparán del castigo"", [Russian Military Historical Society: Ukrainian neo-Nazis "will not escape punishment"], Sputnik, April 20, 2023, accessed May 28, 2023, available at: https://sputniknews.lat/20230420/sociedad-historica-militar-rusa-los-neonazis-ucranianos-no-escaparan-del-castigo-1138343011.html; "UPDATED. Provocation and Disinformation Overview", VoxUkraine, August 13, 2023, accessed May 28, 2023, available at: https://voxukraine.org/en/provocation-and-disinformation-overview; Balanchuk Iryna "Medvedev claims Biden "swore allegiance to neo-Nazi regime"", Ukrainska Pravda, February 20, 2023, accessed May 28, 2023, available at: https://www.pravda.com.ua/eng/news/2023/02/20/7390139/

83 "Putin obeshchayet 'zashchishchat' russkikh' na Ukrayne vsegda" [Putin Promises to 'Defend the Russians' in Ukraine Forever], BBC Russkaya Sluzhba, June 24, 2014, accessed May 28, 2023, available at: https://www.bbc.com/russian/russia/2014/06/140624_putin_deauthorisation_ukraine_reax; von Khayn Mattias, Grunau Andrea, Teize Yevheniy, Ivanova Olexandra, "Kak Putin opravdyvaet vtorzhenie v Ukrainu" [How Putin Justifies the Invasion of Ukraine], Fact-checking DW, March 2, 2022, accessed May 28, 2023, available at: https://www.dw.com/ru/kak-putin-opravdyvaet-vtorzhenie-v-ukrainu-faktchekingdw/a-60960283; Sheremeta Elena, "Yazykovaya zachistka" i "nasil'stvennaya assimilyatsiya" russkogovoryashchikh: tak rossiyskiye SMI vidyat posledstviya prinyatiya zakona "Ob obrazovanii" [Language Purging and Forced Assimilation of Russian Speakers: How Russian Media View the Consequences of the Adoption of the Law "On Education"], Detektor Media, October 26, 2017, accessed May 28, 2023, available at: https://detector.media/rosiiski-zmi/article/165368/2017-10-26-yazykovaya-zachystka-y-nasylstvennaya-assymylyatsyya-russkogovoryashchykh-tak-rossyyskye-smy-vydyat-posledstvyya-prynyatyya-zakona-ob-obrazovanyy/; "Tsena predatel'stva OPZZh. Zachistka russkoyazychnykh merov Ukrainy SBU" [The Price of the Betrayal of the Opposition Platform—For Life. The SBU's Cleansing of Russian-speaking Mayors in Ukraine], Dzen.ru, October 19, 2022, accessed May 28, 2023, available at: https://dzen.ru/a/Y07vF3BZGjM___xi

Russian media[84] and political parties, such as *Opposition Platform for the Life* party (OPZH)[85] and the *Opposition Bloc*[86] also adopted this rhetoric. One of the stated objectives of Vladimir Putin's address on the night of February 24, during which he announced a "special military operation," was the "denazification" of Ukraine.[87]

---

84 "Natsionalisty mitynhuvaly u telekanala 'Nash' s trebovaniyem yoho zakryt. Kanal zastavyv ikh skakat'" [Nationalists Protested at the 'Nash' TV Channel Demanding its Closure. The Channel Made Them Jump], Strana.ua, February 2, 2022, accessed May 28, 2023, available at: https://strana.today/news/374748-natsionalisty-proveli-aktsiju-u-telekanala-nash-s-trebovaniem-eho-zakryt.html; Kramar Ostap, "Natsrada oshtrofuvala 'NASH,' '112 Ukrayina' i NewsOne cherez movu vorozhnetchi ta diskriminatsiyu ZSU v eteri" [The National Council Penalized 'NASH,' '112 Ukraine' and NewsOne for Hate Speech and Discrimination Against the Armed Forces of Ukraine on the Air], Hromadske, May 27, 2021, accessed May 28, 2023, available at: https://hromadske.ua/posts/nacrada-oshtrafuvala-nash-112-ukrayina-i-newsone-cherez-movu-vorozhnechi-i-diskriminaciyu-zsu-v-eteri; " "Pid Natsradu pryishli prykhylnyky ta protyvnyky '112 Ukrayina' i News One" [Supporters and Opponents of '112 Ukraine' and News One Gathered Outside the National Council], UkrInform, September 5, 2019, accessed May 28, 2023, available at: https://www.ukrinform.ua/rubric-society/2773706-pid-nacradu-prijsli-prihilniki-ta-protivniki-112-ukraina-i-news-one.html
85 Lyakhova Yuliya, ""Tak i ne slepili pulyu iz gna": Kiva nazval Ukrainu "kolybel'yu fashizma v Evrope"" ["They Didn't Mold a Bullet out of St": Kiva Called Ukraine the "Cradle of Fascism in Europe"], Segodnya, June 26, 2021, accessed May 28, 2023, available at: https://politics.segodnya.ua/politics/tak-i-ne-slepili-pulyu-iz-g-na-kiva-nazval-ukrainu-kolybelyu-fashizma-v-evrope-1560132.html; Roshchyna Viktoriya, "V Kieve sostoyalsya marsh 'patriotov Kivy' za bor'bu protiv fashizma" [A March of 'Kiva's Patriots' Against Fascism Took Place in Kyiv], Hromadske, May 9, 2021, accessed May 28, 2023, available at: https://hromadske.ua/ru/posts/v-kieve-sostoyalsya-marsh-patriotov-kivy-za-borbu-protiv-fashizma
86 Gayzhevskaya Tatiana, ""Net Boga v dushe": zayavleniyu Muraeva o fashistakh v Ukraine nashli ob"yasneniye," ["No God in the Soul": Murayev's Statement about Fascists in Ukraine Has Been Explained], Obozrevatel, February 8, 2018, accessed May 28, 2023, available at: https://news.obozrevatel.com/politics/zayavleniyu-nardepa-o-fashistah-v-ukraine-nashli-obyasnenie.htm; Sovina Maryna, "Ukraine predrekli global'noye protivostoyniye i raspad strany," [Ukraine Predicted Global Confrontation and the Collapse of the Country], Lenta.ru, October 2, 2021, accessed May 28, 2023, available at: https://lenta.ru/news/2021/10/02/muraev_raspad/
87 "Putin o nachale 'spetsial'noy voyennoy operatsii' v Donbasse. Glavnoye | Novosti Bi-bi-si," [Putin on the Beginning of the 'Special Military Operation' in Donbas. The Main Thing], BBC News — Russian Service, February 24, 2022, accessed May 28, 2023, available at: https://www.youtube.com/watch?v=iPvB_TcItgQ

After Mariupol was captured on 20th May 2022, Russian television showcased several captive Azov soldiers with neo-Nazi tattoos.[88] Separately, it is worth noting the execution of prisoners of war in Olenivka, where the Russian Federation committed a crime by shelling a building that housed Ukrainian prisoners of war, among whom were defenders of Mariupol, including servicemen of the Azov Regiment.[89] Ukrainian journalists proved that this shelling was a direct death penalty for Azov regiment soldiers.[90] The Russian narrative and demonisation of nationalists were vividly illustrated by the statement from the Russian Embassy in the UK following the Olenivka massacre:[91]

---

[88] "Shto oznachayut tatuirovky natsystov s 'Azovstali': Bandera, Gitler, dyavol," [What Do the Tattoos of Nazis with 'Azovstal' Mean: Bandera, Hitler, Devil], Komsomolskaya Pravda, May 31, 2022, accessed May 28, 2023, available at: https://www.kp.ru/daily/27398.5/4595198/

[89] "Russians struck Olenivka to cover up the torture and execution of prisoners — General Staff of the Armed Forces of Ukraine," Ukrainska Pravda, July 29, 2022, accessed May 28, 2023, available at: https://www.pravda.com.ua/eng/news/2022/07/29/7360850/

[90] ""Tse bula tsynichna masova strata". Rik pislya teraktu v Olenivtsi: rodychi polonenykh ob"yednalysya, shchob borotysya za pravdu i svoyikh heroyiv" ["It was a cynical mass execution." A year after the terrorist attack in Olenivka: relatives of prisoners united to fight for the truth and their heroes], Novynarnia, July 07, 2022, accessed November 27, 2023, available at: https://novynarnia.com/2023/07/16/rik-pislya-teraktu-v-olenivczi/; "Strata chy prykryttya v Olenivtsi? Rosiyany zavdaly udaru po v"yaznytsi, de trymaly polonenykh z Azovstali" [Execution or cover-up in Olenivka? The Russians attacked the prison where prisoners from Azovstal were kept], Zaborona, August 11, 2022, accessed November 27, 2023, available at: https://zaborona.com/strata-chy-prykryttya-v-olenivczi-rosiyany-zavdaly-udaru-po-vyaznyczi-de-trymaly-polonenyh-z-azovstali/

[91] Russian Embassy, UK (@RussianEmbassy), "#Azov militants deserve execution, but death not by firing squad but by hanging, because they're not real soldiers. They deserve a humiliating death," Twitter, July 29, 2022, 10:00 PM, accessed May 23, 2023, available at: https://twitter.com/RussianEmbassy/status/1553093117712162828; "Rossiya na ofitsial'nom urovne podyerzhala kazn' boytsov 'Azova' — Soobshchenie Posol'stva," [Russia Officially Supported the Execution of 'Azov' Fighters — Embassy Statement], Dzerkalo Tyzhnya, July 30, 2022, accessed May 28, 2023, available at: https://zn.ua/POLITICS/rossija-na-ofitsialnom-urovne-podderzhala-kazn-bojtsov-azova-soobshchenie-posolstva.html; Bohdanok Olena, "Posol'stvo RF u Velykiy Brytaniyi zaavilo, sho biytsi 'Azova' 'zasluhovuyut na prynyzlyvu smert'," [The Russian Embassy in Great Britain Stated That 'Azov' Fighters 'Deserve a Humiliating Death'], Suspilne, July 30, 2022, accessed May 28, 2023, available at: https://suspilne.media/266

Azov militants deserve execution, but death not by firing squad but by hanging, because they're not real soldiers. They deserve a humiliating death – Russian Embassy in UK, June 29, 2022

It shows perhaps the best example of the dehumanization narrative of Russian propaganda towards Ukrainian nationalists. Under conditions of complete occupation of Ukraine, nationalist movements would likely face repression, and a significant number of their supporters would probably be threatened with physical reprisals, given that they symbolise the "Ukrainian Nazism" against which a "special military operation" was formally declared. A full-scale war emerged as a "unique window of opportunity" for the nationalist movement and, to a certain extent, a natural outcome of their planned focus on military training and constant preparedness for combat against the Russian Federation. However, it remains an open question: *why did these movements aim to form their separate units, and how did they acquire such capacity? Furthermore, why are they mostly discussing highly specialised units rather than regular ones?* Within this context, we can identify several contributing factors: networking, systematic training, an in-house personnel reserve, and the organizational capabilities of the movement's rear echelon.

The role of networking in fostering internal discipline and enhancing professional and ideological training

During the first months of the full-scale invasion (from March to August of 2022), most nationalist military formations were integrated into the DFU. Despite being volunteer-based, these units are notable for their high level of discipline. Most movement supporters attribute this to their heightened motivation and ideological training. The aspect of ideological training is essential and is actively promoted through advertising, particularly emphasising the high quality of training. For instance, the Azov movement

---

083-posolstvo-rf-u-velikij-britanii-zaavilo-so-bijci-azova-zaslugovuut-na-prini zlivu-smert/

employed information campaigns to recruit their units.[92] Specifically, for the 3rd SAB and Azov brigade, multi-episode reports titled "Recruit" are produced.[93] Ideological training and the movement's appeal help reinforce a high level of discipline. This was a crucial component in most nationalist volunteer formations. The DUK-PS, which only became an official brigade of the Armed Forces in the fall of 2022, had its internal disciplinary statute.[94] A primary benefit of ideological training is enhancing moral and psychological motivation. A key factor is viewing the confrontation with Russia as an existential conflict spanned centuries. Historical lectures,[95] conferences,[96] and other civic events have contributed to cultivating motivated movement supporters and their potential mobilisation base.

The activity and ideological training of nationalists generally hinges on a classic portrayal of Ukrainian national history, with a primary emphasis on its military glory. They organise events to

---

[92] 3-tya okrema shturmova bryhada, "Kynu hranatu—perevirymo, chy yakisni u vas okopy: trenuvannya rekrutiv SSO AZOV," [Throw a Grenade—Let's Check the Quality of Your Trenches: Training AZOV Special Operations Forces Recruits], YouTube, September 19, 2022, accessed May 28, 2023, available at: https://www.youtube.com/watch?v=LhAS0UztPRU

[93] AZOV 4308, "Rekrut. Chastyna 2," [Recruit. Part 2], YouTube, January 8, 2019, accessed May 28, 2023, available at: https://www.youtube.com/watch?v=OnGp-womWXA ; AZOV 4308, "Rekrut. Chastyna 3," [Recruit. Part 3], YouTube, January 25, 2019, accessed May 28, 2023, available at: https://www.youtube.com/watch?v=m-Q5qfXUD7w ; 3-tya okrema shturmova bryhada, "168 hodyn vyprobuvan': pershyy tyzhden' KMB v SSO AZOV. Znayomstvo," [168 Hours of Testing: First Week of Basic Training in AZOV Special Operations Forces. Introduction], YouTube, June 19, 2022, accessed May 28, 2023, available at: https://www.youtube.com/watch?v=KeEL7ZVLdak.

[94] Novynarnia, "DUK 'Pravyy sektor' stav 67-yu mekhanizovanoyu bryhadoyu ZSU," [DUK 'Right Sector' Became the 67th Mechanized Brigade of the Armed Forces of Ukraine], December 12, 2022, accessed May 28, 2023, available at: https://novynarnia.com/2022/12/12/duk-pravyj-sektor-stav-67-yu-mehanizovanoyu-brygadoyu-zsu/.

[95] Natsional'nyy Korpus (t.me/nationalcorps), "Zaproshuyemo na vidkrytu lektsiyu do richnytsi utvorennia OUN," [Invitation to an Open Lecture on the Anniversary of the Formation of the OUN], Telegram, January 31, 2022, 14:27, accessed May 28, 2023, available at: https://t.me/nationalcorps/10697 .

[96] Plomin (t.me/plomin), "Onlain-prezentatsiya al'manakhu 'Traditsiya i tradytsionalizm'," [Online Presentation of the Almanac 'Tradition and Traditionalism'], Telegram, January 13, 2021, 15:53, accessed May 28, 2023, available at: https://t.me/plomin/2199 .

honour the students who died fighting against the Russian Red Army in Kruty in 1918,[97] to remember the fighters of the Ukrainian Sich Riflemen (a unit of the Austro-Hungarian Empire's army in World War I),[98] and to commemorate Ukrainian Insurgent Army battles, among others.[99] These practices contribute to fostering cohesion within the community and also shape the arena of mnemonic battles, symbolising (mainly) confrontations with various Russian state formations. For them, confrontation with Russia is a matter of existential survival, a point that is repeatedly stressed at most ideological events.

The most comprehensive ideological training within military units was established in the Azov Movement. Here, lectures continue despite the full-scale invasion,[100] especially among the youth and during lulls in combat.[101] The unit and the political party led

---

97 "Proyshla smoloskypna khoda na chest Heroyiv Krut," [A Torchlight Procession Was Held in Honor of the Heroes of Kruty], Rayon.Lutsk, January 30, 2016, accessed May 28, 2023, available at: https://lutsk.rayon.in.ua/news/5068-proishla-smoloskipna-hoda-na-chest-geroyiv-krut ; "Den' pam"yati heroyiv Krut" [The Day of Remembrance of Heroes of Krut], Svoboda journal, February 3, 2017, accessed May 28, 2023, available at: https://svoboda-news.com/svwp/%D0%B4%D0%B5%D0%BD%D1%8C-%D0%BF%D0%B0%D0%BC%D1%8F%D1%82%D1%96-%D0%B3%D0%B5%D1%80%D0%BE%D1%97%D0%B2-%D0%BA%D1%80%D1%83%D1%82/
98 "Zakarpatska 'Svoboda' vshanuvala marshem heroyiv UPA, Karpatskoi Sichi ta Ukrainskykh Sichovykh Striltsiv (FOTO)," [Transcarpathian 'Freedom' Honored the Heroes of the UPA, Carpathian Sich, and Ukrainian Sich Riflemen with a March (PHOTO)], UNIAN, October 16, 2011, accessed May 28, 2023, available at: https://zakarpattya.net.ua/Partiji/88391-Zakarpatska-Svoboda-vshanuvala-marshem-heroiv-UPA-Karpatskoi-Sichi-ta-Ukrainskykh-Sichovykh-Striltsiv-FOTO
99 "V Ukraini proyshly marshi na chest dnya UPA: yak tse bulo (fotoreportazh, video)," [Marches Were Held in Ukraine in Honor of UPA Day: How It Happened (Photo Report, Video)], UNIAN, October 14, 2014, accessed May 28, 2023, available at: https://www.unian.ua/society/996103-v-ukrajini-proyshli-marshi-na-chest-dnya-upa-yak-tse-bulo-fotoreportaj-video.html
100 Centuria (t.me/centuriaua), "Khto ne znae svoho mynuloho – vtratyt' svoe maibutnie," [Whoever Doesn't Know Their Past Will Lose Their Future], Telegram, April 5, 2023, 19:59, accessed May 28, 2023, available at: https://t.me/centuriaua/1518 .
101 Centuria (t.me/centuriaua), "Pravyl'ni svitohlyadni zasady – tse holovna rysa kozhnoho biytsya molodoyi hvardiyi Centuria," [The Right Worldview Principles Are the Main Characteristic of Every Fighter of the Young Guard 'Centuria'], accessed May 28, 2023, available at: https://t.me/centuria_kr/652

by Andriy Biletskyi commemorate historical events and the recent history of the war with Russia. For instance, a parade[102] and solemn events[103] were held in honour of Mariupol's liberation in 2014 and the so-called "Day of the Dead"—commemorating the fallen soldiers of the Azov movement in the war against the Russian Federation.[104] Additionally, such organisations as "Centuria" are pretty active within the movement, focusing on educational activities[105] physical[106] and street combat training.[107] The "Plomin" publishing house plays a significant role, concentrating on philosophical publications[108] and translations of works by various right-wing

---

102 "Na chest' s'omoyi richnytsi zvil'nennya Mariupolya v misti vidbuvся viys'kovyy parad. FOTO, VIDEO" [In Honor of the Seventh Anniversary of Mariupol's Liberation, a Military Parade Was Held in the City. PHOTO, VIDEO], Novynarnia, June 13, 2021, accessed May 28, 2023, available at: https://novynarnia.com/2021/06/13/mariupol-free/

103 Natsional'nyy Korpus (t.me/natsionalcorps), "Azovtsi peredaly prapor polku do muzeyu Zbroynykh syl Ukrayiny", [Azov Members Transferred the Regimental Flag to the Armed Forces of Ukraine Museum], Jun 13, 2019, accessed May 28, 2023, available at: https://t.me/nationalcorps/4337; Natsional'nyy Korpus (t.me/nationalcorps), "Anons: svyato «Vil'nyy Mariupol'» do richnytsi zvil'nennya mista", [Announcement: "Free Mariupol" Celebration on the Anniversary of the City's Liberation], Jun 13, 2019, accessed May 28, 2023, available at: https://t.me/nationalcorps/4319

104 Reins Oleksii, "Den Mertvykh: shcho vidbuvaietsia na naisakralnishii misterii polku AZOV?," [Day of the Dead: What Happens at the Most Sacred Mystery of the AZOV Regiment?], Bukvy, April 4, 2023, accessed May 28, 2023, available at: https://bykvu.com/ua/mysli/den-mertvykh-shcho-vidbuvaietsia-na-naisakralnishii-misterii-polku-azov/

105 Centuria (t.me/centuriaua), "Proyekt 'Spadshchyna'" [Project "Heritage"], Nov 9, 2021, accessed May 28, 2023, available at: https://t.me/centuriaua/1137

106 Centuria (t.me/centuriaua), "5 prychyn zaymatysya sportom" [5 Reasons to Engage in Sports], Sep 23, 2021, accessed May 28, 2023, available at: https://t.me/centuriaua/1014

107 Centuria (t.me/centuriaua), "Vyshkil 'Vulychnyy protest'" [Training "Street Protest"], Sep 6, 2021, accessed May 28, 2023, available at: https://t.me/centuriaua/953

108 "Ernst Yunher. 'Vohon i krov'," [Ernst Jünger. 'Fire and Blood'], Пломінь [Flame], accessed May 28, 2023, available at: https://plomin.club/product/junger-fire-and-blood/

thinkers, such as Ernst Jünger[109] or Dominique Venner.[110] Moreover, the Oriyentyr press was active,[111] and from the year 2020 immediately, 'RainHouse' also commenced its operations, distinctly concentrating on ideological books for the Azov.[112] The "Freedom" party actively participated in conducting historical lectures. Their analytical centre, "Ukrainian Strategic Studies," organised the "Bandera Readings" conferences.[113] The most recent of these took place in an online format, with party representatives participating from the combat zone.[114] The "Brotherhood" battalion conducted weekly prayers, some personally led by the movement's leader, Dmytro Korchynskyi.[115] Nationalist groups were actively involved in

---

109 "U Lvovi prezentuiut ukrainskyi pereklad povisti pro Pershu svitovu viinu 'Vohon i krov' Ernsta Yunhera," [In Lviv, the Ukrainian Translation of the Tale of the First World War 'Fire and Blood' by Ernst Jünger Is Presented], Novynarnia, February 25, 2019, accessed May 28, 2023, available at: https://novynarnia.com/2019/02/25/u-lvovi-prezentuyut-ukrayinskiy-pereklad-povisti-pro-pers hu-svitovu-viynu-vogon-i-krov-ernsta-yungera/

110 "#plomin_talks: Venneryana i nova pravytsia: sim rokiv postrilu v Notre-Dami," [Wagnerism and New Right: Seven Years After the Shooting in Notre-Dame], Пломінь [Flame] (Youtube Channel), video, May 21, 2020, accessed May 28, 2023, available at: https://www.youtube.com/watch?v=hSNhjZgWn GM

111 "Prezentatsiya knyhy «Shyrokyns'ka operatsiya» proyshla u Poltavi" [The presentation of the book "Shirokyn operation" took place in Poltava], Azov.press, December 07, 2016, accessed November 27, 2023, available at: https://web.archive.org/web/20170219091503/http://azov.press/ukr/prez entaciya-knigi-shirokins-ka-operaciya-proyshla-u-poltavi

112 "Pro nas" [About us], Rainhouse, accessed November 27, 2023, available at: https://rainshouse.com/about

113 Banderivs'ki chytannya, "X Banderivs'ki chytannya: usi dopovidi, dyskusiyi, vystupy, vital'ni slova / 10 lyutoho 2023 roku" [X Bandera Readings: All Reports, Discussions, Speeches, Greetings / February 10, 2023], YouTube, February 13, 2023, accessed May 28, 2023, available at: https://youtu.be/zxj3D56qO K8?t=6260.

114 Banderivs'ki chytannya, "X Banderivs'ki chytannya: usi dopovidi, dyskusiyi, vystupy, vital'ni slova / 10 lyutoho 2023 roku" [X Bandera Readings: All Reports, Discussions, Speeches, Greetings / February 10, 2023], YouTube, February 13, 2023, accessed May 28, 2023, available at: https://youtu.be/zxj3D56qO K8?t=6260.

115 Batal'yon BRATSTVO, "Rankova molytva BRATSTVA" [Morning Prayer of BRATSTVO], YouTube, March 17, 2022, accessed May 28, 2023, available at: https://www.youtube.com/watch?v=BSUO_nkRI6M; Batal'yon BRATSTVO, "Propovid' na Chystyy chetver" [Sermon on Maundy Thursday], YouTube, April 21, 2022, accessed May 28, 2023, available at: https://www.youtube.com/watch?v=ZUTmkFrLot8; Also available at: Dmytro Korchynskiy (t.me/korch-

personnel training. Through their networks, they quickly found exceptional military instructors. The "Hospitaliers" unit of the UDA, highly rated, conducted training in tactical medicine.[116] The "Hospitaliers" cooperated with Separate Tactical Group "Karpatska Sich."[117] Selection by instructors took place regardless of mobilization.[118] The movements frequently conducted firearms training that simulated field conditions. Sokil (youth part of Svododa party),[119] National Corps party, and 300 Centuria 301 (all are parts of the Azov movement) organized such training and boot camps. UNSO maintains its training ground for periodic training camps.[120] The selection and preparation for the 3rd SAB lasted at least three months.[121] The former Azov Regiment conducted firearms courses,[122] boot camps,[123] and assault training courses similar to the

---

ynskiy), Telegram, October 25, 2022, 9:01 p.m., accessed May 28, 2023, available at: https://t.me/korchynskiy/5321.
116 Dziubak Nastya, "Chotyry dni navchannia—y na peredovu, riatuvaty zhyttia. Yak nyni pratsiuiut 'Hospitalyer' y" [Four Days of Training—And to the Frontline to Save Lives. How the 'Hospitallers' are Working Now], Texty.org, April 29, 2022, accessed May 28, 2023, available at: https://texty.org.ua/articles/106515/chotyry-dni-navchannja-i-na-peredovu-rjatuvaty-zhyttja-jak-nyni-pratsjujut-hospitalyery/
117 Karpatska Sich (t.me/karpatsich), "Hospitallers and Karpatska Sich together since 2014" [Hospitallers and Karpatska Sich Together Since 2014], December 8, 2022, 6:53 p.m., accessed May 28, 2023, available at: https://t.me/karpatsich/1331
118 Dziubak Nastya, "Chotyry dni navchannia—y na peredovu, riatuvaty zhyttia. Yak nyni pratsiuiut 'Hospitalyer' y" [Four Days of Training—And to the Frontline to Save Lives. How the 'Hospitallers' are Working Now], Texty.org, April 29, 2022, accessed May 28, 2023, available at: https://texty.org.ua/articles/106515/chotyry-dni-navchannja-i-na-peredovu-rjatuvaty-zhyttja-jak-nyni-pratsjujut-hospitalyery/
119 "V urochyshchi Vovchak vidbudet'sya vyshkil shkoliariv ta litseyistiv," [Training of Schoolchildren and Lyceum Students Will Be Held in Vovchak], Volynski Movyny, May 7, 2018, accessed May 28, 2023, available at: https://www.volynnews.com/news/all/v-urochyshchi-vovchak-vidbudetsia-vyshkil-shkoliariv-ta-litseyistiv/
120 Ukrayins'ka natsionalistychna samooborona, "Polihon UNSO 2019" [Polygon UNSO 2019], YouTube, June 9, 2022, accessed May 28, 2023, available at: https://www.youtube.com/watch?v=IWgEaA8entw.
121 according to one of the members of the 3rd Assault Brigade
122 AZOV. "Recrut 2.0." YouTube, August 31, 2021. Accessed May 28, 2023, available at: https://www.youtube.com/watch?v=cGvdjhqlFHw
123 Natsional'nyy Korpus (t.me/nationalcorps), "Tryvaye nabir na novu zminu u tabir «Slobozhanyn»" [The Recruitment for a New Shift in the Camp

renowned Q-courses for Special Operations Forces.[124] Implementing NATO instructions and standards for personnel training, combat training, and unit hierarchy creation was integral to their work. Units of the "Azov" movement are the clear leaders in compliance with the protocols of NATO countries. TCCC AC protocol requirements were successfully implemented in Azov as early as 2017,[125] and the first military school graduation occurred in 2016.[126] As the structures of the Azov unit evolved, new courses emerged, including the CQB training of the Azov regiment (close combat),[127] which was also used in the 3rd SAB.[128]

Since 2015, the Sergeant's School of the "Azov Movement" (named after Yevhen Konovalts in 2016)[129] began implementing an extensive curriculum. This training course emphasizes the

---

"Slobozhanyn" Continues], July 16, 2017. Accessed May 28, 2023, available at: https://t.me/nationalcorps/403

124 AZOV 4308. "Rekrut. Chastyna 2" [Recruit. Part 2], YouTube, January 8, 2019. Accessed May 28, 2023, available at: https://www.youtube.com/watch?v=On Gp-womWXA ; ZOV 4308. "Rekrut. Chastyna 2" [Recruit. Part 2], YouTube, January 25, 2019. Accessed May 28, 2023, available at: https://www.youtube.com/watch?v=m-Q5qfXUD7w; 3-tya okrema shturmova bryhada. "168 hodyn vyprobuvan': pershyy tyzhden' KMB v SSO AZOV. Znayomstvo" [168 Hours of Testing: The First Week of Basic Military Training in the Special Operations Forces AZOV. Introduction], YouTube, June 19, 2022. Accessed May 28, 2023, available at: https://www.youtube.com/watch?v=KeEL7ZVLdak.

125 "Azov nabyraye rekrutiv na navchal`nyy kurs" [Azov is Recruiting Recruits for the Training Course], Volynski Movyny, May 7, 2018, accessed December 01, 2016, available at: https://www.volynnews.com/news/society/azov-nabyr aye-rekrutiv-na-navchalnyy-kurs/

126 "Viys'kova Shkola Imeni Polkovnyka Yevhena Konoval'tsya" [Military School named after Colonel Yevhen Konovalets], Azov brigade official web-page, accessed May 28, 2023, available at:https://azov.org.ua/military-school/

127 Polk AZOV, "Taktychni pryntsypy CQB v budivli" [Tactical Principles of CQB in the Building], YouTube, July 26, 2016, accessed May 28, 2023, available at: https://www.youtube.com/watch?v=wFAX7rBiQdc.

128 3-tya okrema shturmova bryhada, "Blyzhniy biy v obmezhenomu prostori: trenuvannya SSO AZOV" [Close Combat in Confined Space: SSO AZOV Training], YouTube, December 26, 2022, accessed May 28, 2023, available at: https://www.youtube.com/watch?v=gruHZUVXzvk.

129 Mil'tarnyy, "Interv'yu z Nachal'nykom Viys'kovoyi Shkoly Komandyriv Imeni Polkovnyka Yevhena Konoval'tsya druhom Kirtom" [Interview with the Head of the Military School of Commanders named after Colonel Yevhen Konovalets, Friend Kirt], January 26, 2018, accessed May 28, 2023, available at: https://mil.in.ua/uk/articles/interv-yu-z-nachalnykom-vijskovoyi-shkoly-komandyriv-i-meni-polkovnyka-yevgena-konovaltsya-drugom-kirtom/.

development of qualified sergeants through intensive physical and theoretical training.[130] The program includes comprehensive military training covering aspects such as firearms training, physical training, military tactics, communication skills, and engineering knowledge, focusing on leadership development.[131] As part of the exams, school participants refine Unit Management Procedures (TLP), analyse combat tasks, consider METT-TC factors, conduct OCOKA analysis,[132] and plan actions at the unit/platoon level.[133] Additionally, "Azov" established the School of Special Leadership Training, named after Mykola Sciborsky within the regiment.[134] Leadership schools modelled after the "Axion and Homa School" are also included in the curriculum.[135] Following Azov, the Ukrainian Volunteer Corps "Right Sector" (DUK-PS) and Dmytro Yarosh's UDA established one of the most extensive training infrastructures. Since 2015, the DUK-PS has been conducting training at its bases,[136]

---

130 "Viys'kova Shkola Imeni Polkovnyka Yevhena Konoval'tsya" [Military School named after Colonel Yevhen Konovalets], Azov brigade official web-page, accessed May 28, 2023, available at:https://azov.org.ua/military-school/

131 Mil'tarnyy. "Interv'yu z Nachal'nykom Viys'kovoyi Shkoly Komandyriv Imeni Polkovnyka Yevhena Konoval'tsya druhom Kirtom." January 26, 2018. Accessed May 28, 2023, available at: https://mil.in.ua/uk/articles/interv-yu-z-nachalnykom-vijskovoyi-shkoly-komandyriv-imeni-polkovnyka-yevgena-konovaltsya-drugom-kirtom/.

132 "Dnyamy vidbuvsya vypusk serzhants'koyi shkoly brygady «Azov»."[The graduation of the sergeant school of the 'Azov' brigade took place], Willlive, April 10, 2023, accessed May 28, 2023, available at: https://censor.net/ua/blogs/3271474/horunja_shkola_men_pdpolkovnika_mikoli_stsborskogo https://will-live.com/dnyamy-vidbuvsya-vypusk-serzhantskoyi-shkoly-brygady-azov/

133 "Viys'kova Shkola Imeni Polkovnyka Yevhena Konoval'tsya" [Military School named after Colonel Yevhen Konovalets], Azov brigade official web-page, accessed May 28, 2023, available at: https://azov.org.ua/military-school/

134 Mykola Kravchenko, "Khorunzha shkola imeni pidpolkovnyka Mykoly Stsyborskoho" [The Standard-Bearer School named after Lieutenant Colonel Mykola Stsyborsky], Censor.net, June 15, 2021, accessed May 28, 2023, available at: https://censor.net/ua/blogs/3271474/horunja_shkola_men_pdpolkovnika_mikoli_stsborskogo.

135 Natsional'nyy Korpus, "Shkola Aks'ona i Khomy"—natsionalisty na varti" ["School of Axon and Khoma"—Nationalists on Guard], YouTube, April 27, 2018, accessed May 28, 2023, available at: https://www.youtube.com/watch?v=lX56IeY5iP0

136 Sector Pravdy, "Trenuvannya iz PTRK ta SPG na bazi DUK" [Training with ATGM and SPG on the basis of DUK], YouTube, May 02, 2015, accessed May

covering all known military disciplines, including combat coordination,[137] use of anti-tank missile systems,[138] automatic weapons,[139] armoured vehicles, mortars, position occupying, sniper training,[140] assault operations, and more.

After the dissolution of the "Right Sector," the Ukrainian Volunteer Army, led by Dmytro Yarosh, established similar training bases.[141] According to the movement's leader, since 2017, thousands of volunteers have undergone training at the UDA bases.[142] The most common programme was infantry training, called the "Infantry School."[143] It should be noted that the UDA and DUK educational bases were organised at the organisations' expense.[144]

28, 2023, available at: https://www.youtube.com/watch?v=cy7S8iyRGhc&t=57s.

137 Sector Pravdy, "Trenuvannya biytsiv DUK" [DUK Fighters Training], YouTube, July 10, 2015, accessed May 28, 2023, available at: https://www.youtube.com/watch?v=4f9AwMiRCU8 .

138 Sector Pravdy, "Trenuvannya iz PTRK ta SPG na bazi DUK" [Training with ATGM and SPG on the basis of DUK], YouTube, May 02, 2015, accessed May 28, 2023, available at: https://www.youtube.com/watch?v=cy7S8iyRGhc&t=57s.

139 Sector Pravdy, "Trenuvannya biytsiv DUK" [DUK Fighters Training], YouTube, July 10, 2015, accessed May 28, 2023, available at: https://www.youtube.com/watch?v=4f9AwMiRCU8.

140 Kirilenko, Olha, Mazilyuk Nazariy, "Ne mozhu pity smuzi, znayuchy, shcho Ukrayina stikaye krov'yu. Yak biytsi 'Pravoho sektoru' opanovuyut' amerykans'ku zbroyu" [I Can't Drink Smoothies, Knowing Ukraine Is Bleeding. How 'Right Sector' Fighters Master American Weapons], Ukrayins'ka Pravda, June 1, 2022, accessed May 28, 2023, available at: https://www.pravda.com.ua/articles/2022/06/1/7349896/.

141 "Dmytro Yarosh pokazav trenuval'nu bazu Ukrayins'koyi dobrovol'choyi armiyi" [Dmytro Yarosh Showed the Training Base of the Ukrainian Volunteer Army], Gazeta.ua, April 21, 2017, accessed May 28, 2023, available at: https://www.youtube.com/watch?v=pYcYS7KXano

142 "Yarosh vidkryv navchal'nyy tsentr Ukrayins'koyi dobrovol'choyi armiyi" [Yarosh Opened the Training Center of the Ukrainian Volunteer Army], Ukrinform, February 6, 2017, accessed May 28, 2023, available at: https://www.ukrinform.ua/rubric-regions/2170647-aros-vidkriv-navcalnij-centr-ukrainskoi-do brovolcoi-armii.html.

143 Navchal'nyy Tsentr UDA, "Shkola pikhoti NTs UDA. Vyshkil 2. Den 1" [Infantry School NTs UDA. Training 2. Day 1], YouTube, April 11, 2017, accessed May 28, 2023, available at: https://www.youtube.com/watch?v=EWjLQ9dwbdY.

144 "Navchal'nyy tsentr DUK PS 'Kholodnyy Yar' prodovzhuye pidhotovku biytsiv" [The Training Center DUK PS 'Kholodnyy Yar' Continues the Training of Fighters], Pravyy Sektor, June 19, 2017, accessed May 28, 2023, available at: https://pravyysektor.info/ogoloshennya/navchalnyy-centr-duk-ps-holodn

The Ukrainian National Army's (UNA–UNSO) military training began developing in 1995.[145] After the organisation's revival in 2014-2015,[146] various training sessions were held for its members. UNA-UNSO conducted joint military exercises with various nationalist groups, including meetings with representatives of Taras Deyak's Carpathian Sich in the Lviv region.[147] Training programs included firearms and combat coordination.[148] The Brotherhood Battalion trained all its recruits in 2022 and has been continually training its members since 2015 (formerly known as the St. Mary's Battalion).[149] These pieces of training ensure a high level of combat readiness for all battalion soldiers, enabling their effective field activity. Since 2022, the Brotherhood has also announced the availability of its training centre for preparing recruits for various tasks, including subversive activities.[150] After 2014-15, volunteer training not only allowed for the recruitment of new participants to engage in hostilities but also the continued training of veterans who had distinguished themselves in responsible offensive and

---

yy-yar-prodovzhuye-pidgotovku-biyciv; Dmytro Yarosh, "Yarosh vidkryv navchal'nyy tsentr Ukrayins'koyi dobrovol'choyi armiyi" [Yarosh Opened the Training Center of the Ukrainian Volunteer Army], Ukrinform, February 6, 2017, accessed May 28, 2023, available at: https://www.ukrinform.ua/rubric-regions/2170647-aros-vidkriv-navcalnij-centr-ukrainskoi-dobrovolcoi-armii.html

145 UNSO, "Reportazh pro vyshkil UNSO 1995 r." [Report on UNSO Training in 1995], YouTube, October 29, 2018, accessed May 28, 2023, available at: https://www.youtube.com/watch?v=NM9bQrtHxVU&t=328s

146 UNSO, "Masshtabni viys'kovi treningy na Vinnychchyni" [Large-scale Military Trainings in Vinnytsia Region], YouTube, June 10, 2015, accessed May 28, 2023, available at: https://www.youtube.com/watch?v=ndfwlc8GB1M.

147 Deyak Taras, "Viys'kovyy vyshkil Karpats'koyi Sichi v Ivano-Frankivsku" [Military Training of Karpats'ka Sich in Ivano-Frankivsk], February 6, 2022, accessed May 28, 2023, available at: https://karpatskasich.com/news/item/578-viiskovyi-vyshkil-karpatskoi-sichi-v-ivanofrankivsku

148 Zvedenyy pidrozdil UNSO, "Cherhovyy zymovyy vyshkil UNSO 2020 roku" [Regular Winter Training UNSO 2020], YouTube, October 21, 2022, accessed May 28, 2023, available at: https://www.youtube.com/watch?v=o6hmewUDwnI.

149 Batal'yon Bratstvo, "Nabir do batal'yonu BRATSTVO tryvaye!" [Recruitment to the Battalion BRATSTVO Continues!], YouTube, April 21, 2023, accessed May 28, 2023, available at: https://www.youtube.com/watch?v=3LL3FrVXL0U

150 Batal'yon Svyata Mariya, "Pidhotovka biytsiv" [Training of Fighters], YouTube, July 30, 2015, accessed May 28, 2023, available at: https://www.youtube.com/watch?v=AABX3XU-_8Q.

defensive operations during active engagements within the ATO. These training programs helped instil valuable knowledge and skills in new volunteers, enhancing their contributions to their units' effectiveness.

Socio-Political Movements as Personnel and Reserve

Since 2014, nationalist volunteer military units in Ukraine have actively invested in training and improving their personnel's qualifications. Military training and camps became the key elements of their instruction. Groups like the Ukrainian Volunteer Army and the Right Sector Volunteer Corps have been especially active.

Since the start of 2014, volunteer military units have continuously worked to enhance their personnel's training level. By 2018, at least 23 reserve companies were created within the DUK PS,[151], which likely played a pivotal role in recovering and mobilising new units. Before the Russian invasion in 2022, the UDA successfully deployed reserve battalions and maintained an active battalion-level group of hospitaliers.[152] An active sports lifestyle was a part of the culture of nationalist movements. Local branches of "Azov" organised sports competitions, particularly in boxing[153] and knife fighting.[154] "Sokil," whose members actively joined the "Svoboda"

---

151 Praviy Sektor, "Rezervni sotni DUK PS" [Reserve Hundreds of DUK PS], June 20, 2017, accessed May 28, 2023, available at: https://pravyysektor.info/duk-ps-struktura/rezervni-sotni-duk-ps.

152 Hospitaliers, "About us," accessed May 28, 2023, available at: https://uploads-ssl.webflow.com/621fabdd592ed327753736bd/62bc0c7181d5d6ce528360ed_Hospitallers_EN.pdf.

153 Centuria (t.me/centuriaua), "1 sichnya molod' kryvoriz'koho oseredku Centuria provela turnir z nozhovoho boyu na chest' 114-yi richnytsi vid dnya narodzhennya providnyka Orhanizatsiyi ukrayins'kykh natsionalistiv Stepana Bandery" [On January 1, the youth of the Kryvyi Rih branch of Centuria held a knife fighting tournament in honor of the 114th anniversary of the birth of the leader of the Organization of Ukrainian Nationalists, Stepan Bandera], January 01, 2023, 8:51 p.m., Telegram, accessed May 28, 2023, available at: https://t.me/centuriaua/1406.

154 Centuria (t.me/centuriaua), "1 sichnya molod' kryvoriz'koho oseredku Centuria provela turnir z nozhovoho boyu na chest' 114-yi richnytsi vid dnya narodzhennya providnyka Orhanizatsiyi ukrayins'kykh natsionalistiv Stepana Bandery" [On January 1, the youth of the Kryvyi Rih branch of Centuria held a knife fighting tournament in honor of the 114th anniversary of the birth of the

and "Karpatska Sich" battalions, regularly held boot camps and sports events.[155] Nationalist organisations improved training conditions and arranged additional courses for civilians. These courses included pre-medical training,[156] lectures on the history of the 2014-15 military operations,[157] on the Ukrainian-Russian wars, and the study of recent war history. The introduction of personal reserves aimed to enhance combat coordination, and the UDA/DUK volunteer groups could mobilise equipped, trained, and combat-ready units without placing an additional burden on the Armed Forces manning centres, coordinating their actions with the command of the Defense Forces.

Like other nationalist groups, the Azov movement did not merely create paramilitary or combat units but also quickly became hubs for mobilization 338, formation of volunteer units 339, and territorial defence units 340. This practical preparation for potential conflict became critical to nationalist movements' strategy. This also illustrates the role of military training and mobilisation of nationalist movements in Ukraine. On the eve of a full-scale invasion by the Russian Federation in 2022, special military courses for civilians were developed,[158] in which about 10,000 people participated under the "Azov" civil defence program. This programme succeeded significantly in cities like Kharkiv, Kyiv, and Mariupol.[159] The

---

leader of the Organization of Ukrainian Nationalists, Stepan Bandera], January 01, 2023, 8:51 p.m., Telegram, accessed May 28, 2023, available at: https://t.me/centuriaua/1406.
155 SOKIL, "Vstupay v Sokil!" [Join Sokil!], YouTube, April 28, 2016, accessed May 28, 2023, available at: https://www.youtube.com/watch?v=9Fd9pnjvpgk.
156 National Corps (t.me/nationalcorps), "Tyzhnevyy daydzhest novyn vid Natsional'noho Korpusu" [Weekly Digest of News from the National Corps], Telegram, February 7, 2022, 12:25, accessed May 28, 2023, available at: https://t.me/nationalcorps/10791
157 National Corps (t.me/nationalcorps), "Tyzhnevyy daydzhest novyn vid Natsional'noho Korpusu" [Weekly Digest of News from the National Corps], Telegram, February 21, 2022, 15:52, accessed May 28, 2023, available at: https://t.me/nationalcorps/10976
158 "Ne panykuy! Gotuysya! | Vyshkil z tsyvil'noyi oborony u Kyievi 6 lutoho" [Don't panic! Be prepared! | Civil defense training in Kyiv on February 6], Naatsional'nyy Korpus, February 3, 2022, accessed May 28, 2023, available at: https://www.youtube.com/watch?v=3DX_QxSf3cA
159 According to the anonymus interview with one of leader of Azov movement

ATEK base, which formally belonged to representatives of the nationalist movement, served as a site for conducting exercises[160] and courses for the military, including veterans.[161] Organizations such as Pravy Sektor and VMO Sokil, including veterans of SVOBODA, also conducted similar training.[162] Following the onset of the Russian invasion, most members of nationalist organisations, especially veterans, joined units of the AFU, NGU, and TDF. It is worth noting that these units demonstrated high coordination on the battlefield.[163] The military units of nationalist movements comprised people of varying ethnic, religious, and political backgrounds, underlining the diverse nature of these movements. After the full-scale invasion in 2022, most nationalist movements mobilised their human resources in regular units, ranging from small special groups to large units of 5000 or even more. However, it is possible to join these units without any ideological or political affiliation with the nationalists. These military units formed the basis of elite battalions, regiments, brigades, and special-purpose units. All of this underscores once more the significant role of nationalist movements in Ukraine's military mobilisation and defence against the Russian Federation's invasion.

---

160 Naatsional'nyy Korpus (t.me/nationalcorps), "Koordynatsiyni tsentry z formuvannya dobrovol'chykh pidrozdiliv dlya zakhystu rehioniv Ukrayiny" [Coordination centers for the formation of volunteer units to protect regions of Ukraine], Telegram, February 24, 2022, 16:07, accessed May 28, 2023, available at: https://t.me/nationalcorps/11004

161 "U Kyievi vidbuvsya druhyy velykyy vyshkil z tsyvil'noyi oborony | Ne panykuy! Gotuysya!" [The second large-scale civil defense training took place in Kyiv | Don't panic! Be prepared!], Naatsional'nyy Korpus, February 7, 2022, accessed May 28, 2023, available at: https://www.youtube.com/watch?v=6n5jC2sQWUA

162 Pravyy Sektor (t.me/pravijofficial), "Tsiy nedili z 12:00 do 16:00 chleny NVR 'Pravyy sektor' provedut vidkrytyy povtornyy vyshkil dlya usikh okhochykh u Kyievi" [This week from 12:00 to 16:00, members of the NVR 'Right Sector' will conduct an open retraining for all interested in Kyiv], Telegram, February 19, 2022, 14:20, accessed May 28, 2023, available at: https://t.me/pravijofficial/1416.

163 Based on numerous interviews and communication with different veterans and active servicemen of DFU

Education, Sports, and Military Training

In the context of nationalist movements in Ukraine, their strategy of attracting and training young people features aspects that differentiate them from other groups. This process is closely linked with patriotic and sports education for youth and teenagers. Nationalist groups have combat veterans and contract service members capable of conducting lectures and training sessions on the history of the 2014-2015 military operations.[164] In addition, they offer training courses in basic military affairs, which include, among other things, the analysis of firearms and pair movement tactics. However, the role of patriotic sports schools and competitions is more important, for example, mobile games like the "Terrenovi ihry" (field games) where the primary task of two teams is to capture the opponent's flag. Numerous games are held systematically, including "Zvytyaga," organised by the regional organisation "National Alliance,"[165] and "Hurby Antonivtsiv," organised by the Youth National Congress.[166] These competitions act as the initial stage of selection and incentivise participation in more complex games, such as "Legionnaire," which is essentially a military training camp.[167] Undoubtedly, children's training camps, such as "Strength and Honour" from the "National Alliance,"[168] are implemented with the support of the Ukrainian government. The aforementioned "Gurby

---

164 Sokil Info (t.me/sokil_info), "ZNOVU STRIL'BY" [SHOOTING AGAIN], Telegram, February 1, 2022, 10:24, accessed May 28, 2023, available at: https://t.me/sokil_info/4712.
165 "Zvityaha-2017: yak tse bulo. FOTO" [Zvityaha-2017: how it was. PHOTO], VolynPost, May 10, 2017, accessed May 28, 2023, available at: https://www.volynpost.com/news/89087-zvytiaga-2017-iak-ce-bulo-foto
166 Fuk Rostyslav, "Na Ternopil'shchyni provodyat' terenovu hru 'Gurby-Antonivtsi'" [In Ternopil region, they are conducting the field game 'Gurby-Antonivtsi'], Suspilne, May 7, 2021, accessed May 28, 2023, available at: https://suspilne.media/128731-na-ternopilsini-provodat-terenovu-gru-gurbi-antonivci/.
167 KVVT Lehion, "Legion 21 vyshkil" [Legion 21 training], YouTube, August 21, 2020, accessed May 28, 2023, available at: https://www.youtube.com/watch?v=guVm_fD77ks.
168 "Zustrich z predstavnykamy «Sich: Syla i Chest» — terenova hra v Kholodnomu Yaru — Cherkaska obl." [Meeting with representatives of "Sich: Power and Honor" — field game in Kholodny Yar — Cherkasy region], Facebook, September 21, 2018, accessed May 28, 2023, available at: https://www.facebook.com/watch/?v=1032080733640366.

Antonivtsiv" and "Zvytyaga" received various stages' backing from the Ministry of Youth and Sports of Ukraine.[169] The "Sokil" games, held with the support of the regional administration of national-patriotic education in the Cherkasy region, are one example.[170] The Lviv regional state administration also supported a similar youth game.[171] These gatherings, activities, and camps promote a culture of a healthy lifestyle and present alternative, more attractive, and exciting approaches to military preparation. This is especially crucial when basic familiarisation with military affairs in schools and universities is poor quality.

The Azov movement is also actively involved in developing sports infrastructure. Since its inception, the National Corps and its youth organisations have opened gyms in major cities in Ukraine, particularly in big cities like Kyiv,[172] Dnipro,[173] Kharkiv,[174] and

---

169 "«Shcho robyty, yakscho ne vystachaie adrenalinu v krovi? Yikhaty na Zvityahu!», Viddil natsional'no-patriotychnoho vykhovannia Minmolodsporu" ["What to do if there's not enough adrenaline in the blood? Go to Zvityaha!", Department of National-Patriotic Education of the Ministry of Youth and Sports], Facebook, April 27, 2021, accessed May 28, 2023, available at: https://www.facebook.com/viddilnpvmms/posts/pfbid0z1bsAKhryAUqnidW4J4xJ1DXACFZCqnf7vvKADgHXYu1uuumqJhN9rxkm7fodfuZl?locale=uk_UA; and see also: "Zvityaha. Orhanizator" [Zvityaha. Organizer], accessed May 28, 2023, available at: http://zvytjaga.org.ua/orhanizator/.
170 "Na Cherkashchyni rozpochavsya oblasnyy etap Vseukrayinskoyi viyskovo-patriotychnoyi hry 'Sokil' ('Dzhura')," Press-service of Cherkasy Regional State Administration, June 2, 2022, accessed May 28, 2023, available at: https://ck-oda.gov.ua/novyny-cherkaskoyi-oblasti/na-cherkashhini-rozpochavsya-oblasnij-etap-vseukrayinskoyi-vijskovo-patriotichnoyi-gri-sokil-dzhura/.
171 "Oblasna terenova hra 'Lohenda UPA' vpyate zbere shkoliariv Lvivshchyny" [Regional Ground Game 'Lohenda UPA' Once Again Gathers Schoolchildren of Lviv Region], Press-service of Lviv Regional State administration, September 26, 2018, accessed May 28, 2023, available at: https://old.loda.gov.ua/news?id=39649.
172 Naatsional'nyy Korpus, "Lider partiï Natskorpys Andrii Biletskyi na vidkrytti sotsialnoho sportzalu," [National Corps Leader Andrii Biletskyi at the Opening of a Social Gym], Youtube, December 19, 2018, accessed May 28, 2023, available at: https://www.youtube.com/watch?v=JAWAAIvNYlE
173 Natsional'nyy Korpus (t.me/nationalcorps), "Sportyvnomu Korpusu 'Avanhard' u Dnipri vypovnyuyet'sya 2 roky!" [The 'Avanhard' Sports Corps in Dnipro Turns 2!], May 28, 2019 at 15:00 accessed May 28, 2023, available at: https://t.me/nationalcorps/4152
174 Natsional'nyy Korpus—Kharkiv "Promo 'Sportyvnyi Korpus' Kharkiv," Natsionalnyi Korpus—Kharkiv [Promo 'Sports Corps' Kharkiv], Youtube,

smaller regional centres like Sumy,[175] and Mykolaiv.[176] and also in regional towns such as Pavlohrad,[177] and Mukachevo.[178] However, the most common approach is the development of sports competitions and open martial arts training (mainly boxing and MMA) held on rented infrastructure.[179] The National Corps also attempted to establish the infrastructure for scouting schools and camps under "Youth Corps," but the initiative quickly collapsed and did not gain widespread adoption.[180] Such infrastructure is an alternative to

---

September 10, 2018, accessed May 28, 2023, available at: https://www.youtube.com/watch?v=Bh4CuAPLmS4

175 "Natsionalnyi korpus Sumy vidkryv sportyvnyi zal," [National Corps Sumy Opens Sports Hall], Sumski debaty, June 20, 2018, accessed May 28, 2023, available at: https://debaty.sumy.ua/news/natsionalnyj-korpus-sumy-vidkryv-sportyvnyj-zal

176 Natsional'nyy Korpus (t.me/nationalcorps), "Natsional'nyy Korpus ye odnym iz zasnovnykiv ta spivorhanizatoriv turniru z pauerliftynhu 'Zalizna Natsiya'," [The National Corps is one of the founders and co-organizers of the "Iron Nation" powerlifting tournament], December 07, 2020 at 14:27, accessed May 28, 2023, available at: https://t.me/nationalcorps/8189

177 Natsional'nyy Korpus (t.me/nationalcorps), "U Pavlohradi zanepadaye bezkoshtovnyy sportzal: rozpochavsya zbir koshtiv na rekonstruktsiyu," [A free sports hall is collapsing in Pavlograd: fundraising for reconstruction has begun], August 22, 2019 at 13:29, accessed May 28, 2023, available at: https://t.me/nationalcorps/4783

178 Natsional'nyy Korpus (t.me/nationalcorps), "U Mukachevi na bazi volonters'koho shtabu 'Kel't' vidkryly sotsial'nyy sportyvnyy zal," [A social sports hall was opened in Mukachevo on the basis of the volunteer headquarters 'Celt'], May 31, 2022 at 13:58, accessed May 28, 2023, available at: https://t.me/nationalcorps/12370

179 Natsional'nyy Korpus (t.me/nationalcorps), "Zalizna Natsiya VIII [Iron Nationa VIII], Dec 9, 2021 at 17:25, accessed May 28, 2023, available at: https://t.me/nationalcorps/10450; Natsional'nyy Korpus (t.me/nationalcorps), "Natskorpus u Chervonohradi orhanizuvav turnir z MMA pam"yati azovtsya Barreta," [The National Corps in Chervonohrad organized an MMA tournament in memory of Azov's Barrett], Feb 4, 2020 at 17:57, accessed May 28, 2023, available at: https://t.me/nationalcorps/5917; Natsional'nyy Korpus (t.me/nationalcorps), "U Mykolayevi proyde mizhnarodnyy turnir z MMA 'Dorohu neskorenym V'," [An international MMA tournament 'Road to the Unconquered V' will take place in Mykolayiv], Jul 24, 2019 at 14:39, accessed May 28, 2023, available at: https://t.me/nationalcorps/4754; Natsional'nyy Korpus (t.me/nationalcorps), "Natsional'nyy Korpus L'vivshchyny zaproshuye na turnir pam"yati azovtsya Yuriya Luhovs'koho," [The National Corps of the Lviv region invites you to a tournament in memory of Azov's Yuriy Luhovsky], Mar 4, 2021 at 15:24, accessed May 28, 2023, available at: https://t.me/nationalcorps/8622.

180 "Tabory" [Camps], Yunatskyi Korpus, accessed May 28, 2023, available at: http://youngcorpus.com/camps/; Iryna Kononenko and Andriy Lysak,

military-patriotic education, conducted as a state policy in many countries worldwide. In Ukraine, it is an additional preparation for young men, which was traditionally in decline and was a de facto remnant of the Soviet systems of preparation for mass-term service in the army. For instance, in most training programs for pre-conscription preparation, the main aspects considered are military training and theoretical knowledge concerning types of weapons (mainly Soviet models)[181] and basic types of weapons (chemical, radioactive, small arms, etc.).[182] There are also field trips, but these often bear a more symbolic character, sometimes with the possibility of a one-time shooting session with one type of weapon or another.[183] However, this standard is conditional in the program and only sometimes adhered to. There is also no infrastructure for adequate military preparation—such teaching is usually held in school gymnasiums or on sports fields, rarely using a shooting range, usually organised in the basements of Soviet-era buildings.

"Derev'yanyy AK-47 i 'zapovidy natsionalista'. Yak pratsyuye dytyachyy tabir 'Azovets' pid Kyevom" [Wooden AK-47 and 'nationalist commandments'. How the children's camp 'Azovets' works near Kyiv], Radio Svoboda, August 14, 2018, accessed May 23, 2023, available at: https://www.radiosvoboda.org/a/29433188.html

181 Baka Mykhailo et al., Pidruchnyk dlia 10-11 kl. zahalnoosvit. navch. zakladiv [Textbook for 10-11 grades of general education institutions] (Kyiv: Vezha, 2006), 448 p., accessed May 28, 2023, available at: http://www.marganets-ctpu m.edukit.dp.ua/Files/downloads/%D0%97%D0%B0%D1%85%D0%B8%D1% 81%D1%82%20%D0%92%D1%96%D1%82%D1%87%D0%B8%D0%B7%D0%B D%D0%B8%2010-11%20%D0%BA%D0%BB%D0%B0%D1%81%D1%81.pdf

182 Ministry of Education and Science of Ukraine, 'Pro instruktyvno-metodychni rekomendatsii shchodo orhanizatsii osvitnoho protsesu ta vykladannia navchalnykh predmetiv/intehrovanykh kursiv u zakladakh zahalnoi serednoi osvity u 2022/2023 navchalnomu rotsi' [On instructional and methodological recommendations for organizing the educational process and teaching subjects/integrated courses in general secondary education institutions in the 2022/2023 academic year], document No. #1/9530-22, August 19, 2022, accessed May 23, 2023, available at: https://mon.gov.ua/storage/app/media/zagalna%20serednya/metodichni%20recomendazii/2022/08/20/01/Dodato k.13.zakhyst.Ukrayiny.20.08.2022.pdf

183 Ministry of Education and Science of Ukraine, "Zakhist Ukrainy. 10—11 klasy. Riven' standartu" [Defense of Ukraine. 10—11 grades. Standard Level], Document No. 698, p.3, August 3, 2022, accessed May 23, 2023, available at: https://mon.gov.ua/storage/app/media/zagalna%20serednya/programy-10-11-klas/2022/08/15/navchalna.programa-2022.zakhyst.Ukrayiny-10-11-standart.pdf

Another example is the training of young men at the institutional level within the infrastructure of the Ministry of Education and Science, regulated by the Ministry of Defence of Ukraine in military lyceums, 364, as well as with the support of regional state administrations (ODA).[184] The latter focuses on the population's socially vulnerable sections (large families, orphans, semi-orphans, etc.).[185] In contrast, the military lyceums primarily focus on training young people before entering higher military educational institutions.[186] Despite changes and reforms since 2014, the focus of these academic institutions is more social, and they are essentially a transformation of cadet buildings (also known as "Suvorov schools"). An example of how nationalist camps and other activities are on par with conscription preparation (in its former state) is the cooperation in some field games where students of military schools participate in additional activities within the framework of the educational process, including representatives from regional military lyceums of Ukraine.[187]

---

184 "Pryznachennia ta zavdannia litseiu" [Appointment and Tasks of the Lyceum], Volynskyi oblasnyi litsei z posylenoiu viiskovo-fizychnoiu pidhotovkoiu imeni Heroyiv Nebesnoi Sotni, accessed May 28, 2023, available at: https://vvl.org.ua/about/mission/; "Pro nas" [About Us], Oblasnyi litsei z posylenoiu viiskovo-fizychnoiu pidhotovkoiu v m. Ostroh imeni Kostiantyna Ivanovycha Ostroz'koho Rivnenskoi oblasnoi radi, accessed May 28, 2023, available at: http://vl.rv.ua/about.html; "Istoriia stvorennia" [History of Creation], Kamyane-ts-Podilskyi litsei z posylenoiu viiskovo-fizychnoiu pidhotovkoiu Khmelnytskoi oblasti, December 15, 2021, accessed May 28, 2023, available at: http://kpml.com.ua/pro-litsei/istoriia-stvorennia

185 The same and see also: Viys'kove telebachennya Ukrayiny, "Kyyivskyy viys'kovyy licey" [Kyiv Military Lyceum], YouTube video, 4:47, July 5, 2012, accessed May 28, 2023, available at: https://www.youtube.com/watch?v=iSX0ES-RTnQ&t=287s

186 Cabinet of Ministers of Ukraine, "Pro zatverdzhennya Polozhennya pro viys'kovyy (viys'kovo-mors'kyy, viys'kovo-sportyvnyy) litsey, litsey iz posylenoyu viys'kovo-fizychnoyu pidhotovkoyu" [On the Approval of the Regulations on Military (Naval, Military-Sports) Lyceum, Lyceum with Enhanced Military-Physical Training], Resolution No. 672, June 30, 2021, accessed May 28, 2023, available at: https://zakon.rada.gov.ua/laws/show/672-2021-%D0%BF#Text Viys'kove telebachennya Ukrayiny, "Kyyivskyy viys'kovyy licey,"[Kyiv Military Lyceum], YouTube video, 4:47, July 5, 2012, accessed May 28, 2023, available at: https://www.youtube.com/watch?v=iSX0ES-RTnQ&t=287s

187 Natsionalnyy Alyans, "«Zvityaha 2017» — vseukrayinska viysko-patriotychna terenova hra" ["Victory 2017" — All-Ukrainian Military-Patriotic Terrain Game],

In conclusion, it can be posited that nationalists adeptly capitalised on the low level of pre-conscription training, a legacy maintained mainly from Soviet times without significant modernisation. This scenario facilitated the establishment and efficacy of nationalist youth camps and training programs, predominantly through the voluntary engagement of interested individuals. These camps and programs served dual purposes: they disseminated alternative ideological narratives and imparted fundamental military knowledge. As a result, the movement garnered support and effectively functioned as an alternative framework for military training. The adoption and replication of nationalist practices by state institutions serve as a testament to the efficiency and impact of these methods.

Improving and Transforming Logistics

At the beginning of 2019, the Armed Forces of Ukraine began implementing several significant changes to their logistics system to modernise and meet NATO standards. Logistics, which encompass a wide range of tasks including planning, supply, storage, repair, maintenance, operational control, disposal of surplus, and military transport—all these critical areas for the armed forces were undergoing reformation.[188] The status of the reform as of 2022 is still being determined, as well as the results of the integration into a unified logistics system for the new phase of the war. This reform created a new "J-4" structure called the AFU's Command of the Logistics

---

YouTube, July 21, 2017, accessed May 28, 2023, available at: https://www.youtube.com/watch?v=FGdapZEoSk0; Support AZOV (t.me/AZOVsupport), "Support AZOV razom z 'Centuria' ta biytsyamy 3-yi OSHBr provely viys'kovyy vyshkil u Rivnomu" [Support AZOV together with "Centuria" and fighters of the 3rd OSHBr conducted military training in Rivne], accessed May 28, 2023, available at: https://t.me/AZOVsupport/1468

188 Karpuk Hennadiy, "Lohistyčne zabezpechennya armiyi: chomu v suchasnykh viynakh vse vyrishuye shvydkist'" [Logistic Support of the Army: Why Speed Decides Everything in Modern Wars], Rubryka, April 9, 2019, accessed May 28, 2023, available at: https://rubryka.com/blog/logistychne-zabezpechennya-armiyi/?fbclid=IwAR35eRZMe-KHuQx3T_9_mEW8BF5-Y61yOKyXydd7dQEKqANuxbEVYpcEp5Q;

Forces.[189] A vital aspect of this process is the separation of strategic and operational functions in logistics support. The Armed Forces of Ukraine are also diligently engaged in implementing supply systems standards akin to those of NATO and in unifying rear support and armaments into a single, pragmatic structure. They employ LOGFAS software and are focused on provisioning, supplying, and conducting logistical operations for all DFUs. By the end of 2020, the Armed Forces planned to complete the establishment of the Command of Logistics Forces, which conforms to NATO standards.[190] This major reform envisages merging the Rear and Armaments of the Armed Forces of Ukraine. This large-scale reform aims to abandon outdated Soviet algorithms and technologies in favour of a more modern military service. Consequently, the Armed Forces strive to create an effective logistics system that supports all components of the defence forces following modern requirements and standards. However, the burden on the logistics and support of the Armed Forces of Ukraine, within the framework of an almost threefold increase in personnel (to approximately 1,300,000), could only function with issues at the grassroots level. One example of such problems is the intensification and growth of the volunteer movement in Ukraine, as well as the development and multiple expansion of the activities of charitable funds to help the army. For instance, one of the most significant army aid funds, "Come Back Alive," which has been operating since 2014, collected about 200

---

189 "Dlya stvorennia Komanduvan' logistyky ta morskoyi pikhoti utochneno perelik generals'kykh posad" [For the Establishment of Logistics Command and Marine Infantry, the List of General Positions Is Specified], Ukrainian Military Pages, February 23, 2018, accessed May 28, 2023, available at: https://www.ukrmilitary.com/2018/02/generals.html

190 Ministry of Defence of Ukraine "Osnovni Polozhennya lohistychnoho zabezpechennya Zbroynykh Syl Ukrayiny" [Basic Provisions of logistic support of the Armed Forces of Ukraine], accessed May 28, 2023, available at: http://arcdrmis.rit.org.ua/WWW/arch_mod/docs/05_%D0%9E%D1%81%D0%BD%D0%BE%D0%B2%D0%BD%D1%96_%D0%BF%D0%BE%D0%BB%D0%BE%D0%B6%D0%B5%D0%BD%D0%BD%D1%8F_%D0%BB%D0%BE%D0%B3%D1%96%D1%81%D1%82%D0%B8%D1%87%D0%BD%D0%BE%D0%B3%D0%BE_%D0%B7%D0%B0%D0%B1%D0%B5%D0%B7%D0%BF%D0%B5%D1%87%D0%B5%D0%BD%D0%BD%D1%8F_%D0%97%D0%A1%D0%A3.pdf

million UAH (about 10 million dollars) by 24.02.22.[191] Meanwhile, as of May of 2023, the fund has collected over 7 billion hryvnias, or more than 185 million dollars.[192] Other large organizations focused on supporting the army were also formed—the Serhiy Prytula Foundation, (raised more than $100 millions)[193] the Kyiv School of Economics Foundation, (more than $50 millions)[194] and the United24 Foundation (more than $350 millions),[195] "Razom for Ukraine" Foundation ($100 millions)[196] which collect tens or even hundreds of millions of dollars to help Ukrainians and the army. Foundations and other volunteers bought military equipment such as bulletproof vests, helmets, and drones. These funds even purchase military equipment and obtain licenses for dual-purpose goods[197] and military-specific equipment, such as armoured

---

191 "Za rik povnomashtabnoyi viyny fond 'Povernys' zhyvym' zibrav ponad 27 milyardiv dlya ZSU" [For a year of full-scale war, the "Come Back Alive" fund has collected over 27 billion for the Armed Forces of Ukraine], Ukrinform, May 26, 2023, accessed May 28, 2023, available at: https://www.ukrinform.ua/rubric-society/3714655-za-rik-povnomasstabnoi-vijni-fond-povernis-zivim-zibrav-ponad-7-milardiv-dla-zsu.html

192 "Come Back Alive Donations," Come Back Alive, accessed May 28, 2023, available at: https://report.comebackalive.in.ua/public/dashboard/e4f44bc7-05f4-459b-a10b-cc10e6637217?date=past8years~

193 Kuleba Alina, "Fond Prytuli nazvav sumu donativ, zibranykh za rik povnomashtabnoyi viyny" [The Prytula Foundation announced the amount of donations collected during the year of full-scale war], 24 Channel, March 3, 2023, accessed May 28, 2023, available at: https://24tv.ua/skilki-groshey-zibrav-fond-prituli-za-rik-povnomasshtabnoyi-viyni_n2267040

194 KSE Foundation, Main page, accessed May 28, 2023, available at: https://foundation.kse.ua/

195 United24, Main page, accessed May 28, 2023, available at: https://u24.gov.ua/uk

196 "Yak otrymaty zasoby taktichnoyi medytsyny abo zv'yazku vid BF 'Razom dlya Ukrayiny'?" [How to obtain tactical medical supplies or communication from the charity foundation 'Razom dlya Ukrayiny'?], Razom for Ukraine, accessed June 28, 2023, available at: https://www.razomforukraine.org/ua/zapyt/

197 "Come Back Alive Obtained a License to Purchase Lethal Weapons," Come Back Alive Foundation, June 22, 2022, accessed May 28, 2023, available at: https://savelife.in.ua/materials/news/povernys-zhyvym-otrymav-litsenziyu-na-za/

vehicles,[198] unmanned systems like Bayraktar TB2,[199] or machine guns[200] and mortars.[201] In May of 2022, Deputy Minister of Defence of Ukraine Hanna Maliar said that civil volunteers and charity foundations purchased around 44% of all bulletproof jackets.[202] A critical dimension of the specialised training within nationalist units is the metamorphosis of civil and political organisations into robust support mechanisms for these units. Civil activities were channelled solely toward charitable endeavours to bolster the combat divisions. In many aspects, the Azov movement provides a striking example. It established a patronage service called "Angels of Azov." The "Angels of Azov" patronage service emerged in 2014 as an initiative to assist Ukrainian soldiers and has since expanded its operations.[203] Since February 2022, the service has treated over

---

[198] "'Narodni Bron'ovyky'" [People's Armored Vehicles], Prytula Foundation, accessed on May 28, 2023, available at: https://prytulafoundation.org/about/projects/archive/treba-brati; "«Come Back Alive» purchased 11 armored vehicles for the 36th Marine Brigade," Come Back Alive, September 8, 2022, accessed May 28, 2023, available at: https://savelife.in.ua/materials/news/povernys-zhyvym-prydbav-11-bronovanykh-m/

[199] Solonyna Yevhen, "The Come Back Alive Foundation Bought and Transferred a Bayraktar TB2 Complex to the Ukrainian Military," Come Back Alive Foundation, July 26, 2022, accessed May 28, 2023, available at: https://savelife.in.ua/materials/news/povernys-zhyvym-kupyv-ta-peredav-viyskov/; "Three Bayraktars from Prytula campaign arrive in Ukraine," Ukrainska Pravda, September 5, 2022, accessed May 28, 2023, available at: https://www.pravda.com.ua/news/2022/09/5/7366201/

[200] "Come Back Alive Foundation acquires 1,460 7.62mm machine guns for the Armed Forces," Militarnyi, April 24, 2023, accessed May 28, 2023, available at: https://mil.in.ua/en/news/come-back-alive-foundation-acquires-1-460-7-62mm-machine-guns-for-the-armed-forces/

[201] "Pershi 'DOVHI RUKY' uzhe v TrO" [The first 'LONG ARMS' are already in the JFO], Militarnyi, May 30, 2023, accessed May 28, 2023, available at: https://mil.in.ua/uk/news/pershi-dovgi-ruky-uzhe-v-tro/

[202] "Vid pochatku viyny 56% bronezhyletiv biytsyam zabezpechylo Minoborony, reshtu — volontery, — Malyar" [Since the beginning of the war, 56% of the body armor for the soldiers was provided by the Ministry of Defense, the rest by volunteers, — Malyar], 24 channel, May 12, 2022, accessed May 28, 2023, available at: https://24tv.ua/vid-pochatku-viyni-56-bronezhiletiv-biytsyam-zabezpechilo-minoboroni_n1977814

[203] Buket Yevhen, "«Yangoly Azovu» — shlyakh u dev'ять rokiv sluzhinnya Ukrayini" [«Azov's Angels» — the path of nine years of serving Ukraine], ArmiyaInform, April 29, 2023, accessed May 28, 2023, available at: https://armyinform.com.ua/2023/04/29/yangoly-azovu-shlyah-u-devyat-rokiv-sluzhinnya-ukrayini/

1,700 soldiers.[204] It is aiding approximately 700 soldiers from the NGU "AZOV" brigade, the third separate assault brigade of the Armed Forces of Ukraine, and the particular unit of the GUR MO "KRAKEN."[205]

"Angels of Azov" also extends support and assistance to over 1,500 families of deceased and captured soldiers.[206] Olena Tolkachova, the founder and head of the service, began her voluntary work during the Revolution of Dignity and refocused her efforts on assisting the front after initiating the anti-terrorist operation.[207] The former head of the service is Olga Tkachenko, the widow of one of the movement's ideologues and the battalion's founders, Mykola Kravchenko.[208]

On July 5, 2022, the "Support Azov" project was launched in Kyiv, aimed at aiding combat units, injured soldiers, and families of deceased, wounded, and captured Ukrainian defenders.[209] The

---

204 Buket Yevhen, "«Yangoly Azovu»—shlyakh u dev'ять rokiv sluzhinnya Ukrayini" [«Azov's Angels»—the path of nine years of serving Ukraine], ArmiyaInform, April 29, 2023, accessed May 28, 2023, available at: https://armyinform.com.ua/2023/04/29/yangoly-azovu-shlyah-u-devyat-rokiv-sluzhinnya-ukrayini/

205 Buket Yevhen, "«Yangoly Azovu»—shlyakh u dev'ять rokiv sluzhinnya Ukrayini" [«Azov's Angels»—the path of nine years of serving Ukraine], ArmiyaInform, April 29, 2023, accessed May 28, 2023, available at: https://armyinform.com.ua/2023/04/29/yangoly-azovu-shlyah-u-devyat-rokiv-sluzhinnya-ukrayini/

206 Buket Yevhen, "«Yangoly Azovu»—shlyakh u dev'ять rokiv sluzhinnya Ukrayini" [«Azov's Angels»—the path of nine years of serving Ukraine], ArmiyaInform, April 29, 2023, accessed May 28, 2023, available at: https://armyinform.com.ua/2023/04/29/yangoly-azovu-shlyah-u-devyat-rokiv-sluzhinnya-ukrayini/

207 Buket Yevhen, "«Yangoly Azovu»—shlyakh u dev'ять rokiv sluzhinnya Ukrayini" [«Azov's Angels»—the path of nine years of serving Ukraine], ArmiyaInform, April 29, 2023, accessed May 28, 2023, available at: https://armyinform.com.ua/2023/04/29/yangoly-azovu-shlyah-u-devyat-rokiv-sluzhinnya-ukrayini/

208 Buket Yevhen, "«Yangoly Azovu»—shlyakh u dev'ять rokiv sluzhinnya Ukrayini" [«Azov's Angels»—the path of nine years of serving Ukraine], ArmiyaInform, April 29, 2023, accessed May 28, 2023, available at: https://armyinform.com.ua/2023/04/29/yangoly-azovu-shlyah-u-devyat-rokiv-sluzhinnya-ukrayini/

209 Kinsha Dar'ya, Yaroslav Pryshchepa, "Dopomogty voyinam ta ikhnim rodynam: U stolytsi prezentuvaly proyekt 'SUPPORT AZOV'" [Help the soldiers and their families: A project "SUPPORT AZOV" was presented in the capital],

project's initiator is Andriy Biletskyi, the founder of the "Azov" regiment.[210] Oleh Petrenko, head of "SUPPORT AZOV," stated that the project aims to create a platform for everyone who wants to assist Azov units and those in captivity.[211] The project's website will have three main sections: support for fighters, help for the wounded, and support for families.[212] On February 23, 2023, the "Azov" brigade commanders established the public organisation, "Azov. One", to financially support and provide for their new brigade.[213] The primary goal of Azov. One is to unify and centralise fundraising to optimise donations and their rational use and prevent fraudulent fundraising activities under the pretence of supporting Azov.[214]

Suspilne, July 5, 2022, accessed May 28, 2023, available at: https://suspilne.med ia/257453-dopomogti-voinam-ta-ihnim-rodinam-u-stolici-prezentuvali-proekt -support-azov/

210 Kinsha Dar'ya, Yaroslav Pryshchepa, "Dopomogty voyinam ta ikhnim rodynam: U stolytsi prezentuvaly proyekt 'SUPPORT AZOV'" [Help the soldiers and their families: A project "SUPPORT AZOV" was presented in the capital], Suspilne, July 5, 2022, accessed May 28, 2023, available at: https://suspilne.med ia/257453-dopomogti-voinam-ta-ihnim-rodinam-u-stolici-prezentuvali-proekt -support-azov/

211 Kinsha Dar'ya, Yaroslav Pryshchepa, "Dopomogty voyinam ta ikhnim rodynam: U stolytsi prezentuvaly proyekt 'SUPPORT AZOV'" [Help the soldiers and their families: A project "SUPPORT AZOV" was presented in the capital], Suspilne, July 5, 2022, accessed May 28, 2023, available at: https://suspilne.med ia/257453-dopomogti-voinam-ta-ihnim-rodinam-u-stolici-prezentuvali-proekt -support-azov/

212 Kinsha Dar'ya, Yaroslav Pryshchepa, "Dopomogty voyinam ta ikhnim rodynam: U stolytsi prezentuvaly proyekt 'SUPPORT AZOV'" [Help the soldiers and their families: A project "SUPPORT AZOV" was presented in the capital], Suspilne, July 5, 2022, accessed May 28, 2023, available at: https://suspilne.med ia/257453-dopomogti-voinam-ta-ihnim-rodinam-u-stolici-prezentuvali-proekt -support-azov/

213 Klischuk Liudmyla, "Komandiry 'Azovu' stvoryuyut HO Azov One. Tse—yedyna platforma dlya zboru koshtiv na potreby bryhady" [The commanders of 'Azov' are creating the NGO Azov One. It is the only platform for raising funds for the brigade's needs], Novynarnia, February 23, 2023, accessed May 28, 2023, available at: https://novynarnia.com/2023/02/23/komandyry-azovu-stvor yuyut/.

214 Klischuk Liudmyla, "Komandiry 'Azovu' stvoryuyut HO Azov One. Tse—yedyna platforma dlya zboru koshtiv na potreby bryhady" [The commanders of 'Azov' are creating the NGO Azov One. It is the only platform for raising funds for the brigade's needs], Novynarnia, February 23, 2023, accessed May 28, 2023, available at: https://novynarnia.com/2023/02/23/komandyry-azovu-stvor yuyut/.

Battalion teams actively participate in informational activities, primarily focusing on combat operations and fundraising coverage. Most of the Telegram channels officially associated with volunteer units systematically conduct fundraising. This activity stands out from similar efforts by other foundations and opinion leaders, as fundraising primarily occurs within the network of nationalists and their supporters. The availability of various and diverse information channels, such as Telegram[215] and YouTube[216] enables battalions to utilize their audience to recruit new participants and raise additional funds. For this purpose, videos from drones are used[217] (often for fundraising for drones[218] or as a report on the activity of drones for which funds were raised),[219] videos of assault actions

---

215 Khroniki Ridika (t.me/hroniki_ridika). Telegram. Accessed May 28, 2023. https://t.me/hroniki_ridika ; UDAROV (t.me/kristianudarov). Telegram. Accessed May 28, 2023. https://t.me/kristianudarov; Khimikdavid (t.me/khimikdavid4308). Telegram. Accessed May 28, 2023. https://t.me/khimikdavid4308; Zhorin z Azovu (t.me/MaksymZhorin). Telegram. Accessed May 28, 2023. https://t.me/MaksymZhorin ; Chyli i Ko Kharkiv (t.me/chilli_1654). Telegram. Accessed May 28, 2023. https://t.me/chilli_1654; Andriy Biletsky (t.me/BiletskyAndriy). Telegram. Accessed May 28, 2023. https://t.me/BiletskyAndriy; KHODAKOVSKY (t.me/BKhodakovsky). Telegram. Accessed May 28, 2023. https://t.me/BKhodakovsky.
216 Batal'yon BRATSTVO, YouTube channel, accessed May 28, 2023, available at: https://www.youtube.com/@BatalionBratstvo; Dmytro Korchynskyi, YouTube channel, accessed May 28, 2023, available at: https://www.youtube.com/@korchynskyi/videos
217 Support AZOV (t.me/AZOVsupport), "Ne zabuvayte pro chudovu formulu, yaka stovidsotkovo pratsyuye: vy robyte donaty na nashykh biytsiv = vony dvukhsotyat' rusnyu" [Don't forget about the wonderful formula that works one hundred percent: you make donations to our fighters = they kill the Russians], Telegram, November 9, 2022 at 12:47, accessed May 28, 2023, available at: https://t.me/AZOVsupport/376; Support AZOV, "Biytsi 1-ho shturmbatu 3-yi OSHBr vidknuly rosiyan vid 'Dorohy zhyttya'" [Fighters of the 1st assault battalion of the 3rd Separate Assault Brigade repelled Russians from the "Road of Life"], Telegram, April 25, 2023 at 17:33, accessed May 28, 2023, available at: https://t.me/AZOVsupport/1250
218 Support AZOV (t.me/AZOVsupport), "Pidrozdil aerorozvidky TERRA 3-yi OSHBr vidpravlyaye vorohu 'podarunky' z neba na Bakhmut s'komu napryamku" [The aerial reconnaissance unit TERRA of the 3rd Separate Assault Brigade sends "gifts" from the sky to the enemy on the Bakhmut direction], Telegram, May 14, 2023 at 15:15, accessed May 28, 2023, available at: https://t.me/AZOVsupport/1358 .
219 Batal'yon BRATSTVO (t.me/BatalionBratstvo), "Biytsi batal'yonu BRAT STVO vyslovlyuyut' shchyru podyaku usim nebayduzhnym metsenatam ta dobrym

from cameras like GoPro,[220] tubes from anti-tank systems, etc.[221] Initially created for activist activities, the fundraising system is now entirely reoriented to mobilise resources for the needs of combat units. Nationalist formations also possess significant experience in various aspects of military service, which is used to popularise units and create educational content. They create video materials about using and maintaining weapons,[222] customizations of military equipment, etc.[223] Such extensive media work requires significant media coverage, including video editing and the involvement of specialists in advertising, marketing, crowdfunding, and other related areas. Collected resources are also used to generate aid for

---

khrystyyanam, yaki dopomohly prydbaty neobkhidnyy dron MATRICE-30T" [Fighters of the BRATSTVO battalion sincerely thank all concerned patrons and good Christians who helped to buy the necessary drone MATRICE-30T], Telegram, November 7, 2022 at 22:57, accessed May 28, 2023, available at: https://t.me/BatalionBratstvo/636.

220 Andriy Biletsky (t.me/BiletskyAndriy), "Shturm vorozhykh pozytsiy na Bakhmut s'komu napryamku. Pratsyuye 1 shturmovyy batal'yonUA3 OSHBr. Video z GoPro komandyra druhoho shturmovoho viddilennya tret'oyi shturmovoyi roty Sticha" [Assault of enemy positions on the Bakhmut direction. The 1st assault battalion of the 3rd Separate Assault Brigade is working. Video from GoPro of the commander of the second assault platoon of the third assault company, Stich], Telegram, June 6, 2023 at 19:28 accessed May 28, 2023, available at: https://t.me/BiletskyAndriy/5128.

221 Dmytri Korchynskiy (t.me/korchynskiy), "Shanovni pidpysnyky ta pidpysnytsi. Nashi druzi, pidrozdil Syl Spetsial'nykh Operatsiy Shalena Z'hraya, shcho prodovzhuyut' trymaty oboronu na Bakhmut s'komu napryamku, zbyrayut' 100'000 hryven' na drony Chimera 7" [Dear subscribers. Our friends, the Special Forces unit Shalena Zhraya, who continue to hold the defense on the Bakhmut direction, are collecting 100,000 hryvnia for the Chimera 7 drones], Telegram, June 4, 2023 at 17:45 accessed May 28, 2023, available at: https://t.me/korchynskiy/6537

222 Karpatska Sich "NLAW, instructsii" [NLAW Instructions], YouTube video, March 18, 2022, accessed May 28, 2023, available at: https://www.youtube.com/watch?v=tfI3Li0YyVw&t=21s.

223 3-ya okrema shturmova bryhada [3rd Separate Assault Brigade], "Aphreyd stvola: yak azovtsi modernizuyut' svoyu zbroyu" ["Barrel Upgrade: How Azov Soldiers Modernize Their Weapons"], YouTube video, January 10, 2023, accessed May 28, 2023, available at: https://www.youtube.com/watch?v=kgxupuFOR2o&t=66s. 3-ya okrema shturmova bryhada [3rd Separate Assault Brigade], "Boiove sporjadzhennia shturmovykiv: haĭd vid kombata 3 OSHBr" ["Combat Equipment of Stormtroopers: A Guide from the Commander of the 3rd Separate Assault Brigade"], YouTube, March 1, 2023, accessed May 28, 2023, available at: https://www.youtube.com/watch?v=BI_uBaz0bUU&list=PLnJ_asQaAbl3CiQQ0931UWeOuUEcfNg6D&index=1&t=14s.

their units, serving as alternative logistical support. Therefore, the nationalist units have an additional channel to meet their own needs, provide supplies, rehabilitate the wounded, and assist the families of the deceased.

Conclusions

Since the onset of the Russian-Ukrainian conflict in 2014, Ukrainian nationalist movements have emerged as pivotal actors in the country's military mobilisation and resistance efforts. Evolving from their initial status as political fringe elements, these groups have become integral components of the Armed Forces of Ukraine, ultimately serving as a robust reservoir of highly skilled military specialists and motivated enlistees. Upon examining the factors driving this transformation, several key elements stand out. First, nationalist organisations effectively leveraged their extensive mobilisation networks, focusing them on military objectives. This facilitated the recruitment and training of a substantial volunteer force. Second, these movements implemented comprehensive training programs encompassing physical, professional, and ideological elements, assembling highly specialised military personnel contingents. Armed with a diverse range of capabilities—from seasoned veterans to in-house engineers and technological innovations—these groups exhibited remarkable adaptability to the evolving conditions of warfare. Their consistent success on the battlefield corroborates this.

It is noteworthy that these formations, despite originating from oppositional political stances, have seamlessly integrated into the hierarchical structure of the Armed Forces, adjusting their ideologies and attitudes to align with the difficulties of real-world combat. Additionally, nationalist movements were among the most prepared entities, their ideological framework having long anticipated large-scale military engagement with the Russian Federation. This underscores their readiness for national solidarity and defence during critical junctures. Their principal guiding value—and a cornerstone of their brand identity—is a pronounced emphasis on professionalism, rendering their units markedly more egalitarian than their initial political orientations. As for the first section of the article, which seeks to "rationalise" the nationalists' active support, it is impossible to overlook the unmistakable reality that this conflict is existential for most of Ukraine's population. This pertains not just to the state's survival but also to its citizens' well-being. Distinguishing the nationalist movement from other societal sectors since 2022 is not solely their elevated level of combat readiness and organisational infrastructure but also—and perhaps more critically—their motivational orientation for this preparedness. The ethos underpinning their initiatives is fundamentally rooted in confronting the Russian Federation as both a realistic and immutable threat.

These are the foundational principles of all Ukrainian nationalist movements, which may sometimes be seen as an "overreaction" to perceived threats during the 1990s. However, the Ukrainian scenario is a compelling example of how radicalisation can be context-specific, particularly in response to the political elite's inadequate attention to and understanding of national security and defence. These movements employ narratives to illuminate pressing yet unresolved social issues. It should be recognised that, for the majority, the threat from the Russian Federation was considered to be marginal. The possibility of a major war in Europe during the 2020s was widely viewed as a speculative risk, manipulated in various ways by different political actors. However, these once-hypothetical fears have now come to fruition. To further elucidate this point, it is premature to draw any definitive conclusions regarding the transformation of nationalist movements in Ukraine, most of which are currently engaged in existential battles. However, the events of February 24, 2022, served as a watershed moment, drastically altering Ukraine's political landscape and the trajectory of its social movements. Nationalist groups responded by organising paramilitary units, capitalising on and accentuating the potential threat posed by Russia's imperial ambitions and the spectre of revisionism while drawing inspiration from historical entities like the OUN organisation and various resistance forces.

While some may criticise these movements for employing rhetoric mainly to galvanise support, it is essential to acknowledge that many of their supporters genuinely hold and believe in these views. These movements have not merely engaged in traditional activism; they have participated in democratic processes and established institutional frameworks and practices that proved valuable in the ongoing regional conflict since 2014 and arguably the most devastating war in contemporary history. Hence, it is evident that Ukraine's far-right movements have undergone a fascinating metamorphosis—from politically inconsequential entities in electoral terms to an effective apparatus for recruiting and training combatants. Their integration into the Ukrainian Defence Forces has further concentrated their attention on military resistance against external aggressors, as opposed to previous domestic political confrontations. These groups are now prepared to disavow totalitarian ideologies, comply with the apolitical statutes of the Armed Forces, and conduct unbiased recruitment among civilians, irrespective of ideological or ethnic background. In doing so, Ukrainian nationalists offer a case study where radical narratives about societal threats, such as the imperative for comprehensive military preparedness against the Russian Federation, have helped Ukrainian people to adapt to the existential risks, positively affecting the Ukrainian state and the well-being and survival of its populace in a short-term perspective. In many respects, this represents a novel direction in institutionalising public movements. These groups have managed to construct an infrastructure that serves not merely as a façade for political contestation during times of peace or relative stability but also as a productive mechanism for conducting full-scale military operations. This transformation of nationalists into a mobilisation reserve, built upon the foundation of a social movement, presents an uncommon, if not unique, example in contemporary strategies for preparing mobilisation reserves within the armed forces of democratic nations.

Therefore, considering these factors, it is evident that the nationalist movement has evolved into a significant personnel reserve for the Ukrainian Armed Forces and a source of highly trained specialists for warfare. Nonetheless, exploring the role and impact of nationalist formations in the military conflict with Russia warrants further investigation. Continued study is essential for a more comprehensive and nuanced understanding of this phenomenon, which could serve as a critical benchmark for evaluating theories of organisational structure and understanding the motivations and mechanics of the transformation of radical movements into social institutions.

4 Has the Azov Regiment Depoliticized? An Analysis from the Structure to Individual Trajectories

Bertrand de Franqueville[1]

The aim of this chapter is to better evaluate and understand the level of politicisation of the Azov regiment[2], *i.e.* when the activities of this armed formation acquire a political orientation, including a radical ideological nature. Since its foundation in 2014, the politicisation of this military organisation has been at the heart of public debates, controversies, and questions in media and academia because of its symbolism and the political orientation of its founders.[3]

---

1 I would like to particularly thank Dominique Arel, Anastasia Fomitchova, Lou Raisonnier, Katerina Sviderska, and Alexandra Wishart for their precious advice. As well as the editors for their confidence and their insightful comments. The statements remain my own.
2 In February 2023, Azov became a brigade. For the sake of understanding and to consider Azov's long trajectory, including the pre-2022 period on which I'm focusing more, I've decided to keep the designation "regiment". See: Kuznetsova, K 2023 'Do shturmovikh brigad "Gvardiya nastupu" vzhe doluchilosya ponad 500 divchat — MVS', TSN, February 8, viewed 14 June 2023 <https://tsn.ua/ukrayina/do-shturmovih-brigad-gvardiya-nastupu-uzhe-doluchilosya-ponad-500-divchat-mvs-2261017.html> ; Mazurenko, A 2023 '"Azov" rasshirilsya do brigady v sostave Natsgvardii', Ukrainska Pravda, 9 February, viewed 14 June 2023, <https://www.pravda.com.ua/rus/news/2023/02/9/7388707/>.
3 Coynash, H 2014 '"Azov" — What's the problem?', Kharkiv Human Rights Protection Group, 9 September, viewed 31 December 2022, <https://khpg.org/en/1410395276>; Colborne, M 2021 'Why Designating the Azov movement as an FTO is Ineffective', *Fair Observer*, 2 June, viewed 31 December 2022 <https://www.fairobserver.com/region/europe/micheal-colborne-azov-movement-terrorist-designation-us-ukraine-far-rght-news-35212/>; Colborne, M 2022 *From the Fires of War: Ukraine's Azov Movement and the Global Far right*, Ibidem, Stuttgart, 180 p.; de Franqueville, B, & Nonjon, A 2022 'Mémoire et sentiment national en Ukraine', *La Vie des Idées*, 17 May, viewed 31 December 2022, <https://laviedesidees.fr/Memoire-et-sentiment-national-en-Ukraine.html>; de Franqueville, B, & Nonjon, A 2022 'L'extrême droite ukrainienne existe et elle est déjà bien documentée', *La Croix*, 21 March, viewed 31 December 2022, <https://www.la-croix.com/Debats/Lextreme-droite-ukrainienne-existe-deja-bien-documentee-2022-03-21-1201206132>; John, T, & Lister, T 2022 'A far-

Indeed, the regiment traces part of its origins to the paramilitary organization Patriot of Ukraine, connected to a political party, the Social-National Assembly (SNA)[4]. Moreover, several veterans of the regiment have moved into the civil and political sphere through the creation of the non-governmental organisation "Civil Corps of Azov", and then in October 2016 of a party, the National Corps. With the creation of ultra-nationalist political spaces and aims connected with the regiment's legacy, the Azov movement was born. This development might have suggested a politico-military scenario similar to the initial structuring of the Patriots of Ukraine and the SNA. Several international experts expressed concern about the politicisation of a military unit and its ideological orientation. The idea is then to understand if the Azov regiment is politicised, and its aim would go beyond its military investment in defending

---

right battalion has a key role in Ukraine's resistance. Its neo-Nazi history has been exploited by Putin' *CNN*, 30 March, viewed 31 December 2022, <https://edition.cnn.com/2022/03/29/europe/ukraine-azov-movement-far-right-intl-cmd/index.html>; Kuzmenko, O 2022 '@BBCRosAtkins should've covered the relationship between Biletsky's far-right Azov movement and the Azov Regiment. THREAD.' [Twitter], 27 March. Available from: https://twitter.com/kooleksiy/status/1507902044069416960 [Accessed 31 December 2022]; Kuzmenko, O 2022 'In the Azov Regiment's magazine"Black sun", fighters, AR figures contemporaneously wrote that the launch of a political wing was meant to allow the Regiment to influence politics.' [Twitter], 18 May. Available from: https://twitter.com/kooleksiy/status/1526972935646371841 [Accessed 31 December 2022]; Kuzmenko, O 2022 'National Corps' senior leader Maksym Zhorin, a champion of the bill, is now a commander in SOF Azov Regiment fighting against Russian aggression.' [Twitter], 12 June. Available from: https://twitter.com/kooleksiy/status/1536017241011109889 [Accessed 31 December 2022]; Ourdan, R 2023 'Un an après la bataille de Marioupol, la brigade ukrainienne Azov retourne au combat sur le front de Zaporijia', *Le Monde*, 10 June, viewed 12 June 2023, <https://www.lemonde.fr/international/article/2023/06/10/un-an-apres-la-bataille-de-marioupol-la-brigade-ukrainienne-azov-retourne-a u-combat-sur-le-front-de-zaporijia_6177026_3210.html>; Shekhovtsov, A 2022 'How the West enabled genocide in Mariupol with its misguided Azov obsession', *Euromaidan Press*, 2nd April, viewed 31 December, <https://euromaidanpress.com/2022/04/02/how-the-west-enabled-genocide-in-mariupol-with-its-misguided-azov-obsession/>.

4   Patriot of Ukraine is a paramilitary organization created in 1999 as the armed wing of the far-right Social-National Party of Ukraine. It was disbanded in 2004 and rebuilt in 2005 in Kharkiv under the initiative of Mykola Kravchenko, Oleh Odnorozhenko, Yaroslav Babych and Andriy Biletsky. In 2009, they created their own political party, the Social National Assembly.

Ukraine in the face of Russian aggression. The question is to what extent the structure is politicised.

My approach avoids dichotomous compartmentalisation and an over-generalized, caricatured explanation of the regiment. Consequently, I'm positioning the Azov regiment on a politicisation/de-politicization spectrum, which allows us to appreciate more nuances between two ideal types where an armed group can take a trajectory in either direction. I argue that professionalisation and integration into the State have led the regiment to a greater depoliticization, seeking to meet the standards of a professional army corps by relegating political issues to the civilian sphere, even if some far-right elements can still be found in the structure. Rather than a structural approach, which tends to overestimate the place of ideology in the regiment, it is ultimately through the individual trajectories of combatants that we can gain a clearer understanding of the political perspectives of engagement. I will introduce this chapter by presenting my analytical framework and methodology. Based on these approaches, I will start by examining the factors of politicization and the influence that the group can have on the shaping of the individual *habitus*[5] of its members. In a third section, I will examine the way the professionalization of the regiment and the military imperatives can overtake the ideological stakes of the founders and some officers, leaving more room for a separation of the political and military aims. I will then emphasise that it is difficult, in the long term, to situate the group in a radical trajectory. A bottom-up approach will remind us of the differentiated perceptions between the members. Knowing that already in 2015, 10-20% of the unit was considered neo-Nazi that this contingent might have decreased over time, it is then, finally, in the individual paths of the combatants that we can obtain a clearer understanding of the political perspectives of their commitment.[6] Therefore, in the last

---

5   Bourdieu defined habitus as "structured structures predisposed to function as structuring structures", *i.e.*, the internalization of specific norms and values that limit worldviews. See: Bourdieu, P 1980, *Le sens pratique*, Paris, Éditions de Minuit (coll. «Le Sens commun»), p. 88.
6   Colborne, M 2022 *From the Fires of War: Ukraine's Azov Movement and the Global Far right, Ibidem*, Stuttgart, p62.

section, rather than adopting an approach by the structure, it seems more interesting to look at the level of individual trajectories. We can better assess the political significance of their long-term commitment, which can be seen in the continuous trajectory from pre-regiment activism, the following engagement in the regiment, to the choices they make once they withdraw. At this level, we note a diversity of profiles. While there are indeed soldiers with a continuous trajectory of commitment at the extreme right of the political spectrum (for example, from Patriots of Ukraine to the National Corps), not all of them have this profile, and the motivations for commitment can be multiple, often marked by the emergency of war. Azov has managed to attract extra-political motivations by integrating a wide range of profiles into its ranks.

Theoretical framework and methodology

The debate about the politicization of Azov does not date back to 2022 and is the result of a long-standing ambiguity regarding its political origins, as well as the continued political commitment of some of its members and veterans. As highlighted by Arel and Driscoll, "Two volunteer battalion "brands" in particular acquired outsized political visibility after the front stabilised: Pravyi sektor, for a while, but particularly Azov".[7] This blur is even more critical since the movement originated from the regiment has spun off several organizations that appear to be paramilitary or rather vigilante, such as the *Natsional'ny Druzhyni*. This movement carries an aggressive image, contributing to this challenging apprehension for anyone striving to constitute clear categories with well-defined borders.

Such a difficulty results from this double initial development of Azov, interweaving political ambitions with military issues. However, this categorical blurring is not an isolated phenomenon. It can be found in many military formations, within a spectrum ranging from professional armies to more paramilitary or militia

---

[7] Arel, D, & Driscoll, J 2023 *Ukraine's Unnamed War: Before the Russian Invasion of 2022*, Cambridge: Cambridge University Press, p186.

organizations competing frontally with the state. By spectrum, I mean a polarisation between these two types of military formations without making a strict binary categorisation to apprehend different degrees of (de) politicisation. Politicisation occurs when the activities of an armed formation acquire a political orientation, including a radical ideological nature. On the one hand, we have non-professional armies, militias or paramilitaries with clear, asserted political goals. Combatants are non-state actors. These armies may act as auxiliary forces to the state, or as opposition forces. On the other side of the spectrum, we have professional armies, in which the political dimension is relegated to the private, civilian life of the soldiers, who are state actors. There is no official political stripe, and political pluralism (from an individual and personal point of view) is accepted. The army follows the logic of the continuity of the state, not of the people who run it. The state controls it and symbolises its monopoly of the legitimate use of physical force. The idea of a spectrum implies the possibility of a trajectory including different degrees of politicisation, and relationships to the state, which prevents us from locking ourselves only into ideal types but more as tendencies towards these models. This allows us to embrace nuance in our categorical classifications. Moreover, we can include military groups that may present themselves as auxiliary forces of a state without representing a state army, but also military forces that are instrumentalised by a state to resolve domestic political conflicts. Finally, this framework allows us to think in terms of shifting trajectories over time. On the one hand, a depoliticizing trajectory (towards professionalization), and on the other, a politicising trajectory (see Figure 1)

Figure 1: The politicisation spectrum.

The point is to examine the place of politics. On one part of this spectrum, in professional armies, politics is not necessarily absent among soldiers, but the structure does not carry a particular ideology. Indeed, it is not uncommon to see scandals arise regarding the politicalaspirations of specific soldiers. While these institutions may claim to be neutral and apolitical, the soldiers remain politicised. Of course, they have as much right as their fellow citizens to vote and contribute to the democratic life of their country. However, some of them sometimes go beyond their duty of discretion and openly display their neo-Nazi orientation. Koehler highlights various cases of collusion between elite soldiers and extreme right-wing circles.[8] It was one of the reasons why the Canadian Airborne Regiment was disbanded in the 1990s. Imbeault, in discussing the links between the Canadian army and the far-right, notes that extremists are often attracted to a fantasized representation of the army.[9] For him, the army is not a natural home for those holding far-right beliefs, although it can be more conservative. The newspaper *Mediapart* also published in 2021 a whole report on "neo-Nazis in the French army".[10] And on December 14, 2022, several extreme far-right activists, including military personnel, were arrested as they were about to commit violence during the France-Morocco World Cup semi-final.[11] While this may be a cause for great concern, it is wrong to consider the French army as a neo-Nazi army because of the disparity of its personnel and structural non-commitment to these ideologies. Koehler clarifies that "the large majority of soldiers and officers in these units serve with the utmost dedication, commitment, professionalism, and integrity" and warns

---

8   Koelhler, D 2022 'From Superiority to Supremacy: Exploring the Vulnerability of Military and Police Special Forces to Extreme Right Radicalization", *Studies in Conflict & Terrorism*, p2. Some of these elite soldiers are members of the Ku Klux Klan, have supremacist tattoos or train neo-Nazi groups.
9   Imbeault, M 2021 'L'extrême droite et l'armée au Canada et au Québec', *Collège militaire royal de Saint-Jean*, <https://www.cmrsj-rmcsj.forces.gc.ca/cb-bk/art-art/2021/art-art-2021-1-fra.asp>.
10 Bourdon, S, Brabant, J, & Suc, M 2021, 'Néonazis dans l'armée: la longue litanie des «cas isolés»', Mediapart, 16 March, viewed 31 December 2022, <https://www.mediapart.fr/journal/france/160321/neonazis-dans-l-armee-la-longue-litanie-des-cas-isoles>; Bourdon, S, Brabant, J, & Suc, M 2021, 'Une filière néonazie au sein de l'armée française', *Mediapart*, 16 March, viewed 31 December 2022, <https://www.mediapart.fr/journal/france/160321/une-filiere-neonazie-au-sein-de-l-armee-francaise>
11 Albertini, A, Souillier, L, & Schittly, R 2022 'Qui sont les militants d'extrême droite interpellés après le match France-Maroc?', *Le Monde*, 15 December, viewed 31 December 2022, <https://www.lemonde.fr/societe/article/2022/12/15/qui-sont-les-militants-d-extreme-droite-interpelles-a-paris-le-soir-de-france-maroc_6154609_3224.html>

against creating stigmatization and stereotypes.[12] However, this raises the question of the infiltration of the army by the far right. More in the centre of the spectrum, we can find groups with openly neo-Nazi soldiers too, such as the paramilitary group Wagner, whose founder Dmitri Outkine didn't hide his affiliation to Nazism.[13] This structure represented a certain attraction for a part of the far right because it did not belong to the institutional framework of the Russian army. Moreover, the mutiny perpetrated at the end of June 2023 might have shown a more political dimension. Finally, on the other side of the spectrum, some movements can display this dual military and political presence, like the Lebanese Hezbollah or Irish Republican groups. Others show increased militarism through vigilante actions. The degree of politicisation of the military can then be determined on a spectrum ranging from professional and regular armed formations at one end to openly politically oriented armed formations at the other.

Characterising the Azov regiment is challenging because its relation to the state and politics has evolved since 2014. On the one hand, its foundation as a paramilitary unit at the end of Maidan, considered a supplementary force to the regular Ukrainian army, underlines quite precise far-right initial ideological intentions, leaving doubts about the State's capacity to maintain control over it.[14] On the other hand, even in the early days of the battalion and later the regiment, several soldiers emphasised different reasons for joining it (interpersonal links, the defence of the motherland).[15] Also, the effort to integrate Azov into the Ukrainian forces in the fall of 2014 legitimises them as a regular force. It has strengthened state

---

12 Koehler, D 2022 'From Superiority to Supremacy: Exploring the Vulnerability of Military and Police Special Forces to Extreme Right Radicalization", *Studies in Conflict & Terrorism*, p3.
13 Courrier International, 2022 'Dans le Donbass, la danse macabre des "musiciens" du groupe Wagner', *Courrier International*, 29 October, viewed 31 December 2022, <https://www.courrierinternational.com/article/reportage-dans-le-donbass-la-danse-macabre-des-musiciens-du-groupe-wagnerozhu>.
14 Aliyev, H 2016 'Strong militias, weak states and armed violence: Towards a theory of 'state-parallel' paramilitaries', *Security Dialogue*, vol. 47, no. 6, pp. 498-516.
15 Colin Lebedev, A 2017 *Les combattants et les anciens combattants du Donbass: profil social, poids militaire et influence politique*, Études de l'IRSEM, 2017, no. 53.

control, seemingly forcing a specific military/political compartmentalisation favourable to greater professionalization.[16] In practice, however, several Azov combatants continued to display symbols or make statements that can be identified as far right. International media and Russian propaganda have seized on this evidence to make generalisations that at times border on the caricatural.[17]

The aim here is to propose a nuanced observation of the political ambitions of the regiment. The idea is then to understand to what extent the Azov regiment is (de) politicised. In my approach, I aim to limit overly structural positions by identifying agency within group settings. While a structure constrains an actor, he also has autonomy, influence over it, and his decision-making capacity. In this respect, I draw the structuration theory which highlights, according to Giddens, that «the constitution of agents and structures are not two independently given sets of phenomena, a dualism, but represent a duality. (...). Structure is not "external" to individuals: as memory traces, and as instantiated in social practices, it is in a certain sense more "internal" than exterior to their activities.».[18] Therefore, it seems essential to analyse more precisely the politicization of the actors within the regiment. First, through the impact of the structure on the ideological orientation of the soldiers, but also their understanding and perception of political and military issues, as well as the meaning attributed to their commitment. Combining the logic of engagement with the analysis allows us to understand better the agency dynamics of the soldiers, as well as the differentiated life paths that help us to move away from an overly structural perspective. Moreover, this approach can also help to understand their level of radicalisation, if any. Understood here in a similar way to Sommier or Della Porta & Haupt, I analyse radicalisation as a social process of progressive acceptance of illegitimate violence (in comparison to the idea of legitimate violence of the

---

16 Käihkö, I 2018 'A nation-in-the-making, in arms: control of force, strategy and the Ukrainian Volunteer Battalions', *Defence Studies*, vol. 18, no. 2, pp. 147-166.
17 Colin Lebedev, A 2017 *Les combattants et les anciens combattants du Donbass: profil social, poids militaire et influence politique*, Études de l'IRSEM, 2017, no. 53, p149.
18 Giddens, A 1984, *The constitution of society: outline of the theory of structuration*, Polity Press, Cambridge [Cambridgeshire], p25.

State) as a legitimate tool for political action.[19] In this respect, clandestine logic, *i.e.*, the development of underground and extra-legal actions outside the scope of state surveillance, can help to identify this. Then, it might be useful to question the logic of clandestinity and the profiles of radicality of (and in) the group, which could testify to an extreme ideologization reinforcing the risk factors of increased politicization of the regiment.[20]

Based on these approaches, I believe that where Azov could have taken the path of radicalisation by maintaining its militia dynamic inherited from the Patriot of Ukraine, the efforts of professionalisation and state integration have led the regiment to move closer to the other end of the politicization spectrum by seeking the standards of a professional army that relegates political issues to the civilian sphere, even if some far-right elements can still be found in the structure. This is what we will see in the following sections. I will provide some insights on the subject based on non-participant observation and semi-structured interviews during two separate fieldwork visits to Kyiv and Mariupol in 2016 and 2017. These fields allowed me to collect information on the background of 17 fighters. Four active and 13 veterans (9 involved in the civil structure, three who disengaged from the party and criticised it, and one remaining sympathizer), and to benefit from the point of view of 3 people involved in the movement, three uncommitted sympathisers and three opponents. It allows me to highlight, already at that time,

---

19 Della Porta, D, & Haupt, HG 2012 'Patterns of Radicalization in Political Activism: An introduction', *Social Science History*, vol. 36, no. 3, pp. 311-320; Sommier, I 2012 'Engagement radical, désengagement et déradicalisation. Continuum et lignes de fracture', *Lien social et Politiques*, no. 68, pp. 15-35; Sommier, I 2015 'Sentiments, affects et émotions dans l'engagement à haut risque', *Terrains/Théories*, no. 2.; Sommier, I 2019 'Radicalization Processes' in I Sommier, G Hayes & S Ollitrault (eds.), *Breaking Laws. Violence and Civil Disobedience in Protest*, Amsterdam University Press, pp. 61- 84.

20 Bosi, L, Della Porta, D, & Malthamer, S 2019 'Organizational and Institutional Approaches: social movement studies perspectives on political violence', in E. Chenoweth (ed.), *The Oxford Handbook of Terrorism*, Oxford Handbooks, pp.137-147; Della Porta, D, & Haupt, HG 2012 'Patterns of Radicalization in Political Activism: An introduction', *Social Science History*, vol. 36, no. 3, pp. 311-320; Sommier, I 2019 'Radicalization Processes' in I Sommier, G Hayes & S Ollitrault (eds.), *Breaking Laws. Violence and Civil Disobedience in Protest*, Amsterdam University Press, pp. 61- 84.

some trends that I will explain below. Afterwards, I pursued my research based on online monitoring of Azov's activities, as well as an analysis of the activist and academic literature. I will also rely on data gathered during two fieldwork visits conducted between May-August 2022 and March-April 2023, allowing me to add twenty semi-structured interviews lasting from one to four hours, completed by multiple informative interviews on the question of both far-right and left movements in Ukraine. Thus, I obtained the point of view of opposition groups which also feeds my thoughts.

The structuring influence of Azov

At its origin, Azov did not hide its political aspirations and was part of the Ukrainian nationalist far-right. The symbolic dimension of the regiment reminds us of this legacy, which is directly in line with imagery spread by traditional far-right networks. Above all, several founding members came directly from the Social-National Assembly and Patriot of Ukraine before constituting a volunteer battalion to supplement the army's weakness in the war in the Donbas and then joining the Ukrainian National Guard in the fall of 2014 to comply with the Minsk Protocol. Subsequently, several veterans, including the first commander of Azov, Andriy Biletsky, moved away from military activity to form a Civil Corps with the aspiration to defend the interests of the regiment but also to establish a first channel of political influence. Some flyers distributed and consulted at that time mentioned the military defence of Ukraine, such as the return of the Ukrainian nuclear shield or the strengthening of its forces. Others revealed political ambitions related to the defence of the right to carry weapons or the establishment of a Natiocracy. This new political regime would seek to assert the primacy of the Nation. Gradually, this Civil Corps became a political party, the National Corps, on October 14, 2016.

If structurally, the two entities (the military body, that is, the regiment and the political body, that is, the National Corps) were separated, it is necessary to note that essential links remained between both until 2022.[21] In 2020, Kuzmenko underlined the persistence of the political affiliations of the regiment.[22] He thus explained that "it is clear that the regiment has failed in its alleged attempts to 'depoliticise'". Throughout the year 2022, he offered several analyses on his Twitter page to emphasise the political and ideological affiliations of the regiment. He reminds us that some figures in the armed corps maintain the idea of the need for a political wing. Moreover, several regiment leaders are original members: Prokopenko, Palamar, and Berkal.[23] For example, Denys Prokopenko, current commander, hero of Ukraine and former prisoner of the Russian forces after the defence of the Azovstal factory in Mariupol, is still considered close to the former leaders of the regiment, such as Biletsky.[24] Biletsky would also retain privileged access to the regiment, participating in several of their ceremonies. For example, Colborne notes that he was at the head of a column representing the regiment during the Independence Day parade on 24 August 2020.[25] Within the regiment itself, Kuzmenko underlined the presence of Yuriy Mykhalchyshyn, a prominent far-right figure,

---

21 In the *Financial Times*, Oleksandr Alfyorov, former spokesman of the group, explains that the National Corps suspended its political activities because of the engagement in the war. See Schipani, A & Olearchyk, R 2022 'Don't confuse patriotism and Nazism': Ukraine's Azov forces face scrutiny' *Financial Times*, 29 March, viewed 31 December 2022, <https://www.ft.com/content/7191ec30-9677-423d-873c-e72b64725c2d>. It's also worth noting that some of Azov's veterans, namely members of the National Corps including Biletsky, were at the origin of the 3rd Assault Brigade (formerly SSO Azov) in 2022.
22 Kuzmenko, O 2020 'The Azov Regiment has not depoliticized', *Atlantic Council*, 19 March, viewed 31 December 2022, <https://www.atlanticcouncil.org/blogs/ukrainealert/the-azov-regiment-has-not-depoliticized/>.
23 Kuzmenko, O 2022 'In the Azov Regiment's magazine "Black sun", fighters, AR figures contemporaneously wrote that the launch of a political wing was meant to allow the Regiment to influence politics.' [Twitter], 18 May. Available from: https://twitter.com/kooleksiy/status/1526972935646371841 [Accessed 31 December 2022].
24 John, T, & Lister, T 2022 'A far-right battalion has a key role in Ukraine's resistance. Its neo-Nazi history has been exploited by Putin' *CNN*, 30 March, viewed 31 December 2022, <https://edition.cnn.com/2022/03/29/europe/ukraine-azov-movement-far-right-intl-cmd/index.html>.
25 Colborne, M 2022 *From the Fires of War: Ukraine's Azov Movement and the Global Far right, Ibidem*, Stuttgart, p459.

which would thus contradict the idea of withdrawing radical members from the military unit.[26]

Furthermore, while individual affinity can be explained by typical trajectories and a similar experience at the frontline that strengthens interpersonal ties, for Kuzmenko a particular ideological link can also be found between the National Corps and the regiment. In this regard, the journalist points to the existence of the Mykola Stsiborskiyi Khorunzhyys School (named after the theorist of Natiocracy), which is said to oversee the political and ideological training of the regiment's officers.[27] Launched in 2017 and still active in 2023, the training would involve, according to Kuzmenko, who cites the regiment's website, an "ideological" block. Furthermore, in 2019, he highlighted the support of some of the regiment's soldiers for the National Corps, directly linking their function as military personnel with the party's political involvement.[28] On the other hand, Colborne recalls the use of the same buildings in Kyiv between the regiment and the Civil Corps (the ATEK base) and the party's claim to have a military wing.[29] All these elements would indicate stronger links between the armed and political bodies. This would not ultimately fit with the idea that the regiment has been depoliticised for several years.[30] In an online media article,

---

26 Kuzmenko, O 2022 'In the Azov Regiment's magazine "Black sun", fighters, AR figures contemporaneously wrote that the launch of a political wing was meant to allow the Regiment to influence politics.' [Twitter], 18 May. Available from: https://twitter.com/kooleksiy/status/1526972935646371841 [Accessed 31 December 2022].

27 Kuzmenko, O 2022 'In the Azov Regiment's magazine "Black sun", fighters, AR figures contemporaneously wrote that the launch of a political wing was meant to allow the Regiment to influence politics.' [Twitter], 18 May. Available from: https://twitter.com/kooleksiy/status/1526972935646371841 [Accessed 31 December 2022].

28 Kuzmenko, O 2019 'Apparent active duty soldiers with firearms & Ukraine's National Guard Azov Regiment patches send regards' [Twitter], 14 march. Available from: https://twitter.com/kooleksiy/status/1106352054489006080 [Accessed 1 January 2023].

29 Colborne, M 2022 *From the Fires of War: Ukraine's Azov Movement and the Global Far right, Ibidem*, Stuttgart, p63.

30 Kuzmenko, O 2022 '@BBCRosAtkins should've covered the relationship between Biletsky's far-right Azov movement and the Azov Regiment. THREAD.' [Twitter], 27 March. Available from: https://twitter.com/kooleksiy/status/1507902044069416960 [Accessed 31 December 2022]; Kuzmenko, O 2022 'In the

Kuzmenko explains: "I believe they're absolutely part of the same movement, and I have been presenting evidence thereof"[31], a sentiment that Colborne seems to share.[32] The idea of the politicization of the regiment is also supported by more disturbing general statements by Katchanovstki, who laments the fact that "Nazis" (in his words) were national heroes and helped to pressure President Zelensky to refuse any peace agreement. He forgets that the responsibility for the war remains on the aggressor: Russia. Katchanovski thus deplores the denial of the presence of neo-Nazis in Ukraine, although he measures his discourse by refuting the idea that Ukraine is a Nazi state.[33] For Shekhovtsov, however, these links are more the result of an instrumentalisation of the political party and political movements of the "Azov" label and their military capacities than of a real politicisation of the regiment as such.[34] Colborne also highlights this instrumentalization: "Azov clearly uses the issue of veterans to cloak itself and its activities in a veneer of

---

Azov Regiment's magazine "Black sun", fighters, AR figures contemporaneously wrote that the launch of a political wing was meant to allow the Regiment to influence politics.' [Twitter], 18 May. Available from: https://twitter.com/kooleksiy/status/1526972935646371841 [Accessed 31 December 2022]; Kuzmenko, O 2022 'National Corps' senior leader Maksym Zhorin, a champion of the bill, is now a commander in SOF Azov Regiment fighting against Russian aggression.' [Twitter], 12 June. Available from: https://twitter.com/kooleksiy/status/1536017241011109889 [Accessed 31 December 2022]; Ourdan, R 2023 'Un an après la bataille de Marioupol, la brigade ukrainienne Azov retourne au combat sur le front de Zaporijia', *Le Monde*, 10 June, viewed 12 June 2023, <https://www.lemonde.fr/international/article/2023/06/10/un-an-apres-la-bataille-de-marioupol-la-brigade-ukrainienne-azov-retourne-au-combat-sur-le-front-de-zaporijia_6177026_3210.html>.

31   Marcetic, B 2022 'Whitewashing Nazis Doesn't Help Ukraine', *Jacobin*, 7 July, <https://jacobin.com/2022/04/ukraine-russia-putin-azov-neo-nazis-western-media>.
32   Colborne, M 2022 *From the Fires of War: Ukraine's Azov Movement and the Global Far right*, *Ibidem*, Stuttgart, p148.
33   Mastracci, D, & Cosh, A 2022 'Media Once Called Azov Neo-Nazis. Now They Hide That Fact', *Passage*, 24 August, viewed 31 December 2022, <https://readpassage.com/media-once-called-azov-neo-nazis-now-they-hide-that-fact/>.
34   Shekhovtsov, A 2022 'How the West enabled genocide in Mariupol with its misguided Azov obsession', *Euromaidan Press*, 2nd April, viewed 31 December, <https://euromaidanpress.com/2022/04/02/how-the-west-enabled-genocide-in-mariupol-with-its-misguided-azov-obsession/>.

patriotism to make what they do more presentable for the mainstream".[35]

However, the fact remains that some soldiers in the regiment maintained a political perspective. In 2016 and 2017, some of them, veterans or still serving combatants, shared with me a rhetoric of the dual enemy: an external enemy that makes armed struggle on the front necessary and an internal enemy that requires political engagement.[36] VO15 was also a former activist of Patriot of Ukraine who chose to remain in the regiment, showing, in his case, a trajectory of continuous activist and military commitment. In this respect, the split in perceptions of the world between an "us" and a "them" was strongly noted and tends to be reinforced within the armed structure. Indeed, the group aspires to solidify the unity of the members of the regiment through physical (establishment of a body discipline with the adoption of a military *hexis*, specific salutes), aesthetic (symbolic and clothing standardization), and oral (discourse of uniqueness and exceptionalisation of the group) mechanisms. The transition to the use of a "war name" could also symbolise the entry into a new social life.[37] In addition to this dimension, a set of symbolic rewards can contribute to staying in the structure.[38] First, the social valorization of the fighting experience. But also, the affective dimension that can be found with the multiple references to "a new family" and to "brotherhood".[39] These dynamics can be seen as vectors for radicalisation, especially when there is an ideological aspect that is deployed in a relatively closed

---

35 Colborne, M 2022 *From the Fires of War: Ukraine's Azov Movement and the Global Far right, Ibidem*, Stuttgart, p145.
36 Interview with VO17 & VO15.
37 Sommier, I 2012 'Engagement radical, désengagement et déradicalisation. Continuum et lignes de fracture', *Lien social et Politiques*, no. 68, pp. 15-35.; Sommier, I 2019 'Radicalization Processes' in I Sommier, G Hayes & S Ollitrault (eds.), *Breaking Laws. Violence and Civil Disobedience in Protest*, Amsterdam University Press, pp. 61- 84.
38 Gaxie, D 1977 'Économie des partis et rétributions du militantisme', *Revue française de science politique*, vol. 27, no. 1, pp. 123-154.
39 Sommier, I 2015 'Sentiments, affects et émotions dans l'engagement à haut risque', *Terrains/Théories*, no. 2.; Sommier, I 2019 'Radicalization Processes' in I Sommier, G Hayes & S Ollitrault (eds.), *Breaking Laws. Violence and Civil Disobedience in Protest*, Amsterdam University Press, pp. 61- 84.

social environment. Referring to Likhachev, Colborne underlines that "There reportedly has been at least some degree of indoctrination of far-right ideas in the Regiment; there have been reported cases of young men, seemingly apolitical, entered in the Regiment and within six months becoming neo-Nazis".[40] Thus, the Regiment itself tends to unify individual *habitus*[41] and may contribute to shaping the actors' perceptions reinforced by the dynamics of a high-risk commitment.[42]

Nevertheless, as Colin Lebedev rightly noted, the markers mentioned above of unity "can be found in many other Ukrainian armed corps and do not allow one to conclude that there is a specificity of practices within Azov".[43] As we shall see below, in the actors' discourse, representations placed great emphasis on the exceptionalism of their operational skills directed against Russian forces. These different elements could be more a result of unification related to operational challenges and reflect relatively standard configurations of the volunteer battalions formed in 2014, which the state gradually tried to regularise.[44] Therefore, the regiment's professionalization efforts could tend to relegate the political perspectives of some of their members to the background or civilian life. If any of the characteristics mentioned above can be traced back to a group's radical trajectory, an essential factor of radicality could be based on clandestinity, which was not observed.[45] The integration

---

40   Colborne, M 2022 *From the Fires of War: Ukraine's Azov Movement and the Global Far right*, Ibidem, Stuttgart, p63.
41   See footnote 5 for a definition.
42   Crettiez, X 2011 '« *High Risk Activism* » : essai sur le processus de radicalisation violente (première partie)', *Pôle Sud*, 2011, n° 34, no 1, pp. 45-60.; Crettiez, X 2011 '« *High Risk Activism* » : Essai sur le processus de radicalisation violente: (seconde partie)', *Pôle Sud*, 2011, n° 35, no 2, pp. 97-112.
43   Colin Lebedev, A 2017 *Les combattants et les anciens combattants du Donbass : profil social, poids militaire et influence politique*, Études de l'IRSEM, 2017, no. 53., p66. All the French sources quoted in this chapter have been translated by the author.
44   Fomitchova, A 2021 'Les volontaires dans la formation de l'appareil militaire urkainien (2014-2018)', *Revue d'études comparatives Est-Ouest*, vol.1, no. 1, pp. 137-170.
45   This does not remove the possibility of a clandestine dimension in Azov's actions (as there is for the movement's political groups). But it has not been observed within the Regiment. It appears as an official state structure, which removes its clandestine character against the state. See: Bosi, L, Della Porta, D, &

of Azov and the professionalization of this armed corps could lead to a more nuanced understanding of its politicisation.

Military professionalization and differentiated approaches to commitment

In 2016, Karagiannis explained that "the gradual professionalization of the battalions is likely to attract a different group of volunteers shortly".[46] Shekhovtsov agrees, stating that: "Azov today is a highly professional special operations detachment. Not a political organization, not a militia, not a far-right battalion.".[47] The Azov regiment would no longer be a political organization and its command structure remains to be distinguished from the National Corps, which gave the image of a political arm to an armed corp. If ties continue, this would be more the result of instrumentalist political propaganda of the National Corps than an empirical reality equally promoted by the regiment. An article by Davidzon in the online media *Tablet* highlights the rapid dilution of the original post-Maidan composition of the regiment and emphasises the political will to "normalise" Azov. For him, "even the unit's 'right-wing' ideological heritage has diminished, as circumstances have forced it to professionalise".[48] Similar findings are made by

---

Malthamer, S 2019 'Organizational and Institutional Approaches: social movement studies perspectives on political violence', in E. Chenoweth (ed.), *The Oxford Handbook of Terrorism*, Oxford Handbooks, pp. 137-147; Sommier, I 2019 'Radicalization Processes' in I Sommier, G Hayes & S Ollitrault (eds.), *Breaking Laws. Violence and Civil Disobedience in Protest*, Amsterdam University Press, pp. 61- 84.

46 Karagiannis, E 2016 'Ukrainian volunteer fighters in the eastern front: ideas, political-social norms and emotions as mobilization mechanisms', *Southeast European and Black Sea Studies*, vol. 16, no. 1, p143.

47 Shekhovtsov, A 2022 'How the West enabled genocide in Mariupol with its misguided Azov obsession', *Euromaidan Press*, 2nd April, viewed 31 December, <https://euromaidanpress.com/2022/04/02/how-the-west-enabled-genocide-in-mariupol-with-its-misguided-azov-obsession/>.

48 Davidzon, V 2022 'The Defenders of Mariupol', *Tablet*, 18 May, viewed 31 December 2022, <https://www.tabletmag.com/sections/news/articles/defenders-of-mariupol-azov>.

Likhachev.[49] From his standpoint, while the regiment's beginnings showed a transparent far-right extremist background, not all members and founders shared it. Even more, most of the far-right members left at the end of 2014. He then insists on the diversity of the members of the armed corps, specifies that there is no direct relation between both structures and that "the Armed Forces of Ukraine and the National Guard are outside of politics". Regarding positions within Azov in 2016, VO6, a veteran representing the Civil Corps at the time of our meeting, was insistent that there was diversity in terms of education, religion, and ethnicity:

> We officially have 1,500 people in Azov. 76% are Christian, Orthodox and Greek-Catholic. There are a few Catholics and a few Greek Catholics, but the majority are Orthodox. 19% are pagans. There's one Buddhist and one Muslim. But these were anonymous surveys. Most are Ukrainian, there are ethnic Russians — Ukrainian but ethnic Russian —, and Ukrainian Belarussians. There are some Polish Ukrainians, a few Jews, and a few gypsies.

Since 2014, Azov has been integrated into the National Guard, paving the way for gradual control by the Ukrainian state. As Colin Lebedev says, the integration into the Ministry of the Interior "transformed the identity of the group of fighters who had to align with the rules and norms of the regular armed forces".[50] This has helped to start the professionalisation of the regiment, which forces the armed corps to no longer be able to follow the same basis as before. According to Aliyev at the time, Azov was a "state parallel militia", benefiting from the weakness of the regular army, from representatives on the political scene, from funding that allowed them a certain independence and from an agenda that aimed to legitimise their actions.[51] In this context, for Aliyev, "as long as state interests relate to militias' goals, paramilitaries avoid challenging or

---

49   Likhachev, V 2022 'Euromaidan SOS: honest answers to the most common questions about AZOV in the West', *CCL*, 3 April, viewed 31 December 2022, <https://ccl.org.ua/en/claims/euromaidan-sos-honest-answers-to-the-most-common-questions-about-azov-in-the-west/>.

50   Colin Lebedev, A 2022 *Jamais frères? Ukraine et Russie : une tragédie postsoviétique*, Seuil, Paris, p185.

51   Aliyev, H 2016 'Strong militias, weak states and armed violence: Towards a theory of 'state-parallel' paramilitaries', *Security Dialogue*, vol. 47, no. 6, pp. 498-516.

replacing the government".[52] And thus, Azov sometimes refused to follow the orders of the military hierarchy, as was the case in April 2015 in Shirokino.[53] However, as Käihkö points out, the Ukrainian state undertook a dynamic of "undermining", "co-opting", "incorporation" and "coercion" of the volunteer battalions, thus helping to maintain and strengthen its authority.[54] This generally appears to have been effective since Fomitchova explains that "we do not see a phenomenon of territorialization of armed groups after 2015, nor the emergence of "warlords".[55] In this perspective, the regiment was withdrawn from the frontline in 2015, it maintained only occasional missions over there. For VO12, a veteran and former activist of the National Corps when we met, this was a restoration of control by the authorities: "The authorities understood that they made a big mistake by leaving the soccer ultras unwatched. So, they took Azov out of the war zone and are now keeping them in the training camp. They can't do anything". Journalist Ponomarenko also asserts that this withdrawal could be a political choice, testifying to the state's desire for greater control over the regiment.[56] This disengagement of the regiment seems to have been respected, showing a certain degree of subordination.[57]

---

52 Aliyev, H 2016 'Strong militias, weak states and armed violence: Towards a theory of 'state-parallel' paramilitaries', *Security Dialogue*, vol. 47, no. 6, p503.
53 The regiment was deployed there during a counter-offensive towards Ilovaïsk. Nevertheless, they refused to flee the village and succeeded in imposing this choice to their commanders.
54 Käihkö, I 2018 'A nation-in-the-making, in arms: control of force, strategy and the Ukrainian Volunteer Battalions', *Defence Studies*, vol. 18, no. 2, pp. 147-166.
55 Fomitchova, A 2021 'Les volontaires dans la formation de l'appareil militaire urkainien (2014-2018)', *Revue d'études comparatives Est-Ouest*, vol.1, no. 1, pp. 137-170.
56 Ponomarenko, I 2018 'Even confined to base, controversy dogs Azov Regiment', *Kyiv Post*, 16 January, viewed 31 December 2022, <https://www.kyivpost.com/ukraine-politics/even-confined-base-controversy-dogs-azov-regiment.html>.
57 Ponomarenko, I 2017 'After 2 years of training, Azov Regiment itches to return to war', *Kyiv Post*, 1st September, viewed 31 December 2022, https://www.kyivpost.com/ukraine-politics/two-years-training-azov-regiment-itches-return-war.html; Ponomarenko, I 2018 'Even confined to base, controversy dogs Azov Regiment', *Kyiv Post*, 16 January, viewed 31 December 2022, <https://www.kyivpost.com/ukraine-politics/even-confined-base-controversy-dogs-azov-regiment.html>; Ponomarenko, I 2019 'After more than 3 years in bases, Azov Regiment returns to front ', *Kyiv Post*, 1 February, viewed 31 December 2022,

Yet, this demobilisation appears to have brought some fractures in the political perspectives attached to the regiment, contributing to the reinforcement of an image more focused on military issues. Indeed, conservative values and far-right views can be found and are visible in the trajectories of some of the people I met. However, with the withdrawal from the front, several soldiers decided to leave for political reasons. VO11 demobilised at the end of 2015, and an active National Corps member explained to me: "I didn't want to stay and wait and do nothing. Now the government wants us to avoid fighting. I feel more useful here. If necessary, I will go back to fight". VO15 made a similar observation, but who decided to remain in the military:

> It's a kind of play between our government and the guys. We are forbidden to go to the frontline. We just cannot do it. We should follow the rules we don't want to follow. This is why some guys decided that they can be employed in Kyiv, be a part of the National Corps than being here, sitting here and very often without some action.

VO17 added: "And there are some guys who were born as military.". Thus, if the political orientation of these soldiers is, in these cases, undeniable, these testimonies let us see an essential aspect of the understanding of the meaning of their military commitment: for those who remain within the regiment, the priority is given to military combat. In this respect, they make a clear distinction in their commitments. If they want to continue within the regiment, it is for military reasons. Political commitment is part of civilian life:

> VO15: But in case I would decide that I will be more useful in Kyiv, I will for sure move to Kyiv (or Kharkiv says VO16). But now I'm a part of the military regiment. Not a political party.
> Me: And why do you prefer to stay in the military part?
> VO15: It was my decision. Somebody should be here.

A year earlier, in 2016, VO10 shared this same compartmentalisation with me:

<https://www.kyivpost.com/ukraine-politics/after-more-than-three-years-in-bases-azov-regiment-returns-to-front.html>.

HAS THE AZOV REGIMENT DEPOLITICIZED? 157

> You know... We are soldiers for now. And the regiment hum... Can't take part in politics. So the regiment has no relationship with the government. It has commandments, it has orders but there is Civil Corps that has some political action, some relationship. But not the regiment.

This differentiation between a strictly military activity and a civilian one does not necessarily indicate an absence of politicization. This is especially true since "the boundary between civilians and soldiers was very blurred in the first phase of the war".[58] However, the insistence on this distinction tends, already in 2016 and 2017, to make the political perspective less prominent as a perspective of military action, relegated to the second place of the dynamic of the regiment. This reminds us of the expectations observed in the regular armed forces, which tend to reiterate this differentiation. However, in Azov like in other armed forces, it would be absurd to think that a soldier removes his/her civilian and political coat and gives up his/her individual views once he/she wears his/her uniform. The dichotomies between the civilian and military selves seem artificial and are often rhetorical procedures that are difficult to apply daily. Moreover, we must be careful about language's false neutralisation (or depoliticisation).[59] This makes it necessary to rethink our view of apoliticism: even in the regular armed forces,[60] people are not immune to the power relations at work in the society in which they are embedded.[61] This is also the case in Ukraine, where it's

---

58   Colin Lebedev, A 2022 *Jamais frères? Ukraine et Russie : une tragédie postsoviétique*, Seuil, Paris, p174.
59   Bleiker, R, & Chou, M 2010 'Nietzsche's Style: On Language, Knowledge and Power in International Relations', in C. Moore and C. Farrands (eds.), *International Relations Theory and Philosophy: Interpretive Dialogues*, Routledge, New York, pp. 8-19.; Shapiro, M 1989 'Textualising Global Politics', in J Der Derian & M Shapiro (eds.), *International/Intertextual Relations: Postmodern Readings of World Politics*, Lexington Books, Lexigton, pp. 11-22.
60   Golby, J, & Karlin, M 2020 'The case for rethinking the politicization of the military', *Brookings*, 12 June, viewed 31 December 2022, <https://www.brookings.edu/blog/order-from-chaos/2020/06/12/the-case-for-rethinking-the-politicization-of-the-military/>.
61   Allen, H 2012 'Gender, Sexuality and the Military Model of U.S. National Community' In T. Mayer (ed), *Gender Ironies of Nationalism: Sexing the Nation*, Routledge, London, pp. 82-101; Spike Peterson, V 2010 'Gendered Identities, Ideologies, and Practices in the Context of War and Militarism' in L Sjboerg &

impossible for anyone to completely lose their situated point of view in their armed engagement, and it might influence some specific behaviours. However, the political perception is not the driving force behind their operational action. Moreover, surviving on the frontline, the importance of military experience, and the ability to manage stress are often underlined priorities in armed units. This is particularly noticeable in the interviews conducted since 2022, where it is, above all, survival that is emphasized by the people I met, beyond any ideological dimension. And this is also what Ourdan highlighted in his recent report about the Azov brigade.[62]

Of course, we should keep in mind that, unlike in regular armies, ideological training still seems to be practised within the structure. However, if some have been able to radicalise within the group, it is difficult to establish the systematic level of ideological receptivity of the soldiers compared to the military dimension of their training. Anecdotally, VO10 also told me that the reading material provided by the regiment did not necessarily constitute their primary sources of information, preferring external sources — emphasised as plural but refusing to name them — found using the internet[63]. On one of their military bases at this time, active in Mariupol, apart from the explicit symbolism of their chevron, the visible references underlined more the perspective of inscribing the regiment in a military history specific to Ukraine. The murals observed sought to mark a continuity from the knights and then Cossack forces to the contemporary soldiers. The common point of these murals is to refer to movements of struggle against invading forces and is part of the national autonomist memory of Ukraine.[64]

S Via (eds.), *Gender, War, and Militarism: Feminist Perspectives*, Praeger, Santa Barbara, pp. 17-29.

62 Ourdan, R 2023 'Un an après la bataille de Marioupol, la brigade ukrainienne Azov retourne au combat sur le front de Zaporijia', *Le Monde*, 10 June, viewed 12 June 2023, <https://www.lemonde.fr/international/article/2023/06/10/un-an-apres-la-bataille-de-marioupol-la-brigade-ukrainienne-azov-retourne-au-combat-sur-le-front-de-zaporijia_6177026_3210.html>.

63 As such, sources found and shared on the internet may be a more important factor of influence than the regiment itself.

64 de Franqueville, B, & Nonjon, A 2022 'Mémoire et sentiment national en Ukraine', *La Vie des Idées*, 17 May, viewed 31 December 2022, <https://laviedesidees.fr/Memoire-et-sentiment-national-en-Ukraine.html>.

However, if we observe the sharing of the Ukrainian national imaginary, it does not allow us to evaluate a political radicality, even less neo-Nazi, nor to establish a caricatural generalisation. On the other hand, the power dynamics observed demonstrated a certain virilism, which again does not allow us to establish the politically exceptional character of the regiment. Regarding references to Nazism, they were either declined by the soldiers or, if observed, were associated with "trolling" in response to Russian propaganda. This denial of structural neo-Nazism has been raised in many analyses of Azov, such as the research of Karagiannis[65] or Colborne[66]. However, we should not forget the difficulty for the researcher to access subcultural references delivered in restricted circles and which mark the border between outsider and insider.[67] For example, the nuance regarding the possibility of a double discourse, an official one for outsiders and a less polished one for insiders, is visible within the National Corps, and it is important to remain mindful of this.[68] Still, the discourse of the distinction between civilian and military fields of action, added to the state control over the regiment, could corroborate the perspective of a professionalisation desired and put forward by the soldiers. In particular, because of the need for legitimacy, military action is considered to be inescapable from the political decisions of the Ukrainian authorities. This desire for

---

65   Karagiannis, E 2016 'Ukrainian volunteer fighters in the eastern front: ideas, political-social norms and emotions as mobilization mechanisms', *Southeast European and Black Sea Studies*, vol. 16, no. 1, pp. 139-153.
66   Colborne, M 2022 *From the Fires of War: Ukraine's Azov Movement and the Global Far right*, Ibidem, Stuttgart.
67   Gomza, I, & Zajaczkowski, J 2019 'Black Sun Rising: Political Opportunity Structure Perceptions and Institutionalization of the Azov Movement in Post-Euromaidan Ukraine', *Nationalities Papers*, vol. 47, no. 5, p789.
68   This is particularly true of the Azov logo, claimed to be an I and an N intertwined, but reminding us of the Wolfsangel, and the use of the black sun. The continued use of these references remains questionable. However, in addition to the fact that the far-right imagery associated with the logo might have probably not been reconsidered, it is above all the regiment's military success that has contributed to giving the logo a new meaning (heroism, symbol of resistance, remembrance of the common struggle). This may explain why it has been maintained over time. See also Colborne, M 2022 *From the Fires of War: Ukraine's Azov Movement and the Global Far right*, Ibidem, Stuttgart.

legitimacy is reflected in the words of VO6 and contrasts with the discourse of the dual enemy that others emphasised to me:

> It is the General Staff that directs all actions and parts of the army. We are part of the national guard. They tell us to come closer, to move away, to rush there or there. But inside Azov, we decide what to do ourselves. But we are part of the army and the organization of the Ukrainian army basically. We do what we have to do. We are subject to general orders.

Therefore, there is this will to show, at least from a military point of view, the control of the State. This discourse contrasts with other volunteers or the political approach of military action. We can also note that in military matters, soldiers and veterans stressed this professionalization a lot. First, they wanted to show me their operational capacities. During a visit to their base, within the limits of confidentiality, the soldiers I met valued their material resources above all. But this was also reflected in their speeches, especially when they insisted on their motivation compared to the Ukrainian army and other volunteer battalions, and when they narrated their military prowess. They also emphasised on their NATO standards and "Western-style special forces training".[69]

It is mainly the acquired skills of the regiment's soldiers and the operational quality of the structure that has conferred their legitimacy to act over the last years. The operational redeployment of Azov in 2019 to the front and the departure of Avakov on 13 July 2021 finally seemed to complete this dynamic of state control over the regiment, while the National Corps and affiliated vigilante structures continued their activities and protest actions against the new authorities in place.[70] Finally, considering the trajectory of the regiment, we see that where Azov could have taken the path of radicalisation, it is instead a path of normalisation or even

---

69 Ponomarenko, I 2018 'Even confined to base, controversy dogs Azov Regiment', *Kyiv Post*, 16 January, viewed 31 December 2022, <https://www.kyivpost.com/ukraine-politics/even-confined-base-controversy-dogs-azov-regiment.html>.

70 Ponomarenko, I 2019 'After more than 3 years in bases, Azov Regiment returns to front ', *Kyiv Post,* 1 February, viewed 31 December 2022, <https://www.kyivpost.com/ukraine-politics/after-more-than-three-years-in-bases-azov-regiment-returns-to-front.html> .

regularisation[71]. While it may be acknowledged that the use of militias can be seen as "a cheap instrument for the projection of state power" and that "the proliferation of armed groups may also undermine state authority" (through violence, instrumentalisation by an elite, and the risks of destabilisation in a post-war society, it would appear that this was not the case with the Azov regiment).[72] State control may have helped to reduce the risks. In this regard, several analyses highlight that repression can be a factor of radicalisation but also in the de-escalation of violence.[73] Yet while combatants and veterans may have employed the register of repression, it did not lead to protest movements within the regiment that reinforced the empowerment and clandestinely of the structure by supporting violent dynamics and a total loss of control. Moreover, the movement's low political success could testify to a rather low level of social acceptance of violence, which would contribute to diminishing the regiment's legitimacy if it were politically engaged.[74] These signs seem indicative of a weakened political dynamic within the regiment. But then, how can we understand and better grasp the importance and impact of the ideological dimension for the actors? It is especially the meaning of the commitment that some soldiers explained to me that can show a greater or lesser ideological strength of Azov. At least, ideology appeared as a non-systematic motive of engagement.

---

71 Moreover, the creation of the 3rd Assault Brigade (formerly SSO Azov) suggests different paths, albeit close.
72 Jentzsch, C, Kalyvas, SN, & Schubiger, LI 2015 'Militias in Civil Wars', *Journal of Conflict Resolution*, vol. 59, no. 5, p764.
73 Bosi, L, Della Porta, D, & Malthamer, S 2019 'Organizational and Institutional Approaches: social movement studies perspectives on political violence', in E. Chenoweth (ed.), *The Oxford Handbook of Terrorism*, Oxford Handbooks, pp. 137-147; Sommier, I 2019 'Radicalization Processes' in I Sommier, G Hayes & S Ollitrault (eds.), *Breaking Laws. Violence and Civil Disobedience in Protest*, Amsterdam University Press, pp. 61- 84.
74 Bosi, L, Della Porta, D, & Malthamer, S 2019 'Organizational and Institutional Approaches: social movement studies perspectives on political violence', in E. Chenoweth (ed.), *The Oxford Handbook of Terrorism*, Oxford Handbooks, pp. 137-147.

An ideological commitment to be nuanced: what emerges from individual trajectories

It has been recalled many times that the far-right remains relatively marginal in Ukrainian politics. Goujon reminds us that the representatives of Right Sector and Freedom "obtained only 0.7% and 1.16% of the votes in the presidential elections of May 2014, and then 1.8% and 4.7% (6 deputies) in the parliamentary elections of October 2014".[75] Although visible, and especially in the streets, their overestimation is more related to propaganda effects.[76] AA1, an anarchist volunteer of the Territorial Defence Forces, also explained to me in July 2022 that "what we need to say is that the rumours, circulating among European left, about total dominance of far-right both in Ukrainian politics in general and in the streets in particular — are false, although nationalism is wide-spread and Nazis/rightwing radicals are visible". The electoral success of far-right movements did not increase during the years of war. The various joint movements and parties were limited to around 2% in the presidential and parliamentary elections of 2019. On the scale of Ukrainian society, this political weakness shows their continued marginalisation, failing to capitalise on the military to increase their success.

Amongst the incentives for some soldiers to enrol, we can also find the marginalisation of the ideological dimension affiliated with the far-right. Nationalism, in its relation to the defence of the country, has become more mainstream but does not contribute to an *ipso facto* agreement with the more extreme ideological principles that the National Corps may carry in their political program and perspective.[77] Certainly, many of the soldiers in the early days of the regiment were part of a continuing commitment originating from

---

75 Goujon, A 2022 *L'Ukraine de l'indépendance à la guerre*, Le Cavalier Bleu, Paris, p106.
76 Colin Lebedev, A 2022 *Jamais frères? Ukraine et Russie : une tragédie postsoviétique*, Seuil, Paris, 222p.
77 de Franqueville, B, & Nonjon, A 2022b 'Mémoire et sentiment national en Ukraine', *La Vie des Idées*, 17 May, viewed 31 December 2022, <https://laviedesidees.fr/Memoire-et-sentiment-national-en-Ukraine.html>

Patriot of Ukraine, hooligan circles (estimated between 50% and 65% of the fighters at the time), and pre-existing ultra-nationalist networks whose recruitment may have been strengthened by social ties developed during the Maidan.[78] As said earlier, 10-20% of the unit was considered neo-Nazi in 2015.[79] Some soldiers perceived the Azov movement as a complementary whole, an agent of a larger social movement. VO9 and VO10, both soldiers when we met, explained to me:

> VO10: I thought about that thing. But Azov had a head target. After war change the society, but without machine guns, without riffles.
> VO9: Nowadays, Civil corps is maybe the largest social movement in the country. It tries to influence politics. In a country about corruption. You know...

However, nuances remain necessary. According to Karagiannis, far-right forces participate in the construction of motivations for engagement through ideas (the framing of the conflict), social and political norms (the sense of duty and responsibility), and emotions (the love of the country and the will to defend it, or solidarity for the populations under attack).[80] Nonetheless, the meaning given to these elements is not necessarily the same for all actors. Moreover, this construction does not demonstrate mechanisms exclusive to the far-right. Other soldiers were motivated by a desire to contribute to the fight against Russian aggression and a logic of political opposition to Putin, considered a common basis for recruitment at the time. This point is still emphasised today by veterans, including those from Azov, for whom the "foremost concern was resisting an external and vastly more powerful aggressor".[81] Furthermore, in the engagement process of some soldiers, it is instead the

---

78 Colborne, M 2022 *From the Fires of War: Ukraine's Azov Movement and the Global Far right*, Ibidem, Stuttgart, pp.33-34.
79 Colborne, M 2022 *From the Fires of War: Ukraine's Azov Movement and the Global Far right*, Ibidem, Stuttgart, p62.
80 Karagiannis, E 2016 'Ukrainian volunteer fighters in the eastern front: ideas, political-social norms and emotions as mobilization mechanisms', *Southeast European and Black Sea Studies*, vol. 16, no. 1, pp. 139-153.
81 Mogelson, L 2022 'How Ukrainians Saved Their Capital', *New Yorker*, 9 May, viewed 31 December 2022, <https://www.newyorker.com/magazine/2022/05/09/how-ukrainians-saved-their-capital>.

operational quality of Azov and its apparent legalism that may have been an essential factor of attractiveness almost since its beginning. For example, VO1, who, unlike others quoted afterwards, did not continue within the movement, explained to me in 2015 that in addition to his feeling of resisting Russian aggression, he chose to join Azov because his friends had gone there. He also said: "At the beginning, there was much choice between the different troops. There were battalions with high salaries (...). But I saw in Azov a good organisation and I had a good image of it. I think I made the right choice because many volunteer battalions no longer exist". He then added: "But since Azov presented itself in practice as the best battalion as an organisation etc., that they did a better job than the others, people noticed this and perhaps dissatisfied with the management of their command, came and changed for Azov". For their part, VO5, VO11 and VO17, continued their commitment to the Civil Corps and then the National Corps. And VO16, a foreign fighter, did not hide his familiarity with pre-existing extreme right-wing networks. However, they also expressed certain motivations other than ideology in their choice to join Azov:

> VO5: I'm Russian. And I came to war for my Ukrainian brothers and against Putin regime. Because some of my neighbors went to war in the east of Ukraine on the Russian side, on the separatist side. And they... hum... Russian military... They became Russian military contractors, and they went to fight. After I know this, I think "Yes Russia is waging war against Ukraine and trying to take some part of their land. Putin's regime... hum... make slaves of Russians and he wants to return Ukrainians to slavery too, in the Soviet Union".
>
> VO11: There was a problem with legality, and they didn't have weapons. In Azov, we were offered help for the family if I ever died. Then it was part of the national guard. Being part of it meant that you had weapons and tanks. And there was an opportunity for growth.
>
> VO14: No. I was choosing between Pravy Sektor and Azov. But I thought that Azov was better organized in a more open and transparent way. So I chose Azov.
>
> VO16: Because our friend from this other Ukrainian nationalist organization, he has a good character, we trusted him and thought he is a good person. And we ask him if he knew anything about where we could help more. And... It was more... hum... we could have been in any organization. We

could have been in... I don't know Donbas, Pravy Sektor. No, it was the organization of Azov because we could have the opportunity... And... Our good friend went there, and he asked us. If we had a good friend who came to another organization, I think we would have just ended up there.

VO17: I had three real reasons for choosing Azov. The first was that friends went there. Second, Azov was the armed group that liberated the city. And then, they really had the better organization.

While some of the fighters and veterans interviewed in 2016 and 2017 did not necessarily say they were at odds with the political dimension of the Azov movement, this was not one of the primary motives for their involvement, which can be plural.[82] This aligns with the same analyses provided and confirmed by Fomitchova, who also highlights the "unpreparedness and lack of resources of the regular armed forces" as motivations to join volunteer units.[83] The reasons for the choice of a structure are plural and the units to be joined. Indeed, the outbreak of war in the Donbas in 2014 contributed to the emergence of multiple volunteer battalions. Colin Lebedev points out that if around thirty battalions were created in March-April 2014, only a minority came from "ultranationalist movements, such as Right Sector, partly coming from the eponymous group on the Maidan, or Azov (...).".[84] According to Karagianis there were four types of battalions: ones formed by local authorities, ones by private citizens, ones acting as police patrol, and ones related to far-right parties.[85] It is instead an ideological diversity that one finds at the level of the individuals joining the army or the various voluntary formations. For example, before 2022, structurally, leftists were unable to develop in the war effort, especially

---

82 Colin Lebedev, A 2022 *Jamais frères? Ukraine et Russie : une tragédie postsoviétique*, Seuil, Paris, pp.171-172.
83 Fomitchova, A 2021 'Les volontaires dans la formation de l'appareil militaire urkainien (2014-2018)', *Revue d'études comparatives Est-Ouest*, vol.1, no. 1, p149.
84 Colin Lebedev, A 2022 *Jamais frères? Ukraine et Russie : une tragédie postsoviétique*, Seuil, Paris, p171.
85 Karagiannis, E 2016 'Ukrainian volunteer fighters in the eastern front : ideas, political-social norms and emotions as mobilization mechanisms', *Southeast European and Black Sea Studies*, vol. 16, no. 1, p143.

in terms of armed participation. Individual mobilisation was much more visible, and they joined different units.[86]

In this plurality, Azov has developed military skills that attract beyond ideological logics. Several authors underline a variety of political profiles within the regiment, like Umland.[87] In this regard, Colborne explains that "the ideological orientations of those who fight and have fought within the Regiment isn't always as clear-cut as assumed".[88] In an interview with the French newspaper *Libération*, Likhachev points out that "even in the summer of 2014, not all the fighters in Azov were from the ultra-right. I knew an anarchist who served in Azov and a former participant in Anti-Maidan (...), for whom Russian aggression had become inappropriate".[89] In 2022-2023, too, the people I met told me that priority in the military was given to combat experience and operational quality, considering that ideologies would no longer matter if everyone died. Thinking about political divisions is then seen as a question for the rear. B6, in connection with Azov, explained to me that most soldiers are in the east, fighting Russia. Many have joined because of the regiment's elite image[90]. AA2, an anti-authoritarian activist I met in 2023, explained to me the case of an anarchist who decided to join Azov because they were the only ones recruiting when he was looking to change units to join the front in 2022. For this

---

86 Channell-Justice, E 2022 *Without the State? Self-Organization and Political Activism in Ukraine*, University of Toronto Press, Toronto, 280 p.
87 Umland, A 2019 'Irregular Militias and Radical Nationalism in Post-Euromaydan Ukraine: The Prehistory and Emergence of the 'Azov' Battalion in 2014.' *Terrorism and Political Violence*, vol. 31, no. 1, pp. 105–31
88 Colborne, M 2022 *From the Fires of War: Ukraine's Azov Movement and the Global Far right, Ibidem*, Stuttgart, p62.
89 Monaco, C, & Horn, A 2022 'Quelle est l'importance du régiment Azov, cette unité ukrainienne fondée par des proches de la mouvance néonazie?', *Libération*, 8 March, viewed 31 December 2022, <https://www.liberation.fr/checknews/quelle-est-limportance-du-regiment-azov-cette-unite-ukrainienne-fondee-par-des-proches-de-la-mouvance-neonazie-20220308_6UPAODEHPVCCBA5Z5BQ2QQZKTQ/>.
90 As Ourdan also points out: Ourdan, R 2023 'Un an après la bataille de Marioupol, la brigade ukrainienne Azov retourne au combat sur le front de Zaporijia', Le Monde, 10 June, viewed 12 June 2023, <https://www.lemonde.fr/international/article/2023/06/10/un-an-apres-la-bataille-de-marioupol-la-brigade-ukrainienne-azov-retourne-au-combat-sur-le-front-de-zaporijia_6177026_3210.html >.

anarchist, it wasn't a question of ideology but of common resistance for their survival. AA2 explained, "Like you know, closer you're coming to the frontline, more of... like... Political borders are smashed, blurred". AA1, the anarchist fighter of the Territorial Defence Forces mentioned earlier, would tend to confirm this diversity. His oppositional relationship with the far-right allows him to appreciate the threat it may represent accurately. However, he offered a relatively nuanced view that tends to summarise the question of Azov's politicisation:

> In Azov, there are a lot of apolitical people who just wanted to join the unit with big reputation. However, in this unit, the positions of nazis are still very strong including command, without saying about affiliated political bodies like National Corps which I have very negative opinion about. However, I appreciate heroic resistance of Azov in besieged Mariupol[91].

Thus, the contribution and operational respect are underlined. The sense of oppositional political commitment is expressed not against the regiment itself but against the political organizations that claim affiliation. This is not to deny the presence of radicals but rather to provide a more nuanced approach. This tendency towards diversity of profiles has continued as the regiment has become more professional and the National Corps has developed. The passage through the armed corps may have constituted factors of radicalisation, especially with its totalising aspect, the tools of justifications of violence that can be brought and the emotional experience that this commitment generates.[92] However, this radicality does not necessarily turn into a political radicality that is openly linked to the ideological drivers of the party. Even more, it would seem that the paths and logic of engagement highlight different trajectories that sometimes deviate from the dynamics of radicalisation. In this sense, it seems more relevant to consider the political career of individuals and question the continuation of the commitment to the

---

[91] It should be noted here that the use of the term "Nazi" is often employed in movements opposed to the far-right, in the same way as "fascism", and is the result of a process of labeling that goes beyond the simple precise ideological definition of the groups they oppose.

[92] Della Porta, D, & Haupt, HG 2012 'Patterns of Radicalization in Political Activism: An introduction', *Social Science History*, vol. 36, no. 3, p315.

National Corps as a more explicit manifestation of the radicality of a veteran.[93] A phenomenon that also implies questioning the logic of disengagement.

Indeed, several veterans of the regiment continued to demonstrate an extreme right-wing, even neo-Nazi, logic in their political involvement upon their return to civilian life. For example, Colborne points out in his book that a "private night of Hitler worship in Kyiv" was organised by the neo-Nazi network Wotanjugen led by Azov Regiment veterans, who have an extended extreme political commitment to their return to civilian life, a sign of their radicality.[94] In this respect, the National Corps was essential in the continuity of a radical activist career. The same is true of the various organisations or sub-groups of the "Azov Movement". Indeed, these groups offer privileged spaces for converting military capital into activist capital and contribute to the reintegration of veterans who perceive continuity of a necessary struggle in their commitment. Using the notion of "military capital" helps us understand how this specific form of capital allows a veteran to benefit from a particular aura and a position of power not only in the political structure but also in the broader political field.[95] As such, the movement attempts to capitalise on the prestige of the regiment as a strategy for political insertion. Several veterans explained their transition in this way, such as VO17, who testifies to a similar path as VO11 I mentioned above:

> In the end, I wanted to go back to civilian life. The government was not sending me to the front anymore and I didn't want to stay at the base doing nothing. My chief then offered me a career change within the party. I had

---

93 Della Porta, D, & Haupt, HG 2012 'Patterns of Radicalization in Political Activism: An introduction', *Social Science History*, vol. 36, no. 3, pp.311-320.
94 Colborne, M 2022 *From the Fires of War: Ukraine's Azov Movement and the Global Far right, Ibidem*, Stuttgart, p.48.
95 Bourdieu, P 1976 'Les modes de domination', *Actes de la recherche en sciences sociales*, vol. 2, n°2, pp. 122-132; Bourdieu, P 1981 'La représentation politique [Éléments pour une théorie du champ politique]: Éléments pour une théorie du champ politique', *Actes de la recherche en sciences sociales*, vol. 36, no. 1, pp. 3-24; Bourdieu, P 2011 [1985-1986] 'Champ du pouvoir et division du travail de domination: Texte manuscrit inédit ayant servi de support de cours au Collège de France, 1985-1986', *Actes de la recherche en sciences sociales*, vol. 190, no. 5, pp. 126-139.

gradually climbed the ranks within the armed group. That's how I got my responsibilities in the local office of the National Corps in Mariupol.

VO11, VO17 and several other veterans I met had a continuous trajectory from the regiment to the Civil Corps and/or the National Corps, and the existing solidarity links between the fighters and veterans can facilitate the reconversion of civilian life. The skills acquired at the front are then reused in civilian activities where veterans can continue to develop their warrior *ethos*. First, this was done through the strong emphasis on the military that can be found in the political program of the National Corps, but also through all the aggressive aesthetics and memorial inscriptions that the movement demonstrates in its multiple public manifestations. Second, vigilante activities were developed in the different groups. For example, street activism is exercised by *Natsional'ny Druzhyni* whose patrols, borrowing from military referential, aim to ensure "their" social order.[96] Several violent actions have been carried out against Roma populations[97], banks and betting places[98]. Gorbach thus describes movement members as entrepreneurs of political violence "where violence resources become a crucially important capital asset".[99] They are "prepared to mobilise their violent resources for the advancement of their positions." Finally, this was done through the transmission of military knowledge provided to the younger generation. The insistence on educating young people, to whom political theories, combat sports and weapons manipulation are taught,

---

96 Favarel-Garrigues, G, & Gayer, L 2016 'Violer la loi pour maintenir l'ordre: Le vigilantisme en débat', *Politix*, vol. 115, no 3, pp. 7-33.
97 Miller, C 2018 'With Axes And Hammers, Far-Right Vigilantes Destroy Another Romany Camp In Kyiv', *RFE/RL*, June 8, viewed 10 January 2022, <https://www.rferl.org/a/ukraine-far-right-vigilantes-destroy-another-romany-camp-in-kyiv/29280336.html>.
98 Rudenko, E, & Sarakhman, E 2018 'Al'truyisty na marshi. Yak vlashtovani "Natsdruzhyny", i chy potribno yikh boyatysya', *Ukrayins'ka Pravda*, 6 February, viewed 1 January 2023, <http://www.pravda.com.ua/articles/2018/02/6/7170686/>.
99 Gorbach, D 2018 'Entrepreneurs of political violence: the varied interests and strategies of the far-right in Ukraine', *openDemocracy*, 16 October, viewed 31 December 2022, <https://www.opendemocracy.net/en/odr/entrepreneurs-of-political-violence-ukraine-far-right/>.

can thus constitute a "first step in the radical commitment".[100] With that, the National Corps can have several potential recruits that it trains under a particular ideological orientation, interweaving a martial universe with political perspectives faithful to the will to build a new, more militarised, and hierarchical society thought to be "healthier". A language that goes beyond the warfare context.

However, this emphasis on the martial dimension as a common ground for engagement also suggests an ideological diversity that reflects a more scattered movement while still adhering to a far-right identity. As Colborne points out, there is an "ideologically heterogenous far-right movement" with multiple influences "from Ukrainian nationalists like Stsiborskyi, international influences like the German "Conservative Revolution" and the French *Nouvelle Droite*, as well as outright neo-Nazis and advocates of violence and terror".[101] In 2017, the interest expressed by some members of the National Corps for National-Anarchism, a political perspective that differs from already existing movements in Ukraine[102], to increase their militant base, led me to think of a form of "catch-all nationalism". Moreover, the collision between militarisation, the path of reconversion for veterans, and this ideological disparity can also suggest disillusionment that contributes to the disengagement of some activists. Three veterans I met who had joined the National Corps explained that they had finally decided to leave despite the costs, not feeling in agreement with the ideological orientation (or rather, the lack of orientation). Although he denies the actual belief in neo-Nazi ideology within the movement, VO12 explained to me one of the problems he felt: "For example, their stupid nationalism without foundations. Nationalism is reasonable for intelligent people. But it can also be for stupid people". He shared with me his disillusionment with the lack of control over the movement's image, the

---

100 Dorronsoro, G, & Grojean, O 2004 'Engagement militant et phénomènes de radicalisation chez les Kurdes de Turquie', *European Journal of Turkish Studies*.
101 Colborne, M 2022 *From the Fires of War: Ukraine's Azov Movement and the Global Far right*, Ibidem, Stuttgart, p38.
102 Wishart, A 2019 *The Radical Left in Ukraine since Maidan: The Case of the National Anarchist Movement*, Master Thesis, University of Glasgow and National University of Kyiv Mohyla Academy, 289 p.

use of neo-Nazi symbolism by some members without understanding its deeper meaning, and a lack of ideological clarity. However, if he has distanced himself from political commitment, he doesn't forget his loyalty to the regiment and his pride in fighting in it. The distinction between the armed commitment and the political perspectives of the movement is thus also marked here. This attachment to the regiment is also noted by VO1, whom I met on several occasions and who never pursued political activities, preferring to develop his civilian organisation projects linked to the war effort. On the other hand, I had no news from VO9 and VO10 when I returned to Mariupol from one year to the next, although they indicated they were considering continuing their involvement in the movement. It seems that they have finally moved away from it. Both expressed a desire for change in their country. Finally, the different veterans do not show similar career patterns. Some did pursue a continued commitment from the regiment to the political movement, reinforcing a specific radical career. However, others have moved away from it. And if they remember their commitment to the regiment with pride, it is understood as different from their commitment to the rest of the political movement. A passage through the "careers" allows us to perceive this plurality of profiles and reduces the sensation of a far-right radicalism maintained and developed uniformly within the regiment. It is indeed the consideration of a trajectory going from the previous commitments, the commitment within the regiment and the continuity of a radical career within the inherited political movements which delivers us a more precise outlook of the ideological framings operated within the regiment.

Conclusion

This chapter aimed not to show to what extent the regiment remains politicised or not, but to try to develop a more nuanced approach to this issue. It is not a question of calling for a clear-cut view but rather trying to highlight the multiple and complex logics of engagement and power dynamics that make a strict and established categorisation challenging. As such, the Azov regiment borrows different elements from a spectrum ranging from a militia to a professional military corps, notably because of its trajectory since its creation. However, the efforts of the Ukrainian state to control it and the perspective of professionalisation do not allow it to be established as the armed wing of an openly radical far-right political movement. Above all, the logic of commitment within it reveals multiple paths that tend to distance the regiment from the image of a structure that necessarily reinforces a radical career. If it can participate in it, it does not necessarily contribute to it, and considering the militant and/or military careers allows us to perceive this dynamic with more measure. In the end, it is the continuity of the commitment to a radical career more than the commitment to the Azov regiment that testifies to the politicisation of the fighters and veterans. In addition, many of the profiles I met had a continuous trajectory, notably because of my strategy of insertion in the field through the Civil Corps and then the National Corps (which is also, in a way, indicative of the links maintained). However, despite this bias, differentiated commitment profiles have been, at the very least, noted and confirmed by the existing literature. Nonetheless, an entire article would be necessary to specify this diversity of trajectories further. At the of writing, Ukraine continues to be massively shelled and attacked by Russia. The atrocities of war are a reality that we follow daily. One thing is sure: my support for Ukraine is full, and my solidarity is unbreakable, and international solidarity and financial and military support remain the only possible way to counter despicable aggression. Let us not misunderstand the blame game. The responsibility for the invasion belongs to Russia. The disproportionate interest in Azov, which is at most a domestic political issue, should make us question the propaganda mechanisms. They require the highest degree of caution concerning the distortions this leads to. We also make efforts to counter it by always seeking to refine our binary analyses, which sometimes run the risk of exposing abusive generalisations.

5 Ze Double
A Psychodramatic Interpretation of the Azov's Role in the Russo-Ukrainian War

Ivan Gomza

> *And when you are near,*
> *I will tear your eyes out and place them instead of mine...*
> Jacob Moreno, "Invitation to an Encounter"

Overture

On July 28, 2022, a "kinetic event" obliterated the POW camp at Olenivka, killing around 50 prisoners, most of them members of the Azov battalion captured by Russians at the Azovstal Industrial Complex (Mariupol). As horrendous images of charred bodies melted in metal beds flooded the Internet, a media performance took place. First, Russian media condemned Ukrainians for targeting the camp with artillery.[1] Next, the Russian MoD upgraded the accusation, blaming Ukrainians for using "US-made HIMARS."[2] Finally, Russian senator Vladimir Dzhabarov (*United Russia*) clarified: "[Ukrainians] are exterminating their captured soldiers and militants to shut them up, a typical Nazi approach."[3] The narrative became clear: Ukrainian Nazis at large kill Ukrainian Nazis in captivity with US weaponry to cover up their crimes.

Ukrainians, for their part, condemned Russia for a deliberated war crime—an artificial explosion aiming "to hide the torture of prisoners and executions."[4] When an independent investigation concluded that "available visual evidence appears to support the

---

1 https://t.me/rian_ru/172616
2 https://regnum.ru/news/polit/3655714.html
3 https://t.me/senatorDzhabarov/931
4 https://www.facebook.com/GeneralStaff.ua/posts/373703864942698

Ukrainian claim,"[5] Russians added a new twist. The Russian Embassy in the UK tweeted that "Azov militants deserve execution, but death not by firing squad but by hanging because they're not real soldiers. They deserve a humiliating death."[6] The message was a verbal matryoshka-doll: the embassy ostensibly cited some Mariupol dwellers allegedly traumatised by Ukrainian shelling at *Azovstal*. It was quickly flagged as inappropriate by *Twitter*. This, however, was not a tweet that went rogue. Earlier in May 2022, Chairman of the State Duma Committee on International Affairs Leonid Slutsky declared that "Ukrainian nationalists deserve nothing but the execution."[7] Likewise, Head of the Republic of Crimea Sergey Aksyonov promised to "shoot most Azov militants and pardon a few substituting the firing squad with heavy labour"[8] and the plenipotentiary of the Federation Council in the Constitutional Court of Russia Andrey Klishas suggested shipping Azov prisoners "either to Luhansk People's Republic or to Donetsk People's Republic since there is no moratorium for the capital punishment."[9] Thus, there was another narrative: Azov military personnel were war criminals to be dealt with accordingly.

Together, two Russian narratives represent a typical *logique du chaudron* famously illustrated by Freud:

> A. borrowed a copper kettle from B. and after he had returned it was sued by B. because the kettle now had a big hole[...] His defence was: 'First, I never borrowed a kettle from B. at all; secondly, the kettle had a hole in it already when I got it from him; and thirdly, I gave him back the kettle undamaged.' *Each one of these defences is valid in itself, but taken together they exclude one another.*[10]

---

5   *Institute for Study of War.* (2022). Russian Offensive Campaign Assessment, July 29. Available at: https://www.understandingwar.org/backgrounder/russian-offensive-campaign-assessment-july-29
6   https://twitter.com/RussianEmbassy/status/1553093117712162828
7   https://www.dw.com/ru/plennye-s-azovstali-grozit-li-im-v-rossii-smertnaja-kazn/a-61840660
8   https://ura.news/news/1052555078
9   https://t.me/andreyklishas/320
10 Freud, Sigmund. (1990). *Jokes and Their Relations to the Unconscious.* New York: W. W. Norton & Company, 27. (Emphasis added–I.G.)

Tragedy at Olenivka, however, has an additional symbolic dimension: cadavers, which Russia tried to put under the door of Ukrainian authorities, belonged to the Azov battalion. The alleged "Nazi butchers" were deliberately killed in the middle of the night to be used as evidence of Ukrainian crimes. This event point to the fact that Azov's ghost is ubiquitous in the Russo-Ukrainian war: Russia invaded Ukraine to de-nazify it and used Azov as proof that there were Nazis in Ukraine; Russia obliterated Mariupol to expunge the Azov battalion from the city where it came to fame; Russia performed extra-judiciary executions against anyone surmised to have ties to Azov. Eventually, the Azov-battering traumatised ordinary Ukrainians to the point that they rallied with the slogans "We are all Azov"[11] and organised an art exhibition to commemorate "the angels of the town of Maria."[12] Clearly, Azov is not just a military unit, a nationalist organisation, or a political party in the ongoing war; it signifies something bigger. This study aims to explore some additional representative dimensions of Azov in the Russo-Ukrainian War.

Introducing the Character: Achievements and Limitations of Existing Literature on Azov

The history of Azov has been retold many a time.[13] Several contributors to this volume also present it perfectly, so there is no need to recount the well-known tale: born out of the tinderbox of the first Russian invasion, the Azov movement became prominent in Ukrainian politics. Since 2014, scholars have elaborated on three approaches to treating Azov.

---

11   http://www.golos.com.ua/news/166547
12   https://zmist.pl.ua/news/teper-my-vsi-azovstal-112-portretiv-geroyiv-yaki-zagynuly-u-mariupoli-predstavyly-u-poltavi-fotoreportazh
13   See: Umland, A. (2019). "Irregular Militias and Radical Nationalism in Post-Euromaydan Ukraine: The Prehistory and Emergence of the "Azov" Battalion in 2014." *Terrorism and Political Violence* 31:1, 105-131; Heinemann-Grüder, A. (2019). "Geiselnehmer oder Retter des Staates? Irreguläre Bataillone in der Ukraine." *Osteuropa* 3-4: 51-80; and for a concise outline see Klein, M. (2015.) "Ukraine's volunteer battalions—advantages and challenges." *RUFS Briefing* No. 27.

First, academics put the organisation into a broader perspective of transnational crime and terrorism. Soufan was among the first to allege that because of Azov, Ukraine was "becoming a haven for an array of white supremacy extremist groups to congregate, train, and radicalise."[14] Afterward, numerous scholarly publications stipulated that Azov represented "political-criminal convergence in political violence under the disguise of community protection against crime and norm-breaking"[15] and pursued "an internationalist strategy [to] promote a conservative "Reconquista" against the liberal West"[16] concomitants with "far-right extremist groups in the United States and Europe actively [seeking] out relationships with representatives of the far-right in Ukraine, specifically the National Corps."[17]

Second, scholars focused on the domestic dimensions of Azov activities. Specialists were generally anxious that the powerful far-right movement could substantially challenge democratic consolidation in Ukraine. Observing how the Azov battalion branched out into politics and established a social movement and a party, some feared that "pro-government 'government challengers'... are more efficient than the government in the provision of security and in promoting the incumbent's ideology."[18] Many admitted that Azov "contributed significantly to saving the sovereignty of the

---

14 The Soufan Center. (2019). "White Supremacy Extremism: The Transnational Rise of the Violent White Supremacist Movement." *The Soufan Center*, 32. Available at: https://thesoufancenter.org/wp-content/uploads/2019/09/Report-by-The-Soufan-Center-White-Supremacy-Extremism-The-Transnational-Rise-of-The-Violent-White-Supremacist-Movement.pdf
15 Laryš, Martin. (2022). "Far-Right vigilantes and crime: law and order providers or common criminals? the lessons from Greece, Russia, and Ukraine." *Southeast European and Black Sea Studies*, 6.
16 Rekawek, Kacper et al. (2020). "Violent Right-Wing Extremism and Terrorism—Transnational Connectivity, Definitions, Incidents, Structures and Countermeasure." *Counter Extremism Project*, 15. Available at: https://www.counterextremism.com/sites/default/files/CEP%20Study_Violent%20Right-Wing%20Extremism%20and%20Terrorism_Nov%202020.pdf
17 Lister, Tim. (2020). "The Nexus Between Far-Right Extremists in the United States and Ukraine." *CTC Sentinel* 13:4. Available at: https://ctc.westpoint.edu/the-nexus-between-far-right-extremists-in-the-united-states-and-ukraine/
18 Aliyev, Huseyn. (2022). "Pro-government Anti-government Armed Groups? Toward Theorizing Pro-government 'Government Challengers'." *Terrorism and Political Violence* 34:7, 1369-1385.

Ukrainian state in 2014–2015, but may also have created conditions for challenges to the same state further down the road"[19] because the Azov case illustrates a powerful trend toward "extra-institutional control of the security sector."[20] Even recognising that the Azov Battalion was integrated into the regular military forces in 2015, scholars warned it could "continue to play a role in both the Ukrainian society and security sector to the unforeseeable future."[21] Third, a subset of both academic and journalistic publications struggled to grasp the nature of Azov's ideology. Some unwaveringly declare it "clearly a fascist organisation,"[22] some resort to more neutral terms like "right-wing"[23] or "far-right nationalist,"[24]. In contrast, other scholars explain that "there are absolutely no grounds for accusations that neo-Nazis serve in the Azov regiment."[25]

As informative as the three approaches might be, none explains the tragedy of Olenivka and, in a broader sense, Azov's role in the Russo-Ukrainian war. After all, as a party, *National Corps* is non-consequential: it opted out of parliamentary elections in 2019, and at the local elections of 2020, it secured 18 out of 43122 seats contested in local councils. As an actor in street politics, the *National Corps* made much noise in 2019-2022 but failed to sway the decision-makers. As a military detachment, the National Guard Unit

---

19 Bukkvoll, Tor. (2019). "Fighting on behalf of the state – the issue of pro-government militia autonomy in the Donbas war." *Post-Soviet Affairs* 35:4, 293-307.
20 Puglisi, Rosaria. (2015). "A People's Army: Civil Society as a Security Actor in Post-Maidan Ukraine." *Istituto Affari Internazionali*, 17.
21 Käihkö, Ilmari. (2018). "A nation-in-the-making, in arms: control of force, strategy and the Ukrainian Volunteer Battalions." *Defence Studies* 18:2, 147-166.
22 Melanovski, Jason. (2022). "Ukraine's neo-Nazi Azov Battalion attempts rebranding." *World Socialist Web Site*. Available at: https://www.wsws.org/en/articles/2022/06/03/ykgh-j03.html
23 Raghavan, Sudarsan et al. (2022). "Right-wing Azov Battalion emerges as a controversial defender of Ukraine." *Washington Post*. Available at: https://www.washingtonpost.com/world/2022/04/06/ukraine-military-right-wing-militias/
24 Mapping Militant Organizations. (2022). "Azov Movement." Stanford University. Available at: https://cisac.fsi.stanford.edu/mappingmilitants/profiles/azov-battalion
25 Lykhachov, Vyacheslav. (2022). "Honest Answers to the Most Common Questions about Azov in the West." *Center for Civil Liberties*. Available at: https://ccl.org.ua/en/claims/euromaidan-sos-honest-answers-to-the-most-common-questions-about-azov-in-the-west/

No. 3057 (Azov battalion's official designation) comprises circa 2000 troops. They are considered military elite, but the 1 million people dwarf the number mobilised since February 2022,[26] and even by the 261 thousand-strong army envisaged by the Ukrainian authorities in January 2022.[27] In other words, the obsession with Azov has little to do with its impact on politics and warfare.

To diagnose the persistent Russian preoccupation with Azov, scholars should move beyond examinations of its transnational, national, and ideological aspects, each unable to explain the intricate nature of the phenomenon. In February-September 2022 — as Russian troops enveloped Mariupol, besieged the *Azovstal* complex, captured 2000 of its defenders (including circa 500 members of the Azov Battalion), and threatened to organise a trial on "Nazi criminals," only to release some of them in a POW-exchange deal — Azov was a protagonist of an immense collective psychodrama. People cheered for Azov's blood and wept for its victimhood. I argue that studying Azov as a psychodrama should give the scholarly community essential insights.

Setting the Stage: Reasons to Study Azov as a Psychodrama

The word "psychodrama" has two meanings that are not necessarily related. First, a mundane speech describes some tense situation and "an ongoing psychological struggle."[28] Hence, commentators mention "the Bush-McCain psychodrama,"[29] the Iranian hostage crisis "played out in terms of national psychodrama,"[30] the French

---

26 https://forbes.ua/news/ponad-1-mln-lyudey-u-formi-zabezpechuyut-oboronu-ukraini-reznikov-08072022-7072
27 The Ukrainian army size is regulated by a special law amended in January 2022 thus enlarging it: https://zakon.rada.gov.ua/laws/show/1703-20#Text
28 Merriam-Webster Dictionary. (2022). Entry: "*Psychodrama.*" https://www.merriam-webster.com/dictionary/psychodrama#learn-more
29 Corn, David. (2001). "McCain in vain?" *The Nation* 272: 25, 5-6.
30 Sick, Garry. (1985). *All fall down: America's fateful encounter with Iran*. London: I.B. Tauris & Co.

national debate on the Muslim veil as "a big psychodrama,"[31] a psychodrama of a troubled presidential term[32], "the daily White House psychodrama"[33] around the nuclear deal or even "Brexit psychodrama."[34]

However, there is a second, more specialised sense of the notion. For instance, a description of mental health professionals running psychodrama groups in Pristina to ensure reconciliation between Serbs and Albanians[35] refers not to an intense psychological struggle but something entirely different. In psychological studies, "psychodrama" is a therapeutic technique that combines elements of dramatic performance and ensuing group dynamics to reveal and intervene in psychological issues.[36] Unlike much more famed psychoanalysis, which focuses on talking out psychological problems, psychodrama helps participants express their emotions through acting and take a different perspective on their actions through role-playing.

The method has a variety of applications: overcoming adverse outcomes of traumatic experiences like abuse,[37] PTSD,[38] or child

---

31 Winter, Bronwyn. (2008). *Hijab & the republic: uncovering the French headscarf debate*. Syracuse, N.Y.: Syracuse University Press.
32 "The CFK psychodrama." (2014). *The Economist* 411: 8882, 26.
33 Power, Cassidy and Samuels, Remy. (2018). "Former ambassador examines Iran nuclear deal." *The Pitt News*. https://pittnews.com/article/128195/news/former-ambassador-examines-iran-nuclear-deal/
34 Hughes, Brian. (2019). *The Psychology of Brexit: From Psychodrama to Behavioural Science*. Springer International Publishing.
35 Veljković, Jasna and Despotović, Vera. (2017). "The Sociodrama Narrative: Political Aspects." *Serbian Political Thought* 1, 101.
36 Jones, Phil (2017). "Psychodrama" in *The SAGE Encyclopedia of Abnormal and Clinical Psychology*, Vol. 4. Ed. A. Wenzel. Thousand Oaks: SAGE Publications, 2711
37 Bucuță, Mihaela et al. (2018). "'When you thought that there is no one and nothing': The value of psychodrama in working with abused women." *Frontiers in psychology* 9, 1518-1518; Yiftach, Ron and Yanai, Liat (2021). "Empowering Through Psychodrama: A Qualitative Study at Domestic Violence Shelters." *Frontiers in psychology* 12, 600335.
38 Scott, Giacomucci and Marquit, Joshua. (2020). "The Effectiveness of Trauma-Focused Psychodrama in the Treatment of PTSD in Inpatient Substance Abuse Treatment." *Frontiers in psychology* 11, 896-896.

neglect,[39] fostering positive emotions,[40] helping with fear management,[41] or even preparing for emotionally taxing jobs.[42] In general, the professional community deems psychodrama to be effective.[43] Besides, there is clinical evidence of psychodrama's positive outcomes, like a significant drop in cortisol, a depression-related human hormone,[44] or reducing the intake of opioids by addicted patients who practice the technique.[45]

A subtype of psychodrama, referred to as "sociodrama," deliberately focuses not on individual patients but on communities to empower them to deal with the negative communal experience. Kellermann distinguishes five fields of desirable sociodrama application.[46] (1) *Crisis sociodrama* works on collective traumas provoked by natural disasters, ethnic cleansing, or terrorist attacks; (2) *political sociodrama* tackles strains stemming from unequal power distribution like class struggle; (3) *diversity sociodrama* helps to reveal, examine, and dispel prejudices like racism, bigotry, intolerance and

---

39 Mutafchieva, Milena. (2020). "Psychodrama with children in foster care units in Bulgaria: challenges and reflections: Psychodrama with children along the basic needs of children." *Zeitschrift für Psychodrama und Soziometrie* 19:2, 313-329.
40 Parlak, Simel and Oksuz Gul, Feride (2021). "Psychodrama oriented group therapy for forgiveness in university students." *The Arts in psychotherapy* 73, 101761.
41 Bayrı Bingöl, Fadime et al. (2022). "Psychodrama as a new intervention for reducing fear of childbirth: a randomised controlled trial." *Journal of obstetrics and gynaecology*
42 Oflaz, Fatih et al. (2011). "Psychodrama: an innovative way of improving self-awareness of nurses" *Journal of psychiatric and mental health nursing* 18:7, 569-575; Lennie, Sarah-Jane et al. (2021). "Psychodrama and emotional labour in the police: A mutually beneficial methodology for researchers and participants." *Methods in Psychology* 5.
43 Kipper, David and Ritchie, Timothy. (2003). "The effectiveness of psychodramatic techniques: a meta-analysis." *Group Dynamics* 7:1, 13-25; Wieser, Michael. (2007). "Studies on treatment effects of psychodrama psychotherapy." In *Psychodrama: Advances in theory and practice*, Eds C. Baim, J. Burmeister, and M. Maciel. London, England: Brunner/Routledge, 271-292; Lim, Mengyu et al. (2021). "Surveying 80 Years of Psychodrama Research: A Scientometric Review." *Frontiers in Psychiatry* 12, 9.
44 Erbay, Lale et al. (2018). "Does Psychodrama Affect Perceived Stress, Anxiety-Depression Scores and Saliva Cortisol in Patients with Depression?" *Psychiatry Investigations* 15:10, 970-975.
45 Uğurlu, Tuğçe et al. (2020). "Effect of Psychodrama Group Therapy on Remission and Relapse in Opioid Dependence." *Noro Psikiyatr Ars* 57:3, 197-203.
46 Kellermann, Felix. (2007). *Sociodrama and collective trauma*. London and Philadelphia: Jessica Kingsley Publishers.

other adverse outcomes of othering; (4) *sociodrama for conflict management* promotes non-violent ways to settle conflicts; and (5) *post-conflict sociodrama* offers ways to reconcile fractured communities and warring nations.

Both psychodrama and sociodrama help participants externalise their negative experiences, critically examine them, and work on them. Both are contingent upon a group effort to alleviate either individual or communal anguish. Finally, both use specific dramatic techniques (more on them in the next section) to conjure and exorcise the inner demons of a personal or collective psyche. So, although therapists differentiate the two types for their professional needs, I will use the notion of "psychodrama" even when referring to group-related processes.

The ongoing Russo-Ukrainian war brought misery and suffering unseen in Europe since 1945. A mounting wave of hatred and dehumanisation engulfs Ukrainians and Russians, resulting from artillery barrages and obliterated cities, mass graves and personal losses, rotting corpses, and the exodus of millions... This experience is traumatic by definition. Thus, one might expect purposeful applications of psychodrama to overcome at least a fraction of human suffering. However, most of such interventions, especially those targeting the Russo-Ukrainian reconciliation, will be possible solely after the cessation of the hostilities.

Nevertheless, the war brought an intriguing act of directionless psychodrama titled "Azov." For almost seven months (February-September 2022), two nations watched over and participated in two dramatic performances. Since the early days of the invasion, Russians were intent on "cleansing the neighboring state from Nazism" and installing a friendly regime in Kyiv. Instead, they got bogged down around Mariupol by the personification of the Evil they boasted of evicting—the Azov battalion. The 80-day showdown with the archenemy took a massive toll on the Russian army. Having finally managed to capture Azov's stronghold, an immense souterrain metallurgical plant, they promised to put the captured fascists on trial. However, the months of preparation finished unexpectedly with a prisoner exchange on September 21, when 200 captives, including the Azov battalion chief Denys Prokopenko, were liberated, causing chagrin among Russians thirsty for a show.

During the same period, Ukrainians co-experienced a valiant defense of the "Azovstal" by a heroic set of memorable characters: a gifted pianist, a tender singer, a pregnant woman, an inspiring warrior, and others. Their *noms de guerre* like "Bird" (*Пташка*) and "Guelder-Rose" (*Калина*) became household names. The 3-month long siege brought into being a new badge of honor, "Azov means Steel" (a pun on the *Azovstal*) and a new identity, "We are all Azov." The following months of captivity inflicted anxiety, pain, and distress as revelations of torture and inhumane conditions trickled down to the Ukrainian public. It all distilled into the immense outpouring of collective jubilation on September 21.

The two narratives refer to the same factual events. However, the ways the two nations acted out these events deserve a closer examination. As I argue, the fate of the Azov battalion became a psychodrama for Ukrainian, Russian, and international communities. The way people treated real Azov fighters, depicted them in media and referred to them in official and informal speeches changed the factual Azov into "Azov," with the quotation marks signifying the added psychodramatic dimension. "Azov" reveals some concealed truths about both Ukrainian and Russian communities, their desires, phantasms, and fears. As such, "Azov" is much more significant and exciting than the Azov itself. After all, the organisation's history has been retold many a time; the script of the collective psychodrama, on the other hand, is deciphered for the first time.

Examining the Repertoire: Theoretical Premises of Psychodramatic Technique

According to Jacob Moreno, the founder of the psychodramatic technique, "the method explores the truth of one's soul through action,"[47] deliberately bringing together the theatre and therapy. The

---

47 Moreno, Jacob. (1959). *Gruppenpsychotherapie und Psychodrama: Einleitung in die Theorie und Praxis*. Stuttgart: Thieme, 77.

logic behind using theatrical action to reveal some hidden truth of a psyche is straightforward. Humans are prone to internal conversations. We imagine possible ways to address upcoming situations and re-play alternative scenarios of past events. In addition to those "what ifs," maintaining inner dialogues, people espouse different positions, acting out both pros and contras of any choice, opinion, or judgment we are working on.

Psychodrama purposefully projects inner exchanges and highlights motivations, values, and oppositions by granting each a role. Hence, "shame" and "grief," a "domineering mother" and a "lost sibling," a "quest for a better job," and an "opportunity for revenge" all are reenacted or represented during psychodramas. With a proper effort, any social situation—alongside underlying principles and inbuilt conflicts—gets a suitable role.[48] For this article, I consider Ukrainian nationalism, Russian culture, maltreatment of POWs, and deliberate targeting of non-combatants as *roles* in a psychodramatic sense. They are **illuminated projections of values and motives** proper to collective psyches.

There are five constitutive elements of a psychodrama:

1. *The stage*. Initially, Moreno resorted to real elevated platforms, but later elaborations tended to use any space proper for collective reenactment. The stage for the "Azov" psychodrama is of digital nature: its actors emit their opinion, act out their frustrations, stage their confrontations, and collaborate in most other conceivable ways in social media and via the Internet. I consider the digital space as a proper form of psychodrama stage because of an intriguing similarity:

> the psychodrama stage is an instrument having three time dimensions: past, present, and future, and also as an instrument that does not differentiate between fantasy and reality [...] There is also no differentiation of kinds of realities with one regarded as more real, valid or true than another. Surplus

---

48 Veljković, Jasna and Despotović, Vera. (2017). "The Sociodrama Narrative: Political Aspects." *Serbian Political Thought* 1, 100.

reality can be defined as an intersection between different realities, known and unknown, where the ability to control and distinguish ceases.[49]

It is precisely this *sense of multiple realities* — when *Azovstal* simultaneously is being held by Ukrainians and captured by Russians, a Mariupol Drama theater is serving as "a safe zone for civilians" and "a stronghold for fascists," Olenivka POW camp has been targeted by "the Ukrainian artillery" and "torched out by Russians from within" — constitutes a digital stage for "Azov."

2. *The protagonist*. This figure's passions are projected onto the stage for educational goals. During clinical sessions, protagonists are often recipients of psychodrama-induced therapeutic effects. However, as psychodramatists emphasise, "every protagonist play is ultimately group-oriented,"[50] for each group member is expected to relate to some parts of the play and find them relevant to their situations. More to the point, the protagonist's "symptoms, behaviour and feelings reveal the hidden corners of the past"[51] to teach a meaningful lesson for any human participating in or even observing the action. Hence, the significance of a protagonist is complex: on the one hand, s\he is the one who (as the word's origins suggest) "undergoes the test." On the other hand, just as Oedipus' and Orestes' sufferings reveal some hidden truth about destiny not only to them but also to spectators, protagonists face their inner demons on stage for the sake of the community. This interpretation has a hidden trap: it tempts to consider an actual human being as a vehicle to promote a group's interests. Thus, psychodrama practitioners take necessary steps to ensure personal and group interests. However, in the "Azov" case, actual humans, Azov fighters, were harmed while alive and digitally paraded when deceased. Azov,

---

49 Blomkvist, Leif and Rützel, Thomas. "Disintegration Its role in personality integration" in *Psychodrama since Moreno: Innovations in theory and practice* (eds. Paul Holmes, Marcia Karp, and Michael Watson). London and New York: Routledge, 2005, 168.
50 von Ameln, Falko and Becker-Ebel, Jochen. (2020). *Fundamentals of Psychodrama*. Singapore: Springer Nature, 21.
51 Moreno, Jonathan. "Psychodramatic moral philosophy and ethics" in *Psychodrama since Moreno: Innovations in theory and practice* (eds. Paul Holmes, Marcia Karp, and Michael Watson). London and New York: Routledge, 2005, 69.

therefore, is the protagonist in a psychodrama enacted by other participants to its very real detriment.

3. *The group*. Aptly conceptualized by von Ameln and Becker-Ebel, psychodrama is an action *in the group* (it takes place in a group setting), *by the group* (the group is used as a therapeutic agent), *for the group* (the effects are not limited to the actors on stage and benefit those not directly involved) and *of the group* (the intra-group relations change due to the psychodramatic work).[52] Moreover, there is a subset of psychodrama, sometimes referred to as sociodrama, which focuses on groups even further. As Moreno himself stipulated, psychodrama is "a deep action method dealing with *inter-personal* relations and *private* ideologies, and sociodrama is a deep action method dealing with *inter-group* relations and *collective* ideologies."[53] Since ordinary psychodrama reveals previously concealed motivations, emotions, and values of an interpersonal conflict, sociodrama discloses the drivers of an inter-group conflict.[54] To do it effectively, sociodrama's "working tools are representative types within a given culture and not private individuals."[55] Hence, "Ukrainian fascist thugs," "Russian heroes," "blood-thirsty maniacs," and other labels used during the Azov psychodrama refer not to personal characteristics of actual individuals but serve as signifiers populating the collective culture of a heterogeneous group—Ukrainians, Russians, and foreigners who followed the Azov's fate.

4. *Auxiliaries*. These group members enter the stage to cooperate with the participant and represent the protagonists' relationships, values, abstract entities, things, or other elements required for a more convincing play.[56] Essentially, in "a group-centered or

---

52   von Ameln, Falko and Becker-Ebel, Jochen. (2020). *Fundamentals of Psychodrama*. Singapore: Springer Nature, 24-25.
53   Moreno, Jacob. (1943). "The Concept of Sociodrama: A New Approach to the Problem of Inter-Cultural Relations" *Sociometry* 6:4, 436. (Emphasis added–I.G.)
54   Ulon, Siyat. "Collective shadows on the sociodrama stage." *International Journal of Jungian Studies*, 10:3 (2018), 222.
55   Moreno, Jacob. (1943). "The Concept of Sociodrama: A New Approach to the Problem of Inter-Cultural Relations" *Sociometry* 6:4, 438.
56   Kellermann, Felix. "Cornerstones of role reversal" in *Psychodrama since Moreno: Innovations in theory and practice* (eds. Paul Holmes, Marcia Karp, and Michael Watson). London and New York: Routledge, 2005, 196-197.

theme-centered sociodrama, each member is an auxiliary ego."[57] In particular, they are vital for crucial psychodrama techniques. Practitioners distinguish 350 unique techniques, including role reversal, soliloquy, improvisation, and the empty chair within psychodrama.[58] However, for this study, I focus on three of them. First, auxiliaries participate in *doubling*. Doubling occurs when a group member makes statements suggesting thoughts or feelings that participants may not be conscious of, may not be expressed, or may be unable to express. The person receiving this statement can accept or reject it, but a key aim of doubling is "to support insight and the richness of the exploration of the presenting problem."[59] Doubling, in other words, serves as a comment during the act, a spontaneous introspection or observation of what is going on. Second, auxiliaries practice *mirroring* when they replay what they have just seen for the protagonist. This technique aims "to enable the protagonist to use the device of seeing himself or herself being depicted, rather than being an actor within the scene."[60] As a result, s/he can conform correct interpretations ("yes, I truly loved that memory"), reject it ("no, I suffered at that moment"), or amend it ("rather, I was paralysed with anticipation, not with fear"). One way or another, mirroring helps the protagonist and the group better grasp the experience. Third, entering the stage, auxiliaries *enact desired roles* when they "play the role of their ideal self, i.e., slip[ping] into the role of the person they always wanted to be"[61] and eventually reveal their inner values.

In the "Azov" case, anyone who comments on the unit, its ideology, its role in the war, or the alleged motivations of Azov fighters acts as an auxiliary. Given the natural limitations of the chapter, the number of participants, and the novelty of the task, I decided to

---

57 von Ameln, Falko and Becker-Ebel, Jochen. (2020). *Fundamentals of Psychodrama*. Singapore: Springer Nature, 22.
58 Giacomucci, Scott. (2021). *Social Work, Sociometry, and Psychodrama*, Singapore: Springer Nature, 254.
59 Jones, Phil. (2017). "Psychodrama" in *The SAGE Encyclopedia of Abnormal and Clinical Psychology*, Vol. 4. Ed. A. Wenzel. Thousand Oaks: SAGE Publications, 2712
60 Ibid.
61 von Ameln, Falko and Becker-Ebel, Jochen. (2020). *Fundamentals of Psychodrama*. y Singapore: Springer Nature, 43.

focus solely on Russian auxiliaries and their performance, mostly leaving Ukrainians and foreigners for further study. Nevertheless, as described below, focusing on doubling, mirroring, and enacting the desired roles of Russian participants contributes to a more nuanced understanding of the war because it reveals the motives and values participants are animated with.

5. *The director.* In clinical psychodrama, this is a certified specialist who facilitates the process facilitator. The director is not demiurge designing the psychodrama according to his preferences; instead, he provides expertise and interventions to push the event in a desirable direction. Obviously, there is no such facilitator in the "Azov" psychodrama, which makes it less predictable and more hectic. Besides, devoid of a director able to stop the performance once it reaches some dangerous or violent point, "Azov" transgressed any safety limits typically devised in clinical settings.

There are other notable differences. For instance, unlike a standard psychodrama that typically develops as a three-stage process (warm-up, enactment, and sharing), "Azov" jumped directly into action. Moreover, it is performed in a non-therapeutic context with little benefit for the participants—at least not yet.

These differences notwithstanding, I believe that actions and verbal struggle surrounding the Azov battalion represent a psychodrama. Admittedly, I do not put "psychodrama" in a pure therapeutical sense. However, noteworthy similarities exist between the psychodramatic assumptions and the collective reenactment of Azov's fate. Resorting to role enactment, doubling, and mirroring **commentators on Azov follow the general psychodramatic rule "to act out 'their truth,' as they feel and perceive it, in a completely subjective manner (no matter how distorted this appears)."**[62] Moreover, psychodrama grants spontaneity during action the utmost importance because of spontaneity's revelatory nature. We know that "Moreno noted an etymological link between *spon*taneity and re*spon*sibility. Linguistically, he was wrong, but his error

---

62 Kellermann, Felix. "Cornerstones of role reversal" in *Psychodrama since Moreno: Innovations in theory and practice* (eds. Paul Holmes, Marcia Karp, and Michael Watson). London and New York: Routledge, 2005, 196-197.

provides some insight into his implicit moral philosophy linking the two."[63] The moral dimension of spontaneity is easy to comprehend: through impulsive acts, participants expose their nature, values, and beliefs to bear responsibility for what they failed to conceal. By a lucky coincidence, the digital realm of almost immediate comments provides a convenient shortcut to the collective moral universe. Finally, there is an additional heuristic benefit in treating Azov as psychodrama: psychodramatic performance intentionally blurs the lines between "the past, near past, or present, as well as things that did happen and things that may happen in the future"[64] to reveal hidden motives. Russian soldiers, thus, perform a discernable psychodramatic act, adorning their tanks with St. George's stripes and pretending to re-play the fateful events of WWII, actually fighting in the exact geographical locations as their forbearers eighty years earlier. Therefore, I assume that "Azov" psychodrama should offer valuable insight into Russian collective culture and the origins and realities of the ongoing war.

Enacting the Drama: "Azov" on the Russian Digital Stage

For this study, I define the Azov psychodrama (hereafter, "Azov") as **(quasi)spontaneous reactions to the events related to the unit's performance and fate by the inhabitants of the Russian digital universe**. Since the eruption of hostilities, *Telegram* messenger has substituted other social media as a preferred communication tool. Accordingly, since February 2022, I have constantly been monitoring Russian *Telegram* channels for references to the Azov battalion. I used posts in channels and ensuing conversations and comments to collect material. The primary sources of this study are listed in the table:

---

63 Moreno, Jonathan. "Psychodramatic moral philosophy and ethics" in *Psychodrama since Moreno: Innovations in theory and practice* (eds. Paul Holmes, Marcia Karp, and Michael Watson). London and New York: Routledge, 2005, 74.
64 Gershoni, Jacob. *Psychodrama in the 21st Century: Clinical and Educational Applications*. Ney York: Springer Publishing Company, 2003, 10-11.

Title	Owner	Affiliation	Address	Followers
СОЛОВЬЁВ – Telegram	Vladimir Solovyov	Russia-1	https://t.me/s/SolovyovLive	1396276
WarGonzo	Semen Pegov	Main Directorate of the General Staff of the Armed Forces	https://t.me/wargonzo	1337413
Сладков +	Alexander Sladkov	The Russian Television and Radio Broadcasting Company	https://t.me/s/Sladkov_plus	1037816
Поддубный | Z|O|V| edition	Evgeny Poddubny	Russia-24 TV	https://t.me/s/epoddubny	943628
Kotsnews – Telegram	Alexander Kots	Komsomolskaya Pravda	https://t.me/s/sashakots	681310
Александр Ходаковский – Telegram	Alexander Khodakovsky	Vostok Battalion	https://t.me/aleksandr_skif	549084
Маргарита Симоньян – Telegram	Margarita Simonyan	Rossiya Segodnya	https://t.me/margaritasimonyan	509972
Военкор Котенок Z	Iuri Kotenok	Rossiya Segodnya	https://t.me/s/voenkorkotenok	432790
Grey Zone	Wagner mercenary group	Wagner mercenary group	https://t.me/s/grey_zone	342458
Репортёр Руденко V	Andrei Rudenko	The Russian Television and Radio Broadcasting Company	https://t.me/s/RtrDonetsk	276423
Murado	Murad Gadziyev	Russia Today	https://t.me/s/msgazdiev	33619

Data obtained at https://telemet.me/ as of November 9, 2022

As a group, these eleven channels share several crucial features. First, they represent a set of propaganda peddlers and military correspondents (*voyenkors*) who enjoy a wide readership. As a result, their ideas are communicated to millions of people, and their posts incite comments of hundreds. Second, they produce significant digital content (see table 2). Each channel generated more than 1.5 gigabits of digital content; Solovyov's channel alone contained 125 HTML-pages of archived text.

Title	Followers	Posts
СОЛОВЬЁВ – Telegram	1396276	138876
Kotsnews – Telegram	681310	37060
Военкор Котенок Z	432790	31493
Grey Zone	342458	15719
Поддубный |Z|O|V| edition	943628	13568
Маргарита Симоньян – Telegram	509972	12414
Репортёр Руденко V	276523	10621
WarGonzo	1337413	8104
Сладков +	1037816	6548
Александр Ходаковский – Telegram	549084	2444
Murado	33619	1094

Third, all cultivate ties with the Russian military or media establishment, thus representing not only their owners' private views but also conveying interpretations instrumental to the Russian regime. Therefore, the way leading military correspondents like Pegov, Sladkov, and others describe and interpret the war serves as a proxy psychodrama of the Russian ruling elites.

The initial step to studying the Azov psychodrama in Russian digital space was to establish whether the psychodrama occurred at all. For this purpose, I charted all the mentions of Azov (as a generalised description, a unit, a movement, or a party) in four chosen channels: (1) that of Vladimir Solovyov, a TV anchor and a journalist with close ties to Kremlin; (2) that of Margarita Simonyan, editor-in-chief of the *Russia Today* outlet; (3) that of Alexandr Kots, a *voyenkor* employed by one of the most prominent Russian newspapers *Komsomolskaya Pravda* and regularly covering the events from battlefields; (4) that of the Russian private military company *Wagner* directly engaged in operations against the Ukrainian army in general and the Azov unit in particular. Combined, the four channels offer a triangulated view. Solovyov comments on events and ceaselessly reposts almost all other media warriors, implying that reading his channel provides a meaningful way to account for trends in the Azov-related coverage. Symonyan offers more custom-made interpretations infused with information from *Russia Today* and other outlets (like *RIA-novosti* and *Zvezda*). Kots personally visited *Azovstal* and other Azov-related topography, so his reports give some first-hand experience. Finally, *Grey Zone* is almost devoid of propaganda, offering raw emotion by fighters who faced Azov in battle.

The visualisation comprises the period between Winter 2019 and Fall 2022. I opted for these particular chronological limits for two reasons. First, the 3-year time span provides enough space to trace trends. Second, in the Winter of 2019, Ukraine entered a new electoral cycle (due to presidential and parliamentary elections), and it seemed logical to consider Russian opinions on Azov after Zelensky and his party came to power and set the political agenda. As both charts illustrate,[65] Azov received only sporadic attention before Winter 2022. Instead, Russian media discourse focused on different topics, from educational reforms to the COVID-19 pandemic, whereas the *Wagner* group was busy fighting in the Middle East and Africa and ignoring Azov altogether.

The minor spike occurred in Spring-Summer 2021 with Protasevich's case. This Belarusian oppositional journalist was imprisoned after his plane *en route* from Athens to Vilnius had been forcefully landed by the Belarusian military when passing Belarus' airspace. The public outcry against the violation of civil aviation rules was met with a concerted retort by Russian propaganda emphasising that Protasevich cultivated ties with Azov, thus being not a peaceful activist but a Neo-Nazi. After the case, the Russian digital sphere went again silent on Azov. Then, it erupted with a torrent of messages in Winter 2022, reached a crescendo in Spring (coinciding with the siege of Mariupol), and calmed down in the Fall after the Azov prisoners exchange. Arguably, the same pattern should be discernable with other Telegram channels. The data suggest that in Winter-Fall 2022, there was a period of abnormally intense coverage and comments on Azov, constituting the psychodrama stage.

---

65 I visualized the data in two charts because with Solovyov being much more digitally active, his posts exist in different order of magnitude. If combined, his results would flatten the others.

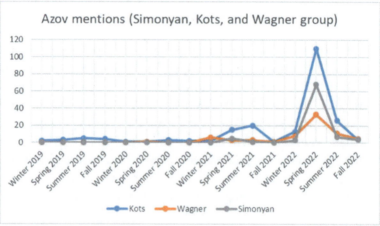

Next, I examined Azov's role in the torrent of mentions and references. As a reminder, being a *protagonist*, Azov served as a screen on which the psychodrama participants (*auxiliaries*) projected their values and fears. I discerned three techniques performed by auxiliaries reporting on Azov: (1) *doubling* or observations on what is going on, which, for this study, I understand as **comments on the ongoing war and the role Azov plays in it**; (2) *mirroring* or reenactments of what auxiliaries claim the protagonist himself performs, interpreted here as **acts committed by the Russians themselves yet attributed to Azov**. In addition, I briefly consider (3) the *enactment*

of desired roles performed by the participants. Unsurprisingly, doubling occupies the most significant part of the commentary, but accounting for the other two techniques significantly nuances the picture.

It is also essential to recognise that most notes refer to noteworthy pieces of war-related news like the conquest of Mariupol (including the infamous cases of the local Drama Theater and Maternity Hospital No. 2 bombings), the siege of *Azovstal*, the Bucha massacre, the strike on the Olenivka prison, the Russian retreat from Kharkiv region and ensuing discovery of torture chambers and mass graves in Izum and Balakliya, and the prisoner exchange that extracted several hundreds of Azov troops, including its leaders, from captivity. For analytical purposes, I treated these events as *psychodrama vignettes*: more or less open settings in which auxiliaries can freely express themselves. It is impossible to provide factual information in this study, so readers are invited to consult other sources for the general context.

The *voyenkors'* war coverage reveals a typical psychodramatic feature: participants plunged into enacting desired roles. Hence, Russian soldiers are represented as noble liberators who painstakingly avoid inflicting damage on non-combatants. Correspondingly, reporters explain, "The reason Russia is conducting not a war, but a special operation is obvious: our goal is only to expel the enemy, so we are careful not to target civilians and the vital infrastructure."[66] Another desired role is the reincarnation of Soviet soldiers during WWII. Most often—and somewhat incongruously—*voyenkors* evoke Stalingrad; for instance, they describe "the Mariupol kettle, currently cut in two, just as it was at Stalingrad"[67] and allege that "Mariupol is Stalingrad of the ongoing war because the capitulation of the Azovstal garrison provoked the psychological crisis similar to that of Hitler's troops in January-February 1943."[68]

Since the Russo-Ukrainian war is interpreted as the newest instalment of WW2, Russian troops are bound to be fighting against

---

66 https://t.me/rt_special/401
67 https://t.me/Sladkov_plus/5100
68 https://t.me/andrew_kots/181

Nazis. Predictably, this is Azov's role. "We see the reincarnation of the traditional plot," waxes a reporter, "Russian soldiers vanquish Nazism. Naturally, it is ludicrous to compare the Third Reich, then the most powerful army on the planet [sic], with that of Ukraine. However, there is one similarity — Azov. It is the purest reincarnation of SS-troops because both had religious cults, political programs, and a quest for victimhood."[69] Azov's war conduct befits Nazis: they use "6000 hostages, citizens of 16 foreign states, as a human shield,"[70] they regularly shell Ukrainian civilians,[71] primarily humanitarian corridors, [72] and nurture a predilection for devastating hospitals[73] and churches.[74]

Azov's alleged tactic is simple and vicious: "They are intent on transforming Mariupol, Kharkiv, and other Ukrainian cities into killing grounds, not for the Russian troops but the local populations."[75] Consequently, during the siege of Mariupol, Azov fighters contended to barricade themselves in civilian housing deliberately.[76] Likewise, Azov reportedly organised a barrack in Maternity Hospital No. 2,[77] intentionally provoking a public outcry when Russian troops destroyed it. Next, Azov cynically "staged the devastations in the hospital doctoring some photos and forcing poor actresses to poise amidst the rubbles."[78]

Just as the German Nazis did in 1941-1943, Azov reportedly singled out one group to humiliate — the Russian speakers. "When they controlled Mariupol, they were malicious... Sometimes they asked for a cigarette in Russian, and when you respond in Russian, they would physically harm you,"[79] a Mariupol dweller confides. Other eye-witnesses inquired by Russian reporters unanimously

---

69 https://t.me/romagolovanov/8199
70 https://t.me/rian_ru/153079
71 https://t.me/swodki/46662
72 https://t.me/SolovievLive/91650
73 https://rossaprimavera.ru/news/100bd442
74 https://t.me/rt_russian/102991
75 https://t.me/SolovievLive/91650
76 https://t.me/vzglyad_ru/47923
77 https://t.me/SolovievLive/92519
78 https://t.me/SolovievLive/92289
79 https://t.me/rt_russian/106415

blamed the Azov personnel, "those mad maniacs who committed genocide in Mariupol."[80] In a gory parallel with German Nazis, who infamously conducted medical experiments on prisoners, Azov fighters ostensibly "used the elderly veterans of WWII to practice martial art." Simonyan, who reports this incredible incident, adds rhetorically: "Who needed the flourishment of Neo-Nazism in Ukraine? How transformed the villains become heroes? Is this the limit to dehumanising Russians and Russian speakers in Ukraine?".[81]

When performing *doubling*, Russian auxiliaries refer to Azov in two distinct ways: (1) to illustrate the ever-growing chasm of moral depravity and (2) to indicate fractionalisation within the Ukrainian military.

The first topic encompasses the bulk of comments during the siege of Mariupol. Following a typical strategy proper to any belligerent nation to dehumanise the enemy, Russian voyenkors focus on Azov as the incarnation of pure wickedness allegedly inherent in Ukrainian nationalism. Azov fighters are hardly humans: they are tattooed ("as if branded"[82]) products of "intense zombification, operated on de-Christianized youth forced to practice paganism."[83] Usually, they fight under the influence of alcohol or drugs, which is why their fortified positions "are littered with syringes and methadone"[84] or at least with "hundreds of cigarette butts, empty bottles, and beer cans, and these indices unmistakably betray the dispositions of nationalists."[85] They are social marginals, "people without proper education, often living with parents even when adults. They can improve their self-esteem only by wearing a uniform and bellowing 'Glory to Ukraine! Glory to the heroes,' and enjoying unlimited power while murdering helpless victims."[86] *Russia-24* correspondent Evgenii Poddubny uses the story of one Azov fighter,

---

80 https://t.me/SolovievLive/94839
81 https://t.me/margaritasimonyan/10856
82 https://t.me/maximgrigoryev/1042
83 https://t.me/SolovievLive/102271
84 https://t.me/rossia_3/4626
85 https://t.me/msgazdiev/885
86 https://t.me/kremlinprachka/18129

Artem Demyd, as a parable of Azov personnel in general: "he joined the Nazi youth organization [sic] 'Plast,' and in Winter 2014 he participated in the destruction of Kyiv and incinerated riot policeman [*Berkut*] alive."[87] Poddubny's stratagem used the image of Ukrainian nationalism to tie together two ostensibly despicable events of the recent Ukrainian history, the Euromaidan revolution and the "Special Military Operation." Another Azov soldier, captured at the *Azovstal*, "confesses he was ordered to film violent murders of Russian POWs[...]to provoke fear and opposition to redeployment in Ukraine by Russians soldiers."[88] The unflattering coverage, in general, offers an unmistakable message: "Azov fighters are beasts unable to distinguish between Good and Evil,"[89] therefore "any soldier who served in Azov—as well as Aidar, Tornado, or any other breeding grounds for butchers—by default has no right to be considered a human. There must be no pity for them."[90]

Tragically, the Azov-bashing extended to bystanders. When the underground caves of the *Azovstal* complex sheltered both a Ukrainian garrison and civilians fleeing the Russian onslaught, Sladkov informed: "up to 800 *Azovstal* workers enlisted into Azov to pocket both a salary and service money."[91] Gadziev concurred: "there are no 'civilians' at the *Azovstal*, only relatives of nationalists from Azov, officers from Ukrainian security services, and pro-Kyiv officials who humiliated Mariupol common folk for years. All these people made the *Azovstal* their shelter while Nazis were busy obliterating the city."[92]

The demonization of Azov had a significant consequence: within the psychodramatic settings, Azov became a synonym for anything wrong in Russia. For example, a *voyenkor* indignantly recounted that his Z-emblazoned car had been vandalised. He explained: "The filthy being who nailed the car is, in essence, an Azov

---

87   https://t.me/epoddubny/11323
88   https://t.me/RtrDonetsk/7956
89   https://t.me/komsomolec_z/68
90   https://t.me/Sladkov_plus/3830
91   https://t.me/Sladkov_plus/5100
92   https://t.me/msgazdiev/906

fighter, a coward, a bastard, and a terrorist-in-the-making."⁹³ On a much bigger scale, Azov incarnated the malicious spirit when the daughter of a pro-Kremlin intellectual, Aleksandr Dugin, was killed in an explosion supposedly targeting the father himself. Russian security services were quick to blame Azov for the assassination.⁹⁴ Likewise, Russian media reported that an old lady shouted "Glory to Azov" and set a private car owned by a Russian military official on fire in Moscow. Later, her relatives alleged, "she was hypnotised and induced into a crime via a telephone call from Ukraine."⁹⁵ It is more likely that the lady committed the act of civil disobedience, but her relatives took a line from the psychodramatic playbook and blamed Azov for wrongdoing.

Inconsistently with demonisation, Azov personnel were constantly ridiculed. Kadyrov boasted that "they are running like jackals with tails between their legs" ⁹⁶ after Chechen troops entered Mariupol. In contrast, another *voyenkor* filmed a short movie showing "Azov fighters attempting to flee Mariupol disguised in female clothing — a strategy taught by their British instructors."⁹⁷ Most unconvincingly — because of an 80-days-long defence action exerted by besieged personnel and utterly out of resonance with the emphasis on intense Nationalist indoctrination — Russian propaganda informed after *Azovstal* had been taken that "militants had enough food and water, they could have hung on for a longer period. However, the Nazis were psychologically broken [...] having no faith and ideals."⁹⁸

However incongruent, this allegation and alike suggest that in Spring 2022, Azov grew to symbolise the depth of moral depravity — represented by the intentional murder of civilians, cravenness, psychological degradation, brutal vindictiveness, or ideological zeal. Analysed systematically, such characteristics do not make

---

93 https://t.me/vysokygovorit/8069
94 https://www.kommersant.ru/doc/5524691
95 В Москве сожгли BMW сотрудника Генштаба. *Gazeta.ru*. August 28, 2022. https://www.gazeta.ru/social/2022/08/28/15342554.shtml?updated
96 https://t.me/RKadyrov_95/1480
97 https://www.youtube.com/watch?v=24qRsgV-ejg
98 https://t.me/MedvedevVesti/9639

sense because no soldiers can be fierce and cowardly, imbued with irrational ideas and lacking principles simultaneously. Yet, suppose one interprets the outburst of incompatible adjectives as acts of psychodramatic doubling. In that case, the picture becomes clear: **Russian auxiliaries acted in a narrow set of separate vignettes trying to convey and provoke the collective sense of outrage with Azov—not to construct a coherent picture.**

The second crucial feature of doubling relates to efforts to use Azov to blunt the Ukrainian war effort. The general strategy was to frame Azov as an extraneous factotum injected into Ukrainian body politics to promote foreign interests. Solovyov used this figure as far as in 2019 when he explained: "Azov does not follow orders from the Ukrainian Ministry of Internal Affairs [...] Azov's main function is to recruit, train, and season troops for private military companies [...] because Azov is affiliated with the Polish PMC that in turn represents financial interests of some people from the US Democratic party."[99] In 2022, however, the strategy received a particular twist to antagonize Azov and the Ukrainian Army (ZSU). In a set of vignettes, Azov represented Evil, not for the Russian people but for Ukrainian soldiers. First of all, Azov appeared as a very unreliable unit. ZSU was alleged to "have attacked the Azov for insubordination"[100] or complained about being "left exposed after Azov had quietly retreated from their positions."[101] Besides, Azov plays a grim role: a POW from ZSU supposedly testified that "his unit was put under the command of Azov and ordered to fight regardless of their opinions whether it was feasible."[102] To enforce compliance, "Azov serves as barrier troops firing in the backs of ordinary soldiers, which is responsible for numerous exchanges of gunfire between the former and the latter."[103] *Voyenkors* signalled deep hatred between Azov and ZSU to the point that "Ukrainian POWs want to have nothing in common with Azov."[104]

---

99 https://t.me/SolovievLive/9228
100 https://t.me/SolovievLive/90854
101 https://t.me/msgazdiev/943
102 https://t.me/urallive/8901
103 https://t.me/margaritasimonyan/10944
104 https://t.me/Sladkov_plus/5251

However, by May 2022, the attempts to provoke a rupture between Azov and other ZSU units proved hopeless. As a result, the commentaries switched to the generalised blame of the Ukrainian Army. For instance, a Russian military expert, German Kulikovski, opined: "Any 'human being' in Ukrainian military fatigue is a bastard and a murderer without exception. It is time to abandon efforts to look for differences between Nazis and ZSU soldiers under a microscope. They are the same, so we have to destroy them all."[105] Another author concurs: "We failed to fathom the extent of fascistization proper to the Ukrainian society [...] ZSU fighters are as brutal as other Nazis."[106] It remains an open question whether there was a genuine conviction that only Azov represented the segment of the Ukrainian military with the most entrenched anti-Russian ideas, or whether this was just a typical divide-and-rule strategy. Arguably, Russian generals expected at least some ZSU soldiers to rebel, as Putin himself requested Ukrainian military personnel not to oppose the invasion in his February speech.[107] With resolute Ukrainian defence on display not only around the Azov's headquarters at Mariupol but all over Ukraine, it became evident that Ukraine entered a patriotic war, and any efforts to oppose nationalist organisations and the Ukrainian nation itself were deemed unnecessary. The Azov psychodrama fittingly subsided, ceding place to a generalised attempt to wipe out Ukraine.

"Azov's" final act was played in September 2022, when Moscow, having been boiling the public for months with promises to put "Azov terrorists" on trial, suddenly reversed itself and exchanged 215 Azov prisoners for a Ukrainian politician (and Putin's crony) Medvedchuk and 55 Russian POWs. Until Fall 2022, the Kremlin refused even to consider such an exchange,[108] and *voyenkors* ridiculed a "brilliant idea by the Ukrainian President to exchange one Ukrainian citizen for dozens of Ukrainian citizens."[109]

---

105 https://t.me/vysokygovorit/9575
106 https://svpressa.ru/war21/article/329794/
107 https://www.bloomberg.com/news/videos/2022-02-24/putin-orders-special-military-operation-for-ukraine-video-l00nw4qc
108 https://ria.ru/20220523/obmen-1790126204.html
109 https://t.me/kremlinprachka/18434

Instead, the Russian public relished an upcoming reenactment of the Nuremberg trials, vaguely hinted at by officials. With notorious Azov leaders spirited away to Turkey, auxiliaries in Russia exploded.[110] "F[...] this de-Nazification: we captured the Nazis, lectured them a little bit, and let them out," exclaimed one user. "Shall we terminate the 'Special Military Operation' as it turns out that Azov is not Nazi after all?" wondered another. Beneath the outrage, however, the Azov psychodrama revealed Russian opinions on the war. One user preached what he considers a proper treatment of Azov's POWs: "We should have smeared prisoners with Novichok and sent them to die in Turkey or simply poison them, especially the leaders." Another suggested, "not to take any commanding officers as POWs and simply kill them." A third demanded to "kill all those responsible for the ignominious exchange," while another considered "finishing all those cowards returned to Russia, for they were too comfortable in captivity and got fat." The downpour of indignation suggests that Russian psychodrama auxiliaries experienced unadulterated hatred toward Azov, easily redirected to anyone not participating in the collective frenzy.

The discontent was dangerous to the Kremlin itself. Azov was swiftly erased from the agenda to regain control of the situation. The psychodrama finished, followed by a candid observation by *voyenkor* Kashevarova: "We made of Azov the biggest villainous hero."[111] It is true. Azov was just one unit among dozens of others within the Ukrainian army fighting the Russian invasion. It served as a screen on which Russians projected their views on the Ukrainian political project, Ukrainian culture, and Ukrainian nationhood. There lies the real, though unrealised, function of doubling.

Mirroring revealed another truth regarding the Russian way of war. Since February 2022, Russian troops have systematically committed war crimes, which suggests these were not mere excesses by individual soldiers but deliberate coercive practices. The UN Commission established "summary executions, unlawful

---

110 The following quotes are taken from the comments at *Grey Zone* channel. It is technically impossible to provide individual references per each.
111 https://t.me/akashevarova/5382

confinement, torture, ill-treatment, rape and other sexual violence committed in areas occupied by Russian armed forces."[112] Germany, France, Australia, Spain, and the US, among others, submitted documentation to the International Court of Justice accusing Russia of genocide.[113] The OSCE Office for Democratic Institutions and Human Rights deposited a 108-page long report documenting violations of the humanitarian law in Ukraine primarily perpetrated in the zones under Russia's control.[114] Besides, leading human rights organisations signaled that Russian forces were responsible for extrajudicial executions of civilians,[115] forceful transfer of children,[116] and sexual violence.[117] Recognizing the war crimes committed by the Russian side, the International Criminal Court issued an arrest warrant for Putin on March 17, 2023.[118]

In response to the mounting evidence, the Kremlin applies two strategies. First, it counters systematic documentation of Russian war crimes with alternative testimonies by rogue operators. For instance, it used Adrian Bocquet, a French ex-military and a humanitarian volunteer working at Kyiv region in Spring 2022, who declared: "The only war crimes I saw during the days I was there were perpetrated by Ukrainian forces, and not by Russian forces."[119] Later, investigations revealed that Bocquet had systematically

---

112 https://www.ohchr.org/sites/default/files/2022-10/A-77-533-AUV-EN.pdf
113 https://www.icj-cij.org/en/case/182
114 https://www.osce.org/files/f/documents/f/a/515868.pdf
115 https://www.amnesty.org/en/latest/news/2022/04/ukraine-russian-forces-extrajudicially-executing-civilians-in-apparent-war-crimes-new-testimony/
116 https://www.amnesty.org/en/latest/news/2022/11/ukraine-russias-unlawful-transfer-of-civilians-a-war-crime-and-likely-a-crime-against-humanity-new-report/
117 https://www.hrw.org/news/2022/04/03/ukraine-apparent-war-crimes-russia-controlled-areas
118 https://www.icc-cpi.int/news/situation-ukraine-icc-judges-issue-arrest-warrants-against-vladimir-vladimirovich-putin-and
119 https://www.youtube.com/watch?v=ZoKnhXnp-Zk&t=1353s

falsified his accounts, inflating his military experience,[120] and he fabricated evidence regarding war crimes committed by Ukrainians.[121]

Another strategy available to Russia was *mirroring*. Since the first days of the invasion, the psychodrama auxiliaries were busy accusing Azov of war crimes. In Mariupol, Azov allegedly "mined the *Azovstal* plant to blast the compound with all the workers if the city is captured."[122] It also "prevented civilians from leaving the city [...] and was methodically obliterating the city's infrastructure to stage Russian artillery strikes."[123] In Kharkiv, "Azov planned to detonate the experimental nuclear facility blaming Russia."[124] Besides, Azov was reported to intentionally shoot civilian cars,[125] violate laws of war while organizing headquarters at civilian infrastructure,[126] take hostages, [127] wantonly destroy Russian-speaking cities,[128] and organize torture chambers.[129] During the psychodrama, Russian observers attributed to Azov almost all horrendous acts committed by Russian war criminals.

In most cases, Azov is used for deflection, that is, as a generalised source of unspecified atrocities like "shelling" or "executions." Deflection goes so far that Chairman of the State Duma Vyacheslav Volodin tried to intimidate US President Biden with Hague Courte because "Azov is being supplied with US weapons instrumental in the killing of simple civilians, whose blood befalls on US President."[130]

---

120 https://www.liberation.fr/checknews/adrien-bocquet-a-aussi-menti-sur-son-passe-militaire-20220607_JUFIZ2SAFFC43IVQFYEFXDRMOY/
121 https://www.francetvinfo.fr/monde/europe/manifestations-en-ukraine/guerre-en-ukraine-le-cliche-cense-prouver-la-presence-a-kiev-de-l-ex-militaire-francais-adrien-bocquet-est-un-photomontage_5201524.html
122 https://t.me/SolovievLive/90512
123 https://t.me/SolovievLive/92344
124 https://t.me/SolovievLive/91583
125 https://t.me/genshab/419
126 https://t.me/SolovievLive/94167
127 https://t.me/kremlinprachka/17809
128 https://t.me/epoddubny/8847
129 https://t.me/SolovievLive/1366
130 https://t.me/duma_gov_ru/70

However, sometimes Azov is accused of specific crimes committed by Russians themselves. To cite one example, after the Ukrainian counter-offensive had liberated Kupiansk, an Azov fighter shared footage taken from a phone of a Russian captive documenting several executions. Psychodramatic auxiliaries rushed to condemn "Ukrainian fascist murderers who filmed their crime."[131] Another concurred that "they will simply re-play the scrip already tried in Bucha, Irpin, and Izum,"[132] alleging that all those well-documented war crimes had been staged. Yet another auxiliary drew a political lesson: "these are Russian people executed by Nazi bastards, executed because those people believed us, joined us, dared to speak Russian and belong to the Russian world [...] The horrendous murder is not simply a crime of a Nazi filth from Azov. It is our Russian sin."[133]

The psychodramatic theory conceptualizes mirroring as a technique that helps participants to recognize their selves and continue a scene they are unwilling or unable to do because of intense negative feelings.[134] Following this insight, I suggest interpreting Russian comments on the war crimes not just as cynical obfuscating, which it often is, but also as a sign of the psychological strain *voeynkors* are experiencing. These individuals report horrors and suffering often inflicted on non-combatants by their compatriots. To express these events, auxiliaries resort to a ruse: they attribute actual crimes to the incarnation of moral depravity, Azov. Remarkably, some judgments are profoundly ironic: they invite the substitution of Azov for Russia and decipher what is actually happening. Take, for instance, the following statement: "Nazis are locked in their echo chamber; thus, everything we find repulsive is normal for them."[135]

The point is not to commiserate with Solovyov, Simonyan, and alike: they are building glamorous careers peddling

---

131 https://t.me/Marinaslovo/4755
132 https://tlgrm.ru/channels/@sashakots/36393
133 https://t.me/c/1641504762/189
134 Giacomucci, Scщee. (2021). *Social Work, Sociometry, and Psychodrama*, Singapore: Springer Nature, 256.
135 https://t.me/Marinaslovo/4746

propaganda and genuine human misery online. Instead, I propose interpreting mirroring as the first step for unwilling subjects to recognize their transgressions. The next step is not necessarily repentance; on the contrary, mirroring might contribute to a full-blown recognition: "Yes, it is me, and I am proud of it."

This is likely to be happening in some segments of the Russian digital space. For example, Igor Mangushev was a political operator close to Prigozhyn, *Wagner*'s owner, and the man reportedly responsible for introducing Z as Russian military insignia.[136] After a tour of duty as a mercenary somewhere in Ukraine, Mangushev gave a speech at a Moscow nightclub. Holding a human skull, he explained that the remains belonged to "a guy besieged in *Azovstal*." Mangushev elaborated that a similar fate awaits all Ukrainians because "we are fighting not against people, but against the idea of independent Ukraine."[137] Mangushev, in other words, all but acknowledged the physical extermination of Ukrainians as the preferable way to fight Ukraine into submission. Egor Kholmogorov, another journalist and the author of the notion "Russian Spring,"[138] is even more candid. He opines:

> We have to annihilate Ukraine even if this means total destruction of all factories, poisonous pollution of all chernozem, crippling of the Russian economy, and death of our young men [...] Our goal is to terminate the gestation of Ukrainian nation [...] We will either reap our victory, becoming a superpower or yield our role in history forever.[139]

These revelations are far from unique. In August 2022, the Russian Ambassador to Austria Mikhail Ulyanov tweeted, "No Mercy to the

---

136 Буква Z—официальный (и зловещий) символ российского вторжения в Украину. *Meduza*. March 15, 2022. https://meduza.io/feature/2022/03/15/bukva-z-ofitsialnyy-i-zloveschiy-simvol-rossiyskogo-vtorzheniya-v-ukrainu-my-popytalis-vyyasnit-kto-eto-pridumal-i-vot-chto-iz-etogo-poluchilos
137 The performance can be seen here: https://www.youtube.com/watch?v=KusjrW5auYw
138 Холмогоров, Егор. (2014.) Воздух русской весны. *Взгляд: деловая газета*. https://vz.ru/columns/2014/4/10/681367.html
139 https://t.me/holmogortalks/24528

Ukrainian population,"[140] provoking a diplomatic scandal[141] (he later deleted the message). In October, after massive rocket strikes hit 40% of power infrastructure in Ukraine, leaving up to 10 million people without energy, anonymous users on *Telegram* were pleased "to see Ukrainians freeze." German Kulikovski concurred with delight: "There will be no pausing in attacks against vital Ukrainian infrastructure, so in the foreseeable future, the country will enjoy the realities of steampunk by the end of November [...] which will be a perfect result."[142] Solovyev's post about a strike against Odesa's hydro power plant elicited 15 thousand likes[143]. Little by little, Russians approve of the Kremlin's intentions to wreak havoc and destruction in Ukraine to achieve its political goals. These instances have no relation to Azov; still, they share the same logic proper to the "Azov psychodrama": Russian commentators are disdainful of all things Ukrainian and eagerly blame Ukraine for crimes they have committed or are still nurturing.

Coda

During the first seven months of the Russian invasion, a relatively small military unit, the Azov battalion, played a central role in Russian war coverage. The focus on Azov could not possibly be explained by its battle performance. Arguably, Azov was singled out because of its ideology, microculture, and symbolic repertoire, granting the Kremlin convenient proof of the need to "de-Nazify" Ukraine. However, profusely describing Azov, Russian military correspondents made much more than posited its "fascist nature."

As I have argued, the outburst of collective passions centred on Azov in Spring-Fall 2022 constitutes a form of group action resembling psychodrama, a collective performance focused on the

---

140 https://twitter.com/amb_ulyanov/status/1560756872709382145?s=21&t=TnpYUs3QIJM1JoraL13-OQ
141 Stewart, David. (2022). "Austria summons Russian ambassador for tweeting, «No mercy for the Ukrainian people«." *News 360*. https://www.msn.com/en-us/news/world/austria-summons-russian-ambassador-for-tweeting-%C2%A Bno-mercy-for-the-ukrainian-people%C2%BB/ar-AA10SGHj
142 https://t.me/vysokygovorit/10010
143 https://t.me/SolovievLive/137259

trials of a protagonist but aiming to alleviate psychological traumas inflicted on all participants. Highlighting spontaneity, the psychodramatic method urges participants to express their preoccupations and values as they see fit. When Russians rushed to comment on Azov, they followed the psychodramatic guidelines.

First, on many occasions, participants accused Azov of their documented wrongdoings. Moreover, they attributed to Azov issues that faced Russia—as when ridiculing the weapon system used by the battalion, "junk and trash supplied by the Western partners."[144] However, Russian troops were reduced to using "D-20 artillery and T-80BV tanks dating from the Soviet era"[145] or even the overtly obsolete T-62.[146] Seemingly illogical accusations against Azov are grounded in a mechanism known in the cognition theory as a *simulation*: during simulation, people use themselves as a model for understanding other individuals.[147] Alternatively, it is dubbed *projection* in clinical psychology, where specialists see it as "a defence mechanism by which unacceptable psychological impulses and traits in oneself are attributed to others."[148] If my interpretation is valid, during "Azov psychodrama," participants projected onto the unit the morally reprehensible features of the Russian invasion of Ukraine. No Ukrainian policy toward the Russian-speaking populations reached the extent of coercion and outright genocidal indentions as compared to executions of pro-Ukrainian activists, destruction of cultural heritage, including Ukrainian

---

144 https://t.me/diza_donbass/839
145 https://www.bloomberg.com/news/articles/2022-06-14/russia-turns-to-old-tanks-as-it-burns-through-weapons-in-ukraine
146 https://www.mil.gov.ua/en/news/2022/05/23/the-operational-update-regarding-the-russian-invasion-on-06-00-on-may-23-2022/
147 Gordon, Robert. (1986). "Folk psychology as simulation." *Mind & Language* 1: 158–171.
148 Costa, Rui. (2017). "Projection (Defense Mechanism)." In: Zeigler-Hill, V., Shackelford, T. (eds) *Encyclopedia of Personality and Individual Differences*. Springer, Cham. https://doi.org/10.1007/978-3-319-28099-8_1413-1

printed books, and other measures envisioned by the Kremlin[149] or currently in motion at the Russian-occupied territories.[150]

Second, a bulk of Azov-related reportages blamed Azov for moral depravity ranging from pusillanimity to fanaticism, from substance abuse to calculated targeting of non-combatants. However, artificial inflation of Azov's image to the point when it started representing the villainous archenemy, propaganda suffered a massive backlash when the Kremlin exchanged many of the alleged "war criminals" earmarked for a public trial in a POW swap. The public outcry in the Russian digital space suggested that Azov's fate eventually became important for Russia itself. Paradoxically, anti-Russia-representing Azov became near and dear to Russians because, as a counter-model, it reinforced Russian identity. For this reason, Russian participants resort to reenacting their preferred roles when performing psychodrama. Most apparent is the effort to revitalise WW2 heroism. This is almost inevitable given the cult of the Great Victory,[151] the composition of political elites, where Soviet-related nomenklatura constitutes a staggering 60%,[152] the return to Soviet practices,[153] and the identification of contemporary Russians more with the Soviet state than Russia itself.[154] As a result, the WW2 shadow is ubiquitous. Commentators see fascists

---

149 For details, consult a project of de-Ukrainization prematurely aired by the Russian political operator T. Sergeitsev "What Russia Should Do With Ukraine," *Ria-novosti*: https://ria.ru/20220403/ukraina-1781469605.html

150 For a comprehensive analysis of deliberate brutality of Russian troops: Watling, Jack, Danylyuk, Oleksandr and Reynolds, Nick (2023). "Preliminary Lessons from Russia's Unconventional Operations During the Russo-Ukrainian War, February 2022–February 2023." Royal United Services Institute for Defence and Security Studies, https://rusi.org/explore-our-research/publications/special-resources/preliminary-lessons-russias-unconventional-operations-during-russo-ukrainian-war-february-2022

151 Polegkyi, Oleksii. (2016). "Russia's new 'religion': The cult of the 'Great Victory'." *New Eastern Europe*: https://neweasterneurope.eu/2016/05/25/russias-new-religion-the-cult-of-the-great-victory/

152 Snegovaya, Maria and Petrov, Kirill. (2022). "Long Soviet shadows: the nomenklatura ties of Putin elites." *Post-Soviet Affairs* 38(4): 329-348.

153 Kryshtanovskaya, Olga. (2009). "Sovietization of Russia, 2000-2008," *Eurasian Review* 2: 95-133.

154 Whitefield, Stephen and Chaisty, Paul. (2022). "Putin's Russia: people increasingly identify with the Soviet Union—here's what that means." *The Conversation*: https://theconversation.com/putins-russia-people-increasingly-identify-with-the-soviet-union-heres-what-that-means-181129

everywhere and attempt to discern the watershed moment of Stalingrad in any insignificant battle. The geography of the Russo-Ukrainian war also contributes to building parallels, for towns like Kharkiv, Kupiansk, Izium, and Mariupol witnessed important fighting back in 1941-45. In addition, Russian participants pretend to play the favourite roles borrowed from a broader national hagiography like "protectors of the Orthodox faith" and "champions of the oppressed populations." In the dreamscape of psychodrama, such role-playing, however cynical it may seem, helps participants expose their values for public display to have them scrutinised and evaluated as proper or improper for eventual work with traumas.

Finally, although an exhibition of one's inner demons might have therapeutic effects for a participant, psychodrama's real target is the community. With the "Azov" psychodrama being only a small scene within a broader act of Russo-Ukrainian relations, I believe the involved group transcends the Ukrainian and Russian communities. The global community observed, participated in, and is likely to be transformed by the experience. Sure enough, I do not suggest that Canadians or Chileans following the fateful siege of Mariupol are bound to profound metamorphosis. Instead, I am implying that several significant projections of values and motives (roles) inherited from the painful experiences of WWII, the Cold War, and the post-Soviet transitions will not endure. Signs of the changes are abundant: Western universities grew more aware of in-built pro-Russian bias in their curricula and are trying to amend them. Central European warnings that Russian imperialism might challenge the EU, typically derided as history-induced traumas by Western political circles, are being vindicated. The inaptitude of international organisations like the UNO, the ICRC, and the IAEA to promote peace, POWs rights, and nuclear security, respectively, urge to erect new pillars of international world order. Russia's military power is being degraded to the point where no one accepts the notion of "the world's second-most prominent army" at face value. These events point to not-so-subtle alterations within the global community already provoked by the war. Roles played by Russia and Ukraine, memories of 1945 and 1991, regional politics in the post-Soviet region — much will change for humanity, and the Azov psychodrama is one of the locomotives of the shift.

6 The War in Ukraine and the Transnational Far-right Extremist Movement

Mollie Saltskog

Introduction

While the conflicts of the 1980s, 1990s, and 2000s presented individuals adhering to Salafi-jihadi ideology with opportunities to travel and fight for their "cause," similar opportunities were scarce for those in extreme far-right milieus. Until 2014. When war broke out as a result of Russia's illegal invasion and annexation of Crimea and occupation of areas in eastern Ukraine, the extreme far-right movement had, for the first time since the Croatian War of Independence (1991-1995), a conflict with an extreme far-right ideological pull, in this sense, it is easy to trace Ukraine's transformation into a hub for the far-right since 2014. The war provided battlefield opportunities for local far-right individuals fighting on both sides of the conflict and the foreigners who travelled to join them. It also placed unprecedented attention and focus on Ukraine among the transnational far-right—something that individuals and groups in the country have seized upon to establish their positions in the contemporary movement. The conflict also brought with it opportunities for the Russian Federation to continue building inroads and providing support for far-right movements outside its borders. However, the on-the-ground realities are not as clear-cut.

The emergence of Ukraine as a key hub for the far-right movement must first be considered within the broader context of the increasing trans-nationalization of extremist movements. In addition, as the conflict has waxed and waned in intensity since 2014, the on-the-ground dynamics, coupled with Ukrainian government policy to address the issues of extremist individuals in its armed forces and volunteer groups, have impacted how far-right movements interact with organisations and groups present in Ukraine. Lastly,

Russia's attempted full invasion of Ukraine on February 24, 2022, dramatically changed the nature of the conflict and the role of far-right individuals and groups. Today, it appears that Russia is likely the primary country utilising extremist actors in the conflict, including far-right groups like the Wagner Group, Rusich Group, and Russian Imperial Movement (RIM).[1] These broader dynamics are essential to keep in mind to examine the current far-right landscape in Ukraine and understand how it has emerged as a critical node in the transnational far-right movement. This chapter argues that this node is not an exception to the rule. Instead, it is a by-product of the contemporary extremist landscape, Russia's illegal war, and the opportunities that conflict often presents to non-state actors.

This chapter should not be used as evidence for the Kremlin's disinformation narratives about Ukraine, which has served as a pretext for the brutal and illegal war unleashed by Putin on Ukraine and its citizens. Instead, the situation should be analysed within the broader context of the rise of far-right ideology in the West, including in the armed forces of Western countries. In 2020, Germany's defence minister disbanded a unit of the Command Special Forces (KSK) over reports of right-wing extremism, including neo-Nazism and white supremacism, within its ranks.[2] According to data produced by George Washington University's Program on Extremism, 118 of the over 900 defendants charged in connection with the January 6, 2021 attack on the US Capitol have a military background.[3]

---

1 "Foreign Fighters, Volunteers, and Mercenaries: Non-State Actors and Narratives in Ukraine" (The Soufan Center, April 4, 2022), https://thesoufancenter.org/research/foreign-fighters-volunteers-and-mercenaries-non-state-actors-and-narratives-in-ukraine/.
2 Scott Neuman, "Germany Disbands Elite Military Unit Following Reports Of Right Wing Extremism," *NPR*, July 1, 2020, sec. Europe, https://www.npr.org/2020/07/01/886458028/germany-disbands-elite-military-unit-following-reports-of-right-wing-extremism;
3 "GWUPOE Jan6 Demographics Tracker," Tableau Software, accessed December 30, 2022, https://public.tableau.com/views/GWUPOEJan6Demographics Tracker/StateDashboard?:embed=y&:showVizHome=no&:host_url=https%3A%2F%2Fpublic.tableau.com%2F&:embed_code_version=3&:tabs=no&:toolbar=yes&:animate_transition=yes&:display_static_image=no&:display_spinner=no&:display_overlay=yes&:display_count=yes&:language=en-US&publish=yes&:loadOrderID=0;

Far-right extremism has infiltrated armed forces across the Western world, likely because of the operational advantage for groups and movements to have those with military experience in their ranks. Similar reasons help explain why far-right extremists, or other extremists, have travelled to gain combat experience during the war in Ukraine.

The Rise of the Transnational Contemporary Extreme Far-Right Movement

The threats from far-right terrorism and extremism are pronounced and growing in many parts of the Western world. The United Nations (UN) has noted that between 2014 and 2018, there was a 320 per cent increase in attacks conducted by individuals the UN categorized as "affiliated with "right-wing terrorism".[4] In the United States, the threats posed by domestic violent extremists, primarily those espousing ideologies within the far-right terrorism umbrella, are assessed to have surpassed that of international terrorism, such as those espousing Salafi-jihadi ideology.[5] In the United Kingdom, law enforcement authorities have noted that the country is facing a growing terrorist threat from the violent far-right, with 41 per cent of counter-terrorism arrests in 2021 categorised as "extreme right-wing suspects".[6] Other European countries still identify Islamist terrorism as the biggest threat, but far-right extremism presents a growing terrorism threat on the radar of law enforcement. For example, the November 2022 terrorism threat assessment from the Netherlands's National Coordinator for Counterterrorism and

---

4 "Terrorist Attacks on the Basis of Xenophobia, Racism and Other Forms of Intolerance, or in the Name of Religion or Belief," Report of the Secretary-General (The United Nations, August 3, 2022), https://documents-dds-ny.un.org/doc/UNDOC/GEN/N22/450/52/PDF/N2245052.pdf?OpenElement;

5 "(U) Domestic Violent Extremism Poses Heightened Threat in 2021" (Office of the Director of National Intelligence, March 1, 2021), https://www.dni.gov/files/ODNI/documents/assessments/UnclassSummaryofDVEAssessment-17MAR21.pdf;

6 Vikram Dodd, "Terrorism in the UK: The Rising Threat of Far-Right Extremists," *The Guardian*, May 16, 2022, sec. UK news, https://www.theguardian.com/uk-news/2022/may/16/terrorism-in-the-uk-the-rising-threat-of-far-right-extremists;

Security stated: "The nature of the terrorist threat has changed over the past few years: the threat in and to the Netherlands has become more multifaceted and more diffuse." The assessment noted that "Jihadism remains the principal terrorist threat," but because of "the rise of right-wing extremist accelerationism, terrorist attacks prompted by this inherently violent ideology have also become conceivable".[7]

The increasingly pronounced threat from violent far-right extremism has been accompanied with a notable trans-nationalization of the movement. The US Office of the Director of National Intelligence noted in a 2021 Domestic Violent Extremism (DVE) threat assessment that:

> U.S. [Racially and Ethnically Motivated Violent Extremists (REMVE)] who promote the superiority of the white race are the [Domestic Violent Extremist] actors with the most persistent and concerning transnational connections because individuals with similar ideological beliefs exist outside of the United States and these [extremists] frequently communicate with and seek to influence each other."[8]

The UN Counter-Terrorism Committee Executive Directorate (CTED) declared in April 2020 that it had been "alerted by Member States to their increasing concern at the growing and increasingly transnational threat posed by extreme right-wing terrorism."[9]

The transnationalisation of the contemporary extreme right-wing movement is highlighted in how far-right mass casualty attacks are inspired and ultimately perpetrated within this network through online manifestos that reference other terrorists and their grievances. For example, Brenton Tarrant, the perpetrator of the

---

[7] "Terrorist Threat Assessment for the Netherlands 57" (National Coordinator for Security and Counterterrorism, November 7, 2022), https://english.nctv.nl/documents/publications/2022/11/07/terrorist-threat-assessment-for-the-netherlands-57.

[8] "(U) Domestic Violent Extremism Poses Heightened Threat in 2021" (Office of the Director of National Intelligence, March 1, 2021), https://www.dni.gov/files/ODNI/documents/assessments/UnclassSummaryofDVEAssessment-17MAR21.pdf;

[9] "'Member States Concerned by the Growing and Increasingly Transnational Threat of Extreme Right-Wing Terrorism,'" CTED Trends Alert (United Nations Security Council Counter-Terrorism Committee Executive Directorate, April 2020);

2019 New Zealand Mosque attacks—in which 51 worshippers lost their lives—was, to some extent, inspired by the Norwegian terrorist Anders Behring Breivik. Breivik committed the 2011 attack on Utoya Island that killed 77 people, the majority of them children and youths. In a self-styled interview before the attack, Tarrant claimed, "I have only had brief contact with Knight Justiciar Breivik, receiving a blessing for my mission after contacting his brother knights".[10] However, this claim was later disputed by both Norwegian and New Zealand law enforcement authorities, as well as Tarrant himself, who said this claim was meant to lead law enforcement astray in their investigations. The *Report of the Royal Commission of Inquiry into the Terrorist Attack on Christchurch Masjidain on 15 March 2019*, however, discussed how and to what extent Tarrant was inspired by Breivik and his written manifesto, noting that "the individual was significantly influenced by the Oslo terrorist." Specifically, the Royal Commission concluded that Tarrant's preparations for the atrocities he committed were, to a large extent, consistent with the written guidance offered by Breivik to future terrorists, and that, in examining Tarrant's actions prior to and during the attacks, "the guidance offered by the Oslo terrorist was largely operational in nature.".[11]

Violent far-right extremists who have conducted mass-casualty attacks in the United States have also referenced Breivik, Tarrant, and other attackers in their manifestos and in symbolism used during their atrocities. Most recently, the shooter who carried out a mass-casualty attack targeting Black Americans at a supermarket in Buffalo, NY, on May 14, 2022, killing 10, seemingly drew inspiration from Breivik, Tarrant, and other violent far-right attackers.

---

10 Adam Taylor, "New Zealand Suspect Allegedly Claimed 'Brief Contact' with Norwegian Mass Murderer Anders Breivik," *Washington Post*, March 15, 2019, https://www.washingtonpost.com/world/2019/03/15/new-zealand-suspect-allegedly-claimed-brief-contact-with-norwegian-mass-murderer-anders-breivik/;

11 "Ko Tō Tātou Kāinga Tēnei: Royal Commission of Inquiry into the Terrorist Attack on Christchurch Masjidain on 15 March 2019" (Ko tō tātou kāinga tēnei: Royal Commission of Inquiry into the terrorist attack on Christchurch masjidain on 15 March 2019, December 8, 2020), https://christchurchattack.royalcommission.nz/the-report/download-report/download-the-report/;

Similar to Tarrant, the shooter inscribed his weapons with names and references to other extreme far-right killers, including Breivik and Tarrant. ("Buffalo Shooter's Weapons Covered in White Supremacist Messaging," 2022).[12] It is evident that the inspiration for and calls to violence within the contemporary violent far-right movement has become transnational.

Apart from violent attacks, other aspects of the contemporary far-right extremist movement have also become transnational, including ideological, organisational, and financial factors. Far-right extremist ideologues that call for violence utilise the internet and in-person organised events to spread their hateful creed to organisations and individuals in other countries. In neo-Nazi and accelerationist online chat forums, neo-Nazi ideologue James Mason's writings from the 1980s, compiled in the 600+ pages publication entitled SIEGE, have become mandatory reading for those seeking to gain entry into certain accelerationist organisations and groups in the United States and Europe.[13] Mason notoriously fixated on terrorism and race war, which is reflected in his writings and the groups that they inspire. In 2019, American far-right extremist ideologue Greg Johnson was deported from Norway, where he was due to speak at a far-right conference in Oslo. Authorities cited that Johnson had expressed "respect" for the far-right terrorist Breivik.[14] The Scandza Forum that Johnson was set to speak at was founded in 2017 and brings together far-right extremists from all over Europe and North America for in-person conferences in Scandinavian countries.[15] Similar in-person events—including conferences,

---

12 "Buffalo Shooter's Weapons Covered in White Supremacist Messaging," *ADL Center on Extremism*, May 15, 2022, https://www.adl.org/resources/blog/buffalo-shooters-weapons-covered-white-supremacist-messaging;
13 "The Atomwaffen Division: The Evolution of the White Supremacy Threat" (The Soufan Center, August 12, 2020), https://thesoufancenter.org/research/the-atomwaffen-division-the-evolution-of-the-white-supremacy-threat/;
14 Liam Stack, "American White Nationalist Is Arrested in Norway," *The New York Times*, November 4, 2019, sec. World, https://www.nytimes.com/2019/11/04/world/europe/greg-johnson-arrested-white-nationalist.html;
15 Chuck Tanner, "Sons of Vanguardism: American White Nationalists at the Scandza Forum ⋆ Institute for Research and Education on Human Rights," *Institute for Research and Education on Human Rights*, October 15, 2019,

marches, and concerts — attracting far-right extremists from different countries have occurred in other parts of Europe, including Germany[16], Bulgaria (Colborne, 2020)[17], and Poland (Higgins, 2021).[18]

Transnational organisational aspects are also present in the contemporary extreme far-right movement. A 2020 special report by The Soufan Center on the Atomwaffen Division (AWD), a Neo-Nazi organisation founded in the United States, mapped cells and affiliated and inspired organisations in over a dozen countries. Some cells and affiliated organisations had somewhat regular contact with the US-based cells. They pledged allegiance to AWD in a similar manner to how al-Qaeda affiliates across the globe historically pledged allegiance to Central al-Qaeda.[19]

The contemporary far-right extremist movement also leverages transnational connections to fund activities. While criminal activities and more conventional fundraising activities, including membership dues and donations, are still used by some individuals and groups, experts and researchers have noted how cryptocurrency, donations via crowdfunding, and e-commerce sales have become critical sources of financing for the extreme far-right movement.[20] A 2021 Southern Poverty Law Center investigation found

---

https://www.irehr.org/2019/10/15/sons-of-vanguardism-american-white-nationalists-at-the-scandza-forum/;

16 Richard Engel and Luke Denne, "Neo-Nazis form U.S. and Europe Build Far-Right Links at Concerts in Germany," *NBC News*, March 22, 2020, https://www.nbcnews.com/news/us-news/neo-nazis-u-s-europe-build-far-right-links-concerts-n1165266;

17 Michael Colborne, "Neo-Nazis Failed to March in an EU Capital This Week — but Their Network Is Growing," *Haaretz*, February 26, 2020, https://www.haaretz.com/world-news/europe/2020-02-26/ty-article/.premium/neo-nazis-failed-to-march-this-week-but-theyre-network-is-growing/0000017f-e579-da9b-a1ff-ed7f9bba0000;

18 Andrew Higgins, "As Poland Celebrates Its Independence Day, Far-Right Groups Stage Rallies across the Country.," *The New York Times*, November 11, 2021, sec. World, https://www.nytimes.com/2021/11/11/world/europe/poland-independence-day-far-right-protests.html;

19 "The Atomwaffen Division: The Evolution of the White Supremacy Threat" (The Soufan Center, August 12, 2020), https://thesoufancenter.org/research/the-atomwaffen-division-the-evolution-of-the-white-supremacy-threat/;

20 Jason Blazakis, "Far-Right Online Financing and How to Counter It — Global Center on Cooperative Security," *Global Center on Cooperative Security* (blog),

that over 600 crypto addresses were associated with known far-right extremist individuals or groups.[21] A 2020 investigation found that at least 24 extreme far-right groups and individuals use one or more online fundraising services, such as Amazon, DonorBox, and Stripe.[22] Terrorism finance researcher and expert Jessica Davis noted, "Merchandise sales and donations are critical aspects of Proud Boys' financing and remain a viable source of funds for the group".[23] Following the January 6, 2021 attack on the US Capitol, in which several members of the Proud Boys participated, their chapter in the UK seemingly used the attention and resulting influx of members in its Telegram channel to fundraise. As early as February 2021, Proud Boys UK-affiliate merchandise started arriving at different US chapters, indicating some form of likely financial ties or exchange between the UK-based and US-based chapters.[24]

This is not to say that the transnational aspect of the extreme far-right movement is entirely novel and unique to the contemporary movement. Indeed, there are documented instances of fascist and Nazi organisations and parties in Europe during the 1930s that sported connections across country borders.[25] In addition, the Rhodesian Bush War (1964-1979) is estimated to have attracted hundreds of far-right extremists from over 15 countries 685 that

---

August 1, 2022, https://www.globalcenter.org/resource/far-right-online-financing-and-how-to-counter-it/;

21 "How Cryptocurrency Revolutionized the White Supremacist Movement," *Southern Poverty Law Center* (blog), December 9, 2021, https://www.splcenter.org/hatewatch/2021/12/09/how-cryptocurrency-revolutionized-white-supremacist-movement;

22 Alex Kotch, "Funding Hate: How Online Merchants and Payment Processors Help White Nationalists Raise Money" (Center for Media and Democracy, April 24, 2020), https://www.exposedbycmd.org/wp-content/uploads/2020/04/Funding-Hate-Report-by-CMD.pdf.;

23 Jessica Davis, "Proud Boys Financing," June 10, 2021, https://newsletter.insighttthreatintel.com/p/proud-boys-financing;

24 "A Perfect Storm: Insurrection, Incitement, And The Violent Far-Right Movement," *The Soufan Center* (blog), October 4, 2021, https://thesoufancenter.org/research/a-perfect-storm-insurrection-incitement-and-the-violent-far-right-movement/;

25 Nathaniël Kunkeler and Martin Kristoffer Hamre, "Conceptions and Practices of International Fascism in Norway, Sweden and the Netherlands, 1930-40," *Journal of Contemporary History* 57, no. 1 (January 1, 2022): 45–67, https://doi.org/10.1177/00220094211031992;

travelled to fight in the conflict, something that is still invoked and celebrated on far-right extremist chat forums today.[26] It is essential to recognise the impact of emerging technologies on the contemporary far-right extremist movement by allowing grievances, goods, ideas, tactics, techniques, and procedures to travel across borders at an unprecedented speed and rate.[27] Previously, far-right extremists and groups primarily focused on building a national or domestic identity and associated activities. For many of the contemporary extreme far-right, primarily white supremacists, the harnessing of emerging technologies has allowed for these barriers to be broken down in favour of a more globalised approach.[28]

An excellent example of this is how the war in Ukraine has emerged as a conflict with a clear ideological pull for the transnational far-right extremist movement and how technology has aided in bringing information, debate, and tips on how to travel to join the conflict. Following the 2014 Russian annexation of Crimea and the war in eastern Ukraine, far-right groups and individuals took to the internet to share information on the war and advice on how to join different sides of the conflict.[29] As the war intensified due to Russia's illegal full-scale invasion of Ukraine in February of 2022, it has continued to be a hot-button topic on far-right extremist message boards and chat forums. Interestingly, however, the movement is not a monolith in how it views the war and what side it

---

26 Simon Purdue, "Foreign Fighters and the Global War for White Supremacy — Centre for Analysis of the Radical Right," *Centre for Analysis of the Radical Right* (blog), February 22, 2020, https://www.radicalrightanalysis.com/2020/02/22/foreign-fighters-and-the-global-war-for-white-supremacy/;
27 "Strategic Framework for Countering Terrorism and Targeted Violence" (Department of Homeland Security, September 2019), https://www.dhs.gov/sites/default/files/publications/19_0920_plcy_strategic-framework-countering-terrorism-targeted-violence.pdf;
28 "CONFRONTING VIOLENT WHITE SUPREMACY (PART III): ADDRESSING THE TRANSNATIONAL TERRORIST THREAT" (One Hundred Sixteenth Congress: U.S. Government Publishing Office, September 20, 2019), https://www.govinfo.gov/content/pkg/CHRG-116hhrg37975/html/CHRG-116hhrg37975.htm;
29 Mollie Saltskog and Colin P. Clarke, "Rebuttal: Ukraine Is Emerging as Critical Node for White-Supremacy Extremists | Russia Matters," *Russia Matters* (blog), September 24, 2020, https://www.russiamatters.org/analysis/rebuttal-ukraine-emerging-critical-node-white-supremacy-extremists#_ftn1;

supports. While some individuals and groups venerate the Ukrainian side's fighting spirit and protection of their sovereignty, other groups and individuals support the Russian side and claim Putin is the "saviour of the white race." Yet, some groups and individuals have expressed concern that this conflict involves whites fighting and killing whites, which is contradictory to preserving the white race.[30]

Ukraine as a Node in the Transnational Contemporary Far-Right Extremist Movement

It is within this broader context that we must examine the extreme far-right movement and the conflict in Ukraine to understand why the country has become a node in the contemporary, transnational far-right extremist network. Specifically, how the conflict in Ukraine, prompted by Russia's illegal invasion in 2014, facilitated this development. In examining this phenomenon, two, at times contradictory, arguments emerge. First, just as jihadists used conflicts in Afghanistan, Chechnya, the Balkans, Iraq, and Syria to share tactics, techniques, and procedures and to solidify transnational networks, so too have far-right extremists on both sides utilised the Ukraine conflict. Second, Ukraine is not unique in having a far-right extremist movement that has become an essential node in the contemporary transnational network. Instead, it is but one example of how the contemporary far-right extremist movement is becoming a pronounced, transnationalised extremist threat across the Western world.

Foreign Fighters and Volunteers

The 2014 war in Ukraine brought with it an influx of foreign fighters who sought to join the war on both sides of the conflict. According to research published by The Soufan Center, between 2014 and

---

30 Foggett, S., Saltskog, M. and Clarke, C.P. (2022) *How Are Putin's Far-Right Fans in the West Reacting to His War?*, *War on the Rocks*. Available at: https://warontherocks.com/2022/03/how-are-putins-far-right-fans-in-the-west-reacting-to-his-war/ (Accessed: 21 May 2023);

2019, an estimated 17,000 individuals from over 50 countries travelled to participate in the Ukrainian conflict.[31] By comparison, between 5,000 and 10,000 foreign fighters travelled to Afghanistan in 1980.[32] However, over 44,000 foreign fighters are estimated to have travelled to Syria following the outbreak of the 2011 civil war.[33]

Perhaps unsurprisingly, the vast majority of the foreign fighters that joined the conflict in Ukraine were Russian nationals that primarily joined the pro-Russian side, amounting to around 15,000, or 88 per cent, of the 17,000. However, of the 1,000 from Western countries, 880 joined the Ukrainian side.[34] Researchers have established that no single ideology defined the foreign nationals who travelled to join the conflict, and those adhering to similar ideological strands still occasionally fought on opposing sides. But both the Ukrainian and pro-Russian sides have a documented presence of far-right extremist foreign fighters. According to field research by far-right extremist researcher and expert Kacper Rekawek, an estimated 50-80 per cent of the around 1,000 Westerners who travelled to fight in the conflict likely espouse some form of far-right extremist ideology.[35]

In the early days of the war in 2014 and 2015, on the Ukrainian side of the conflict, volunteer battalions served an essential purpose in strengthening the defence of Ukraine against Russian aggression.

---

31 "White Supremacy Extremism: The Transnational Rise of the Violent White Supremacist Movement," The Soufan Center, September 2019, https://thesoufancenter.org/research/white-supremacy-extremism-the-transnational-rise-of-the-violent-white-supremacist-movement/;

32 Thomas Hegghammer, "Should I Stay or Should I Go? Explaining Variation in Western Jihadists' Choice between Domestic and Foreign Fighting," *American Political Science Review* 107, no. 1 (February 2013): 1–15, https://doi.org/10.1017/S0003055412000615;

33 Richard Barrett, "Beyond the Caliphate: Foreign Fighters and the Threat of Returnees" (The Soufan Center, October 2017), https://thesoufancenter.org/research/beyond-caliphate/;

34 "White Supremacy Extremism: The Transnational Rise of the Violent White Supremacist Movement," The Soufan Center, September 2019, https://thesoufancenter.org/research/white-supremacy-extremism-the-transnational-rise-of-the-violent-white-supremacist-movement/;

35 Kacper Rekawek, "Career Break or New Career? Extremist Foreign Fighters in Ukraine" (Counter Extremism Project, May 4, 2020), https://www.counterextremism.com/press/new-cep-report-career-break-or-new-career-extremist-foreign-fighters-ukraine;

Early in the conflict, while these volunteer battalions were not formally part of Ukraine's armed forces, they proved to be some of the most influential forces on the frontlines.[36] Because of the nature of these volunteer battalions, accepting members on a volunteer basis, it became relatively easy for foreigners to sign up and join without much scrutiny or due process. As a result, many of these battalions included a diverse cadre of volunteer fighters, with European, Canadian, American, and South American nationals fighting alongside ethnic Tatars and Chechens. In several of these volunteer battalions, individuals adhering to extreme far-right ideology could also be found, including within the Azov Battalion, Right Sector, and Aidar Battalion. Several Western nationals espousing far-right extremist beliefs have been documented fighters in these battalions, including Swedish, Norwegian, Italian, Australian, and U.S. nationals.[37]

Little evidence exists that any of the volunteer battalions had an explicit or stated goal to recruit foreigners with extreme far-right beliefs or excluded individuals based on ethnicity or religion.[38] Nonetheless, simply because volunteer battalions were neither monolithic nor espoused an explicit adherence to neo-Nazi ideology or other forms of far-right extremist ideology does not negate the fact that individuals in the ranks of these volunteer battalions espoused such ideologies. The mujahideen in Afghanistan were not all adherents of Salafi-jihadist ideology. Likewise, units in Ukraine

---

36 Michael Cohen and Matthew Green, "Ukraine's Volunteer Battalions," *Infantry Online*, 2016, https://www.benning.army.mil/infantry/magazine/issues/20 16/APR-JUL/pdf/16)%20Cohen_UkraineVolunteers_TXT.pdf;

37 John Færseth, "Ukraine's Far-Right Forces," *Hate Speech International*, February 3, 2015, https://www.hate-speech.org/ukraines-far-right-forces/; FashCast, *The Fash Cast Anthology Without Images*, accessed December 30, 2022, http://archive.org/details/TheFashCastAnthologyWithoutImages; Sean Rubinsztein-Dunlop, Suzanne Dredge, and Michael Workman, "Former Neo-Nazi Returns to Australia after Fighting in Foreign War," *ABC News*, April 30, 2018, https://www.abc.net.au/news/2018-05-01/foreign-fighters-return-to-australia-with-military-training/9696784;

38 Huseyn Aliyev, "Is Ukraine a Hub for International White Supremacist Fighters? | Russia Matters," *Russia Matters* (blog), May 13, 2020, https://www.russiamatters.org/analysis/ukraine-hub-international-white-supremacist-fighters;

draw fighters adhering to diverse sets of beliefs—including far-right extremism.

The now-called Azov Regiment, frequently referred to as the Azov Battalion, is perhaps the most well-known Ukrainian volunteer battalions that included individuals, locals and foreigners adhering to far-right extremist ideology. The Azov Regiment was a volunteer militia formed on May 5, 2014, in Mariupol to fight pro-Russian rebels and forces in eastern Ukraine ("Історія формування полку АЗОВ," n.d.).[39] It is important to note, as other authors of this book have, that the Azov Battalion is one part of the three-pronged Azov Movement—including the National Corps (Political Movement) and the National Militia (street movement). Since the start of the war, the Azov Battalion, along with the two other pillars that make up the Azov Movement, has been accused of espousing neo-Nazi ideology, committing human rights abuses, and recruiting like-minded foreigners to which it is transnationally connected.[40] Interviews with members of the Azov Battalion in Mariupol in the early days of the war clearly illustrate adherence to neo-Nazi and other far-right extremist ideologies and symbolism, both among local as well as foreign fighters.[41] Leaked posts from the now defunct fascist Iron March chat forum (active 2011 to 2017) show the fascination neo-Nazis and white supremacists from around the globe had with Ukraine, which even included exchanging advice on how to travel to join the Azov and Right Sector volunteer battalions.[42] Other far-right extremist groups active on Iron

---

39 "Історія формування полку АЗОВ," accessed December 28, 2022, https://azov.org.ua/pro-nas/;
40 "Report on the Human Rights Situation in Ukraine 16 February to 15 May 2016" (Office of the United Nations High Commissioner for Human Rights, June 3, 2016), https://www.ohchr.org/sites/default/files/Documents/Countries/UA/Ukraine_14th_HRMMU_Report.pdf;
41 Shaun Walker, "Azov Fighters Are Ukraine's Greatest Weapon and May Be Its Greatest Threat," *The Guardian*, September 10, 2014, sec. World news, https://www.theguardian.com/world/2014/sep/10/azov-far-right-fighters-ukraine-neo-nazis;
42 Jacques Singer-Emery and Rex Bray III, "The Iron March Data Dump Provides a Window Into How White Supremacists Communicate and Recruit," *Lawfare* (blog), February 27, 2020, https://www.lawfareblog.com/iron-march-data-dump-provides-window-how-white-supremacists-communicate-and-recruit;

March indicated they planned on sending fighters to Ukraine, with AWD founder Brandon Russel writing, "At the start of next year, we will be sending guys over to Ukraine".[43]

Since the volunteer battalions' formal incorporation into Ukraine's armed forces or its Ministry of Interior (a process that commenced in or around late 2014), it has become harder for foreign nationals to travel and join pro-Ukrainian forces on the frontlines, thereby stymieing the influx of far-right extremist fighters on this side. Several initiatives adopted by the Ukrainian government between late 2014 and 2016 exerted more government control over the volunteer battalions, professionalised their code of conduct and operations, and weeded out undesired foreign fighters.[44] These policy changes, coupled with a general freezing of the conflict following the height of fighting in 2014 and 2015, reduced the number of foreign nationals travelling to Ukraine to gain battlefield experience, including those exhibiting far-right extremist ideologies. Still, evidence suggests that some of the foreigners with far-right extremist beliefs who originally joined these volunteer battalions were still present on the battlefield after these policies were implemented.[45] In addition, far-right extremists continued to travel or tried to travel to Ukraine to train and gain combat experience. In 2019 and 2020, two US citizens were apprehended ahead of planned trips to Ukraine, with both seemingly adhering to far-right extremist ideologies.[46] The continued fascination that the conflict in eastern Ukraine exerts on the transnational far-right extremist milieu

---

43 Reid Ross, A. and Bevensee, E. (2019) *Transnational White Terror: Exposing Atomwaffen And The Iron March Networks, bellingcat*. Available at: https://www.bellingcat.com/news/2019/12/19/transnational-white-terror-exposing-atomwaffen-and-the-iron-march-networks/ (Accessed: 21 May 2023);
44 Huseyn Aliyev, "Is Ukraine a Hub for International White Supremacist Fighters? | Russia Matters," *Russia Matters* (blog), May 13, 2020, https://www.russiamatters.org/analysis/ukraine-hub-international-white-supremacist-fighters;
45 Mollie Saltskog and Colin P. Clarke, "Rebuttal: Ukraine Is Emerging as Critical Node for White-Supremacy Extremists | Russia Matters," *Russia Matters* (blog), September 24, 2020, https://www.russiamatters.org/analysis/rebuttal-ukraine-emerging-critical-node-white-supremacy-extremists#_ftn1;
46 John Lewis et al., "White Supremacist Terror: Modernizing Our Approach to Today's Threat" (George Washington University and the Anti-Defamation Leauge, 2020), https://doi.org/10.4079/poe.04.2020.00;

illustrates the symbolism of the conflict for the contemporary movement. Ukraine, however, does not stand out as an anomaly when looking at the history of conflict and the role of non-state actors exhibiting extremist beliefs and ideologies. Just as Salafi-jihadist fighters flocked to conflicts in Afghanistan, former Yugoslavia, Iraq, and Syria, so have far-right extremists sought opportunities to gain battlefield experience and credibility for participating on the frontline in Ukraine.

This is the by-product of conflict. To extremists, these conflicts offer a chance to train, network, and acquire hands-on knowledge, including bomb-making, surveillance detection, and operational security. These are all key components in refining the tactical capabilities of terrorists and other violent extremists. For the extremist elements present in the former volunteer battalions-turned-formal defence forces, the situation in Ukraine should also not be considered unique or a sign that Ukraine is overrun by individuals adhering to far-right extremism.

While perhaps not the focus of this volume, it is essential to note that pro-Russian forces have also attracted and trained foreigners espousing far-right extremist beliefs. For example, Russian groups like the RIM and its paramilitary unit, the Imperial Legion volunteer unit, have attracted and trained foreign fighters motivated by far-right extremist beliefs. RIM has hosted paramilitary training camps in St. Petersburg and Moscow for Russian and foreign nationals and cultivated ideological and financial contacts with like-minded organisations in Europe and the United States.[47] Two Swedish nationals who trained with RIM in St. Petersburg in 2019 later returned to Sweden to carry out acts of violence, including bombing a refugee centre.[48] In addition, RIM cultivated ideological and financial links with Matthew Heimbach, a US citizen who was a key organiser of the 2017 Unite the Right Rally in

---

47 "Inside The Russian Imperial Movement: Practical Implications of U.S. Sanctions," The Soufan Center, April 23, 2020, https://thesoufancenter.org/research/inside-the-russian-imperial-movement-practical-implications-of-u-s-sanctions/;
48 The Court of Western Sweden, Department 4, Division 43, Case Number B3668-17, September 22, 2017;

Charlottesville, Virginia.[49] In 2017, Heimbach hosted a delegation of Russian RIM members in the United States, including Washington D.C. 709, and reportedly received funding from RIM.[50] Likewise, in or around 2015, the Nordic Resistance Movement (NRM), a Scandinavian-based neo-Nazi organization, also reportedly received funding from the RIM. That same year, RIM's leader, Stanislav Anatolyevich Vorobyev, spoke at an annual conference organized by NRM, where he said that "a full-scale war against the traditional values of Western civilisation" was imminent, and that he and his men were fighting "the Jewish oligarchs in Ukraine" on the side of pro-Russian extremists in Eastern Ukraine.[51]

In April 2020, the US Department of State designated RIM as a Specially Designated Global Terrorist (SDGT) entity under Executive Order (E.O.) 13224. The State Department also designated three of the group's leaders, Stanislav Anatolyevich Vorobyev, Denis Valliullovich Gariev, and Nikolay Nikolayevich Trushchalov under the same E.O. According to the State Department: "RIM has provided paramilitary-style training to white supremacists and neo-Nazis in Europe and actively works to rally these types of groups into a common front against their perceived enemies. RIM has two training facilities in St. Petersburg, which are likely used for woodland and urban assault, tactical weapons, and hand-to-hand combat training. RIM is led by Vorobyev, its founder and overall leader. Gariyev is the head of RIM's paramilitary arm, the Imperial Legion. Trushchalov is RIM's Coordinator for External Relations" ("Designation of the Russian Imperial Movement," 2020). The designation was significant in that it was the first time the United States designated a white supremacist terrorist group. It

---

49   Elizabeth Grimm and Joseph Stabile, "Confronting Russia's Role in Transnational White Supremacist Extremism," Just Security, February 6, 2020, https://www.justsecurity.org/68420/confronting-russias-role-in-transnational-white-supremacist-extremism/;
50   "Inside The Russian Imperial Movement: Practical Implications of U.S. Sanctions," The Soufan Center, April 23, 2020, https://thesoufancenter.org/research/inside-the-russian-imperial-movement-practical-implications-of-u-s-sanctions/;
51   "Nordendagarna 2015," Nordfront.Se, September 7, 2015, accessed April 3, 2020, https://www.nordfront.se/nordendagarna-2015.smr;

also illustrates how far-right extremist organisations in Russia, which likely operate with the tacit approval of the Kremlin, have utilised the conflict in Ukraine to train foreigners and make inroads into the broader transnational far-right extremist milieu.

Transnational Ties of Ukraine's Far-Right Extremist Ecosystem Outside of the Battlefield

Apart from the battlefield, what the conflict represents to the contemporary far-right extremist milieu and how Ukraine has emerged as a critical node in this network should not be underestimated. The far-right extremist ecosystem in Ukraine has been dramatically transformed thanks to the prominence of former volunteer battalions, like Azov, and their connections to far-right extremist organisations inside and outside of Ukraine. Before the war, the Ukrainian far-right extremist movement looked to Europe for inspiration and validation. Today, Ukraine is seen as a beacon for adherents of these ideologies and a place for followers of far-right extremism from around the world to travel for opportunities to network, swap tactics on recruitment and funding and learn from the perceived success of the Ukrainian ultra-nationalist establishment.

While, as previously discussed, the Azov Battalion has become more legitimised and sought to purge extremist elements, the broader three-pronged Azov Movement has capitalised on the conflict to network and organise within the broader transnational far-right extremist milieu. The Azov movement has documented ties to far-right extremist organisations in the US and Europe, including those whose members have been convicted for violent attacks and crimes of terrorism—including the Atomwaffen Division (USA), National Action (UK), and the Rise Above Movement (USA).[52]

At the centre of these efforts sits Olena Semenyaka, a self-styled spokeswoman for the broader Azov Movement. Semenyaka

---

52 "Kaleb Cole Extreme Risk Protection Order—DocumentCloud," September 26, 2019, https://www.documentcloud.org/documents/6498181-19-2-25260-0-sub1-132497-Encrypted.html; Matthew Collins, "Recruiting for Ukraine," HOPE Not Hate (blog), 2018, https://hopenothate.org.uk/research-old/state-of-hate-2018/violence/recruiting-for-ukraine/;

has made concerted efforts to connect with the transnational far-right extremist milieu in Europe and the United States. She has travelled across Europe to speak at prominent international far-right conferences and events, where she promotes Azov's geopolitical ideology and ambitions.[53] In an undated interview published in 2018 with members of the NRM, Semenyaka describes the Azov Battalion as part of Ukraine's National Guard, with a goal to eventually establish a "foreign legion" within the Azov Regiment.[54] There is little evidence to suggest that the Azov Battalion, or any other former volunteer battalion, attained this goal.[55] However, Semenyaka's statement signals the intent of far-right extremist individuals in Ukraine to connect and network with like-minded organisations and individuals in the broader transnational movement, including by using the conflict as a magnet.

Far-right extremist individuals, ideologues, and organisations in both Europe and the United States have flocked to Ukraine to network, train, and participate in events. According to organisers of Asgardsrei, an annual "National Socialist black metal" festival put on by individuals linked to the Azov movement, close to 1,000 foreigners attended the festival in December 2018. Among the foreign attendees were members of far-right extremist groups, including the US-based Atomwaffen Division, Italy's CasaPound, and Germany's The Third Way.[56] The Asgardsrei festival no longer exists in its previous form and has been replaced by another festival

---

53 interregnum-intermarium, "The Azov Movement in the West: Achievements in 2019," April 2019, https://interregnum-intermarium.tumblr.com/post/184469943719/the-azov-movement-in-the-west-achievements-in;
54 FashCast, *The Fash Cast Anthology Without Images*, accessed December 30, 2022, http://archive.org/details/TheFashCastAnthologyWithoutImages;
55 Mollie Saltskog and Colin P. Clarke, "Rebuttal: Ukraine Is Emerging as Critical Node for White-Supremacy Extremists | Russia Matters," *Russia Matters* (blog), September 24, 2020, https://www.russiamatters.org/analysis/rebuttal-ukraine-emerging-critical-node-white-supremacy-extremists#_ftn1;
56 Tim Hume, "It's Not All Bad: Coronavirus Shut Down Europe's Neo-Nazi Music Festival Scene," *Vice* (blog), May 7, 2020, https://www.vice.com/en/article/qj4dex/its-not-all-bad-coronavirus-shut-down-europes-neo-nazi-music-festival-scene;

THE WAR IN UKRAINE 227

known as the Heretic Fest.[57] Some reports suggest that the organiser Alexey Levkin and his group known as the "Militant Zone," who initially founded the Asgardsrei festival in Moscow in 2012, has reportedly taken steps to distance himself from the Azov Movement; however, this author could not independently verify those reports.

Far-right extremist ideologues have also travelled to Ukraine to network and share their extremist ideology. In October 2018, at the invitation of the National Corps (Azov's political wing), US far-right extremist ideologue Greg Johnson travelled to Kyiv to lecture at a National Corps-organized event.[58] Apart from having previously expressed respect for Norwegian terrorist Breivik, which resulted in Norway deporting Johnson on national security grounds, he also believes in creating a white ethno-state. To that end, Johnson has regularly promoted the Azov Movement's nationalist achievements on his platforms, as he did during his 2018 lecture in Kyiv (RECONQUISTA Україна, 2018).

Members of the US-based RAM, including its founder Robert Rundo, have cultivated ties with several different far-right extremist groups and individuals in Ukraine. Rundo cooperates with Ukraine-based Russian national and far-right extremist Denis Kapustin (Denis "Nikitin") on a joint podcast and a collaboration between his clothing brand and Kapustin's clothing company "White Rex." In 2018, Rundo travelled with other members of RAM to participate in a Mixed Martial Arts (MMA) tournament in Ukraine.[59] Indeed, sports camps, tournaments, and festivals have all been essential events that allow the Ukrainian far-right extremist movement to cement its ideology and political goals.[60] In 2020,

---

57 'HERETIC FEST — Heretic Camp' (no date). Available at: https://heretic.camp/hereticfest/ (Accessed: 21 May 2023);
58 Christopher Miller, "Azov, Ukraine's Most Prominent Ultranationalist Group, Sets Its Sights On U.S., Europe," *Radio Free Europe/Radio Liberty*, November 14, 2018, sec. Ukraine, https://www.rferl.org/a/azov-ukraine-s-most-prominent-ultranationalist-group-sets-its-sights-on-u-s-europe/29600564.html;
59 Ali Winston Thompson A C., "American Hate Group Looks to Make Allies in Europe," ProPublica, accessed December 30, 2022, https://www.propublica.org/article/robert-rundo-denis-nikitin-hooligans-europe-hate-group;
60 Adrien Nonjon, (2021) 'Forging the Body of the New Ukrainian Nation: Sport as a Gramscist Tool for the Ukrainian Far Right', *The Journal of Illiberalism Studies*, 1(2);

RAM member "Robert Smithson" visited Kyiv, where he spoke outside the American Embassy in support of RAM members convicted in the United States.[61] This gathering was led by the Ukrainian far-right extremist group "Tradition and Order," which is known for its anti-LGBTQ attacks and has been described by the US Department of State as a "violent radical group".[62]

Just as Russia's war against Ukraine presented far-right extremists on both sides of the conflict with an opportunity to gain battlefield experience, international outreach by Ukrainian far-right extremist groups and individuals over the past years has likely helped establish Ukraine as a node in the transnational far-right extremist movement. Since 2014, numerous foreign far-right extremist ideologues, individuals, and groups have also established connections off the battlefield with like-minded individuals and organisations in Ukraine.

Still, this phenomenon is not unique to Ukraine, and must be considered within the broader context of the contemporary far-right extremist milieu. Russian far-right extremist individuals and organisations have also capitalised on the war to make inroads with like-minded individuals and organisations in Europe and elsewhere — something that U.S. and European far-right extremists alike have welcomed. In 2015, the Rodina Party organised the International Russian Conservative Forum in St. Petersburg, which attracted several well-known American far-right extremist ideologues, including Jared Taylor, along with representatives and members of European far-right parties such as Golden Dawn (Greece) and Forza Nuova (Italy).[63] Several European nationals

---

61 Oleksiy Kuzmenko, "Ties between American, Ukrainian Far Right Were on Full Display in Kyiv Last Week as Robert Smithson, a Member of American White Nationalist 'Rise Above Movement', Spoke in Front of @USEmbassyKyiv at a Protest in Support of the RAM Organized by a Ukrainian Far-Right Group. THREAD https://T.Co/T6z3hxyQq8," Tweet, *Twitter*, July 15, 2020, https://twitter.com/kooleksiy/status/1283512094739103744;
62 "UKRAINE 2021 HUMAN RIGHTS REPORT" (U.S. Department of State, 2022), https://www.state.gov/wp-content/uploads/2022/04/313615_UKRAINE-2021-HUMAN-RIGHTS-REPORT.pdf;
63 "Inside The Russian Imperial Movement: Practical Implications of U.S. Sanctions," The Soufan Center, April 23, 2020, https://thesoufancenter.org/resea

have travelled to train with Russian far-right extremist organisations, like the RIM.[64] Just as Ukrainian far-right extremist individuals and organisations have hosted music and MMA events, so too have groups in Germany, Bulgaria, Sweden, Italy, and Portugal. As extremism researchers Kacper Rekawek, Alexander Ritzmann, and Dr. Hans-Jakob Schindler have noted: "Music and violent sports events are a common feature of many violent [extreme far-right] scenes transnationally. They aim to provide the movement with finances to sustain its existence and attract previously unconnected individuals as potential recruits to its ranks".[65]

Conclusion

Under the information above and analysis, it is evident that Russia's illegal invasion and war in Ukraine likely catalysed Ukraine to become a prominent node in today's transnational far-right extremist milieu. However, the realities are not that simple. Considering this phenomenon within the broader context of the increasing transnationalisation of the far-right extremist movement is essential. In addition, Ukrainian government policy and the changing dynamics of the conflict, including Russia's further invasion of Ukraine on February 24, 2022, have changed the on-the-ground dynamics and affected how the extreme far-right movement interacts with organisations and groups present in Ukraine. While not the focus of this chapter, research indicates that the inflow of far-right extremist foreign fighters into Ukraine's "Foreign Legion" volunteer battalion following February 24 has not materialised to the extent that researchers and policymakers feared it would.[66] Reporting

---

rch/inside-the-russian-imperial-movement-practical-implications-of-u-s-sanctions/;
64 "Inside The Russian Imperial Movement: Practical Implications of U.S. Sanctions," The Soufan Center, April 23, 2020, https://thesoufancenter.org/research/inside-the-russian-imperial-movement-practical-implications-of-u-s-sanctions/;
65 Kacper Rekawek, Alexander Ritzmann, and Dr Hans-Jakob Schindler, "Violent Right-Wing Extremism and Terrorism—Transnational Connectivity, Definitions, Incidents, Structures and Countermeasures," no. 732 (2020);
66 Egle E. Murauskaite, "Foreign Fighters in Ukraine: What Concerns Should Really Be on the Agenda?," *Russia Matters*, August 18, 2022, https://www.russia

and research from the field appear to indicate that Russia is likely the primary country utilising extremist actors in the conflict, as exemplified by mercenaries in the Wagner Group and foreign fighters in the Ruisch paramilitary group (*Foreign Fighters, Volunteers, and Mercenaries*, 2022).[67] Therefore, it is essential to dispute the Kremlin's disinformation narratives unequivocally and vehemently, which utilise false arguments about the "de-Nazification" of Ukraine as a pretext and justification for Russia's ongoing war and illegal occupation of Ukraine. Indeed, the ability to grasp two nuanced concepts simultaneously is critical in the complex on-the-ground dynamics created by war, including how extremist non-state actors interact with and capitalise on a conflict. First, to recognise how far-right extremist actors have capitalised on the conflict to carve out a node centred on Ukraine within the contemporary transnational movement. Second, policymakers, experts, and researchers can work to support Ukraine while still being realistic about the presence of extremist elements on both sides of the conflict, on and off the battlefield, and work to stymie the ability of these actors to capitalize on the chaos that war ultimately produces.

---

matters.org/analysis/foreign-fighters-ukraine-what-concerns-should-really-be-agenda;

67 "Foreign Fighters, Volunteers, and Mercenaries: Non-State Actors and Narratives in Ukraine" (The Soufan Center, April 4, 2022), https://thesoufancenter.org/research/foreign-fighters-volunteers-and-mercenaries-non-state-actors-and-narratives-in-ukraine/.

7 No "Far Right Al-Qaeda" Azov's Foreign Fighters

Kacper Rekawek

In 2020, the current author co-led the writing process of a report on the transnational connectivity of the extreme right-wing scenes of different Western countries[1]. During its preparation, it was becoming clear to the authors that Western extremists no longer saw their Eastern or Central-Eastern European (CEE) brethren as unworthy or subpar wannabe counterparts[2]. Instead, many perceived the region as a proverbial "Shangri-la" of far-right extremism. Some travelled there to praise its homogeneity, traditionalism, and conservatism as a welcome distraction from the reality in the West[3]. To some extent, one could argue that this fascination is a result of a prolonged process of discovering CEE, a region close to the West but, in the minds of some of its visitors, very much unlike its Western neighbours. This discovery process might have been hastened by the media exposure of high-profile far-right events in the CEE, such as Poland's 11 November Independence Day March, Day of Honour in Hungary, or the Lukov March in Bulgaria, which attracted outsized international, if not global, attention[4]. These helped create an image of "strong nations" opposed both to the European Union

---

1 Rekawek, K. and Ritzmann, A. and Schindler, H. J. (2020). Violent Right-Wing Extremism and Terrorism—Transnational Connectivity, Definitions, Incidents, Structures and Countermeasures. Berlin: Counter Extremism Project, https://www.counterextremism.com/sites/default/files/CEP%20Study_Violent%20Right-Wing%20Extremism%20and%20Terrorism_Nov%202020.pdf
2 Colborne, M. (2022). From the Fires of War: Ukraine's Azov Movement and the Global Far Right. Berlin: ibidem press.
3 Rekawek, K. (2021a). Looks can be deceiving: Extremism meets paramilitarism in Central and Eastern Europe. Berlin: Counter Extremism Project, https://www.counterextremism.com/sites/default/files/2021-06/CEP%20Report_Looks%20Can%20Be%20Deceiving_Extremism%20Meets%20Paramilitarism%20in%20CEE_June%202021_1.pdf
4 Reuters (2021). Polish far-right Independence Day march to go ahead despite court ban. 11 November. https://www.reuters.com/world/europe/polish-far-right-independence-day-march-go-ahead-despite-court-ban-2021-11-11/

and Russia, situated to the immediate East of Western Europe[5]. Nonetheless, one of the keys, if not THE key, CEE selling points amongst the Western far right has been the so-called "Azov Battalion", an entity which no longer exists but was transformed into a transnational far-right brand[6].

One look at the current day far-right Telegram channels, including those attempting to recruit fighters for the Russo-Ukrainian war or selling clothes for "angry youth"[7], reveals a long-nurtured fascination with the unit and especially its "prehistory" and activities in 2014[8]. Its logotypes and battlefield prowess are cherished by the subscribers of these channels, who idolise Azov in their posts and almost fetishise its original yellow and blue logo featuring the spinning wheel — kolovrat and the so-called "idea of a nation" or wolfsangel. This fascination has been carried over onto the 2022 stage of the Russo-Ukrainian war when the now Azov Regiment, with a different logo and having less and less in common with its so-called "little black men" of 2014 (Callsign 'Woland,' 2017), stood valiantly during the siege of Azovstal in Mariupol[9]. The fascination, however, continues and ultimately hurts the regiment. At the time of writing this (mid-2023), circa 700 Azov members are still in captivity in Russia, and any lingering doubt about the extremist/far-right nature of the unit in which they served will not help their

---

5 Intermarium Support Group (2022). "The history and the ground for revival today." https://intermarium-support.com/en/program/
6 Colborne, M. (2022). From the Fires of War: Ukraine's Azov Movement and the Global Far Right. Berlin: ibidem press.
7 The author chose not to mention the names nor to provide links to the aforementioned channels in order not to help them disseminate their content to a wider audience. Relevant posts from these channels can be provided by the author upon request.
8 Umland, A. (2019). "Irregular Militias and Radical Nationalism in Post-Euromaydan Ukraine: The Prehistory and Emergence of the "Azov" Battalion in 2014," Terrorism and Political Violence, 31:1, 105-131, DOI: 10.1080/09546553.2018.1555974.
9 Jedrysik, M. (2022). "The Azov Regiment: Neo-Nazis, Football Hooligans or Defenders of Ukraine?." Oko.press, 1 April. https://oko.press/the-azov-regimen t-neo-nazis-football-hooligans-or-defenders-of-ukraine/

chances of winning back their freedom in a Ukraine-Russia exchange of prisoners[10].

In the eyes of some external observers, however, the key to this fascination has never been the logo, the graphics, or Azov's heroics, but instead, the fact that the unit in its original form featured non-Ukrainian and especially Western members[11]. Mostly because of this, much of the last decade saw the names Azov, Azov Movement, Azov Regiment and finally, Azov Battalion turned into transnational, if not global, far-right bogeymen[12] — almost akin to a far-right Al-Qaeda[13]. This chapter will attempt to put this development into context while looking at the genuine Western foreign fighter/volunteer involvement in the ranks of the Azov Battalion (later Regiment). At the same time, it will not study the Azov Movement's ideology, which contains a sizeable transnational pillar or activities of its most outwardly oriented member(s), such as Olena Semenyaka[14], or instances of political tourism when, for example, Azov's ideological brethren from the West visited Kyiv or shared platforms with the movement's representatives[15]. The author deliberately takes this approach so that all these actions and areas of activity are not conflated and lumped together as evidence of Azov's alleged status as a far-right Al-Qaeda. This is not to deny the

---

10 Mazurenko, A. (2022). "An estimated 800 Azov Regiment members are held prisoner, including over 40 women, some pregnant." Ukrainska Pravda, 27 September. https://www.pravda.com.ua/eng/news/2022/09/27/7369333/
11 Harp, S. (2022). "Foreign fighters in Ukraine could be a time bomb for their home countries." The Intercept, 30 June. https://theintercept.com/2022/06/30/ukraine-azov-neo-nazi-foreign-fighter/
12 Rekawek, K. and Ritzmann, A. and Schindler, H. J. (2020). Violent Right-Wing Extremism and Terrorism — Transnational Connectivity, Definitions, Incidents, Structures and Countermeasures. Berlin: Counter Extremism Project, pp. 15-16 https://www.counterextremism.com/sites/default/files/CEP%20Study_Violent%20Right-Wing%20Extremism%20and%20Terrorism_Nov%202020.pdf
13 Rose, M., Soufan, A. H. (2020). "We Once Fought Jihadists. Now We Battle White Supremacists." The New York Times, 11 February. https://www.nytimes.com/2020/02/11/opinion/politics/white-supremacist-terrorism.html.
14 Nonjon, A. (2020). "Olena Semenyaka, The "First Lady" of Ukrainian Nationalism." Illiberalism Studies Programme Working Paper, September. https://www.illiberalism.org/olena-semenyaka-the-first-lady-of-ukrainian-nationalism/
15 Interregnum (2019). "Metapolitics, geopolitics, culture." https://interregnum-intermarium.tumblr.com/post/184469943719/the-azov-movement-in-the-west-achievements-in

movement's transnational appeal or to disregard its activities beyond Ukraine, which will be discussed in other parts of this volume, but rather to dissect the seemingly crucial tenet of its existence: its martial aspect and the attraction it was said to have had for its non-Ukrainian fans and well-wishers. The fact that Azov, a nationalist or far-right socio-political entity based in a country bordering the EU and NATO, seemed to have had "its" military battalion/regiment, in reality: within the ranks of the National Guard of Ukraine (Національна гвардія України), which has been fighting in a war since 2014, was said to have been one of the critical factors in its rise and transnational notoriety[16]. It was widely assumed that external volunteers could join "its" battalion/regiment and, in this sense, enable the vision of a transnational force in the service of a radical, if not extremist, political entity (Azov Movement or its political party, the National Corps, Національний корпус[17]. The fact that so many Western far-right individuals widely praised or referenced the Azov Battalion/Regiment on, for example, their social media only strengthened this notorious image[18]. The Battalion, at that time not yet officially called "Azov," allowed some foreigners, who gravitated to its early incarnation straight from the Euromaidan protests which they either observed as tourists or participated in, to act as their externally oriented spokesmen and recruiters as early as the Summer of 2014[19]. As will be shown, however, this seemingly ominous development led to Azov recruiting a few foreigners. It was contextualised, if not ridiculed, by one who answered the call and initially seemed to have had serious misgivings

---

16 Miller, Ch. (2018). "Azov, Ukraine's Most Prominent Ultranationalist Group, Sets Its Sights On U.S., Europe." RadioFreeEurope/RadioLiberty, 14 November. https://www.rferl.org/a/azov-ukraine-s-most-prominent-ultranationalist-group-sets-its-sights-on-u-s-europe/29600564.html
17 Soufan Center, the. (2019). White Supremacy Extremism: The Transnational Rise of the Violent White Supremacist Movement. September. https://thesoufancenter.org/wp-content/uploads/2019/09/Report-by-The-Soufan-Center-White-Supremacy-Extremism-The-Transnational-Rise-of-The-Violent-White-Supremacist-Movement.pdf
18 Ibid
19 Biloslavo, F. (2014). "Ukraine: Far-Right Fighters from Europe Fight for Ukraine." Eurasianet. 6 August. https://eurasianet.org/ukraine-far-right-fighters-from-europe-fight-for-ukraine

about their decision[20]. In short, looking back on the events when Azov was formed, one concludes that the foreign fighter phenomenon hardly applied to this formation and that alarmist media reports on this very unit have overblown its size. As it turned out, Azov's foreign fighters contingent could not have constituted a sizeable chunk of the alleged 17 000 foreign fighters who appeared in the 2014-15 stage of the Russo-Ukrainian war and most of whom were not Westerners, nor individuals who fought for Ukraine, but were Russian citizens who mobilised or were partly mobilised by the Russian state, in favour of the Ukrainian "separatists"[21]. Unlike the tiny Azovian group, these fighters received far less scrutiny from academics, experts, or policymakers, except Rácz[22], but had more impact on the battlefield than foreigners scattered around different Ukrainian volunteer battalions. This chapter will not discuss the image, real or imagined, of either Azov in general or the Battalion or Regiment in particular. While noting the input, that is, the interest in Azov as a fighting force or the praise it received in far-right circles; it will focus instead on the output or the numbers and the influence of foreigners fighting in its ranks between 2014 and 2022. It will also discuss their post-Azov fates to dissect the extent to which they, just like some of the foreign fighters returning from other conflicts, might have been involved in political violence or outright terrorism upon returning home[23]. As demonstrated, the reality in this respect differs from the proverbial fa- right Al Qaeda

---

20 Löfroos, C. (2022). Vapaaehtoiset—Sotamme Ukrainassa 2014-2015. Tampere: Kiuas.
21 Soufan Center, the. (2019). White Supremacy Extremism: The Transnational Rise of the Violent White Supremacist Movement. September, p.19. https://the soufancenter.org/wp-content/uploads/2019/09/Report-by-The-Soufan-Center-White-Supremacy-Extremism-The-Transnational-Rise-of-The-Violent-White-Supremacist-Movement.pdf
22 Rácz, A. (2017). "The Elephant in the Room: Russian Foreign Fighters in Ukraine." In: Rekawek, K. (ed., 2017). Not Only Syria? The Phenomenon of Foreign Fighters in a Comparative Perspective. Amsterdam: IOS Press.
23 Renard, T. and Coolsaet R. (eds.). 2018. Returnees: who are they, why are they (not) coming back and how should we deal with them? Assessing Policies on Returning Foreign Terrorist Fighters in Belgium, Germany and the Netherlands. Brussels: Egmont. https://www.egmontinstitute.be/app/uploads/2018/02/egmont.papers.101_online_v1-3.pdf?type=pdf

image bestowed on Azov years ago. The chapter proceeds in three sections: the first (The Scale) discusses the actual numbers of foreigners in the ranks while looking at testimonies of the Azov Battalion/Regiment members interviewed by the author. The second (The Fascination) attempts to explain the reasons for this fascination, which, as will be shown, had minimal basis in facts on the ground. The third (The Aftermath) will zoom in on the post-2014 activities of the Azov veterans and primarily focus on one instance in which some of them decided to pick up guns once again — the 2022 resumption of the Russo-Ukrainian war.

The Scale

In the words of one veteran, the foreign members of Azov were predominantly "conservative, on the right" but certainly "not neo-Nazis. These could be counted on the fingers of one hand"[24]. He and his colleagues were allegedly motivated by the opportunity "to work with a professional unit in conditions of war". They did not desire to train themselves into terrorists of the future or Western European far-right militants. At the same time, their numbers were low: "Some Swedes, Croats, a German who was only there for training, Slovaks, etc. We had 10-12 languages, including Russian, Georgian, and Belarusian, as these guys were also here. In total, you could talk about 30-35 Westerners who spent enough time here to be called Azov formers"[25]. The same veteran also remarked that the "separatists" had a relatively similar number of "conservative" Westerners in their ranks. In his view, these paltry numbers could not account for a major security headache for any Western state — "the police can tackle numbers such as these. Ok, yes, suppose one becomes a lone wolf but anything more? No.[26]"

Even if one was to take with a massive pinch of salt the veteran above's account of his and his comrade's ideological underpinnings (especially his understanding of the word "conservative", which,

---

24 Anonymous, #1. (2020). Author's interview with a Swedish former member of the Azov Battalion/Regiment who wished to remain anonymous. 25 January.
25 Ibid
26 Ibid

for some, drifted very much into the territory of the nationalist far right)[27] then, as will also be shown below, his numerical estimate is not off the mark. Neither is his analysis of the scale of the threat such a group of potentially determined returnee foreign fighters could pose to Western countries. There were too few of them and, ironically, it had been the alumni of the other side who proved more entrepreneurial in their post-Ukraine exploits, such as participation in the ill-fated Montenegrin coup, joining of the infamous Wagner Group on its Syrian or Libyan missions, attempts to ingratiate themselves with the Kurdish Peshmerga to fight ISIS or high-visibility presence at the protests of the Yellow Vests in Paris in 2019[28].

The first memoirs of a foreigner in the ranks of Azov (another Swede; as of writing this, the memoirs remain unpublished in English but are a fascinating, and yet not widely known, contemporary source of direct knowledge on the inner workings of the unit) strengthen the point of the first testimony and provide a rather gloomy picture of the Azovian "foreigner group"[29]. Despite the fact that the Battalion "has long been open to accepting foreign nationals", was "the easiest unit to apply for," and "by all account there were many foreign volunteers in the battalion" (who were mostly Russian, Belarusian or Georgian), its "foreigner group," formed in September 2014, numbered around a dozen men or later "a size of two squads," and could fit into two regular cars[30]. Such a view was confirmed to the author by other members of that very "group" who stated that at first it had been "Mike [Mikael Skillt, Azov's early Swedish member], me and a few other guys"[31]. Another

---

27 Friberg, D. (2015). The Real Right Returns: A Handbook for the True Opposition. Budapest: Arktos Media.
28 Rekawek, K. (2019). ""It Ain't Over 'til It's Over": Extreme Right-Wing Foreign Fighters in Ukraine." The CounterPoint Blog. 23 September. https://www.co unterextremism.com/blog/ %E2%80%9Cit-ain%E2%80%99t-over-%E2%80%9 8til-it%E2%80%99s-over%E2%80%9D-extreme-right-wing-foreign-fighters-uk raine
29 Löfroos, C. (2022). Vapaaehtoiset—Sotamme Ukrainassa 2014-2015. Tampere: Kiuas. The author received a manuscript of the English version of the book, which is to be published in 2023, directly from the author.
30 Ibid.
31 Anonymous, #4. (2022). Author's interview with a former Croat member of the Azov Battalion who wished to remain anonymous. 25 July.

fighter, a Frenchman, stated that in total four of his compatriots, and the French were the 2nd largest, after Swedes, group of Westerners in Azov, rotated through the unit at its peak in 2014[32]. His Croat counterpart, upon seeing the author's 2015 estimate that as many as 30 Croats fought on the Ukrainian side in the war and mostly in Azov[33], commented in 2022 that this was "way off the mark as there had been far, far fewer of us.[34]"

Most of the fighters had some form of military experience. Still, the initial rag-tag look of its members, their (dis) organisation, lack of leadership and focus produced a bewildered comment from one of its stalwarts: "Was this the foreign elite Azov had been gathering up?[35]". Interestingly, this group was born out of a larger, company-sized outfit, which had existed before and was led by "Båtsman," a notorious Belarusian member of the Battalion[36] who had under his command the initial small group of Westerners (Swedes and e.g. a single Croat)[37]. At the same time:

> "Russian propaganda had made a big deal out of the fact that there were Western volunteers in Azov from the very beginning. The picture which they painted, however, had made our numbers out to be much larger than it really was. The purpose of course was to turn the Russian speaking population, both in Ukraine and Russia proper, hostile against us. To make Azov in particular and the Ukrainian army in general seem like the foreign,

---

32 Anonymous, #6. (2022). Author's interview with a former French member of the Azov Battalion/Regiment who wished to remain anonymous. April 21.
33 Rekawek, K. (2015). "Neither "NATO's Foreign Legion" Nor the "Donbass International Brigades:" (Where Are All the) Foreign Fighters in Ukraine?." PISM Policy Paper. No. 6 (108), March. https://pism.pl/publications/PISM_Policy_Paper_no__6__108___Neither__NATO_s_Foreign_Legion__Nor_the__Donbass_International_Brigades____Where_Are_All_the__Foreign_Fighters_in_Ukraine_
34 Anonymous, #5. (2022). Author's interview with a former Croat member of the Azov Battalion/Regiment who wished to remain anonymous. April 13.
35 Löfroos, C. (2022). Vapaaehtoiset—Sotamme Ukrainassa 2014-2015. Tampere: Kiuas.
36 Vernyhor, P. (2021). "Anonymous YouTube Video Seemingly Shows Neo-Nazi Sergiy Korotkikh Agreeing to Be An Informant for the Russian FSB." ZABORONA, 13 August. https://zaborona.com/en/anonymous-youtube-video-seemingly-shows-now-nazi-sergiy-korotkikh-agreeing-to-be-an-informant-for-the-russian-fsb/
37 Löfroos, C. (2022). Vapaaehtoiset—Sotamme Ukrainassa 2014-2015. Tampere: Kiuas.

real invading force and thus: Illegitimate. A foreign army from the West, not the least different from the German one which had invaded the Soviet Union back in 1941.[38"]

At the same time, this "illegitimate" force, allegedly full of "merciless mercenaries," featured individuals with rather generic and far from ideological attitudes as to why they fought for Ukraine in its war with Russia. As one Finnish Azovian, quoted in the memoirs mentioned above, attested to his Swedish colleague:

> "I always wanted to see and experience a real war and then, when it started here (Ukraine), it was perfect. The right enemy, the right kind of war and a good reason to fight. A perfect war, at least for my generation. I can help Ukraine in the war, Ukraine can help me get to fight in a war. It as a win-win.[39"]

Ironically, however, not too many foreigners, as Löfroos states in his memoirs[40], developed similar views on their motivations for joining the war. It nonetheless suited Russia to inflate the number of foreigners so that this could delegitimise the Ukrainian war effort. To some extent, Russia repeated the same manoeuvre in 2022 when it spoke of "2,000 foreign mercenaries from the United States, Britain, Poland and other countries are present in the Ukrainian units fighting in the Kharkov Region" (TASS, 2022) — akin to 2014 alleged, "NATO's Foreign Legion" (Rekawek, 2015). As the author of the discussed memoirs attested, this alleged "Legion" (read: "foreigner group") was to "dissipate...soon after Azov was finally withdrawn from the frontline in 2015[41"]. Regardless of its genuine, albeit modest, contribution to the fighting in Shyrokyne in February 2015, the group was not always getting the recognition it deserved, with an officer from another volunteer battalion scornfully telling the Western foreigners in the ranks of the Azov Regiment: "you foreigners are not fighting anyway. You are just here to take photos, a bunch of posers" (*Ibid.*). The comment might have had some merit concerning foreign fighters in general, but, as will be shown, not so

---

38 Ibid.
39 Ibid.
40 Ibid
41 Ibid.

much in relation to this particular group, many of whom returned to fight in Ukraine in 2022.

Regardless of their effectiveness and tenacity, their low numbers in the ranks of Azov were also confirmed to the author by one of the fighters who experienced the siege of Mariupol, Russian captivity and was then released as a part of the prisoner exchange with Russia into Saudi Arabia. He confirmed that at the time of the siege—almost eight years after the founding of the original battalion—there were two Western members, including him, in the ranks of the Azov Regiment[42]. Of course, other foreigners fought alongside them in other Ukrainian formations, such as the marines, and some had even gone through Azov at earlier stages of their military careers in Ukraine. Nonetheless, this paltry number, straight from the person in the know, forces us to seriously reconsider our understanding of the transnational militant connectivity of Azov.

The Fascination

As was shown, the actual paltry scale of Western foreign fighting in Azov's ranks should not merit its lionisation in extremist circles nor its elevation to a status of a critical tenet of a far-right "laboratory" into which Ukraine was allegedly developing[43]. The author then states that six factors contributed to this development, and this section will discuss these. His choice of factors is informed by his eight years of study of foreign fighters in Ukraine, especially his conversations with these individuals. At the same time, it is also derived from his observations of the Russo-Ukrainian war and how many of his contemporary academics and experts perceive this conflict and situate it within the context of other world events. These factors are not discussed in any order. They are open to reinterpretation, especially considering the events of 2022 when Azov is undergoing a thorough public relations makeover as the gallant

---

42 Anonymous, #2. (2022). Author's interview with a Swedish former member of the Azov Battalion/Regiment who wished to remain anonymous. 15 October.
43 Rose, M., Soufan, A. H. (2020). "We Once Fought Jihadists. Now We Battle White Supremacists." The New York Times, 11 February. https://www.nytimes.com/2020/02/11/opinion/politics/white-supremacist-terrorism.html.

defenders of Azovstal in Mariupol and not the 2014 radicals brandishing swastika tattoos[44].

1. The ISIS comparison.

Mobilisation of foreign fighters for the Russo-Ukrainian war, on either side, was happening against the backdrop of some of ISIS' most significant successes in Iraq and Syria. The jihadi organisation took Mosul, Iraq's second-largest city, in late Spring of 2014[45], more or less at the same time as the "Russian Spring" of the separatists in Ukraine—that is, attempts to have more regions of Ukraine "secede" from the country[46]. Shortly afterwards, however, the Ukrainian summer counterattack came close to the eradication of the two Donbas' "people's republics," and foreign fighters began to arrive both in Kyiv and Donetsk to join both sides involved in the conflict. As these began to be paraded or put themselves forward in front of the media, it was hard not to make a connection with the "other" foreign fighters of the time, namely those in the ranks of ISIS and, to a lesser extent those fighting for the Kurds in Syria. There were many differences between these groups of fighters, but they had one thing in common—they both went to war at a similar point in history. Years later, one veteran of the Ukraine-bound group bitterly complained that this comparison destroyed his life in his native Sweden: "We were put on par with the jihadis as if we had anything in common[47]". Despite such protestations, one cannot deny that there exist a few points of ideological convergence between the jihadis and the far-right (the interviewed Azovians all, however, denied belonging to the latter category): fascination with authoritarian or totalitarian governance, cult of violence, affirmation of a specifically, if not regressively, perceived manhood. He also

---

44 Anonymous, #3. (2022) Author's interview with a member of the National Corps party who wished to remain anonymous. 15 June.
45 Clarke, C. (2019). After the Caliphate: The Islamic State & the Future Terrorist Diaspora. New York: Polity.
46 Arutunyan, A. (2022). Hybrid Warriors. Proxies, Freelancers and Moscow's Struggle for Ukraine. London: Hurst.
47 Anonymous, #2. (2022). Author's interview with a Swedish former member of the Azov Battalion/Regiment who wished to remain anonymous. 15 October.

complained that given some of their ideological backgrounds in nationalist/far-right groupings, the media "were happy to turn us into new jihadis, a new terrorist threat"[48]. In short, the non-Ukrainian Azovians were adamant in their conversations with the author that they had not constituted a terrorist threat to their home countries before departing for Ukraine, nor would they morph into one upon return[49]. In this sense, they were not the latest examples of Hegghammer's "cheese bell theory" of foreign fighting, which assumes rebels need to escape abroad to survive as, among other things literally, foreign fighters as they would be crushed at home due to improved surveillance and repressive abilities of their countries of origin[50].

The abovementioned protestations came from an Azov veteran who fought in Ukraine in 2014 and early 2015. In his discussions with the current author, he explained that he did not feel particularly welcome or at ease back in his home country, which, in his view, "hated people like us. Patriotic, traditional", and things allegedly took a turn for the worse after their return from the frontlines. All had "chats" with the Swedish Security Service (Swedish: Säkerhetspolisen, SÄPO), in which they were quizzed about their links with the Nordic Resistance Movement (NRM), the country's then-primary militant far-right organisation. This made it clear to the returning fighters that the security services had a counterterrorism or counter-extremism motive in mind while interviewing them[51]. Ironically, Swedish nationalism, a distinctly anti-Russian phenomenon, with Russia referred to as the traditional or hereditary enemy, underwent a peculiar transition in the second decade of the 21st century. NRM, which emerged as the new and dominant face of the Scandinavian and Swedish far, if not extreme, right seemed infatuated with Russia—a seemingly traditionalist, nationalist, patriarchal and anti-LGBT, anti-immigration/anti-Muslim power. They

---

48 Anonymous, #2. (2022). Author's interview with a Swedish former member of the Azov Battalion/Regiment who wished to remain anonymous. 15 October.
49 Ibid.
50 Hegghammer, T. (2021). "Cheese Bells and Foreign Fighting." War on the Rocks, 6 August. https://warontherocks.com/2021/08/foreign-fighters-and-cheese-bells/
51 Ibid.

also allegedly accepted financial "gifts" from Russian far-right emissaries who were trekking to Stockholm to lure the leading Scandinavian far-right organization into Moscow's orbit[52]. Consequently, such a pro-Russian organization, albeit an ideological home to some of the comrades of the Swedish Azovians, would not permit former members of the regiment in their ranks and SÄPO's worries were misplaced, to say the least.

The phenomenon of describing Azovians as "foreign fighters" seemed less pronounced outside Sweden, but the sheer usage of the term, which came to be synonymous with the jihadis travelling to join ISIS in Syria, was putting veterans of the Russo-Ukrainian war on the spot. Consequently, the likes of the Czech Republic, Italy, Serbia, and Spain arrested and charged "their" fighters with all sorts of criminal activities, ranging from preparation of acts of terrorism to mercenary activities[53]. Pressing such charges seemed prescient, especially concerning foreign fighters from anti-systemic milieus who travelled to either Russia or Ukraine. This predominantly meant individuals from the far-right, represented on both sides of the conflict. As far as the Ukrainian side was concerned, this could have meant members of the Azov Battalion/Regiment, at times seemingly the only outfit happy to enlist foreigners[54]. As was shown, there had never been many such (Western) foreign fighters in the ranks of the uni. Still, some of their countries of origin were making a connection between their professed ideologies, the Azov Battalion/Regiment and its background, and an ongoing war in Europe. The result was a deepened "fascination" with the few

---

52 Finnsiö, M. (2020). "Sweden.", p.115 In: Rekawek, K. and Ritzmann, A. and Schindler, H. J. (2020). Violent Right-Wing Extremism and Terrorism—Transnational Connectivity, Definitions, Incidents, Structures and Countermeasures. Berlin: Counter Extremism Project, https://www.counterextremism.com/sites/default/files/CEP%20Study_Violent%20Right-Wing%20Extremism%20and%20Terrorism_Nov%202020.pdf.

53 Rekawek, K. (2021b). "An effective ban on foreign fighting? Wider implications of the Czech policy towards foreign (terrorist) fighters." RightNow! 20 September. https://www.sv.uio.no/c-rex/english/news-and-events/right-now/2021/an-effective-ban-on-foreign-fighting-wider-implica.html

54 Anonymous, #4. (2022). Author's interview with a former Croat member of the Azov Battalion who wished to remain anonymous. 25 July.

individuals who ventured Eastwards to fight as potential terrorists of the future.

2. Inability to contextualise and consume news from Ukraine.

The fascination might have been strengthened by the inability of Western audiences to comprehend the situation, which was offensively dubbed the "Ukraine crisis", even though Russia was responsible for its outbreak. To many, the war seemed like a "civil war", and the "grievances" put forward by the "separatists" were often taken at face value or given a sympathetic ear[55]. The latter was too often perceived as a righteous underdog which allegedly suffered under the yoke of Ukrainian imperialism. The fact that they spoke Russian legitimised their claim to "statehood" or "separation" from Ukraine. The fact that Russian has also been the political language in Kyiv seemed to escape the attention of some Western observers. In these conditions, any of "our" radicals travelling "there" to fight only compounded Ukraine's public-relations debacle. Again, the presence of equally, if not more, radical fighters on the "separatist" side seemed largely unnoticed[56]. In short, the "white power warrior from Sweden" in Azov's ranks was more coveted in the press than French far-right extremists shopping for units in first Donetsk and then Luhansk People's Republics[57]. This was also down to the fact that it was far more straightforward for a foreign reporter or an observer to reach Kyiv, where one could visit Azov's HQ, than flying to Moscow, then busing to Rostov on the Don and finally, illegally crossing the Russo-Ukrainian border into the so-called "People's Republics." Consequently, more reporting on Ukraine's far- right and its guests made it out into the world,

---

55 Britannica (2014). "Ukraine crisis." https://www.britannica.com/topic/Ukraine-crisis
56 Rekawek, K. (2020). Career Break or a New Career? Extremist Foreign Fighters in Ukraine. Berlin: Counter Extremism Project. https://www.counterextremism.com/sites/default/files/CEP%20Report_Career%20Break%20or%20a%20New%20Career_Extremist%20Foreign%20Fighters%20in%20Ukraine_April%202020.pdf
57 Ibid.

thereby strengthening the suspicion that something radical was indeed brewing on the Ukrainian side of the frontlines.

3. Russian manipulation.

The easiest or laziest of the explanations stipulates that our fascination with Azov is all down to Russian propaganda, which was keen to play up the unit's imagery as a "Nazi" unit and then gladly informed "us," the West, of its unsavoury foreign members. This explanation builds upon an authentic and almost century-old Soviet/Russian tradition of regarding and portraying any real or imagined anti-Soviet and consequently anti-Russian or nationalist Ukrainian action or thought as "fascist," "Banderite" (supporter of the Organisation of Ukrainian Nationalists, OUN, *Організація українських націоналістів*) or in later years, "Nazi"[58]. In this reading of the situation, organisations such as Azov, regardless of whether the Azov Battalion, Regiment, or the Movement, are a symptom of the alleged Ukrainian long-professed fascination with fascist or even Nazi politics. One should not forget that Moscow imposed such a narrative for most of the 20th century on Ukraine and found a considerable number of adherents to this worldview amongst the country's Russian minority and Ukrainian proponents of "Soviet Ukraine[59]". Interestingly, the narrative did not disappear with the downfall of the Soviet Union and pro-Russian political forces within Ukraine found it to have been a useful mobilising tool against the Western-oriented but also "fascist," "post-Banderite" opponents[60].

Given all this, one should not be too surprised that after 2014, Ukrainians would automatically push back against any criticism of entities such as Azov and not judge them on their merit but perceive these as a continuation of Russian smearing against their country. The current author has received such comments from

---

58 Rekawek, K. (2023). Foreign Fighters in Ukraine: Brown-Red Cocktail. Abingdon: Routledge.
59 Riabczuk, M. (2022). Czternasta od końca. Opowieści o współczesnej Ukrainie. Krakow: Znak.
60 Rekawek, K. (2023). Foreign Fighters in Ukraine: Brown-Red Cocktail. Abingdon: Routledge.

Ukrainian academics and experts who would react in a knee-jerk fashion to any criticism of Azov long before it valiantly defended the Azovstal Iron and Steel Works. Such an approach produced an expected pushback from less seasoned observers of the conflict who, instead of being won over by the Ukrainian heated arguments, began to doubt their sincerity. They were put off by the rigid and uncompromising character of the Ukrainian takes on the situation. Ironically, this created a bizarre echo chamber in which Russia's original spin of anything Ukrainian as fascist would be rightly denounced by the Ukrainians. These would, however, grow to be exasperated by the Western inability to unequivocally, in their minds, side with Ukraine.

Moreover, these Westerners anecdotally seemed to have been probing for evidence which would support Russia's inaccurate claims. In short, the more the Ukrainians pushed back, the more difficult it became to convince neutrals of the inaccuracy of the Russian manipulation. This had been inaccurate and misleading, but with time and in line with Moscow's wishes, it hardly mattered for the embittered Ukrainians and the allegedly objective outsiders. The latter found plenty of alarming evidence to doubt Ukrainian claims concerning Azov. The fact that this evidence did not concern Azov's minuscule group of foreign fighters became irrelevant as the critique zoomed in on other non-foreign fighters related issues such as the Azov Movement's political activity.

4. Mistaking the movement for the Regiment?

Azov's members were heard and seen making statements which positioned their movement, or its political party, within the framework of transnationally oriented nationalist or far-right entities of the 21st century[61]. It looked as if they cared not only about Ukraine but also the external affairs. In the case of Azov, the external especially meant the so-called Intermarium, a geopolitical space in between the West and Russia which would allow for the rebirth of

---

61 Colborne, M. (2022). From the Fires of War: Ukraine's Azov Movement and the Global Far Right. Berlin: ibidem press.

their transnational nationalist ideal[62]. Azov's political party, the National Corps (NK, Національний корпус) developed its own "international secretariat" whose members, especially its head — Olena Semenyaka, travelled Europe and spoke at different far-right conferences and other gatherings. While doing so, she seemingly represented the totality of the movement, not just the political party, or at least that had been the impression of the audiences, listeners and interlocutors at least partly drawn to her or her messages because of the "Azov," read: Azov Battalion/Regiment, connection. The party never shied away from utilising the Regiment's fame to boost its image and, at times, referred to it as "ours[63]".

All of this came at a price to be paid primarily on how the Movement was perceived externally. While the NK's "international" personnel clocked up air miles representing a socio-political entity which was said to encompass a former volunteer battalion and did not, or could not, do much to counter such an impression, the whole Movement found itself on the receiving end of a vocal criticism coming from abroad[64]. Moreover, the critique's edge was not only aimed at the party, the Movement's ideology, and its political positions — beyond the pale for a good deal of external observers — but also its transnationalism. In this reading of the situation, trips abroad, speaking at congresses and interviews given by the likes of Semenyaka became proof that this militant entity is forging connections to recruit, train and field foreign fighters in its ranks. This was far from the case, as the "secretariat's" members told the current author[65]. For them, their connections were political and developed to counter Russian influence in the nationalist/far-

---

62 Nonjon, A. (2020). "Olena Semenyaka, The "First Lady" of Ukrainian Nationalism." Illiberalism Studies Programme Working Paper, September. https://www.illiberalism.org/olena-semenyaka-the-first-lady-of-ukrainian-nationalism/
63 National Corps, (2021). "IV International Online Conference "Global Turbulence and the Purpose of Intermarium." 18 December. https://www.youtube.com/watch?v=bQ4zJTTy-ps&t=9619s
64 Miller, Ch. (2018). "Azov, Ukraine's Most Prominent Ultranationalist Group, Sets Its Sights On U.S., Europe." RadioFreeEurope/RadioLiberty, 14 November. https://www.rferl.org/a/azov-ukraine-s-most-prominent-ultranationalist-group-sets-its-sights-on-u-s-europe/29600564.html
65 Rekawek, K. (2023). Foreign Fighters in Ukraine: Brown-Red Cocktail. Abingdon: Routledge.

right circles in the West[66]. However, due to the lingering Azov Regiment connection, their explanations were hardly ever taken at face value. In addition to that, the Azov Movement's, or the National Corps' hosting of certain unsavoury characters, who seemed like readymade transnational far-right troublemakers[67] and not just ideologues, strengthened the impression that the idea behind the transnational outreach was about cooperation of politically violent actors. Ironically, interviewees involved in Azov always stressed that the party was ready to "defend itself" in the streets of Ukraine but became aware of the fact that association with militant figures from abroad brings too much "heat", especially from the U.S. government, for it to be worthwhile[68]. In short, as many commentators and observers were put off by Semenyaka and co.'s politics and events at which she spoke, they incorrectly diagnosed the motives and the actual purpose behind this transnational outreach. Their approach, however, inadvertently added to the Movement's mystique as a far-right equivalent of Al-Qaeda intent on luring impressionable foreign recruits into its fold. The Movement's denials of this fact and the stress these put on the fact that foreigners were barred from service in the National Guard of Ukraine (to which the Azov Regiment belongs) were falling on proverbial deaf ears[69].

66　Rekawek, K. and Ritzmann, A. and Schindler, H. J. (2020). Violent Right-Wing Extremism and Terrorism — Transnational Connectivity, Definitions, Incidents, Structures and Countermeasures. Berlin: Counter Extremism Project, https://www.counterextremism.com/sites/default/files/CEP%20Study_Violent%20Right-Wing%20Extremism%20and%20Terrorism_Nov%202020.pdf.
67　Colborne, M. (2022). From the Fires of War: Ukraine's Azov Movement and the Global Far Right. Berlin: ibidem press.
68　Rekawek, K. (2020). Career Break or a New Career? Extremist Foreign Fighters in Ukraine. Berlin: Counter Extremism Project. https://www.counterextremism.com/sites/default/files/CEP%20Report_Career%20Break%20or%20a%20New%20Career_Extremist%20Foreign%20Fighters%20in%20Ukraine_April%202020.pdf
69　Azov Regiment, (2021). ATTENTION! THE AZOV REGIMENT'S RESPONSE TO THE ALLEGATIONS PUBLISHED IN "TIME" MAGAZINE. 15 April. https://azov.org.ua/the-azov-regiments-response-to-the-allegations-published-in-time-magazine/

5. Not doing itself favours.

The key reason why the Movement's rebuttals were not working as far as recruitment of foreigners was concerned was the public image it (self)acquired after 2014. Semenyaka could dismiss this as the result of the chaos of 2014, during which the future regiment "basically recruited anyone who could hold a weapon in their hands," and that included some "war adventurers[70]". It is undoubtedly true, however, that its first popular emanation, the now) famous Azov Battalion of 2014, contained many individuals who would have been called far-right by Western standards. To add insult to injury, these individuals were not exactly hidden from the view of the visiting journalists or experts. They were happy to engage them in wide-ranging political conversations[71]. Moreover, the backgrounds of the leaders of the nationalist/far-right Ukrainian volunteer battalions and their run-ins with the law before 2013-2014[72] and the imagery of the developing unit (logo, patches, and tattoos of its members) contributed to the formation of a truly perfect storm. In these conditions, conversations between the observers and the observed developed as if on parallel tracks: the Battalion's members would not be asked about their exploits and why they picked up guns in the first place but about their ideology or tattoos, whereas the visiting outsiders would be appalled by the seeming nonchalance with which these soldiers' treated subjects and opinions internationally deemed beyond the pale. In addition to this, external observers would be quick to point out that the unit visibly had some foreign presence within their ranks and that "its" foreigners were coming from milieus deemed extreme in the broader West, including Skillt, a militant member of Swedish far-right

---

70 TIME. (2021). "Inside a White Supremacist Militia in Ukraine." 8 January. https://www.youtube.com/watch?v=fy910FG46C4
71 VICE News, (2014). "We Embedded with the Azov Battalion While They Trained and Conducted a Patrol." 7 September. https://www.vice.com/en/article/qbexvm/russian-roulette-the-invasion-of-ukraine-september-7-123
72 Umland, A. (2019). "Irregular Militias and Radical Nationalism in Post-Euromaydan Ukraine: The Prehistory and Emergence of the "Azov" Battalion in 2014," Terrorism and Political Violence, 31:1, 105-131, DOI: 10.1080/09546553.2018.1555974.

organisations; Gaston Besson, a French veteran of the Yugoslav Wars on the Croat side; and Francesco Fontana, a far-right militant from Italy[73]. These hardly seemed like ideals of decency and respectability according to international media standards. In short, everyone suspected that if a given unit attracted such individuals, it must have something to offer them, and by extension, it automatically seemed suspicious. At that stage, the number of foreign volunteers no longer seemed important—what was key was the fact that a "white power warrior from Sweden" was fighting for Azov[74].

6. Anti-fascism.

The fact that such a "warrior" could be featured in the ranks of any military unit was becoming a cause célèbre in the second decade of the 21st century. This decade first saw Anders Breivik conduct two heinous terrorist attacks in the name of a far-right ideology back in 201. It notionally closed with the 2019 Christchurch massacre by Brenton Tarrant. Violence by right-wing extremists, their views, writings, and political activities were becoming one of the, if not the topic for the international media, especially in the light of the 2015 refugee/migrant crisis, the 2016 Brexit referendum, and the election of Donald Trump as U.S. president. On the one hand, the decade saw a normalisation of far-right discourse and postulates within the mainstream of the political debate. Simultaneously, however, it produced a backlash against this process and a surge of interest in anything related to the far-right to unmask and disrupt its activities. Consequently, organisations and movements which would not have received much coverage in earlier decades were now prime candidates as research subjects or recipients of media inquiries.

One could claim that Azov, a small and politically not very successful socio-political movement existing in a poor country at

---

[73] Biloslavo, F. (2014). "Ukraine: Far-Right Fighters from Europe Fight for Ukraine." Eurasianet. 6 August. https://eurasianet.org/ukraine-far-right-fighters-from-europe-fight-for-ukraine

[74] Newman, D. (2014). "Ukraine conflict: 'White power' warrior from Sweden." BBC News. 16 July. https://www.bbc.com/news/world-europe-28329329

"the gates of Europe"[75], found itself in this position almost by default. Of course, the fact that it fought in the war and undoubtedly made certain unsavoury transnational connections only made things worse for its leadership and members. It seemed logical to be interested in something that looked like a "militia." It functioned in a country with a lot of nationalists seemingly intent on anti-state political violence[76]. Moreover, as was shown, the country hosting these nationalists was being perceived in some quarters, and due to the ongoing prevalence of Russian narratives, as a proverbial nest of far-rightism. In such conditions, the appearance of genuine Western far-right foreign fighters in the ranks of Azov only added to the combustible mix. It might have helped transform the modest numbers "foreigner group" into a nascent far-right Al-Qaeda[77]. In this sense, the number of foreign fighters in Azov's ranks began to look like statistics of "a 320 per cent rise in attacks [in the West] conducted by individuals affiliated with [extreme right wing] movements and ideologies over the past five years[78]". This popular opinion had no basis in data collected by the likes of the author's Centre for Research on Extremism (C-Rex) at the University of Oslo, which suggested that the level of fatal violence due to extreme-right terrorism in Western Europe has been consistently low since the early 2000s onwards[79]. It nonetheless made the headlines, and so did

---

75 Plokhy, S. (2012). The Gates of Europe: A History of Ukraine. New York: Basic Books. Radio Free Europe/Radio Liberty. (2015). "Right Sector Leader Declares 'New Stage Of Ukrainian Revolution'." 22 July. https://www.youtube.com/watch?v=IvDas1ZmzU4
76 Radio Free Europe/Radio Liberty. (2015). "Right Sector Leader Declares 'New Stage Of Ukrainian Revolution'." 22 July. https://www.youtube.com/watch?v=IvDas1ZmzU4
77 Rose, M., Soufan, A. H. (2020). "We Once Fought Jihadists. Now We Battle White Supremacists." The New York Times, 11 February. https://www.nytimes.com/2020/02/11/opinion/politics/white-supremacist-terrorism.html.
78 UN CTED, United Nations Security Council Counter-Terrorism Committee Executive Directorate. (2020). "CTED Trends Alert. April 2020." p.7 https://www.un.org/securitycouncil/ctc/sites/www.un.org.securitycouncil.ctc/files/files/documents/2021/Jan/cted_trends_alert_extreme_right-wing_terrorism.pdf
79 Aasland Ravndal, J., Tandberg, C., Ravik Jupskås, A.., Thorstensen, M. (2022). "RTV Trend Report 2022Right-Wing Terrorism and Violence in Western Europe, 1990−2021." p.5-9, C-Rex Research Report. Oslo: University of Oslo.

Azov's foreign fighters—seemingly perfect fits for a narrative which aimed to situate outlier events, such as attacks conducted by Breivik or Tarrant, among a proverbial tidal wave of similar attacks worldwide and an allegedly unstoppable political current seeing the far-right triumph globally. Consequently, if exposing such fighters seemed like a noble deed, then it has been practised with more zeal and conviction by some of the observers intent on assisting the cause of anti-fascism. Ideologically, they have not entirely missed their mark but, in doing so, exaggerated the magnitude of the phenomenon at hand.

The Aftermath

The fear related to the returns of the foreign fighters from the Azov ranks ran deep. Not only were they seen as potential agents of "Al Qaeda 2.0" by some external observers[80], but it seemed that several security services also took an active interest in "their" returnees. One Swedish former member of Azov remembered that when the local security services questioned him (apparently, this was a standard procedure for all the Azov Swedes[81], he received a question: "Do you want to or plan to carry out religiously motivated terrorist acts in Sweden[82]?" While this question sounded laughable to him, it shows the framework through which some of the security sectors of Europe might have chosen to view such veteran foreign fighters. Such an approach in some, not necessarily Azov-related cases, led to prosecutions and even sentences for the likes of partaking in a criminal organisation, mercenary activities, or preparation of acts of terrorism while in Ukraine (in countries such as Italy or the Czech Republic for the "separatist" foreign fighters). At the

---

    https://www.sv.uio.no/c-rex/english/publications/c-rex-reports/2022/rtv_trend_report_2022.pdf.
80 Rose, M., Soufan, A. H. (2020). "We Once Fought Jihadists. Now We Battle White Supremacists." The New York Times, 11 February. https://www.nytimes.com/2020/02/11/opinion/politics/white-supremacist-terrorism.html.
81 Anonymous, #1. (2020). Author's interview with a Swedish former member of the Azov Battalion/Regiment who wished to remain anonymous. 25 January.
82 Löfroos, C. (2022). Vapaaehtoiset—Sotamme Ukrainassa 2014-2015. Tampere: Kiuas.

same time, and as shown, the fears related to such returnees were mainly misplaced. None got involved in political violence after returning from Ukraine, and one can risk a theory that they also shied away from any militancy. In the words of one foreign Azov veteran: "People who had been losers before coming to Ukraine, they remained losers afterwards. That is not to say they went criminal or anything. They were not doing very well. Others? Some had more luck. Maybe someone started a private protection agency; others went into business[83]"

However, the previous admissions of the Azov veteran interviewed must be scrutinised in more detail. An interviewee from a highly contested and controversial unit, at times even referred to as the far-right equivalent of Al-Qaeda, would have a reputation to protect while talking to the likes of the current author about the post-war activities of his erstwhile colleagues. He would most certainly downplay any controversial aspects in former foreign fighters' life stories after their contribution to the Russo-Ukrainian war. As shown by the author elsewhere, such an approach would align with the characteristics of the "Western foreign fighter secret society" concept (WFFSS). WFFSS is an amorphous entity, a brotherhood or network of fighters who fought together in one conflict and then remained in touch after its conclusion to effectively tip each other off about "the next war"[84]. Outsiders, such as the current author, would have access to the members of the WFFSS but would not be privy to their discussions and would have never—without experience of foreign fighting, at least—been given the same trust by the society's members. In these conditions, one could have expected that many nefarious, if not outright illegal, actions might have escaped the attention of outsiders looking in. Two factors mitigate against this threat: 1. Their counterparts on the pro-Russian or pro-"separatist" side who fought in 2014 developed their own WFFSS, which sometimes even overlapped with the Azovians'

---

83 Anonymous, #7. (2022). Author's interview with a former Swedish member of the Azov Battalion/Regiment who wished to remain anonymous. 11 November.
84 Ibid

participation. As the author has shown elsewhere[85], some of the pro-Russian veteran foreign fighters had the tendency to appear in "interesting places", such as Libya, Somalia, and Syria or while preparing a coup in Montenegro or on the proverbial barricades of the Yellow Vest protests in Paris. Their deeds and mischief, however, have been mainly uncovered, and to date, no similar development has happened for the Azovians, who, one might assume, proverbially kept their heads down; 2. A member of the rival WFFSS and a far-right French militant who fought for Russia in 2014 told the current author in an interview that he and his friends had no plans to participate in any political violence or terrorism upon returning home. He justified it because involvement in these activities would "unite the society behind the police and the state, justify the strengthening of security and authoritarian laws. This is why I can't fight a war here [in my home country] and why I oppose terrorism[86]". One can assume that, instinctively, the Azovians who, as was shown, felt almost hounded by the establishment comparing them to ISIS foreign fighters, could have hardly contemplated a different approach.

Interestingly, the resumption of hostilities in 2022 served to lure some of the Westerners from Azov ranks back into the service. The key figure here was meant to be Mikael Skillt, who resurfaced after a prolonged absence from social media on the one hand and from Kyiv on the other. This was surprising as after 2014 he married a Ukrainian and settled in the country and was a presence in the capital. Throughout 2021, the author's sources within the Azov Movement were convinced that he had gone on some private military contracting missions in Africa and some, anonymously, were ready to speculate that he "could have died there"[87]. His reappearance in early March 2022 in Kyiv and his photo and video session

---

85 Rekawek, K. (2020). Career Break or a New Career? Extremist Foreign Fighters in Ukraine. Berlin: Counter Extremism Project. https://www.counterextremism.com/sites/default/files/CEP%20Report_Career%20Break%20or%20a%20 New%20Career_Extremist%20Foreign%20Fighters%20in%20Ukraine_April%202020.pdf
86 Ibid, p.25
87 Anonymous, #3. (2022) Author's interview with a member of the National Corps party who wished to remain anonymous. 15 June.

with the "Intermarium Support Group" (ISG), an Azovian NGO based in Kyiv[88], then seemed a total surprise to all concerned. He was showcased as a future instructor for elements of Ukraine's International Legion, which were recruited by the personnel of the ISG. Skillt was also featured in a photo which saw all the recruited individuals share a stage with MP Svatoslav Yurash, a vital patron of this recruitment effort[89]. Weeks later, however, it was becoming clear that the Legion was not what its backers had initially hoped for, and these recruitment efforts were yielding modest returns (20-30 recruited)[90], leading Skillt to jump ship directly into a unit of Ukrainian troops fighting around Kharkiv.

Skillt, however, was not the only veteran Westerner who decided to return to the fold. Another veteran, Carolus Löfroos, at some point early in the conflict, participated in a donations call for a group of fighters, which was allegedly constituted of his old 2014-2015 "foreigner group" from that battalion[91]. In his subsequent book, he mentioned a few of its members (nationals of Greece, Finland and France, amongst others) who resurfaced to fight near the capital[92]. In addition to this group, Denis Šeler, one of the original Azov's late arrivals who missed the beginning of the war in 2014, allegedly also reappeared in Kyiv in 2022[93] and was said to have led a group of Croats back into the fight. He was also allegedly the speaker in one of Azov's videos, in which he spoke of "companies" full of foreigners who got to Ukraine to fight Russia. Regardless of

---

88   Intermarium, #2. (2022). Facebook post. 15 March. https://www.facebook.com /intermarium.today/photos/pb.100078455973737.-2207520000./117430144210 263/?type=3
89   Intermarium, #2. (2022). Facebook post. 15 March. https://www.facebook.com /intermarium.today/photos/pb.100078455973737.-2207520000./117430144210 263/?type=3
90   Polskieradio.pl. (2022). "Волонтер: Люди со всего мира приехали воевать за Украину, а их не пускают на фронт." 1 April. shorturl.at/eFN67
91   Carolus. (2022). Twitter post from @fri_skytt. 7 April. https://twitter.com/fri_ skytt/status/1512135749247844352?t=z091KEnagTwgbNsiCS5B2g&s=09
92   Löfroos, C. (2022). Vapaaehtoiset—Sotamme Ukrainassa 2014-2015. Tampere: Kiuas.
93   Bajruši, R. (2022) "'Da, jedan Hrvat je zarobljen i točno znam gdje je pao u ruke Rusa. Sigurno nije u Azovstalu'." Jutarnji List. 7 May. https://www.jutarnji.hr /vijesti/hrvatska/da-jedan-hrvat-je-zarobljen-i-tocno-znam-gdje-je-pao-u-ruk e-rusa-sigurno-nije-u-azovstalu-15194390

these claims, the author's sources in Azov later confirmed that the Croats left Kyiv after the battle for that city was won as they felt "they did the job they had come to do in Ukraine[94]".

Conclusion

Given the numbers of Western foreign fighters in Azov and their post-war deeds and actions, two conclusions become immediately evident: 1. the unit has never been the hub of far-right militancy some thought it morphed into, and 2. its transnational potential has mostly been aspirational (politically for the Azov Movement) and imagined (for the wannabe far-right militants and fanboys dedicated to Azov's imagery). Its Western alumni, who might have somehow aligned ideologically with the original Battalion, did not join it to carry the flame of some far-right militancy/revolution back to their home countries as they have not courted trouble after returning from Ukraine to date. Interestingly, however, given the chance, they re-joined the war effort in 2022, but not necessarily in the ranks of Azov-related units in Ukraine. In this sense, they have demonstrated dedication to the Ukrainian cause and to some of their brothers in arms from earlier years, not to a specific ideology. One might doubt whether they were merely "conservative" or "on the right", but it now seems evident that Azov, a predominantly Ukrainian and Ukraine-oriented (para)military and a socio-political movement[95], would think of them as its external ambassadors sent abroad to wreak proverbial havoc. This chapter, however, discussed reasons why such individuals might have been perceived along these lines as Azov became an object of fascination to many external observers who: a) compared it with its jihadi contemporaries, be it from ISIS or Al-Qaeda; b) failed to contextualise news from Ukraine and often relied on Russian viewpoints to describe the

---

94 Anonymous, #5. (2022). Author's interview with a former Croat member of the Azov Battalion/Regiment who wished to remain anonymous. April 13.
95 Gomza, I. (2022). "Too Much Ado About Ukrainian Nationalists: the Azov Movement and the War in Ukraine." KRYTYKA. April. https://krytyka.com/en/articles/too-much-ado-about-ukrainian-nationalists-the-azov-movement-and-the-war-in-ukraine

situation in the country; c) mistook Azov's politicking for its militancy; and d) situated Azov as an element of a seemingly transnational far-right monolith that is going from strength to strength. At the same time, the original Battalion and then the Movement gave such observers seemingly some reasons to be viewed as the potential equivalent of the far-right Al-Qaeda. It had never come close to this and remains wary of any activity, such as doubling down on its feeble contacts with US extremists, which might, among other things, result in it being declared "terrorist" by the likes of the US State Department, with all the consequences that might follow[96].

---

96 Anonymous, #3. (2022) Author's interview with a member of the National Corps party who wished to remain anonymous. 15 June.

Conclusion
Beyond the Storm:
Much Ado About Nothing?

Christian Kaunert, Alex MacKenzie and Adrien Nonjon

Despite being the focus of attention from an early stage, the Azov phenomenon remains little known, both in terms of its nature and the context in which it emerged. In preparing this book, we wanted to return to this subject by drawing up an overview of this multi-branch organisation from its official founding in 2014 to the beginning of Russia's all-out invasion of Ukraine in 2022. Regarding all previous chapters based on this precise timeline, our first priority in this conclusion must, therefore, be to bring the story of the Azov Brigade right up to the present day by covering how it has evolved during the ongoing war (with mid-2024 being the time of writing). The unit has undergone significant change since the defence of Mariupol in early 2022, given the casualties sustained, prisoners of war still held by Russia, and the unit's expansion, refresh, and return to the theatre of war in mid-2023. Indeed, the conflict has likely accelerated the drifting apart of the Azov Brigade and the Azov Movement (the two are still often conflated by scholars and journalists, even today) or perhaps even eliminated connections altogether, as we discussed in the introduction. It is possible that some newer additions who volunteered between the unit's withdrawal from combat in late 2022 and re-deployment in 2023 as both an Assault Brigade and Spec Ops Unit hold extreme beliefs of various kinds, but their allegiances will be different and a minority in any case. We can be certain that the reality of today's Azov Brigade is far more complicated than it being a unit dominated by extremists; ten years of conflict mean that we are dealing with a transformed entity since it was created by fringe far-right activists in 2014. No comprehensive knowledge of Azov is possible without an awareness of the range of issues that Ukraine has been facing since 2014. While the individual contributions in this book provide a valuable summary, it is nonetheless important to set out a few points for reflection—whether they work in the fields of International Relations, Terrorism Studies, or are area or country specialists—on the future of this unit and, more broadly, of right-wing extremism.

The Azov Brigade During the Russia-Ukraine War, 2022–Today

Russia's war in Ukraine continues unabated with no sign of an end in sight. Both sides remain a long way apart in terms of their objectives and, thus, any landing strip for a negotiated solution, with Russia attempting to grind down Ukrainian forces to grab as much land as possible and Kyiv continuing to fight for a restoration of the pre-2014 settlement (including the Crimean Peninsula being returned by Russia), far off. Russian leaders will likely feel that the longer the conflict goes on, the greater their chance of winning due to its superior manpower reserves and productive capabilities, although this will be a long way from the outright victory optimistically anticipated in early 2022.[1] External events will have a significant bearing on this conflict, especially US and European leaders and their commitments to Ukraine, but the actions of China and other allies of Russia will also matter.

Ever since the war began, heated debates have taken place about how it will end. Unsurprisingly, many expect a negotiated solution.[2] Yet, such an occurrence could embolden Putin depending on the relative positions of the warring parties at such a time in the future. Russia has not proven to be the most reliable negotiating partner over the past two decades given that it has repeatedly failed to respect the sovereignty of states in its vicinity, specifically Ukraine, Georgia, and Moldova. Above other major states, Russia

---

1 RUSI (2024), 'Russian Military Objectives and Capacity in Ukraine 2024', available at: https://www.rusi.org/explore-our-research/publications/commentary/russian-military-objectives-and-capacity-ukraine-through-2024 (accessed on 11th July 2024)
2 Chatham House (2023), 'How to End Russia's War on Ukraine', available at: https://www.chathamhouse.org/2023/06/how-end-russias-war-ukraine/fallacy-1-settle-now-all-wars-end-negotiating-table (accessed on 11th July).

has long been seen as a challenge not only to Eastern Europe but to the democratic and liberal order more generally due to its authoritarian regime and status-based economy.[3] In this respect, Ukraine's victory is more than necessary. If Ukraine does not have a strong presence in future talks with Russia or is starved of Western aid to push it towards a settlement, a future territorial dispute might be created, both of which are well-known causes of interstate war. In other words, the West would not be putting in place a lasting, sustainable peace but instead a temporary armistice against a reinvigorated, emboldened, and untrustworthy Russia.[4] In such circumstances and given Putin's long-held views about Eastern Europe and Russia's role in the world, such as the artificiality of Ukraine and regret about the fall of the USSR, it is difficult not to foresee Moscow striking again before long.[5]

Russia's actions have now caused hundreds of thousands of casualties. However, it is difficult to ascertain precise numbers of either side because of censorship, the need to maintain morale, and disinformation. There can be little doubt that these numbers will increase substantially, given that the conflict will likely run for years to come. Also, Russia shifted towards a strategy based on attrition from about January 2023 during offensives in the Donetsk region as it moved away from a force composed of professional soldiers towards one of mainly conscripts.[6] Not only this, but Russia has faced substantial criticism for atrocities during the war, whether intentional targeting of civilians and infrastructure to

---

3 Michael Mousseau (2019), 'The End of War: How a Robust Marketplace and Liberal Hegemony are Leading to Perpetual World Peace', *International Security*, 44(1), p196; Alexander Motyl (2023), 'Why We Should Not Bet on a Peaceful Russia', available at: https://foreignpolicy.com/2023/08/25/russia-ukraine-putin-prigozhin-negotiation-settlement-deal-peace-war-counteroffensive/ (accessed on 11th July 2024).
4 John Vasquez (2009), *The War Puzzle Revisited* (Cambridge University Press: Cambridge).
5 Fiona Hill (2015), 'How Vladimir Putin's World View Shapes Russian Foreign Policy', in David Cadier and Margot Light (eds.), *Russia's Foreign Policy: Ideas, Domestic Politics, and External Relations* (Palgrave Macmillan: Basingstoke).
6 BBC (2024), 'Russia's Meat Grinder Soldiers – 50,000 Confirmed Dead', available at: https://www.bbc.co.uk/news/world-68819853 (accessed on 29th April 2024).

appalling killings undertaken by supposedly private security companies, such as by what was the Wagner Group before its rebellion in June 2023.[7] War crimes have even been claimed to be 'integral' to Russia's way of war to generate widespread fear and force opponents into submission.[8] Yet, Russia's economy appears to be faring reasonably well considering the stresses of war. It is likely to grow by more than three per cent in 2024, and it possesses deep manpower reserves.[9] By contrast, Ukraine is hugely dependent on Western aid, is fighting on its territory, and is regularly having its infrastructure pummelled by Russian drones and missiles. Estimates from 2023 suggested that the cost of rebuilding the country could cost anywhere between $138 billion to $750 billion—and that this would take decades of peace.[10] Not only this, but Ukraine is attempting to avoid conscripting its youngest men so as not to lose a generation, with the age for mobilisation reduced from twenty-seven to twenty-five only in May 2024 due to manpower shortages.[11]

Moving on to the Azov Brigade's war specifically, much has occurred. Many of its soldiers early in the war were killed or

---

[7] Amnesty International (2024), 'Justice for Ukraine Means Accountability for All War Crimes Committed by Russia Since 2014', available at: https://www.amnesty.org/en/latest/news/2024/02/with-russias-full-scale-invasion-two-years-ago-an-act-of-aggression-that-is-a-crime-under-international-law-the-tragically-familiar-human-rights-catastrophe-extended-acros/ (accessed on 11th July 2024).

[8] Fredrik Wesslau (2024), 'There Must be a Reckoning for Russian War Crimes', available at: https://foreignpolicy.com/2024/02/20/russia-war-crimes-justice-ukraine-putin-children-deportation-torture/ (accessed on 11th July 2024)

[9] Reuters (2024), 'Russian Ministry Sees 2024 GDP at 2.8%, But With Higher Inflation, Weaker Rouble, available at: https://www.reuters.com/world/europe/russian-ministry-sees-2024-gdp-28-with-higher-inflation-weaker-rouble-2024-04-23/#:~:text=The%20International%20Monetary%20Fund%20this,export%20revenues%20in%20spite%20of (accessed on 29th April 2024).

[10] New York Times (2023), "The World's Largest Construction Site': The Race is on to Rebuild Ukraine' available at: https://www.nytimes.com/2023/02/16/business/economy/ukraine-rebuilding.html (accessed on 30th April).

[11] The Guardian (2024), 'I Love my Country, But I Can't Kill': Ukrainian Men Evading Conscription', available at: https://www.theguardian.com/world/article/2024/may/04/i-love-my-country-but-i-cant-kill-ukrainian-men-evading-conscription#:~:text=The%20mobilisation%20age%20was%20reduced,such%20as%20Poland%20and%20Lithuania. (accessed on 11th July 2024).

captured, with about 2,000 of the defenders of Mariupol (including units other than Azov) still held captive by Russia following their surrender in May 2022. However, others have been released in prisoner swaps, including some agreements on individuals sitting out the war under house arrest in Turkey.[12] Before the prisoner swaps and denying that Azov fighters had the right to protection under the Geneva Convention, Russia attempted in occupied Mariupol to arrange show trials for them, with hanging or decades-long incarceration being the punishments meted out. However, these do not appear to have taken place.[13] In mid-2023, the revamped unit, having been expanded to an Assault brigade earlier that year, returned to fighting near Zaporizhzhia – close to the infamous nuclear power station that has been the source of much concern during the conflict. Clearly, at that point, the now Azov 3rd Assault Brigade could not have been composed of the same personnel as was the case even a year earlier, never mind whether many remained from 2014, which likely makes it all the more 'normal' in the Ukrainian armed forces. Despite this, there will be some exceptions, such as officer Denys Prokopenko, who joined the unit in 2017 and has been referred to as a football 'ultra', often seen as holding at least nationalist belief systems.[14] Having said this, Prokopenko does not make his political views public, which may be a further sign of the

---

12 The Guardian (2024), 'Escape From Mariupol: How One Ukrainian Soldier Fled the Azovstal Steelworks Against the Odds', available at: https://www.theguardian.com/world/2024/jan/09/escape-from-mariupol-how-one-ukrainian-soldier-fled-the-azovstal-steelworks-against-the-odds (accessed on 26th April 2024); Le Monde (2023), 'War in Ukraine: A Year on From Siege of Mariupol, The Azov Brigade Returns to Battle', available at: https://www.lemonde.fr/en/international/article/2023/06/13/war-in-ukraine-a-year-on-from-siege-of-mariupol-the-azov-brigade-returns-to-battle_6031209_4.html (accessed on 26th April 2024).
13 Filipe dos Reis and Janis Grzybowski (2023), 'Moving 'Red Lines': The Russian–Ukrainian War and the Pragmatic (Mis-)use of International Law', *Global Constitutionalism*, pp.1-23. doi:10.1017/S2045381723000175
14 Euromaidan Press (2024), '' We Fight Real Nazis of Today': Azov Commander Slams US Weapons Ban in Plea for Aid', available at: https://euromaidanpress.com/2024/04/20/we-fight-real-nazis-of-today-azov-commander-slams-us-weapons-ban-in-plea-for-aid/ (accessed on 30th April 2024); Olga Ruzhelnyk (2024), 'From Football Stadium to Revolution and War Frontlines: Ukrainian Uktras the Conversion of Their Capital', *International Political Science Review*, 45(2), pp.209-223.

professionalisation of the Azov Brigade and it now being firmly under state control.[15]

Today, in mid-2024, the Azov Brigade is based near the Serebryansky forest, which is in the Luhansk Oblast and on the front lines, its numbers now swelled to 5,000 or perhaps more, all of which are believed to be volunteers. Not only this, but it is currently bucking the trend of Ukrainian defeats and holding its ground in the area.[16] In June 2024, the US government lifted its ban from 2015 on supplying the Azov with training and weapons, with the State Department finding 'no evidence of Gross Violations of Human Rights' by the unit. According to the so-called 'Leahy Law', the US cannot train or supply weapons to foreign organisations responsible for such acts.[17] This appears to show a natural consequence of Russian disinformation efforts. Of course, considering the different sources of information, it is difficult to properly grasp the extent to which extremists populate the Azov Brigade and other Ukrainian units. Russian sources will unsurprisingly call Azov "Nazis", whereas the Ukrainian state will be keen to show otherwise. In this light, Putin's insistence that Ukraine is somehow a "Nazi state" appears to grow more hollow by the day. However, we know that Ukraine, since its independence and then the Maydan Revolution, has embraced a wide range of beliefs—some repulsive—in its struggle against Russia.[18] Furthermore, in this

---

15 Ivan Gomza (2024), 'The Azov Movement: The Trajectory of a Far-Right Movement in Post-Euromaidan Ukraine' in Peter Marton, Gry Thomasen, Csaba Bekes, and Andras Racz (eds.), *The Palgrave Handbook of Non-State Actors in East-West Relations* (Palgrave Macmillan: Cham), p6
16 The Guardian (2024), 'Elite Force Bucks Trend of Ukrainian Losses on Eastern Front', available at: https://www.theguardian.com/world/2024/apr/27/elite-force-bucks-trend-of-ukrainian-losses-on-eastern-front (accessed on 30th April 2024); Le Monde (2024), 'Azov Brigade is Once Again at Heart of Fighting in Donbas', available at: https://www.lemonde.fr/en/international/article/2024/05/13/azov-brigade-is-once-again-at-heart-of-fighting-in-donbas_6671268_4.html (accessed on 16th July 2024).
17 CNN (2024), 'Azov: US Lifts Ban on Sending Weapons to Ukraine's Azov Brigade', available at: https://edition.cnn.com/2024/06/12/europe/us-weapons-azov-brigade-ukraine-intl/index.html (accessed 16th July 2024).
18 Politico (2024), 'Ukraine Embraces Far-Right Russian 'Bad Guy' to Take the Battle to Putin', available at: https://www.politico.eu/article/the-good-the-bad-and-the-ugly-of-the-ukraine-war/ (accessed on 30th April).

conflict, it is not always easy to see where nationalists with democratic commitments end and far-right extremism begins in Ukraine, given the total nature of the ongoing struggle against Russia that led to a sacred union and the rise of a strong patriotic feeling. Once again, whatever Ukraine's deficiencies—and it has many—they are dwarfed by Russia's questionable alliances, such as with 'populists' and those further to the right of the political spectrum around the world, far-right units in its armed forces (e.g. the Rusich Group); and permissiveness towards far-right ideologies and extremism at home, as is the case with the Russian Imperial Movement, for example.[19] As the conflict in Ukraine has progressed and given the differences between the behaviours of the two armed forces, with war crimes extensively committed by Russia, we hear far less of claims that Ukraine is a 'Nazi' state.

Through its in-depth and exhaustive exploration of one of the targets of Russian propaganda for the last decade, we are confident that this book goes some way to debunking Russia's claims of Ukraine needing to be 'de-Nazified' for those who are yet to be convinced. Above all, it is interesting that we conclude the book by asking whether the thing we started out studying was materially worthy of study. Quite clearly, we have put the Azov Brigade into some perspective by showing that it is one unit of hundreds in the Ukrainian armed forces and, even today, numbers only in the thousands in an army that has swelled to many hundreds of thousands since Russia's invasion. This points to how effective misinformation efforts can be, primarily when employed against societies that possess little knowledge of a region and are as polarised as many Western states are today. Indeed, there have even been several mainly

---

19   Miroslav Mares, Martin Larys, and Jan Holzer (2019), *Militant Right-Wing Extremism in Putin's Russia: Legacies, Forms, and Threats* (Routledge: London).; Kacper Rekawek, Thomas Renard, and Barbara Molas (eds.) (2024), 'Russia and the Far Right: Insights From Ten European Countries', available at: https://www.icct.nl/sites/default/files/2024-04/Russia%20and%20the%20Far-Right%20Insights%20from%20Ten%20European%20Countries%20-%20A4%20e-book_0.pdf (accessed on 1st May 2024); Anna Kruglova (2024), 'For God, For Tsar, and For The Nation: Authenticity in the Russian Imperial Movement's Propaganda', *Studies in Conflict and Terrorism*, 47(6), pp.645-667; Anton Shekhovtsov (2017), *Russia and the Western Far Right: Tango Noir* (Routledge: London).

leftist outlets that have got carried away into hysteria, reproducing and thereby amplifying concerns about 'Azov Nazies'.[20] The real-world effects of this are that people buy into Russian views of the conflict, meaning a victory of sorts for Putin and his allies, primarily if hesitancy to arm or train Ukrainian forces results, all of which concretely assists Moscow. Indeed, it is well-known how the war has been presented on Russian television, with criticism of the conflict even criminalised.[21] By contrast, the rest of the world has seen significant acts of Russian brutality, whether the notorious sledgehammer incident involving Wagner Group fighters or the especially peculiar and sinister case of the deportation of Ukrainian children in Russia.[22]

Donald Trump-supporting US Republicans have been instrumental in attempting to block aid to Ukraine already. However, that is also partially due to a historical commitment to isolationism as a persisting current in US foreign policy.[23] The great danger here is, given the lack of preparation and economic fragility, that Western aid to Ukraine declines or even ceases, and Russia is emboldened to nibble at other states in the post-Soviet space in the future, perhaps even those that are currently NATO members. It would certainly not help if Trump is in office in Washington, given that he has already pledged to eliminate aid to Ukraine through a 24-hour

---

20 International Centre for Defence and Security (2023), 'Anton Shekhovtsov: Helping Those 'Azov Nazis'?, available at: https://icds.ee/en/anton-shekhovtsov-helping-those-azov-nazis/ (accessed on 26th April 2024).
21 New York Times (2022), 'The War in Ukraine, as Seen on Russian Television' available at: https://www.nytimes.com/interactive/2022/05/06/technology/russian-propaganda-television.html (accessed on 26th April 2024).
22 Politico (2023), 'Behind Enemy Lines: Inside the Operation to Rescue Ukraine's Abducted Children', available at: https://www.politico.eu/article/save-ukraine-children-abduction-russia-war-rescue-operation/ (accessed on 16th July 2024); Reuters (2022), 'Video Shows Sledgehammer Execution of Russian Mercenary, available at: https://www.reuters.com/world/europe/sledgehammer-execution-russian-mercenary-who-defected-ukraine-shown-video-2022-11-13/ (accessed on 16th July 2024).
23 The Guardian (2024), 'Ukraine's War Efforts Already Affected by Block on $60 billion US Aid, Says NATO Chief', available at: https://www.theguardian.com/world/2024/feb/15/ukraines-war-effort-already-affected-by-block-on-60bn-us-aid--nato-jens-stoltenberg#:~:text=Earlier%20this%20week%20the%20Senate,across%20the%20US%2DMexico%20border. (accessed on 19th July 2024).

negotiation that would allegedly lead to peace[24] and pledging not to assist European states deemed to have been under-spending on defence. In early 2024, Trump said that he would allow Russia to do 'whatever the hell they want' to NATO members that do not spend sufficiently on defence, thereby moving away from the alliance's commitment to collective defence.[25] The selection of James (JD) Vance as Trump's running partner (future vice-president) bodes ominously for Ukraine also. In 2022, Vance said 'I don't care what happens to Ukraine one way or the other', that Russia is not a significant threat to Europe, and that his concerns lie more in East Asia than Europe.[26] It is interesting that those on the US right and far-right moved from being fearful of Russia and communism during the Cold War to sympathy and hope for emulation in some respects from the 1990s onwards.[27] Many populists in Europe have even looked to Putin as an inspirational leader and have attempted to sabotage the EU's efforts to assist Ukraine, such as Hungary's Prime Minister Viktor Orban, who has attempted to veto aid.[28] Others who previously claimed to admire Putin, such as Italy's Prime Minister Giorgia Meloni, now condemn him.[29] With the war

---

24 AP News (2024) 'Trump says he can end the Russia-Ukraine war in one day. Russia's UN ambassador says he can't', available at : https://apnews.com/article/trump-russia-ukraine-war-un-election-a78ecb843af452b8dda1d52d137ca893#:~:text=At%20a%20CNN%20town%20hall,and%20Russian%20President%20Vladimir%20Putin. (accessed on 4th August 2024).
25 BBC (2024), 'How America's Allies are Trying to 'Trump-Proof' NATO's Future', available at: https://www.bbc.co.uk/news/articles/c3gr90jnxjvo (accessed on 16th July 2024).
26 Reuters (2024), 'European Alarmed by Trump VP Pick Vance's Opposition to Ukraine Aid', available at: https://www.reuters.com/world/europe/europeans-alarmed-by-trump-vp-pick-vances-opposition-ukraine-aid-2024-07-16/ (accessed on 16th July 2024).
27 George Michael (2019), 'Useful Idiots or Fellow Travelers? The Relationship between the American Far Right and Russia' *Terrorism and Political Violence*, 31(1), pp.64–83.
28 Reuters (2024), 'Brussels Threatens to Hit Hungary's Economy if Orban Vetoes Ukraine Aid', available at: https://www.reuters.com/world/europe/brussels-threatens-hit-hungarys-economy-if-orban-vetoes-ukraine-aid-ft-2024-01-29/ (accessed on 16th July 2024).
29 Politico (2024), 'Putin Can't Count on His Friends in Italy Anymore', available at: https://www.politico.eu/article/vladimir-putin-giorgia-meloni-relationship-russia-italy-not-friends/ (accessed on 16th July 2024).

showing no sign of ending soon, Ukraine's future very likely hinges on aid given to it by outside donors over the long term.

What of the Azov Movement, the organisation with which the Azov Brigade is often conflated? As mentioned, the Azov Battalion was initially established and led by people with far-right views.[30] Widely covered in the media at the start of the Russian incursions into Ukraine in early 2014, the unit has evolved enormously over the last ten years. Quickly brought under the control of the state apparatus following the Minsk Protocol of 5 September 2014, the unit has gradually evolved into a cutting-edge fighting entity. Even as the political remains present in a conceptual form of national patriotism that cannot ignore the long history of Ukrainian nationalism, it merely blends into a vast political spectrum that is essentially the result of Russia's threat to the Ukrainian nation-state. On the other hand, as our authors have shown, if we are to talk about Azov as a political formation, it is preferable to dwell on the various constituents of the National Corps, which, when it came into being on 14 October 2016, intended to give a voice to certain veterans and radical activists. The Azov Movement sprung from this, yet today's Azov Brigade and Azov Movement are separate.[31] The Azov Movement has been presented as trying to penetrate the state and bring about a 'Weimar Germany scenario' – in the sense of gradually filling the state apparatus with loyalists before a takeover. By contrast, others have pointed to its moderation and acceptance of formal democratic rules and processes over time.[32] It is difficult to know whether this trend towards standardisation will continue in the aftermath of the war. The current war has had a profound impact on the Ukrainian far right. Many of their members have died in the conflict, notably Mykola 'Kruk' Kravchenko and key figures have been lost, creating a leadership vacuum in nationalist formations. Indeed, the only one left is Olena Semenyaka, about whom little

---

30 Andreas Umland (2019), 'Irregular Militias and Radical Nationalism in Post-Euromaydan Ukraine: The Prehistory and Emergence of the 'Azov' Battalion in 2014', *Terrorism and Political Violence*, 31(1), pp.105-131.
31 Michael Colborne (2022), *From the Fires of War: Ukraine's Azov Movement and the Global Far Right* (Ibidem: Stuttgart)
32 Ivan Gomza (2024), 'The Azov Movement'.

seems to have been reported since the early 2020s. The movement's future is uncertain as it grapples with the loss of experienced activists and the challenge of maintaining relevance in a rapidly changing political environment. The younger generation of nationalists, more radicalised by the war, could reshape the movement, leading to either a resurgence or further marginalisation[33]. Furthermore, those in the National Corps had been in confrontation with the state for much of the 2010s. However, when the Russian invasion occurred in 2022, the Ukrainian government co-operated with the National Corps, leading to the setting up of several other Azov units that consolidated as the 3rd Independent Assault Regiment, which Biletskyi then commanded.[34] To be clear, the Azov Brigade that is the focus of this book is known as the 12th Special Operations Brigade (Azov). So, at this point, we confusingly have the Azov Movement, units connected to that movement, and a separate military unit under the control of the Ukrainian state.

Ukrainian Paths: Post-war challenges and promises.

This book has provided much food for thought beyond the Azov Brigade and its precursors, especially given historical and ongoing Russian efforts to delegitimise states drifting away from its orbit. There is also much in flux, especially with 2024 likely being a critical juncture in Ukraine's war and the possibility of a far less supportive US administration coming into office following the election in November 2024. Much is uncertain at this point, but several areas warrant further research already or will do in the years to come.

Firstly, more research on Ukrainian political movements could be conducted without the shroud of Russian disinformation efforts. Unsurprisingly, academics are most interested in the extremes, but not all independence movements were so. With full awareness of Russian delegitimisation efforts, research in this new light seems essential. Such research may be more accessible after

---

33   Adrien Nonjon (2023)'The end of Ukrainian nationalism is not here — yet', *Baltic World Journal*, vol.1, no.2, pp. 35-40.
34   Ivan Gomza (2024), 'The Azov Movement'.

the war's end, given that these are sensitive issues at present. Is Ukraine heading towards a more democratic future? How much will the war have damaged Ukraine's fledgling democracy? The problems of censorship and allegiances in desperate circumstances seem essential here. What of the Ukrainian extremes as well? As this book demonstrates, 'nationalists' have been seen as a useful resource by the Ukrainian government during the conflict. Likely being viewed as heroes at the end of the conflict, how will they fare? These will include far-right individuals and movements, such as the Azov Movement. Their international and domestic actions will need to be scrutinised at that point. Much will depend on the war's outcome and external players' responses. If Russia wins and bites off chunks of Ukraine while being starved of Western aid, it would be no surprise if extremes do rise and oppose Russia. Ukraine's far right, after all, has a distinctly anti-Russian flavour. By contrast, if Ukraine reaches a tolerable settlement with a weakened Russia, is backed by its allies, and is accepted or at least assisted by international organisations, it may well have a good chance of calming the extremes and having a healthy, democratic, and prosperous future outside Moscow's influence.

Secondly, more research on the Azov Brigade itself is required. The war renders academic research challenging. While we have some idea of the variety of beliefs within the unit held in the late 2010s from de Franqueville's chapter herein, an update would seem worthwhile, especially given how the war has altered the unit, from expansion to prisoners of war still held in Russia. As Gomza shows, the brigade once featured heavily in Russian propaganda, but this seems to have subsided as the war progressed. It may be the case that this could not be sustained given Russia's atrocities on the battlefields of Ukraine. How, then, does Russia continue to justify its war to its citizens? Also, what changed in the US' calculations? In other words, why did it recently decide to supply weapons and training to the Azov Brigade? It is worth considering what became of the different volunteer battalions, too. Right Sector, a historically far-right unit that retains some independence to this day, seems to peculiarly be absent from debates about the extremes in

Ukraine, except for in a handful of publications.[35] More research must also be undertaken on the foreign fighters in the conflict. Scholars seem to believe that there were more Western extremists among those who fought between 2014-2021 — before the full-scale Russian invasion.[36] By contrast, we have limited information on the roughly 2,000 individuals who have fought since then. Preliminary studies seem to suggest that these fighters were often former soldiers and went to defend Ukraine from Russian aggression.[37] Having said this, it does not mean that all participants behaved impeccably in Ukraine.[38]

Thirdly, it is essential to consider the international aspects of the war in Ukraine. Russian disinformation is an obvious case, with Oksamytna pointing out how its successes in diffusing this has led to Western publics having skewed views of the region, such as that Ukraine would capitulate and Russian troops expecting to enter a state with people that would welcome and see them as liberators.[39] The Azov Brigade also now seems an obvious case given that Russian efforts have led to Western support to this unit only being permitted in 2024. Obviously, there should have been no question of a ban on provision of assistance when the unit was founded by far-right individuals in 2014. This relates to traditional and social medias and how the war has been covered, which surely feeds into

---

35   Khalil Mutallimzada and Kristian Steiner (2023), 'Fighters' Motivations for Joining Extremist Groups: Investigating the Attractiveness of the Right Sector's Volunteer Ukrainian Corps', *European Journal of International Security*, 8(1), pp.47-69.
36   Kacper Rekawek (2023), *Foreign Fighters in Ukraine: The Red-Brown Cocktail* (Routledge: London).
37   RUSI (2023), 'Why Foreign Volunteers Enlist in the Ukrainian International Legion', available at: https://rusi.org/explore-our-research/publications/commentary/why-foreign-volunteers-enlist-ukrainian-international-legion (accessed on 19th July 2024).
38   The Telegraph (2022), 'Allegations of Abuse and Suicide Missions Follow Leaders of Ukraine's Foreign Legion' available at: https://www.telegraph.co.uk/world-news/2022/08/21/allegations-abuse-suicide-missions-follow-leaders-ukraines-foreign/ (accessed on 19th July 2024).
39   Kseniya Oksamytna (2023), Imperialism, Supremacy, and the Russian Invasion of Ukraine' *Contemporary Security Policy*, 44(4), 497–512.

how citizens of states supportive of Ukraine view the conflict.[40] Some have also questioned the 'opportunity costs' of assistance to Ukraine—that is, whether the money given as aid could be more effectively used on other causes.[41] So, what will Ukraine's future relationships look like? A lot will depend on the war, but will Kyiv be successful in its efforts to join NATO in the EU and what will this mean for both organisations? Furthermore, how will Ukraine relate to both the US and Russia, especially the latter given that it may have successfully removed itself from Russia's political, economic, and social orbit? Might that encourage others to break free from Moscow's grasp? There is much to do as Ukraine's future hangs in the balance.

We end this book saying that, for all its faults—of which there are many—Ukrainians appear to have a strong desire to join the West as a member of the EU, perhaps NATO[42], and, above all, further strengthen the country's democratic credentials.[43] Abandoning Ukraine to Russia could lead to more conflict, not less, for the above reasons. It would encourage Russia, which is almost certainly waiting for a Trump administration to push Kyiv towards negotiations that will no doubt work in their favour. Peace should not come at any cost. In this case, Europe would need to significantly increase its support for Ukraine, although this would not completely compensate for the US's withdrawal and capriciousness under Trump. Thus, we take the opportunity to argue for continuing maximum support for Ukraine. Under incredible hardship, its troops and society have held firm for years under the onslaught of a far more powerful and imperialistic enemy. Russia and autocrats worldwide cannot get the impression that the West can be outlasted if conflicts

---

40 Michael Tschirky and Mykola Makhortykh (2024), '#Azovsteel: Comparing Qualitative and Quantitative Approaches For Studying Framing of the Siege of Mariupol on Twitter', *Media, War, and Conflict*, 17(2), pp.163-178.
41 Luke Glanville and James Pattison (2024), 'Ukraine and the Opportunity Costs of Military Aid', *International Affairs*, 100(4), pp.1571-1590.
42 Guardian (2024) 'Should Ukraine join NATO? Open letter' available at: https://www.theguardian.com/commentisfree/article/2024/jul/27/ukraine-nato-membership (accessed on 4th August 2024).
43 Chatham House (2024), 'Democracy in Ukraine', available at: https://www.chathamhouse.org/2023/11/democracy-ukraine (accessed on 19th July 2024).

go on. We must show greater resolve and support than this until a reasonable end point for Kyiv can be reached. Once the fighting is over, Western supporters must also commit to assisting Ukraine in rebuilding and strengthening not just infrastructure but also its society and institutions.

SOVIET AND POST-SOVIET POLITICS AND SOCIETY
Edited by Dr. Andreas Umland | ISSN 1614-3515

1   Андреас Умланд (ред.) | Воплощение Европейской конвенции по правам человека в России. Философские, юридические и эмпирические исследования | ISBN 3-89821-387-0

2   *Christian Wipperfürth* | Russland – ein vertrauenswürdiger Partner? Grundlagen, Hintergründe und Praxis gegenwärtiger russischer Außenpolitik | Mit einem Vorwort von Heinz Timmermann | ISBN 3-89821-401-X

3   *Manja Hussner* | Die Übernahme internationalen Rechts in die russische und deutsche Rechtsordnung. Eine vergleichende Analyse zur Völkerrechtsfreundlichkeit der Verfassungen der Russländischen Föderation und der Bundesrepublik Deutschland | Mit einem Vorwort von Rainer Arnold | ISBN 3-89821-438-9

4   *Matthew Tejada* | Bulgaria's Democratic Consolidation and the Kozloduy Nuclear Power Plant (KNPP). The Unattainability of Closure | With a foreword by Richard J. Crampton | ISBN 3-89821-439-7

5   Марк Григорьевич Меерович | Квадратные метры, определяющие сознание. Государственная жилищная политика в СССР. 1921 – 1941 гг | ISBN 3-89821-474-5

6   *Andrei P. Tsygankov, Pavel A.Tsygankov (Eds.)* | New Directions in Russian International Studies | ISBN 3-89821-422-2

7   Марк Григорьевич Меерович | Как власть народ к труду приучала. Жилище в СССР – средство управления людьми. 1917 – 1941 гг. | С предисловием Елены Осокиной | ISBN 3-89821-495-8

8   *David J. Galbreath* | Nation-Building and Minority Politics in Post-Socialist States. Interests, Influence and Identities in Estonia and Latvia | With a foreword by David J. Smith | ISBN 3-89821-467-2

9   Алексей Юрьевич Безугольный | Народы Кавказа в Вооруженных силах СССР в годы Великой Отечественной войны 1941-1945 гг. | С предисловием Николая Бугая | ISBN 3-89821-475-3

10 Вячеслав Лихачев и Владимир Прибыловский (ред.) | Русское Национальное Единство, 1990-2000. В 2-х томах | ISBN 3-89821-523-7

11 Николай Бугай (ред.) | Народы стран Балтии в условиях сталинизма (1940-е – 1950-е годы). Документированная история | ISBN 3-89821-525-3

12 *Ingmar Bredies (Hrsg.)* | Zur Anatomie der Orange Revolution in der Ukraine. Wechsel des Elitenregimes oder Triumph des Parlamentarismus? | ISBN 3-89821-524-5

13 *Anastasia V. Mitrofanova* | The Politicization of Russian Orthodoxy. Actors and Ideas | With a foreword by William C. Gay | ISBN 3-89821-481-8

14 *Nathan D. Larson* | Alexander Solzhenitsyn and the Russo-Jewish Question | ISBN 3-89821-483-4

15 *Guido Houben* | Kulturpolitik und Ethnizität. Staatliche Kunstförderung im Russland der neunziger Jahre | Mit einem Vorwort von Gert Weisskirchen | ISBN 3-89821-542-3

16 *Leonid Luks* | Der russische „Sonderweg"? Aufsätze zur neuesten Geschichte Russlands im europäischen Kontext | ISBN 3-89821-496-6

17 Евгений Мороз | История «Мёртвой воды» – от страшной сказки к большой политике. Политическое неоязычество в постсоветской России | ISBN 3-89821-551-2

18 Александр Верховский и Галина Кожевникова (ред.) | Этническая и религиозная интолерантность в российских СМИ. Результаты мониторинга 2001-2004 гг. | ISBN 3-89821-569-5

19 *Christian Ganzer* | Sowjetisches Erbe und ukrainische Nation. Das Museum der Geschichte des Zaporoger Kosakentums auf der Insel Chortycja | Mit einem Vorwort von Frank Golczewski | ISBN 3-89821-504-0

20 Эльза-Баир Гучинова | Помнить нельзя забыть. Антропология депортационной травмы калмыков | С предисловием Кэролайн Хамфри | ISBN 3-89821-506-7

21 Юлия Лидерман | Мотивы «проверки» и «испытания» в постсоветской культуре. Советское прошлое в российском кинематографе 1990-х годов | С предисловием Евгения Марголита | ISBN 3-89821-511-3

22 *Tanya Lokshina, Ray Thomas, Mary Mayer (Eds.)* | The Imposition of a Fake Political Settlement in the Northern Caucasus. The 2003 Chechen Presidential Election | ISBN 3-89821-436-2

23 *Timothy McCajor Hall, Rosie Read (Eds.)* | Changes in the Heart of Europe. Recent Ethnographies of Czechs, Slovaks, Roma, and Sorbs | With an afterword by Zdeněk Salzmann | ISBN 3-89821-606-3

24 *Christian Autengruber* | Die politischen Parteien in Bulgarien und Rumänien. Eine vergleichende Analyse seit Beginn der 90er Jahre | Mit einem Vorwort von Dorothée de Nève | ISBN 3-89821-476-1

25 *Annette Freyberg-Inan with Radu Cristescu* | The Ghosts in Our Classrooms, or: John Dewey Meets Ceauşescu. The Promise and the Failures of Civic Education in Romania | ISBN 3-89821-416-8

26 *John B. Dunlop* | The 2002 Dubrovka and 2004 Beslan Hostage Crises. A Critique of Russian Counter-Terrorism | With a foreword by Donald N. Jensen | ISBN 3-89821-608-X

27 *Peter Koller* | Das touristische Potenzial von Kam"janec'–Podil's'kyj. Eine fremdenverkehrsgeographische Untersuchung der Zukunftsperspektiven und Maßnahmenplanung zur Destinationsentwicklung des „ukrainischen Rothenburg" | Mit einem Vorwort von Kristiane Klemm | ISBN 3-89821-640-3

28 *Françoise Daucé, Elisabeth Sieca-Kozlowski (Eds.)* | Dedovshchina in the Post-Soviet Military. Hazing of Russian Army Conscripts in a Comparative Perspective | With a foreword by Dale Herspring | ISBN 3-89821-616-0

29 *Florian Strasser* | Zivilgesellschaftliche Einflüsse auf die Orange Revolution. Die gewaltlose Massenbewegung und die ukrainische Wahlkrise 2004 | Mit einem Vorwort von Egbert Jahn | ISBN 3-89821-648-9

30 *Rebecca S. Katz* | The Georgian Regime Crisis of 2003-2004. A Case Study in Post-Soviet Media Representation of Politics, Crime and Corruption | ISBN 3-89821-413-3

31 *Vladimir Kantor* | Willkür oder Freiheit. Beiträge zur russischen Geschichtsphilosophie | Ediert von Dagmar Herrmann sowie mit einem Vorwort versehen von Leonid Luks | ISBN 3-89821-589-X

32 *Laura A. Victoir* | The Russian Land Estate Today. A Case Study of Cultural Politics in Post-Soviet Russia | With a foreword by Priscilla Roosevelt | ISBN 3-89821-426-5

33 *Ivan Katchanovski* | Cleft Countries. Regional Political Divisions and Cultures in Post-Soviet Ukraine and Moldova| With a foreword by Francis Fukuyama | ISBN 3-89821-558-X

34 *Florian Mühlfried* | Postsowjetische Feiern. Das Georgische Bankett im Wandel | Mit einem Vorwort von Kevin Tuite | ISBN 3-89821-601-2

35 *Roger Griffin, Werner Loh, Andreas Umland (Eds.)* | Fascism Past and Present, West and East. An International Debate on Concepts and Cases in the Comparative Study of the Extreme Right | With an afterword by Walter Laqueur | ISBN 3-89821-674-8

36 *Sebastian Schlegel* | Der „Weiße Archipel". Sowjetische Atomstädte 1945-1991 | Mit einem Geleitwort von Thomas Bohn | ISBN 3-89821-679-9

37 *Vyacheslav Likhachev* | Political Anti-Semitism in Post-Soviet Russia. Actors and Ideas in 1991-2003 | Edited and translated from Russian by Eugene Veklerov | ISBN 3-89821-529-6

38 *Josette Baer (Ed.)* | Preparing Liberty in Central Europe. Political Texts from the Spring of Nations 1848 to the Spring of Prague 1968 | With a foreword by Zdeněk V. David | ISBN 3-89821-546-6

39 *Михаил Лукьянов* | Российский консерватизм и реформа, 1907-1914 | С предисловием Марка Д. Стейнберга | ISBN 3-89821-503-2

40 *Nicola Melloni* | Market Without Economy. The 1998 Russian Financial Crisis | With a foreword by Eiji Furukawa | ISBN 3-89821-407-9

41 *Dmitrij Chmelnizki* | Die Architektur Stalins | Bd. 1: Studien zu Ideologie und Stil | Bd. 2: Bilddokumentation | Mit einem Vorwort von Bruno Flierl | ISBN 3-89821-515-6

42 *Katja Yafimava* | Post-Soviet Russian-Belarussian Relationships. The Role of Gas Transit Pipelines | With a foreword by Jonathan P. Stern | ISBN 3-89821-655-1

43 *Boris Chavkin* | Verflechtungen der deutschen und russischen Zeitgeschichte. Aufsätze und Archivfunde zu den Beziehungen Deutschlands und der Sowjetunion von 1917 bis 1991 | Ediert von Markus Edlinger sowie mit einem Vorwort versehen von Leonid Luks | ISBN 3-89821-756-6

44 *Anastasija Grynenko in Zusammenarbeit mit Claudia Dathe* | Die Terminologie des Gerichtswesens der Ukraine und Deutschlands im Vergleich. Eine übersetzungswissenschaftliche Analyse juristischer Fachbegriffe im Deutschen, Ukrainischen und Russischen | Mit einem Vorwort von Ulrich Hartmann | ISBN 3-89821-691-8

45 *Anton Burkov* | The Impact of the European Convention on Human Rights on Russian Law. Legislation and Application in 1996-2006 | With a foreword by Françoise Hampson | ISBN 978-3-89821-639-5

46 *Stina Torjesen, Indra Overland (Eds.)* | International Election Observers in Post-Soviet Azerbaijan. Geopolitical Pawns or Agents of Change? | ISBN 978-3-89821-743-9

47 *Taras Kuzio* | Ukraine – Crimea – Russia. Triangle of Conflict | ISBN 978-3-89821-761-3

48 *Claudia Šabić* | „Ich erinnere mich nicht, aber L'viv!" Zur Funktion kultureller Faktoren für die Institutionalisierung und Entwicklung einer ukrainischen Region | Mit einem Vorwort von Melanie Tatur | ISBN 978-3-89821-752-1

49 *Marlies Bilz* | Tatarstan in der Transformation. Nationaler Diskurs und Politische Praxis 1988-1994 | Mit einem Vorwort von Frank Golczewski | ISBN 978-3-89821-722-4

50 *Марлен Ларюэль (ред.)* | Современные интерпретации русского национализма | ISBN 978-3-89821-795-8

51 *Sonja Schüler* | Die ethnische Dimension der Armut. Roma im postsozialistischen Rumänien | Mit einem Vorwort von Anton Sterbling | ISBN 978-3-89821-776-7

52 *Галина Кожевникова* | Радикальный национализм в России и противодействие ему. Сборник докладов Центра «Сова» за 2004-2007 гг. | С предисловием Александра Верховского | ISBN 978-3-89821-721-7

53 *Галина Кожевникова и Владимир Прибыловский* | Российская власть в биографиях I. Высшие должностные лица РФ в 2004 г. | ISBN 978-3-89821-796-5

54 *Галина Кожевникова и Владимир Прибыловский* | Российская власть в биографиях II. Члены Правительства РФ в 2004 г. | ISBN 978-3-89821-797-2

55 *Галина Кожевникова и Владимир Прибыловский* | Российская власть в биографиях III. Руководители федеральных служб и агентств РФ в 2004 г.| ISBN 978-3-89821-798-9

56 *Ileana Petroniu* | Privatisierung in Transformationsökonomien. Determinanten der Restrukturierungs-Bereitschaft am Beispiel Polens, Rumäniens und der Ukraine | Mit einem Vorwort von Rainer W. Schäfer | ISBN 978-3-89821-790-3

57 *Christian Wipperfürth* | Russland und seine GUS-Nachbarn. Hintergründe, aktuelle Entwicklungen und Konflikte in einer ressourcenreichen Region| ISBN 978-3-89821-801-6

58 *Togzhan Kassenova* | From Antagonism to Partnership. The Uneasy Path of the U.S.-Russian Cooperative Threat Reduction | With a foreword by Christoph Bluth | ISBN 978-3-89821-707-1

59 *Alexander Höllwerth* | Das sakrale eurasische Imperium des Aleksandr Dugin. Eine Diskursanalyse zum postsowjetischen russischen Rechtsextremismus | Mit einem Vorwort von Dirk Uffelmann | ISBN 978-3-89821-813-9

60 *Олег Рябов* | «Россия-Матушка». Национализм, гендер и война в России XX века | С предисловием Елены Гощило | ISBN 978-3-89821-487-2

61 *Ivan Maistrenko* | Borot'bism. A Chapter in the History of the Ukrainian Revolution | With a new Introduction by Chris Ford | Translated by George S. N. Luckyj with the assistance of Ivan L. Rudnytsky | Second, Revised and Expanded Edition ISBN 978-3-8382-1107-7

62 *Maryna Romanets* | Anamorphosic Texts and Reconfigured Visions. Improvised Traditions in Contemporary Ukrainian and Irish Literature | ISBN 978-3-89821-576-3

63 *Paul D'Anieri and Taras Kuzio (Eds.)* | Aspects of the Orange Revolution I. Democratization and Elections in Post-Communist Ukraine | ISBN 978-3-89821-698-2

64 *Bohdan Harasymiw in collaboration with Oleh S. Ilnytzkyj (Eds.)* | Aspects of the Orange Revolution II. Information and Manipulation Strategies in the 2004 Ukrainian Presidential Elections | ISBN 978-3-89821-699-9

65 *Ingmar Bredies, Andreas Umland and Valentin Yakushik (Eds.)* | Aspects of the Orange Revolution III. The Context and Dynamics of the 2004 Ukrainian Presidential Elections | ISBN 978-3-89821-803-0

66 *Ingmar Bredies, Andreas Umland and Valentin Yakushik (Eds.)* | Aspects of the Orange Revolution IV. Foreign Assistance and Civic Action in the 2004 Ukrainian Presidential Elections | ISBN 978-3-89821-808-5

67 *Ingmar Bredies, Andreas Umland and Valentin Yakushik (Eds.)* | Aspects of the Orange Revolution V. Institutional Observation Reports on the 2004 Ukrainian Presidential Elections | ISBN 978-3-89821-809-2

68 *Taras Kuzio (Ed.)* | Aspects of the Orange Revolution VI. Post-Communist Democratic Revolutions in Comparative Perspective | ISBN 978-3-89821-820-7

69 *Tim Bohse* | Autoritarismus statt Selbstverwaltung. Die Transformation der kommunalen Politik in der Stadt Kaliningrad 1990-2005 | Mit einem Geleitwort von Stefan Troebst | ISBN 978-3-89821-782-8

70 *David Rupp* | Die Rußländische Föderation und die russischsprachige Minderheit in Lettland. Eine Fallstudie zur Anwaltspolitik Moskaus gegenüber den russophonen Minderheiten im „Nahen Ausland" von 1991 bis 2002 | Mit einem Vorwort von Helmut Wagner | ISBN 978-3-89821-778-1

71 *Taras Kuzio* | Theoretical and Comparative Perspectives on Nationalism. New Directions in Cross-Cultural and Post-Communist Studies | With a foreword by Paul Robert Magocsi | ISBN 978-3-89821-815-3

72 *Christine Teichmann* | Die Hochschultransformation im heutigen Osteuropa. Kontinuität und Wandel bei der Entwicklung des postkommunistischen Universitätswesens | Mit einem Vorwort von Oskar Anweiler | ISBN 978-3-89821-842-9

73 *Julia Kusznir* | Der politische Einfluss von Wirtschaftseliten in russischen Regionen. Eine Analyse am Beispiel der Erdöl- und Erdgasindustrie, 1992-2005 | Mit einem Vorwort von Wolfgang Eichwede | ISBN 978-3-89821-821-4

74 *Alena Vysotskaya* | Russland, Belarus und die EU-Osterweiterung. Zur Minderheitenfrage und zum Problem der Freizügigkeit des Personenverkehrs | Mit einem Vorwort von Katlijn Malfliet | ISBN 978-3-89821-822-1

75 *Heiko Pleines (Hrsg.)* | Corporate Governance in post-sozialistischen Volkswirtschaften | ISBN 978-3-89821-766-8

76 *Stefan Ihrig* | Wer sind die Moldawier? Rumänismus versus Moldowanismus in Historiographie und Schulbüchern der Republik Moldova, 1991-2006 | Mit einem Vorwort von Holm Sundhaussen | ISBN 978-3-89821-466-7

77 *Galina Kozhevnikova in collaboration with Alexander Verkhovsky and Eugene Veklerov* | Ultra-Nationalism and Hate Crimes in Contemporary Russia. The 2004-2006 Annual Reports of Moscow's SOVA Center | With a foreword by Stephen D. Shenfield | ISBN 978-3-89821-868-9

78 *Florian Küchler* | The Role of the European Union in Moldova's Transnistria Conflict | With a foreword by Christopher Hill | ISBN 978-3-89821-850-4

79 *Bernd Rechel* | The Long Way Back to Europe. Minority Protection in Bulgaria | With a foreword by Richard Crampton | ISBN 978-3-89821-863-4

80 *Peter W. Rodgers* | Nation, Region and History in Post-Communist Transitions. Identity Politics in Ukraine, 1991-2006 | With a foreword by Vera Tolz | ISBN 978-3-89821-903-7

81 *Stephanie Solywoda* | The Life and Work of Semen L. Frank. A Study of Russian Religious Philosophy | With a foreword by Philip Walters | ISBN 978-3-89821-457-5

82 *Vera Sokolova* | Cultural Politics of Ethnicity. Discourses on Roma in Communist Czechoslovakia | ISBN 978-3-89821-864-1

83 *Natalya Shevchik Ketenci* | Kazakhstani Enterprises in Transition. The Role of Historical Regional Development in Kazakhstan's Post-Soviet Economic Transformation | ISBN 978-3-89821-831-3

84 *Martin Malek, Anna Schor-Tschudnowskaja (Hgg.)* | Europa im Tschetschenienkrieg. Zwischen politischer Ohnmacht und Gleichgültigkeit | Mit einem Vorwort von Lipchan Basajewa | ISBN 978-3-89821-676-0

85 *Stefan Meister* | Das postsowjetische Universitätswesen zwischen nationalem und internationalem Wandel. Die Entwicklung der regionalen Hochschule in Russland als Gradmesser der Systemtransformation | Mit einem Vorwort von Joan DeBardeleben | ISBN 978-3-89821-891-7

86 *Konstantin Sheiko in collaboration with Stephen Brown* | Nationalist Imaginings of the Russian Past. Anatolii Fomenko and the Rise of Alternative History in Post-Communist Russia | With a foreword by Donald Ostrowski | ISBN 978-3-89821-915-0

87 *Sabine Jenni* | Wie stark ist das „Einige Russland"? Zur Parteibindung der Eliten und zum Wahlerfolg der Machtpartei im Dezember 2007 | Mit einem Vorwort von Klaus Armingeon | ISBN 978-3-89821-961-7

88 *Thomas Borén* | Meeting-Places of Transformation. Urban Identity, Spatial Representations and Local Politics in Post-Soviet St Petersburg | ISBN 978-3-89821-739-2

89 *Aygul Ashirova* | Stalinismus und Stalin-Kult in Zentralasien. Turkmenistan 1924-1953 | Mit einem Vorwort von Leonid Luks | ISBN 978-3-89821-987-7

90 *Leonid Luks* | Freiheit oder imperiale Größe? Essays zu einem russischen Dilemma | ISBN 978-3-8382-0011-8

91 *Christopher Gilley* | The 'Change of Signposts' in the Ukrainian Emigration. A Contribution to the History of Sovietophilism in the 1920s | With a foreword by Frank Golczewski | ISBN 978-3-89821-965-5

92 *Philipp Casula, Jeronim Perovic (Eds.)* | Identities and Politics During the Putin Presidency. The Discursive Foundations of Russia's Stability | With a foreword by Heiko Haumann | ISBN 978-3-8382-0015-6

93 *Marcel Viëtor* | Europa und die Frage nach seinen Grenzen im Osten. Zur Konstruktion ‚europäischer Identität' in Geschichte und Gegenwart | Mit einem Vorwort von Albrecht Lehmann | ISBN 978-3-8382-0045-3

94 *Ben Hellman, Andrei Rogachevskii* | Filming the Unfilmable. Casper Wrede's 'One Day in the Life of Ivan Denisovich' | Second, Revised and Expanded Edition | ISBN 978-3-8382-0044-6

95 *Eva Fuchslocher* | Vaterland, Sprache, Glaube. Orthodoxie und Nationenbildung am Beispiel Georgiens | Mit einem Vorwort von Christina von Braun | ISBN 978-3-89821-884-5

96 *Vladimir Kantor* | Das Westlertum und der Weg Russlands. Zur Entwicklung der russischen Literatur und Philosophie | Ediert von Dagmar Herrmann | Mit einem Beitrag von Nikolaus Lobkowicz | ISBN 978-3-8382-0102-3

97 *Kamran Musayev* | Die postsowjetische Transformation im Baltikum und Südkaukasus. Eine vergleichende Untersuchung der politischen Entwicklung Lettlands und Aserbaidschans 1985-2009 | Mit einem Vorwort von Leonid Luks | Ediert von Sandro Henschel | ISBN 978-3-8382-0103-0

98 *Tatiana Zhurzhenko* | Borderlands into Bordered Lands. Geopolitics of Identity in Post-Soviet Ukraine | With a foreword by Dieter Segert | ISBN 978-3-8382-0042-2

99 *Кирилл Галушко, Лидия Смола (ред.)* | Пределы падения – варианты украинского будущего. Аналитико-прогностические исследования | ISBN 978-3-8382-0148-1

100 *Michael Minkenberg (Ed.)* | Historical Legacies and the Radical Right in Post-Cold War Central and Eastern Europe | With an afterword by Sabrina P. Ramet | ISBN 978-3-8382-0124-5

101 *David-Emil Wickström* | Rocking St. Petersburg. Transcultural Flows and Identity Politics in the St. Petersburg Popular Music Scene | With a foreword by Yngvar B. Steinholt | Second, Revised and Expanded Edition | ISBN 978-3-8382-0100-9

102 *Eva Zabka* | Eine neue „Zeit der Wirren"? Der spät- und postsowjetische Systemwandel 1985-2000 im Spiegel russischer gesellschaftspolitischer Diskurse | Mit einem Vorwort von Margareta Mommsen | ISBN 978-3-8382-0161-0

103 *Ulrike Ziemer* | Ethnic Belonging, Gender and Cultural Practices. Youth Identitites in Contemporary Russia | With a foreword by Anoop Nayak | ISBN 978-3-8382-0152-8

104 *Ksenia Chepikova* | ‚Einiges Russland' - eine zweite KPdSU? Aspekte der Identitätskonstruktion einer postsowjetischen „Partei der Macht" | Mit einem Vorwort von Torsten Oppelland | ISBN 978-3-8382-0311-7

105 *Леонид Люкс* | Западничество или евразийство? Демократия или идеократия? Сборник статей об исторических дилеммах России | С предисловием Владимира Кантора | ISBN 978-3-8382-0211-2

106 *Anna Dost* | Das russische Verfassungsrecht auf dem Weg zum Föderalismus und zurück. Zum Konflikt von Rechtsnormen und -wirklichkeit in der Russländischen Föderation von 1991 bis 2009 | Mit einem Vorwort von Alexander Blankenagel | ISBN 978-3-8382-0292-1

107 *Philipp Herzog* | Sozialistische Völkerfreundschaft, nationaler Widerstand oder harmloser Zeitvertreib? Zur politischen Funktion der Volkskunst im sowjetischen Estland | Mit einem Vorwort von Andreas Kappeler | ISBN 978-3-8382-0216-7

108 *Marlène Laruelle (Ed.)* | Russian Nationalism, Foreign Policy, and Identity Debates in Putin's Russia. New Ideological Patterns after the Orange Revolution | ISBN 978-3-8382-0325-6

109 *Michail Logvinov* | Russlands Kampf gegen den internationalen Terrorismus. Eine kritische Bestandsaufnahme des Bekämpfungsansatzes | Mit einem Geleitwort von Hans-Henning Schröder und einem Vorwort von Eckhard Jesse | ISBN 978-3-8382-0329-4

110 *John B. Dunlop* | The Moscow Bombings of September 1999. Examinations of Russian Terrorist Attacks at the Onset of Vladimir Putin's Rule | Second, Revised and Expanded Edition | ISBN 978-3-8382-0388-1

111 *Андрей А. Ковалёв* | Свидетельство из-за кулис российской политики I. Можно ли делать добро из зла? (Воспоминания и размышления о последних советских и первых послесоветских годах) | With a foreword by Peter Reddaway | ISBN 978-3-8382-0302-7

112 *Андрей А. Ковалёв* | Свидетельство из-за кулис российской политики II. Угроза для себя и окружающих (Наблюдения и предостережения относительно происходящего после 2000 г.) | ISBN 978-3-8382-0303-4

113 *Bernd Kappenberg* | Zeichen setzen für Europa. Der Gebrauch europäischer lateinischer Sonderzeichen in der deutschen Öffentlichkeit | Mit einem Vorwort von Peter Schlobinski | ISBN 978-3-89821-749-1

114 *Ivo Mijnssen* | The Quest for an Ideal Youth in Putin's Russia I. Back to Our Future! History, Modernity, and Patriotism according to Nashi, 2005-2013 | With a foreword by Jeronim Perović | Second, Revised and Expanded Edition | ISBN 978-3-8382-0368-3

115 *Jussi Lassila* | The Quest for an Ideal Youth in Putin's Russia II. The Search for Distinctive Conformism in the Political Communication of Nashi, 2005-2009 | With a foreword by Kirill Postoutenko | Second, Revised and Expanded Edition | ISBN 978-3-8382-0415-4

116 *Valerio Trabandt* | Neue Nachbarn, gute Nachbarschaft? Die EU als internationaler Akteur am Beispiel ihrer Demokratieförderung in Belarus und der Ukraine 2004-2009 | Mit einem Vorwort von Jutta Joachim | ISBN 978-3-8382-0437-6

117 *Fabian Pfeiffer* | Estlands Außen- und Sicherheitspolitik I. Der estnische Atlantizismus nach der wiedererlangten Unabhängigkeit 1991-2004 | Mit einem Vorwort von Helmut Hubel | ISBN 978-3-8382-0127-6

118 *Jana Podßuweit* | Estlands Außen- und Sicherheitspolitik II. Handlungsoptionen eines Kleinstaates im Rahmen seiner EU-Mitgliedschaft (2004-2008) | Mit einem Vorwort von Helmut Hubel | ISBN 978-3-8382-0440-6

119 *Karin Pointner* | Estlands Außen- und Sicherheitspolitik III. Eine gedächtnispolitische Analyse estnischer Entwicklungskooperation 2006-2010 | Mit einem Vorwort von Karin Liebhart | ISBN 978-3-8382-0435-3

120 *Ruslana Vovk* | Die Offenheit der ukrainischen Verfassung für das Völkerrecht und die europäische Integration | Mit einem Vorwort von Alexander Blankenagel | ISBN 978-3-8382-0481-9

121 *Mykhaylo Banakh* | Die Relevanz der Zivilgesellschaft bei den postkommunistischen Transformationsprozessen in mittel- und osteuropäischen Ländern. Das Beispiel der spät- und postsowjetischen Ukraine 1986-2009 | Mit einem Vorwort von Gerhard Simon | ISBN 978-3-8382-0499-4

122 *Michael Moser* | Language Policy and the Discourse on Languages in Ukraine under President Viktor Yanukovych (25 February 2010–28 October 2012) | ISBN 978-3-8382-0497-0 (Paperback edition) | ISBN 978-3-8382-0507-6 (Hardcover edition)

123 *Nicole Krome* | Russischer Netzwerkkapitalismus Restrukturierungsprozesse in der Russischen Föderation am Beispiel des Luftfahrtunternehmens „Aviastar" | Mit einem Vorwort von Petra Stykow | ISBN 978-3-8382-0534-2

124 *David R. Marples* | 'Our Glorious Past'. Lukashenka's Belarus and the Great Patriotic War | ISBN 978-3-8382-0574-8 (Paperback edition) | ISBN 978-3-8382-0675-2 (Hardcover edition)

125 *Ulf Walther* | Russlands „neuer Adel". Die Macht des Geheimdienstes von Gorbatschow bis Putin | Mit einem Vorwort von Hans-Georg Wieck | ISBN 978-3-8382-0584-7

126 *Simon Geissbühler (Hrsg.)* | Kiew – Revolution 3.0. Der Euromaidan 2013/14 und die Zukunftsperspektiven der Ukraine | ISBN 978-3-8382-0581-6 (Paperback edition) | ISBN 978-3-8382-0681-3 (Hardcover edition)

127 *Andrey Makarychev* | Russia and the EU in a Multipolar World. Discourses, Identities, Norms | With a foreword by Klaus Segbers | ISBN 978-3-8382-0629-5

128 *Roland Scharff* | Kasachstan als postsowjetischer Wohlfahrtsstaat. Die Transformation des sozialen Schutzsystems | Mit einem Vorwort von Joachim Ahrens | ISBN 978-3-8382-0622-6

129 *Katja Grupp* | Bild Lücke Deutschland. Kaliningrader Studierende sprechen über Deutschland | Mit einem Vorwort von Martin Schulz | ISBN 978-3-8382-0552-6

130 *Konstantin Sheiko, Stephen Brown* | History as Therapy. Alternative History and Nationalist Imaginings in Russia, 1991-2014 | ISBN 978-3-8382-0665-3

131 *Elisa Kriza* | Alexander Solzhenitsyn: Cold War Icon, Gulag Author, Russian Nationalist? A Study of the Western Reception of his Literary Writings, Historical Interpretations, and Political Ideas | With a foreword by Andrei Rogatchevski | ISBN 978-3-8382-0589-2 (Paperback edition) | ISBN 978-3-8382-0690-5 (Hardcover edition)

132 *Serghei Golunov* | The Elephant in the Room. Corruption and Cheating in Russian Universities | ISBN 978-3-8382-0570-0

133 *Manja Hussner, Rainer Arnold (Hgg.)* | Verfassungsgerichtsbarkeit in Zentralasien I. Sammlung von Verfassungstexten | ISBN 978-3-8382-0595-3

134 *Nikolay Mitrokhin* | Die „Russische Partei". Die Bewegung der russischen Nationalisten in der UdSSR 1953-1985 | Aus dem Russischen übertragen von einem Übersetzerteam unter der Leitung von Larisa Schippel | ISBN 978-3-8382-0024-8

135 *Manja Hussner, Rainer Arnold (Hgg.)* | Verfassungsgerichtsbarkeit in Zentralasien II. Sammlung von Verfassungstexten | ISBN 978-3-8382-0597-7

136 *Manfred Zeller* | Das sowjetische Fieber. Fußballfans im poststalinistischen Vielvölkerreich | Mit einem Vorwort von Nikolaus Katzer | ISBN 978-3-8382-0757-5

137 *Kristin Schreiter* | Stellung und Entwicklungspotential zivilgesellschaftlicher Gruppen in Russland. Menschenrechtsorganisationen im Vergleich | ISBN 978-3-8382-0673-8

138 *David R. Marples, Frederick V. Mills (Eds.)* | Ukraine's Euromaidan. Analyses of a Civil Revolution | ISBN 978-3-8382-0660-8

139 *Bernd Kappenberg* | Setting Signs for Europe. Why Diacritics Matter for European Integration | With a foreword by Peter Schlobinski | ISBN 978-3-8382-0663-9

140 *René Lenz* | Internationalisierung, Kooperation und Transfer. Externe bildungspolitische Akteure in der Russischen Föderation | Mit einem Vorwort von Frank Ettrich | ISBN 978-3-8382-0751-3

141 *Juri Plusnin, Yana Zausaeva, Natalia Zhidkevich, Artemy Pozanenko* | Wandering Workers. Mores, Behavior, Way of Life, and Political Status of Domestic Russian Labor Migrants | Translated by Julia Kazantseva | ISBN 978-3-8382-0653-0

142 *David J. Smith (Eds.)* | Latvia – A Work in Progress? 100 Years of State- and Nation-Building | ISBN 978-3-8382-0648-6

143 *Инна Чувычкина (ред.)* | Экспортные нефте- и газопроводы на постсоветском пространстве. Анализ трубопроводной политики в свете теории международных отношений | ISBN 978-3-8382-0822-0

144 *Johann Zajaczkowski* | Russland – eine pragmatische Großmacht? Eine rollentheoretische Untersuchung russischer Außenpolitik am Beispiel der Zusammenarbeit mit den USA nach 9/11 und des Georgienkrieges von 2008 | Mit einem Vorwort von Siegfried Schieder | ISBN 978-3-8382-0837-4

145 *Boris Popivanov* | Changing Images of the Left in Bulgaria. The Challenge of Post-Communism in the Early 21st Century | ISBN 978-3-8382-0667-7

146 *Lenka Krátká* | A History of the Czechoslovak Ocean Shipping Company 1948-1989. How a Small, Landlocked Country Ran Maritime Business During the Cold War | ISBN 978-3-8382-0666-0

147 *Alexander Sergunin* | Explaining Russian Foreign Policy Behavior. Theory and Practice | ISBN 978-3-8382-0752-0

148 *Darya Malyutina* | Migrant Friendships in a Super-Diverse City. Russian-Speakers and their Social Relationships in London in the 21st Century | With a foreword by Claire Dwyer | ISBN 978-3-8382-0652-3

149 *Alexander Sergunin, Valery Konyshev* | Russia in the Arctic. Hard or Soft Power? | ISBN 978-3-8382-0753-7

150 *John J. Maresca* | Helsinki Revisited. A Key U.S. Negotiator's Memoirs on the Development of the CSCE into the OSCE | With a foreword by Hafiz Pashayev | ISBN 978-3-8382-0852-7

151 *Jardar Østbø* | The New Third Rome. Readings of a Russian Nationalist Myth | With a foreword by Pål Kolstø | ISBN 978-3-8382-0870-1

152 *Simon Kordonsky* | Socio-Economic Foundations of the Russian Post-Soviet Regime. The Resource-Based Economy and Estate-Based Social Structure of Contemporary Russia | With a foreword by Svetlana Barsukova | ISBN 978-3-8382-0775-9

153 *Duncan Leitch* | Assisting Reform in Post-Communist Ukraine 2000–2012. The Illusions of Donors and the Disillusion of Beneficiaries | With a foreword by Kataryna Wolczuk | ISBN 978-3-8382-0844-2

154 *Abel Polese* | Limits of a Post-Soviet State. How Informality Replaces, Renegotiates, and Reshapes Governance in Contemporary Ukraine | With a foreword by Colin Williams | ISBN 978-3-8382-0845-9

155 *Mikhail Suslov (Ed.)* | Digital Orthodoxy in the Post-Soviet World. The Russian Orthodox Church and Web 2.0 | With a foreword by Father Cyril Hovorun | ISBN 978-3-8382-0871-8

156 *Leonid Luks* | Zwei „Sonderwege"? Russisch-deutsche Parallelen und Kontraste (1917-2014). Vergleichende Essays | ISBN 978-3-8382-0823-7

157 *Vladimir V. Karacharovskiy, Ovsey I. Shkaratan, Gordey A. Yastrebov* | Towards a New Russian Work Culture. Can Western Companies and Expatriates Change Russian Society? | With a foreword by Elena N. Danilova | Translated by Julia Kazantseva | ISBN 978-3-8382-0902-9

158 *Edmund Griffiths* | Aleksandr Prokhanov and Post-Soviet Esotericism | ISBN 978-3-8382-0963-0

159 *Timm Beichelt, Susann Worschech (Eds.)* | Transnational Ukraine? Networks and Ties that Influence(d) Contemporary Ukraine | ISBN 978-3-8382-0944-9

160 *Mieste Hotopp-Riecke* | Die Tataren der Krim zwischen Assimilation und Selbstbehauptung. Der Aufbau des krimtatarischen Bildungswesens nach Deportation und Heimkehr (1990-2005) | Mit einem Vorwort von Swetlana Czerwonnaja | ISBN 978-3-89821-940-2

161 *Olga Bertelsen (Ed.)* | Revolution and War in Contemporary Ukraine. The Challenge of Change | ISBN 978-3-8382-1016-2

162 *Natalya Ryabinska* | Ukraine's Post-Communist Mass Media. Between Capture and Commercialization | With a foreword by Marta Dyczok | ISBN 978-3-8382-1011-7

163 *Alexandra Cotofana, James M. Nyce (Eds.)* | Religion and Magic in Socialist and Post-Socialist Contexts. Historic and Ethnographic Case Studies of Orthodoxy, Heterodoxy, and Alternative Spirituality | With a foreword by Patrick L. Michelson | ISBN 978-3-8382-0989-0

164 *Nozima Akhrarkhodjaeva* | The Instrumentalisation of Mass Media in Electoral Authoritarian Regimes. Evidence from Russia's Presidential Election Campaigns of 2000 and 2008 | ISBN 978-3-8382-1013-1

165 *Yulia Krasheninnikova* | Informal Healthcare in Contemporary Russia. Sociographic Essays on the Post-Soviet Infrastructure for Alternative Healing Practices | ISBN 978-3-8382-0970-8

166 *Peter Kaiser* | Das Schachbrett der Macht. Die Handlungsspielräume eines sowjetischen Funktionärs unter Stalin am Beispiel des Generalsekretärs des Komsomol Aleksandr Kosarev (1929-1938) | Mit einem Vorwort von Dietmar Neutatz | ISBN 978-3-8382-1052-0

167 *Oksana Kim* | The Effects and Implications of Kazakhstan's Adoption of International Financial Reporting Standards. A Resource Dependence Perspective | With a foreword by Svetlana Vlady | ISBN 978-3-8382-0987-6

168 *Anna Sanina* | Patriotic Education in Contemporary Russia. Sociological Studies in the Making of the Post-Soviet Citizen | With a foreword by Anna Oldfield | ISBN 978-3-8382-0993-7

169 *Rudolf Wolters* | Spezialist in Sibirien Faksimile der 1933 erschienenen ersten Ausgabe | Mit einem Vorwort von Dmitrij Chmelnizki | ISBN 978-3-8382-0515-1

170 *Michal Vít, Magdalena M. Baran (Eds.)* | Transregional versus National Perspectives on Contemporary Central European History. Studies on the Building of Nation-States and Their Cooperation in the 20th and 21st Century | With a foreword by Petr Vágner | ISBN 978-3-8382-1015-5

171 *Philip Gamaghelyan* | Conflict Resolution Beyond the International Relations Paradigm. Evolving Designs as a Transformative Practice in Nagorno-Karabakh and Syria | With a foreword by Susan Allen | ISBN 978-3-8382-1057-5

172 *Maria Shagina* | Joining a Prestigious Club. Cooperation with Europarties and Its Impact on Party Development in Georgia, Moldova, and Ukraine 2004–2015 | With a foreword by Kataryna Wolczuk | ISBN 978-3-8382-1084-1

173 *Alexandra Cotofana, James M. Nyce (Eds.)* | Religion and Magic in Socialist and Post-Socialist Contexts II. Baltic, Eastern European, and Post-USSR Case Studies | With a foreword by Anita Stasulane | ISBN 978-3-8382-0990-6

174 *Barbara Kunz* | Kind Words, Cruise Missiles, and Everything in Between. The Use of Power Resources in U.S. Policies towards Poland, Ukraine, and Belarus 1989–2008 | With a foreword by William Hill | ISBN 978-3-8382-1065-0

175 *Eduard Klein* | Bildungskorruption in Russland und der Ukraine. Eine komparative Analyse der Performanz staatlicher Antikorruptionsmaßnahmen im Hochschulsektor am Beispiel universitärer Aufnahmeprüfungen | Mit einem Vorwort von Heiko Pleines | ISBN 978-3-8382-0995-1

176 *Markus Soldner* | Politischer Kapitalismus im postsowjetischen Russland. Die politische, wirtschaftliche und mediale Transformation in den 1990er Jahren | Mit einem Vorwort von Wolfgang Ismayr | ISBN 978-3-8382-1222-7

177 *Anton Oleinik* | Building Ukraine from Within. A Sociological, Institutional, and Economic Analysis of a Nation-State in the Making | ISBN 978-3-8382-1150-3

178 *Peter Rollberg, Marlene Laruelle (Eds.)* | Mass Media in the Post-Soviet World. Market Forces, State Actors, and Political Manipulation in the Informational Environment after Communism | ISBN 978-3-8382-1116-9

179 *Mikhail Minakov* | Development and Dystopia. Studies in Post-Soviet Ukraine and Eastern Europe | With a foreword by Alexander Etkind | ISBN 978-3-8382-1112-1

180 *Aijan Sharshenova* | The European Union's Democracy Promotion in Central Asia. A Study of Political Interests, Influence, and Development in Kazakhstan and Kyrgyzstan in 2007–2013 | With a foreword by Gordon Crawford | ISBN 978-3-8382-1151-0

181 *Andrey Makarychev, Alexandra Yatsyk (Eds.)* | Boris Nemtsov and Russian Politics. Power and Resistance | With a foreword by Zhanna Nemtsova | ISBN 978-3-8382-1122-0

182 *Sophie Falsini* | The Euromaidan's Effect on Civil Society. Why and How Ukrainian Social Capital Increased after the Revolution of Dignity | With a foreword by Susann Worschech | ISBN 978-3-8382-1131-2

183 *Valentyna Romanova, Andreas Umland (Eds.)* | Ukraine's Decentralization. Challenges and Implications of the Local Governance Reform after the Euromaidan Revolution | ISBN 978-3-8382-1162-6

184 *Leonid Luks* | A Fateful Triangle. Essays on Contemporary Russian, German and Polish History | ISBN 978-3-8382-1143-5

185 *John B. Dunlop* | The February 2015 Assassination of Boris Nemtsov and the Flawed Trial of his Alleged Killers. An Exploration of Russia's "Crime of the 21st Century" | ISBN 978-3-8382-1188-6

186 *Vasile Rotaru* | Russia, the EU, and the Eastern Partnership. Building Bridges or Digging Trenches? | ISBN 978-3-8382-1134-3

187 *Marina Lebedeva* | Russian Studies of International Relations. From the Soviet Past to the Post-Cold-War Present | With a foreword by Andrei P. Tsygankov | ISBN 978-3-8382-0851-0

188 *Tomasz Stępniewski, George Soroka (Eds.)* | Ukraine after Maidan. Revisiting Domestic and Regional Security | ISBN 978-3-8382-1075-9

189 *Petar Cholakov* | Ethnic Entrepreneurs Unmasked. Political Institutions and Ethnic Conflicts in Contemporary Bulgaria | ISBN 978-3-8382-1189-3

190 *A. Salem, G. Hazeldine, D. Morgan (Eds.)* | Higher Education in Post-Communist States. Comparative and Sociological Perspectives | ISBN 978-3-8382-1183-5

191 *Igor Torbakov* | After Empire. Nationalist Imagination and Symbolic Politics in Russia and Eurasia in the Twentieth and Twenty-First Century | With a foreword by Serhii Plokhy | ISBN 978-3-8382-1217-3

192 *Aleksandr Burakovskiy* | Jewish-Ukrainian Relations in Late and Post-Soviet Ukraine. Articles, Lectures and Essays from 1986 to 2016 | ISBN 978-3-8382-1210-4

193 *Natalia Shapovalova, Olga Burlyuk (Eds.)* | Civil Society in Post-Euromaidan Ukraine. From Revolution to Consolidation | With a foreword by Richard Youngs | ISBN 978-3-8382-1216-6

194 *Franz Preissler* | Positionsverteidigung, Imperialismus oder Irredentismus? Russland und die „Russischsprachigen", 1991–2015 | ISBN 978-3-8382-1262-3

195 *Marian Madeła* | Der Reformprozess in der Ukraine 2014-2017. Eine Fallstudie zur Reform der öffentlichen Verwaltung | Mit einem Vorwort von Martin Malek | ISBN 978-3-8382-1266-1

196 *Anke Giesen* | „Wie kann denn der Sieger ein Verbrecher sein?" Eine diskursanalytische Untersuchung der russlandweiten Debatte über Konzept und Verstaatlichungsprozess der Lagergedenkstätte „Perm'-36" im Ural | ISBN 978-3-8382-1284-5

197 *Victoria Leukavets* | The Integration Policies of Belarus and Ukraine vis-à-vis the EU and Russia. A Comparative Analysis Through the Prism of a Two-Level Game Approach | ISBN 978-3-8382-1247-0

198 *Oksana Kim* | The Development and Challenges of Russian Corporate Governance I. The Roles and Functions of Boards of Directors | With a foreword by Sheila M. Puffer | ISBN 978-3-8382-1287-6

199 *Thomas D. Grant* | International Law and the Post-Soviet Space I. Essays on Chechnya and the Baltic States | With a foreword by Stephen M. Schwebel | ISBN 978-3-8382-1279-1

200 *Thomas D. Grant* | International Law and the Post-Soviet Space II. Essays on Ukraine, Intervention, and Non-Proliferation | ISBN 978-3-8382-1280-7

201 *Slavomír Michálek, Michal Štefansky* | The Age of Fear. The Cold War and Its Influence on Czechoslovakia 1945–1968 | ISBN 978-3-8382-1285-2

202 *Iulia-Sabina Joja* | Romania's Strategic Culture 1990–2014. Continuity and Change in a Post-Communist Country's Evolution of National Interests and Security Policies | With a foreword by Heiko Biehl | ISBN 978-3-8382-1286-9

203 *Andrei Rogatchevski, Yngvar B. Steinholt, Arve Hansen, David-Emil Wickström* | War of Songs. Popular Music and Recent Russia-Ukraine Relations | With a foreword by Artemy Troitsky | ISBN 978-3-8382-1173-2

204 *Maria Lipman (Ed.)* | Russian Voices on Post-Crimea Russia. An Almanac of Counterpoint Essays from 2015–2018 | ISBN 978-3-8382-1251-7

205 *Ksenia Maksimovtsova* | Language Conflicts in Contemporary Estonia, Latvia, and Ukraine. A Comparative Exploration of Discourses in Post-Soviet Russian-Language Digital Media | With a foreword by Ammon Cheskin | ISBN 978-3-8382-1282-1

206 *Michal Vít* | The EU's Impact on Identity Formation in East-Central Europe between 2004 and 2013. Perceptions of the Nation and Europe in Political Parties of the Czech Republic, Poland, and Slovakia | With a foreword by Andrea Pető | ISBN 978-3-8382-1275-3

207 *Per A. Rudling* | Tarnished Heroes. The Organization of Ukrainian Nationalists in the Memory Politics of Post-Soviet Ukraine | ISBN 978-3-8382-0999-9

208 *Kaja Gadowska, Peter Solomon (Eds.)* | Legal Change in Post-Communist States. Progress, Reversions, Explanations | ISBN 978-3-8382-1312-5

209 *Paweł Kowal, Georges Mink, Iwona Reichardt (Eds.)* | Three Revolutions: Mobilization and Change in Contemporary Ukraine I. Theoretical Aspects and Analyses on Religion, Memory, and Identity | ISBN 978-3-8382-1321-7

210 *Paweł Kowal, Georges Mink, Adam Reichardt, Iwona Reichardt (Eds.)* | Three Revolutions: Mobilization and Change in Contemporary Ukraine II. An Oral History of the Revolution on Granite, Orange Revolution, and Revolution of Dignity | ISBN 978-3-8382-1323-1

211 *Li Bennich-Björkman, Sergiy Kurbatov (Eds.)* | When the Future Came. The Collapse of the USSR and the Emergence of National Memory in Post-Soviet History Textbooks | ISBN 978-3-8382-1335-4

212 *Olga R. Gulina* | Migration as a (Geo-)Political Challenge in the Post-Soviet Space. Border Regimes, Policy Choices, Visa Agendas | With a foreword by Nils Muižnieks | ISBN 978-3-8382-1338-5

213 *Sanna Turoma, Kaarina Aitamurto, Slobodanka Vladiv-Glover (Eds.)* | Religion, Expression, and Patriotism in Russia. Essays on Post-Soviet Society and the State. ISBN 978-3-8382-1346-0

214 *Vasif Huseynov* | Geopolitical Rivalries in the "Common Neighborhood". Russia's Conflict with the West, Soft Power, and Neoclassical Realism | With a foreword by Nicholas Ross Smith | ISBN 978-3-8382-1277-7

215 *Mikhail Suslov* | Geopolitical Imagination. Ideology and Utopia in Post-Soviet Russia | With a foreword by Mark Bassin | ISBN 978-3-8382-1361-3

216 *Alexander Etkind, Mikhail Minakov (Eds.)* | Ideology after Union. Political Doctrines, Discourses, and Debates in Post-Soviet Societies | ISBN 978-3-8382-1388-0

217 *Jakob Mischke, Oleksandr Zabirko (Hgg.)* | Protestbewegungen im langen Schatten des Kreml. Aufbruch und Resignation in Russland und der Ukraine | ISBN 978-3-8382-0926-5

218 *Oksana Huss* | How Corruption and Anti-Corruption Policies Sustain Hybrid Regimes. Strategies of Political Domination under Ukraine's Presidents in 1994-2014 | With a foreword by Tobias Debiel and Andrea Gawrich | ISBN 978-3-8382-1430-6

219 *Dmitry Travin, Vladimir Gel'man, Otar Marganiya* | The Russian Path. Ideas, Interests, Institutions, Illusions | With a foreword by Vladimir Ryzhkov | ISBN 978-3-8382-1421-4

220 *Gergana Dimova* | Political Uncertainty. A Comparative Exploration | With a foreword by Todor Yalamov and Rumena Filipova | ISBN 978-3-8382-1385-9

221 *Torben Waschke* | Russland in Transition. Geopolitik zwischen Raum, Identität und Machtinteressen | Mit einem Vorwort von Andreas Dittmann | ISBN 978-3-8382-1480-1

222 *Steven Jobbitt, Zsolt Bottlik, Marton Berki (Eds.)* | Power and Identity in the Post-Soviet Realm. Geographies of Ethnicity and Nationality after 1991 | ISBN 978-3-8382-1399-6

223 *Daria Buteiko* | Erinnerungsort. Ort des Gedenkens, der Erholung oder der Einkehr? Kommunismus-Erinnerung am Beispiel der Gedenkstätte Berliner Mauer sowie des Soloveckij-Klosters und -Museumsparks | ISBN 978-3-8382-1367-5

224 *Olga Bertelsen (Ed.)* | Russian Active Measures. Yesterday, Today, Tomorrow | With a foreword by Jan Goldman | ISBN 978-3-8382-1529-7

225 *David Mandel* | "Optimizing" Higher Education in Russia. University Teachers and their Union "Universitetskaya solidarnost'" | ISBN 978-3-8382-1519-8

226 *Mikhail Minakov, Gwendolyn Sasse, Daria Isachenko (Eds.)* | Post-Soviet Secessionism. Nation-Building and State-Failure after Communism | ISBN 978-3-8382-1538-9

227 *Jakob Hauter (Ed.)* | Civil War? Interstate War? Hybrid War? Dimensions and Interpretations of the Donbas Conflict in 2014–2020 | With a foreword by Andrew Wilson | ISBN 978-3-8382-1383-5

228 *Tima T. Moldogaziev, Gene A. Brewer, J. Edward Kellough (Eds.)* | Public Policy and Politics in Georgia. Lessons from Post-Soviet Transition | With a foreword by Dan Durning | ISBN 978-3-8382-1535-8

229 *Oxana Schmies (Ed.)* | NATO's Enlargement and Russia. A Strategic Challenge in the Past and Future | With a foreword by Vladimir Kara-Murza | ISBN 978-3-8382-1478-8

230 *Christopher Ford* | Ukapisme – Une Gauche perdue. Le marxisme anti-colonial dans la révolution ukrainienne 1917-1925 | Avec une préface de Vincent Présumey | ISBN 978-3-8382-0899-2

231 *Anna Kutkina* | Between Lenin and Bandera. Decommunization and Multivocality in Post-Euromaidan Ukraine | With a foreword by Juri Mykkänen | ISBN 978-3-8382-1506-8

232 *Lincoln E. Flake* | Defending the Faith. The Russian Orthodox Church and the Demise of Religious Pluralism | With a foreword by Peter Martland | ISBN 978-3-8382-1378-1

233 *Nikoloz Samkharadze* | Russia's Recognition of the Independence of Abkhazia and South Ossetia. Analysis of a Deviant Case in Moscow's Foreign Policy | With a foreword by Neil MacFarlane | ISBN 978-3-8382-1414-6

234 *Arve Hansen* | Urban Protest. A Spatial Perspective on Kyiv, Minsk, and Moscow | With a foreword by Julie Wilhelmsen | ISBN 978-3-8382-1495-5

235 *Eleonora Narvselius, Julie Fedor (Eds.)* | Diversity in the East-Central European Borderlands. Memories, Cityscapes, People | ISBN 978-3-8382-1523-5

236 *Regina Elsner* | The Russian Orthodox Church and Modernity. A Historical and Theological Investigation into Eastern Christianity between Unity and Plurality | With a foreword by Mikhail Suslov | ISBN 978-3-8382-1568-6

237 *Bo Petersson* | The Putin Predicament. Problems of Legitimacy and Succession in Russia | With a foreword by J. Paul Goode | ISBN 978-3-8382-1050-6

238 *Jonathan Otto Pohl* | The Years of Great Silence. The Deportation, Special Settlement, and Mobilization into the Labor Army of Ethnic Germans in the USSR, 1941–1955 | ISBN 978-3-8382-1630-0

239 *Mikhail Minakov (Ed.)* | Inventing Majorities. Ideological Creativity in Post-Soviet Societies | ISBN 978-3-8382-1641-6

240 *Robert M. Cutler* | Soviet and Post-Soviet Foreign Policies I. East-South Relations and the Political Economy of the Communist Bloc, 1971–1991 | With a foreword by Roger E. Kanet | ISBN 978-3-8382-1654-5

241 *Izabella Agardi* | On the Verge of History. Life Stories of Rural Women from Serbia, Romania, and Hungary, 1920–2020 | With a foreword by Andrea Pető | ISBN 978-3-8382-1602-7

242 *Sebastian Schäffer (Ed.)* | Ukraine in Central and Eastern Europe. Kyiv's Foreign Affairs and the International Relations of the Post-Communist Region | With a foreword by Pavlo Klimkin and Andreas Umland| ISBN 978-3-8382-1615-7

243 *Volodymyr Dubrovskyi, Kalman Mizsei, Mychailo Wynnyckyj (Eds.)* | Eight Years after the Revolution of Dignity. What Has Changed in Ukraine during 2013–2021? | With a foreword by Yaroslav Hrytsak | ISBN 978-3-8382-1560-0

244 *Rumena Filipova* | Constructing the Limits of Europe Identity and Foreign Policy in Poland, Bulgaria, and Russia since 1989 | With forewords by Harald Wydra and Gergana Yankova-Dimova | ISBN 978-3-8382-1649-2

245 *Oleksandra Keudel* | How Patronal Networks Shape Opportunities for Local Citizen Participation in a Hybrid Regime A Comparative Analysis of Five Cities in Ukraine | With a foreword by Sabine Kropp | ISBN 978-3-8382-1671-3

246 *Jan Claas Behrends, Thomas Lindenberger, Pavel Kolar (Eds.)* | Violence after Stalin Institutions, Practices, and Everyday Life in the Soviet Bloc 1953–1989 | ISBN 978-3-8382-1637-9

247 *Leonid Luks* | Macht und Ohnmacht der Utopien Essays zur Geschichte Russlands im 20. und 21. Jahrhundert | ISBN 978-3-8382-1677-5

248 *Iuliia Barshadska* | Brüssel zwischen Kyjiw und Moskau Das auswärtige Handeln der Europäischen Union im ukrainisch-russischen Konflikt 2014-2019 | Mit einem Vorwort von Olaf Leiße | ISBN 978-3-8382-1667-6

249 *Valentyna Romanova* | Decentralisation and Multilevel Elections in Ukraine Reform Dynamics and Party Politics in 2010–2021 | With a foreword by Kimitaka Matsuzato | ISBN 978-3-8382-1700-0

250 *Alexander Motyl* | National Questions. Theoretical Reflections on Nations and Nationalism in Eastern Europe | ISBN 978-3-8382-1675-1

251 *Marc Dietrich* | A Cosmopolitan Model for Peacebuilding. The Ukrainian Cases of Crimea and the Donbas | With a foreword by Rémi Baudouï | ISBN 978-3-8382-1687-4

252 *Eduard Baidaus* | An Unsettled Nation. Moldova in the Geopolitics of Russia, Romania, and Ukraine | With forewords by John-Paul Himka and David R. Marples | ISBN 978-3-8382-1582-2

253 *Igor Okunev, Petr Oskolkov (Eds.)* | Transforming the Administrative Matryoshka. The Reform of Autonomous Okrugs in the Russian Federation, 2003–2008 | With a foreword by Vladimir Zorin | ISBN 978-3-8382-1721-9

254 *Winfried Schneider-Deters* | Ukraine's Fateful Years 2013–2019. Vol. I: The Popular Uprising in Winter 2013/2014 | ISBN 978-3-8382-1725-3

255 *Winfried Schneider-Deters* | Ukraine's Fateful Years 2013–2019. Vol. II: The Annexation of Crimea and the War in Donbas | ISBN 978-3-8382-1726-0

256 *Robert M. Cutler* | Soviet and Post-Soviet Russian Foreign Policies II. East-West Relations in Europe and the Political Economy of the Communist Bloc, 1971–1991 | With a foreword by Roger E. Kanet | ISBN 978-3-8382-1727-7

257 *Robert M. Cutler* | Soviet and Post-Soviet Russian Foreign Policies III. East-West Relations in Europe and Eurasia in the Post-Cold War Transition, 1991–2001 | With a foreword by Roger E. Kanet | ISBN 978-3-8382-1728-4

258 *Paweł Kowal, Iwona Reichardt, Kateryna Pryshchepa (Eds.)* | Three Revolutions: Mobilization and Change in Contemporary Ukraine III. Archival Records and Historical Sources on the 1990 Revolution on Granite | ISBN 978-3-8382-1376-7

259 *Mikhail Minakov (Ed.)* | Philosophy Unchained. Developments in Post-Soviet Philosophical Thought. | With a foreword by Christopher Donohue | ISBN 978-3-8382-1768-0

260 *David Dalton* | The Ukrainian Oligarchy After the Euromaidan. How Ukraine's Political Economy Regime Survived the Crisis | With a foreword by Andrew Wilson | ISBN 978-3-8382-1740-6

261 *Andreas Heinemann-Grüder (Ed.)* | Who Are the Fighters? Irregular Armed Groups in the Russian-Ukrainian War since 2014 | ISBN 978-3-8382-1777-2

262 *Taras Kuzio (Ed.)* | Russian Disinformation and Western Scholarship. Bias and Prejudice in Journalistic, Expert, and Academic Analyses of East European, Russian and Eurasian Affairs | ISBN 978-3-8382-1685-0

263 *Darius Furmonavicius* | LithuaniaTransforms the West. Lithuania's Liberation from Soviet Occupation and the Enlargement of NATO (1988–2022) | With a foreword by Vytautas Landsbergis | ISBN 978-3-8382-1779-6

264 *Dirk Dalberg* | Politisches Denken im tschechoslowakischen Dissens. Egon Bondy, Miroslav Kusý, Milan Šimečka und Petr Uhl (1968-1989) | ISBN 978-3-8382-1318-7

265 *Леонид Люкс* | К столетию «философского парохода». Мыслители «первой» русской эмиграции о русской революции и о тоталитарных соблазнах XX века | ISBN 978-3-8382-1775-8

266 *Daviti Mtchedlishvili* | The EU and the South Caucasus. European Neighborhood Policies between Eclecticism and Pragmatism, 1991-2021 | With a foreword by Nicholas Ross Smith | ISBN 978-3-8382-1735-2

267 *Bohdan Harasymiw* | Post-Euromaidan Ukraine. Domestic Power Struggles and War of National Survival in 2014–2022 | ISBN 978-3-8382-1798-7

268 *Nadiia Koval, Denys Tereshchenko (Eds.)* | Russian Cultural Diplomacy under Putin. Rossotrudnichestvo, the "Russkiy Mir" Foundation, and the Gorchakov Fund in 2007–2022 | ISBN 978-3-8382-1801-4

269 *Izabela Kazejak* | Jews in Post-War Wrocław and L'viv. Official Policies and Local Responses in Comparative Perspective, 1945-1970s | ISBN 978-3-8382-1802-1

270 *Jakob Hauter* | Russia's Overlooked Invasion. The Causes of the 2014 Outbreak of War in Ukraine's Donbas | With a foreword by Hiroaki Kuromiya | ISBN 978-3-8382-1803-8

271 *Anton Shekhovtsov* | Russian Political Warfare. Essays on Kremlin Propaganda in Europe and the Neighbourhood, 2020-2023 | With a foreword by Nathalie Loiseau | ISBN 978-3-8382-1821-2

272 *Андреа Пето* | Насилие и Молчание. Красная армия в Венгрии во Второй Мировой войне | ISBN 978-3-8382-1636-2

273 *Winfried Schneider-Deters* | Russia's War in Ukraine. Debates on Peace, Fascism, and War Crimes, 2022–2023 | With a foreword by Klaus Gestwa | ISBN 978-3-8382-1876-2

274 *Rasmus Nilsson* | Uncanny Allies. Russia and Belarus on the Edge, 2012-2024 | ISBN 978-3-8382-1288-3

275 *Anton Grushetskyi, Volodymyr Paniotto* | War and the Transformation of Ukrainian Society (2022–23). Empirical Evidence | ISBN 978-3-8382-1944-8

276 *Christian Kaunert, Alex MacKenzie, Adrien Nonjon (Eds.)* | In the Eye of the Storm. Origins, Ideology, and Controversies of the Azov Brigade, 2014–23 | ISBN 978-3-8382-1750-5

277 *Gian Marco Moisé* | The House Always Wins. The Corrupt Strategies that Shaped Kazakh Oil Politics and Business in the Nazarbayev Era | With a foreword by Alena Ledeneva | ISBN 978-3-8382-1917-2

278 *Mikhail Minakov* | The Post-Soviet Human | Philosophical Reflections on Social History after the End of Communism | ISBN 978-3-8382-1943-1

279 *Natalia Kudriavtseva, Debra A. Friedman (Eds.)* | Language and Power in Ukraine and Kazakhstan. Essays on Education, Ideology, Literature, Practice, and the Media | With a foreword by Laada Bilaniuk | ISBN 978-3-8382-1949-3

280 *Paweł Kowal, Georges Mink, Iwona Reichardt (Eds.)* | The End of the Soviet World? Essays on Post-Communist Political and Social Change | With a foreword by Richardt Butterwick-Pawlikowski | ISBN 978-3-8382-1961-5

281 *Kateryna Zarembo, Michèle Knodt, Maksym Yakovlyev (Eds.)* | Teaching IR in Wartime. Experiences of University Lecturers during Russia's Full-Scale Invasion of Ukraine | ISBN 978-3-8382-1954-7

282 *Oleksiy V. Kresin* | The United Nations General Assembly Resolutions. Their Nature and Significance in the Context of the Russian War Against Ukraine | Edited by William E. Butler | ISBN 978-3-8382-1967-7

283 *Jakob Hauter* | Russlands unbemerkte Invasion. Die Ursachen des Kriegsausbruchs im ukrainischen Donbas im Jahr 2014 | Mit einem Vorwort von Hiroaki Kuromiya | ISBN 978-3-8382-2003-1

284 „Alles kann sich ändern". Letzte Worte politisch Angeklagter vor Gericht in Russland | Herausgegeben von Memorial Deutschland e.V. | ISBN 978-3-8382-1994-3

285 *Nadiya Kiss, Monika Wingender (Eds.)* | Contested Language Diversity in Contemporary Ukraine. National Minorities, Language Biographies, and Linguistic Landscape | ISBN 978-3-8382-1966-0

286 *Richard Ottinger (Ed.)* | Religious Elements in the Russian War of Aggression Against Ukraine. Propaganda, Religious Politics and Pastoral Care, 2014–2024 | ISBN 978-3-8382-1981-3

287 *Yuri Radchenko* | Helping in Mass Murders. Auxiliary Police, Indigenous Administration, SD, and the Shoa in the Ukrainian-Russian-Belorussian Borderlands, 1941–43 | With forewords by John-Paul Himka and Kai Struve | ISBN 978-3-8382-1878-6

288 *Zsofia Maria Schmidt* | Hungary's System of National Cooperation. Strategies of Framing in Pro-Governmental Media and Public Discourse, 2010–18 | With a foreword by Andreas Schmidt-Schweizer | ISBN 978-3-8382-1983-7

ibidem.eu